Morality and Power

For my children and grandchildren

'Moral seriousness in public life is like pornography: hard to define but you know it when you see it. It describes a coherence of intention and action, an ethic of political responsibility. All politics is the art of the possible. But art too has its ethic' (Tony Judt).

'I would argue that the nature of modern economics has been substantially impoverished by the distance that has grown between economics and ethics' (Amartya Sen).

'We all make ethical choices, often without being conscious of doing so. Too often we assume that ethics is about obeying the rules that begin with "You must not …". If that were all there is to living ethically, then as long as we were not violating one of those rules, whatever we were doing would be ethical. This view of ethics, however, is incomplete. It fails to consider the good we can do others less fortunate than ourselves, not only in our own community, but anywhere within reach of our help. We ought also to extend our concern to future generations and beyond our own species to non-human animals' (Peter Singer).

Morality and Power

On Ethics, Economics and Public Policy

Mike Berry

Emeritus Professor, Centre for Urban Research, RMIT University, Australia

Edward Elgar
PUBLISHING

Cheltenham, UK • Northampton, MA, USA

Published by
Edward Elgar Publishing Limited
The Lypiatts
15 Lansdown Road
Cheltenham
Glos GL50 2JA
UK

Edward Elgar Publishing, Inc.
William Pratt House
9 Dewey Court
Northampton
Massachusetts 01060
USA

A catalogue record for this book
is available from the British Library

Library of Congress Control Number: 2017933401

This book is available electronically in the Elgaronline
Social and Political Science subject collection
DOI 10.4337/9781786435569

MIX
Paper from responsible sources
FSC® C013604

ISBN 978 1 78643 555 2 (cased)
ISBN 978 1 78643 556 9 (eBook)

Typeset by Servis Filmsetting Ltd, Stockport, Cheshire

Printed and bound by CPI Group (UK) Ltd, Croydon, CR0 4YY

Contents

Preface

Halfway through the second decade of the twenty-first century the state of the world is experiencing a degree of political volatility and economic uncertainty not unlike the situation 100 years ago. Admittedly, the main event is not global warfare but the proliferation of regional and civil wars and the aftermath of the Great Recession of 2008 that casts a shadow over what had been the confident predictions of peace and prosperity following the collapse of the communist bloc at the end of the preceding century. Post 9/11 and after 2008 the major Western economies have gone through a decade of stagnation. Economic growth as conventionally measured has been weak or non-existent, even in the capitalist centre, the United States of America. The real material living standard of a majority of citizens in the advanced nations has frozen or gone backward. At the same time, profits have never been higher and the fruits of capitalist enterprise more unequally distributed. There is a pervasive feeling in those societies that something is wrong. It's not supposed to be this way. There appears to be a hollowness at the core of society that overlays the strictly material basis of dissatisfaction. There is, in fact, an ethical crisis – a sense that the things that are valued as aspects of a full social existence and give meaning to life are disappearing.

Economics as a discipline – notwithstanding the genuine commitment of most economists to improve the lives of their fellow human beings – has some responsibility for this state of the world. It is not simply that orthodox economists were blindsided by the Great Recession, unable to foresee and thus forestall the crisis, but that they and the governments they advise have been unable to fix matters after the event. After the initial shock had worn off, it was pretty much business as usual. It was all an aberration, no one could have known what came down the road, just one of those mysteries in life. Most economists shrugged and went back to their models, the very ones that had so dramatically missed the main event. After a brief burst of Keynesian pump priming, the policies of fiscal restraint and austerity were back.

I argue in this book that economics as a social and policy science must make room at the centre for two key frames, two sets of lenses through which to view what is happening and what might happen. First, human beings as social actors are influenced in their complex behaviours by ethical or normative concerns. Values matter at the coalface of economic and social life. Moreover, values emerge within particular, historically defined situations. They are not exogenous data for the purpose of idealized models of reality; they are reality. Second, people engage in economic and other activities from positions of unequal power. This too is an ontological given and must be explained and the consequences accounted for in what is happening and what governments need to know when developing and implementing policy. Ethics matters in another sense. It is not enough for economists and governments to know how values and norms emerge in a community and how they are likely to influence behaviour. Economists and policy makers *should* themselves have a clear normative commitment to guide their actions – what they think it worthwhile to understand and act upon. This is, of course an ethical statement in itself, as the emphasis in the preceding sentence attests.

The approach presented draws upon arguments from contemporary political philosophy concerning social justice, while situating the development of orthodox economics within a tradition of moral philosophy stretching back to the eighteenth century.[1] I have tried to keep the number of references quoted to a manageable level and resisted as much as possible the temptation to indulge in war by endnote. To this end, I have relied upon a limited number of relevant references in the text, though when it seemed useful, directed the reader to further sources in the notes.

NOTE

1. Throughout the book I use the terms orthodox, mainstream and neoclassical economics interchangeably.

Acknowledgements

The debt I owe to the long tradition of critical thinking in this field will be obvious from the text. However, I wish to particularly mention the inspiring contributions of Amartya Sen, John Rawls and Michael Sandel, who have in their different ways stimulated my thoughts and those of others working the seams they first mined. Thanks also to my son Jon for pointing out the relevance of Jonathan Haidt's thought-provoking book, *The Righteous Mind* to many of the themes developed in the book. I spent part of the period when writing this book, as Helen Kam Visiting Fellow at Girton College, University of Cambridge. I thank the Mistress and fellows of the college for welcoming me into their community and for the many fascinating discussions that arose there. I am also grateful for the encouragement of longstanding friends and colleagues Terry Burke at Swinburne University, Michael Harloe at LSE and Chris Ryan at the University of Melbourne. My colleagues at the Centre for Urban Research, RMIT University continue to put up with me and offer an exciting intellectual milieu in which to work. I thank my editors at Edward Elgar, Alex Pettifer, Rachel Downie and Michaela Doyle, for their professional assistance. As always, my wife Deirdre has been my strongest supporter and best mate.

PART I

Foundations

1. Introduction

> Economics relates ultimately to the study of ethics and that of politics, and this point of view is further developed in Aristotle's *Politics*. There is no scope in all this for dissociating the study of economics from that of ethics and political philosophy (Amartya Sen).

Public policy in the advanced economies has undergone a radical shift to the right over the past 40 years. This reflects, in large part, the re-emergence of deep divisions in modern capitalist societies such as the United States of America and the United Kingdom. Class inequalities of privilege, position and power have hardened during these decades and reset the policy agendas of governments, particularly in those countries adhering to a neoliberal faith in free markets and the institutional and ideological frameworks legitimating the resulting policy approaches.

The resulting policy path-dependence has emerged in country after country as a result of interdependent national and international forces. The complex processes of globalization, in their economic, cultural and political phases have impacted differently on particular countries but the overall outcome has been increasing differentiation within most, including those designated 'emerging economies' by commentators and politicians. Clearly, epoch-changing developments like the fall of the Soviet empire and the associated rise of US triumphalism in the 1990s have been decisive in the rise of market fundamentalism in democratic politics. New communication technologies have also played their part in shrinking the world and replicating Western consumerism throughout it.[1] This has not been without challenge, as the rise of nationalist politics and religious fundamentalism in some countries has made only too clear.

Nevertheless, the broad narrative of market-led economic growth predominates in many parts of our increasingly fragile planet, most dramatically in the most dynamic region of the world, Asia. In one important sense, this represents a generalization of development forces unleashed in the Western countries during the nineteenth century and reinforced after World War II. However, it also flows from the reassertion of ideas that first emerged in the eighteenth century, a mix of classical liberalism and the emerging political economy. Utilitarianism and the later subjective turn wrought by neoclassical economics provided the basis on which economics as the emperor of the social sciences captured the policy process after the World War II. Increasingly, the self-confident (and self-interested) pronouncements of economists have come to define and confine political debate and policy outcomes to a narrow concern for material welfare, tracked by conventional measures like per capita gross domestic product. This development is celebrated as a triumph of the scientific cast of economics as a discipline over its historical roots in moral philosophy.

Mainstream economics having colonized the policy arena and posited itself as the solution has, in fact, become part of the problem. An over-reliance on the market and the extension of market criteria to policy fields stretching well beyond the traditional areas of taxation, industry structure, employment and industrial relations and the financial sector, to dictate outcomes in education, health, social welfare and infrastructure, has contributed to growing inequalities of income, wealth and opportunities, while stoking insecurity in various forms and undermining the social bonds on which societies (and market processes) depend for their continuing existence. Far from being the value-free science promoted by its practitioners, orthodox economics expresses particular ethical precepts, while unintentionally repressing alternative value commitments; these moral precepts and absences bias public policy in clearly observable directions, with a range of consequences, some of which are unintended and – depending on an observer's moral viewpoint – undesirable.

The conventional distinction between 'positive' and 'normative' economics neatly proposes an intellectual division of labour between ethics and economics, between the roles of values and analysis in the practice of the discipline. From this position, economists are able to quarantine their analyses of what *is* happening in the economy from what *should* happen. Positive economics employs what Amartya Sen (1987) calls 'the engineering' or 'logistic' approach. The ends and values of agents are given and economics is all about how economic processes result in predictable outcomes. However, to the extent that the ethical sentiments of agents influence *how* they act, economists need to take into account the nature, strength and ranking of those sentiments in explaining actual outcomes. 'If one examines the balance of emphases in the publications of modern economics, it is hard not to notice the eschewal of normative analysis, and the neglect of the influence of ethical considerations in the characterization of actual human behavior' (ibid. p. 7).

In fact, of course, economists do assume a particular narrow set of human motivations in their positive analyses – namely that people seek to pursue their own self-interests, however they conceive them. Traditionally this position has been proposed as self-evident, indeed as a definition of what is *rational*. From this position economists jump easily to the comfortable but value-laden view that policies that maximize the ability of individuals to realize their self-conscious (indeed, self-regarding) interests are *morally* compelling; these are the policies that governments *should* impose. Note the (apparent) contradiction: positive analysis prescribes what ought to be done. 'To see any departure from self-interest maximization as evidence of irrationality must imply a rejection of the role of ethics in actual decision taking (other than some variant or other of that exotic moral view known as "ethical egoism") (ibid. p. 15)'. Economists have further narrowed the ethical scope of their discipline by developing a particular brand of normative analysis known as modern welfare economics that provides both specific tools for assessing public policies and a language for justifying them.

This book seeks to unscramble the logical mess and politically regressive state to which the uncritical application of orthodox economics to public policy has brought us. Throughout I adopt a 'consequentialist' ethical position. That is, I critique orthodox economics and its policy directions and outcomes in terms of its actual deleterious consequences in the real world of power and time and place. In so doing I rely on a wealth of critical studies on the philosophy of economics carried out over the past 40 years and on the much longer philosophical tradition stretching back into the eighteenth century. My aim is to remind or – in cases of unconscious ignorance, instruct – both economists and policy makers that the entrenched policy positions they take have real consequences for real people based on ethical foundations that may not bear the weight placed on them. If Aristotle's injunction that ethics is all about the search for 'the good life', and that economics as the study of wealth is one but only one tool in the hands of the wise legislator, then it behooves all of us as citizens to open up debate about what factors outside the scope of orthodox economics need to inform what our governments should do and don't do. Inevitably, this will downgrade the current pre-eminent position of economists in the public policy realm, a blow to them no doubt but hopefully one that the rest of the citizenry will benefit from. In assuming a consequentialist position I am aware that those operating from an alternative moral framework will find some of my arguments less than compelling. That is how it should be. There are legitimate differences between, say, consequentialist and rights-based traditions.[2] Those pursuing a virtue ethics will have their own critiques of conventional approaches to economic and social policy. It is important to open up the economics discipline to a broader ethical critique, especially as the practice of economics as-we-know-it has major implications for the impact of public policy on the pursuit of 'the good life'. My major point is that, as currently configured and practiced, mainstream economics fails its own implied consequentialist ethical foundation.

The view expressed in this book is of a dualistic conception of the relevance of ethics in public policy. First, in order to understand how and why people act in the ways they do it is necessary to grasp the fact that human behaviour, including those actions and exchanges normally described as economic, are influenced through and through by the normative commitments, beliefs and obligations that they hold dear. Trying to explain economic phenomena without taking into account the values of real people situated in particular social milieu is like attempting to understand why people sacrifice their lives for their children and the defence of their communities without considering the influence of kinship, tribal relations and the constructions of nationalism. Second, ethical analysis is necessary to reflect on and question whether observable behaviours and current policies are justifiable – and if they are, on what grounds and under what conditions. To confine one's gaze to understanding the world in the first sense may satisfy the scholarly instinct but is itself tantamount to taking an ethical position in the second sense; the task is not to change the world but to understand it.[3]

The book is divided into three main parts. Part I examines the ethical tradition from which modern economics as a distinct discipline emerged. This entails focusing on the development of utilitarianism, starting with David Hume's focus on the individual as subject, the conflict of interests and values, the coexistence of self-regarding and other-regarding drivers of human behaviour and the possibility of objectivity in moral judgment. Attention then moves on to the development of classical utilitarianism and its critique by John Stuart Mill as a backdrop to the emergence of neoclassical economics in the last third of the nineteenth century. With the landmark publication of Alfred Marshall's *Principles of Economics* in 1890 economics in its recognizably modern form had arrived. The discipline now promised to provide both a deep understanding of and a set of tools for bringing about a state of affairs in which the material well-being of individuals – as a consequence of their own voluntary interactions – is maximized.

More specifically, Chapter 2 traces the emergence of arguments in the eighteenth century that culminated in the rise of utilitarianism, the ethical foundation of a rationalistic economic science, a century later. It does so by considering the work of the two giants of the Scottish Enlightenment, David Hume and Adam Smith. The importance of considering the thought of long-dead eighteenth-century moral philosophers – as Hirschman (1977), Sen (1987) and Rothschild (2002) have argued – is to recognize the complex interrelations between the passions and the interests that existed before modern economics collapsed the distinction into a reductionist theory of rational choice that rules out the explanatory and policy pay-off resulting from an approach that embraces the pluralistic structure of human nature.

Chapter 3 discusses the influential work of the British legal scholar and philosopher, Jeremy Bentham. His book *An Introduction to the Principles of Morals and Legislation*, published in 1789, laid down the classical theory of utilitarianism, arguably the first secular attempt to divorce morality from a theological base. Later philosophers and political economists, notably, Sidgwick, J.S. Mill and Francis Edgeworth developed and modified Bentham's work. However, none succeeded in resolving certain difficulties associated with the impossibility of measuring utility in ways that allowed aggregation over actions, time frames and people. The chapter goes on to discuss how modern economics came to transform the Benthamite calculus into a system of rational choice based on an ordinal concept of utility, while developing a particular but limited notion of cardinal utility.

Chapter 4 tells how John Stuart Mill sought to shake off the early influence of his father, James Mill, and Bentham to deal with features of classical utilitarianism that he found morally repugnant and politically dangerous. In particular, he objected to the radical egalitarianism implicit in Bentham's theory and the associated view that 'push-pin was as good as poetry'. Mill preferred an evolutionary approach to public policy and constitutional reform that would be governed by the gradual moral elevation of the masses under the benevolent guidance of governments imbued with a sophisticated (that is, Millian) utilitarian ethic.

By the time of his death, Mill's moral philosophy and political economy were about to be eclipsed by 'the marginal revolution'. Chapter 5 discusses how the utilitarian concern with total utility was approached side on by considering the impact on economic outcomes of marginal changes in commodity choices and resource allocations. This allowed economists to focus on the process rather than the outcomes of market interactions, emptying the subject of an explicit moral charge. By the beginning of the twentieth century, economics had moved a long way from its utilitarian roots. The recognized inability to give sense to what it means to maximize utility or net happiness caused economists to narrow their gaze to the more tractable issue of explaining how prices (including wages and interest rates) are formed in freely operating market economies. Left behind, however, was an equal sense of something missing. What was the *value* to human actors of freely operating market systems? What *justified* the nature of economic organization and the social consequences resulting? What role *should* government have in monitoring and, perhaps, intervening in market processes? These are all basic ethical or normative questions the answers to which could not be read off from the utility and cost curves of the new microeconomics.

However, certain seemingly insuperable conceptual and practical difficulties remained if the new science was to guide wise public policy, such as the tricky challenge of comparing the impacts of specific policies on the well-being of different people over different time periods. Part II discusses how this and other challenges were met, resulting in the policy context framing real world developments since the 1970s in countries like the USA. Attention focuses on the narrow definition and treatment of 'economic welfare', the central concept of economic efficiency, the limited and subservient role of distributional factors and the implications of conventional analysis for questions of social justice. The section emphasizes how power has been written out of the narrative, implicitly reflecting and entrenching the interests and policy priorities of privileged sections of society. This can be traced back to a one-sided reading of Adam Smith's *The Wealth of Nations* and a neglect of his *Theory of Moral Sentiments*. This section concludes with a summary pinpointing the key elements of a consequentialist ethical framework for reviewing the outcomes of recent public policies informed by orthodox economics.

Chapter 6 interrogates the way in which the concept of welfare has been defined and applied in economics over the past century. I identify and critique the particular consequentialist cast defining *whose* outcomes count, *which* outcomes count and *how* these outcomes can be aggregated across people and values. Critique focuses on the over-reliance on market values to the exclusion of other value bases and outcomes, and on the inadequacy of formal theories of well being inherent in the revealed preference-driven model of rational choice. This addresses the debate on 'the moral limits of markets' and the non-consequentialist perspectives of rights/obligations and virtue ethics.

Chapter 7 backtracks to uncover the intellectual context from which modern theories of economic welfare developed. I discuss the emergence of the 'old' welfare economics and 'new' welfare economics associated with A.C. Pigou and Vilfredo Pareto, respectively. Most attention is given to the undeservedly neglected work of Pigou; the main critique of Pareto is reserved for the following chapter. It is not possible to fully appreciate the grip of conventional market derived values without considering how Pigou following Alfred Marshall entrenched 'the measuring rod of money' in the normative firmament of the discipline. The chapter also highlights Pigou's major contribution to the moral limits of markets, namely the concept and wide applicability of 'externalities'.

Chapter 8 is a central critical conceptual section of the book, dealing with the major ethical weapon of mainstream economics – the politically influential concept of economic efficiency, derived from the Pareto principle. It is the distributional value judgment inherent in the notion of 'Pareto improvement' that enables the seemingly (misleadingly) technical meaning of 'efficiency' to overwhelm alternative ethical drivers of public policy. The chapter draws out the limitations of the Pareto principle in both its strong and weak forms before addressing the controversial subjects of the theory of second best and the compensation principle. The latter expresses what I have called the 'super strong' Pareto principle providing the normative justification for the economists' familiar tool – cost–benefit analysis. This tool when applied routinely to policy biases outcomes in favour of the well-off and effectively zero-values – in both monetary and non-monetary terms – outcomes that are difficult or impossible to ascribe monetary values to. In effect, by relying on the measuring rod of money the attempt by Pareto to remove cardinal measures of welfare from the scene is defeated and Pigou re-emerges triumphant through the back door – but not in a way that carries much ethical weight for good policy.

Chapter 9 focuses at the societal level, comparing and critiquing alternative theories of social justice and expanding the analysis beyond the debates framed by proponents and opponents of Paretian welfare economics. This carries the analysis beyond theories based on maximizing some social good to considering the role of contested concepts like desert, merit, equality, rights and community. What are the implications of different conceptions of social justice for 'good' policy?

Chapter 10 asks whether democracy is possible and if so, if it is desirable. The chapter begins with the familiar approach of social choice theory and debates over the 'impossibility' of deriving a majoritarian social welfare function. However, I argue that the fixation with the extension of rational choice theory to the societal level diverts attention from the real political economic forces determining the extent of 'effective democracy', in its classical and modern senses, characterizing the role and position of citizens in developed Western societies.

Chapter 11 recapitulates the main conclusions of Part II and outlines a coherent non-utilitarian framework for assessing the social good of public policies. The framework considers issues raised by non-consequentialist moral perspectives – like rights and duty – but from the viewpoint of their outcomes in the lives of people in real existing capitalist societies. This analysis frames (orients) the discussions of policies pertaining to the morally problematic domains covered in Part III.

Part III then turns to a critical account of some of the consequences of policies justified by orthodox economic analysis. The resulting impoverishment of the public realm and attendant threat to the long-term well-being of the bulk of the populations living in societies dominated by market fundamentalism – formalized in and legitimated by the practice of orthodox economics – is addressed through a review of: the increasingly sharp juxtaposition of 'private affluence and public squalor'; increasing economic and social inequality; the increase in macroeconomic insecurity associated with the 'financialization' of capitalism; the growing concerns around population growth and forced mobility and the micro and macro threats to the environment. The final chapter in this section focuses on the multiple threats to democracy resulting from the outcomes identified.

Chapter 12 looks at the results of three decades of privatizing previously public services in countries embracing neoliberal leanings. These policies bring into sharp relief the values inherent in and moral limitations of markets. The blanket claim that by introducing 'contestability', the interests of consumers will be necessarily better served is impossible to establish, either theoretically or empirically. The claim rests on unbridled faith in the efficiency of markets – in the special sense analyzed in Chapter 8 – and on arguments in bad faith put by those associated with financial and investor interests. Also complicit are politicians and policy makers listening to the long-dead voices of 'defunct economists' and looking to a career future in the rarefied world of bankers and lobbyists.

Chapter 13 revisits the moral issues around inequality in the context of the lively current debates unleashed by Thomas Piketty's book *Capital in the Twenty-First Century.* The emphasis is on the moral valuation of the outcomes of inequality in different spheres of life. What moral justifications are there for government intervention to offset the rising trend of economic inequality – and to what extent is this influenced by the impacts of economic inequality on other value spheres? In line with the viewpoint proposed in this book, I highlight the various negative outcomes tied to the increasing economic polarization of society.

Chapter 14 focuses on the ethical problems raised by developments in the financial sector of the advanced capitalist economies in the lead up to and policy responses arising from the 2008 global financial crisis and its lingering aftermath in the USA and Europe. In 2008 the global financial crisis burst on a world and an economics profession that was blind to its possibility. Although initial responses managed to avoid the main mistakes that turned the Wall Street Crash of 1929 into the Great Depression, an untimely reversion to the policy of enforced austerity prolonged the misery among the majority of the peoples of the advanced economies. The crisis uncovered a pervasive ethical malaise at the core of a contemporary capitalism.

Chapter 15 considers concerns around environmental values and justice, both at the micro and macro levels. To what extent are cross-country environmental problems more intractable for policy makers, civil society groups and politicians? These and related questions interact with intergenerational ethical concerns over inequality. To what extent do market approaches – that is, pollution trading schemes – help or hinder a 'thick' understanding of the ethically desirable policies necessary to deal with the concerns? The phenomenon of and threats posed by human-induced climate change raise difficult economic, political and moral challenges for policy makers. It is far from clear that current political institutions and processes are adequate to successfully addressing them.

Chapter 16 looks at a world that is currently undergoing a degree and geographical scope of population mobility not experienced since the immediate aftermath of World War II. Forced migration and displacement is occurring on a scale that threatens to overwhelm the capacities of nation states, their governments and peoples to absorb and adapt to the changing demographic landscape. Conventional migration, refugee and border protection policies are failing and ad hoc responses are seeing the modern equivalent of concentration camps and isolationist rhetoric overwhelming public debates. What are the ethical consequences and questions raised by these developments? How are they feeding into the rising political tide of populist politics?

Chapter 17 revisits a number of the issues raised in Chapter 10 in the light of the arguments presented in Part III. I argue that developments in the neoliberal era raise threats to the future functioning of liberal democracy as the West has come to know it. In the words of a prominent critical economist (Joseph Stiglitz) we live in an era in which democracy itself is in peril.

Each chapter in Part III is structured on a 'what – why – what – so what' basis. I ask what has happened, why did it happen, what are the consequences and what are the normative and policy implications. Sources and references are used sparingly, and provided to assist the reader to follow up the main points made.

It must be stressed that the topics tackled in Part III are very large ones. Each deserves and many have received book-length treatment. My aim is to focus on some of the key aspects of the issues and challenges as a method of illustrating the arguments presented in the first two parts of the book, without claiming to have in any sense exhaustively covered the topics.

The Epilogue provides a final summary of the key arguments of the book and the implications of a renewed ethical commitment to a sustainable social democracy.

The distinguished economist and philosopher Amartya Sen has long stressed the importance of ethical issues for economics. His lectures, published as *On Economics and Ethics* in 1987, summarized the wealth of work done in this field to that point. Since then there has been a veritable explosion in attempts to 'bring' philosophy (especially ethics) into economics. In addition to specialist journals like *Economics and Philosophy* and *Philosophy and Public Affairs* and numerous review articles in outlets like the *Journal of Economic Literature* and the *Journal of Economic Perspectives*, a number of important books have been published on the topic; notably, Hausman and McPherson (1996, 2006), Wight (2015), Little (2002), Gaus (2008), Dutt and Wilber (2013), Reiss (2013) – to name a few.

Why, then, intrude another book into an increasingly crowded field? I do draw on and cite many of the relevant works, recent and earlier – and provide the reader with a brief guide to this literature in chapter endnotes that also extend some of the points made in the text; these additional notes are indicative and not intended to be definitive. I have tried to confine direct quotations in the text to those that I believe best convey the line of argument that I am developing, avoiding the temptation to indulge in debates over alternative interpretations of large topics like utilitarianism, for example. However, I believe that the existing contributions miss a number of important issues and matters of ethical and political import in the context of contemporary public policy in capitalist liberal democracies, due in part to the methodological and institutional framework informing those analyses.

Summarizing, the main differences – and I would argue, positive contributions – of this book are as follows.

First, I attempt (in Part I) to provide an account, albeit selective, of the historical philosophical roots of orthodox economics as it came to dominate the public policy realm from the mid-eighteenth, through the nineteenth and into the twentieth centuries.

Second, the book takes seriously the institutional context within which the capitalist economy operates. The model of rational choice that pervades orthodox economic analysis abstracts from critical social and political factors influencing economic outcomes. The problematic of power in economic life is either ignored or – as in game theory – reduced to a consideration of strategic interaction between individual agents operating in an institutional and cultural vacuum.

Third, I contrast the emergence in the early twentieth century of the 'old' and 'new' economics, associated with two giants in the history of economic thought, Arthur Pigou and Vilfredo Pareto, respectively. In Chapter 8 I subject the concept of Paretian optimality – the bedrock of modern economics – to a rigorous critique; this contrasts with the more limited and disjointed treatments of the notion of economic efficiency found in the existing literature, including the references noted earlier. This chapter is central to the overall thrust of the arguments presented in this book and, I would hazard, one of its main contributions to the lively debates now energizing the discipline and associated social sciences. The contribution resides not in the individual arguments marshaled, as each has, in some degree, been put forward before, but in bringing them together in one place so that the reader can appreciate the collective force of the critique.

Fourth, in Part III, I attempt to demonstrate how recent developments in capitalist economies have ethically significant implications, both for how economics has been practiced and how public policies have unwound. A final word, by way of an epilogue, suggests how things might in future be different. In short, this book offers a more radical political economy approach to the significance of practical ethics in the policy world than is currently available in the literature.

This book is aimed at senior undergraduate and postgraduate students interested in heterodox economics and political economy, and to students and practitioners of public policy. Students in other social sciences and others perplexed by the iron grip of orthodox economics on politicians and policy makers may also find the critical approach advanced here useful.

NOTES

1. There have been many attempts to describe and analyse the manifold facets and causes of the rise of neoliberalism, an essentially contested concept, if ever there was one. For example, see Varoufakis (2011); Berry (2013); Blyth (2013); Quiggin (2010); Cassidy (2009).
2. See, for example, Wight (2015) for a review of non-consequentialist moral traditions and their implications for economics.
3. Frankfurt School critical theorist Theodor Adorno once claimed: 'I established a theoretical model of thought. How could I have expected that people would want to implement it with Molotov cocktails?' (quoted in Jeffries, 2016, p. 1). Adorno's point, apparently, was to interpret the world, not to change it.

2. David Hume's 'judicious spectator'

> It is no exaggeration to say that beginning with the second quarter of the 18th century utilitarianism has more or less succeeded in dominating English moral philosophy . . . In the 20th century, utilitarianism has had far more influence in economics than any other moral philosophy, where it was represented by Marshall and Pigou; only with the 1930s did the hold of the classical doctrine fail. But still today many economists hold what they call a very general form of utilitarianism (Rawls, 2007 p. 393).[1]

Both Amartya Sen (1987) and I.M.D. Little (2002) point to the intellectual roots of modern economics in the philosophical tradition of utilitarianism, associated in particular with the work of Jeremy Bentham, James and John Stuart Mill, Henry Sidgwick and Francis Edgeworth. Utilitarianism in this tradition is uncritically assumed to prioritize the individual's maximization of some good outcome or consequence. However, the philosophical roots of modern economics stretch back further into the eighteenth century, to the Scottish Enlightenment and the foundational contributions of David Hume and Adam Smith. The latter were especially concerned with recognizing the historical and institutional context within which human passions and interests intersected to sustain stable and fulfilling lives. As such, these earlier arguments pre-figured tensions for later variants of utilitarianism, especially those of the classical Benthamite tradition.

Hume in particular focused on the historical reality of societies in which people have legitimate interests and particular moral sentiments, both factors affecting their individual and collective behaviours – and conceptions of *the Good.* Hume's approach, according to John Rawls (2007, p. 177), is characterized by three premises:

1. Moral distinctions and judgments are not based on reason alone but depend also on our sentiments that are socially and culturally nurtured.
2. We (thus) recognize moral distinctions and apply them from a certain point of view – not from 'objective' deductive, inductive or probabilistic arguments.
3. We concur in our moral judgments not as rational and intelligent beings but because we share the same moral sensibilities.

Hume's just society is one in which all or most people accept the rules of a competitive society in which private property is established ensuring security of ownership and transfer and the enforcement of contracts between people. Acceptance is positive in that all or most people publicly recognize that these rules are enshrined in institutions that promote the general good – and accept that (most) others also recognize this. Justice for Hume is based on a convention understood as 'a sense of common interest'.[2]

It is clear that Hume operates with a consequentialist ethical approach. He is concerned with outcomes, with good consequences for people as they themselves judge. Pettit (1991) argues that a consequentialist approach holds that individuals should act to promote and hence maximize the Good. This may create practical challenges. For example, it could lead a liberal government (for whom liberty is the Good) to restrict or ban some actions of groups that can reasonably be seen as threatening the liberty of all. That is, preserving the liberty of the majority over-compensates the loss of liberty by some minorities in consequence. This suggests the possibility of trade-offs, an idea much celebrated by later economists but not often by moral philosophers searching for a rationalist basis for a universalistic ethic. For example, trading off one person's liberty for another's would not be acceptable to strict libertarians who operate with a different conception of the Good, still less to others operating from a non consequentialist or rights-based viewpoint. Consequentialism, according to Pettit, has two parts:

1. Agents face a set of options for acting. Each option has a range of 'prognoses' or outcomes. Every outcome of an option has an impact on the value realized – happiness for utilitarians, freedom for libertarians and so on.
2. Every option has its value fixed by the values of its outcomes.

An agent ranks outcomes in terms of the values realized (prop. 1) and ranks (chooses) options in terms of their outcomes (prop. 2).

Consequentialist moral theory, strictly speaking, requires agents to be exhaustively deliberative, to be human calculating machines, an unrealistic requirement in view of the limitations of human nature. This criticism, Pettit claims, can be met by adopting a 'restrictive consequentialism', whereby agents choose options likely to maximize the value (good) they seek but recognize that this is most likely if they restrict the scope of the options considered.

This more restricted reading – both with respect to potential trade-offs and limited scope of maximization – seems to better fit Hume's rather nuanced analysis of the wellsprings of human behaviour. For Hume, human action is driven not by reason alone but by reason energized and guided by the passions. The latter are classified twofold as: direct, indirect and original, on the one hand, and violent and calm, on the other hand (Rawls, 2000, pp. 26–7). Original passions are instinctually present and when acted upon *give* pleasure or pain and/or emotions of good or evil. They may be expressed 'violently', as in the spur to punish an enemy or satisfy hunger or 'calmly', as in demonstrations of benevolence or acts of kindness to children. Direct passions arise immediately *from* perceptions of pleasure or pain, for example desire and aversion (violent) or a general appetite to good or aversion to evil (calm). Indirect passions arise from pleasure or pain refracted by 'ideas' as well as 'impressions', that is by reflection, as in love and hate (violent) and moral approval or disapproval (calm).[3]

It is this tendency for Hume to equate pleasure and pain with good and evil respectively that moves commentators like Rawls to place him in the utilitarian camp. A further factor pushing in the same direction is Hume's much-celebrated claim that 'reason is the slave of the passions'. By this he means that reason can never be a *motive* for action but can only provide a *rationale* for action spurred by passions, either violently or calmly. Put another way, reason provides the means – the link *perceived* between cause and effect – and passions the ends.[4] Critically, for Hume – and an analytical understanding of the restricted subsequent narrowing of the utilitarian project – the human passions are diverse and are not confined by a commitment to hedonistic or egoistic ends.

> I think for Hume, all kinds of passions may specify ultimate, or final ends: for example, benevolence and kindness to children, pride and shame, our general appetite to good as well as our sense of beauty, and much else, can all specify such ends . . . He doesn't suppose that all our passions are concerned with self-centered objectives (Rawls, 2000, p. 32).

Hume attempts to establish a *psychological* account of morality, based on his analysis of the universal capacity for human sympathy. As a result of repeated observations of and experiences interacting with each other, we each acquire a conception of the fact that other people's passions, desires, fears and aspirations resemble our own. As a consequence of experience and reflection, we each develop a sense of other people's feelings resulting in a *passive* understanding of what they are going through. This comprehension may or may not move us to actively assist them in cases of observed distress. Thus we may help a sick friend, 'knowing' the pain he is suffering, while ignoring the worse plight of millions of starving refugees elsewhere in the world. Sympathy is far from being an impartial propensity: indeed:

> we sympathize more with people as they are like us, close to us, similar to us in culture and language, and so on. Sympathy is not to be mistaken for the love of mankind as such – there is no such thing – and it extends beyond our species, since we sympathize with animals (ibid. p. 87).

Consequently, for Hume, sympathy alone does not provide an adequate base for realizing binding moral judgments and commitments across a society with diverse, often conflicting interests and localized loyalties. Fortunately, human beings also possess the capacity to reason and imagine themselves in a distanced point of view from which they can come to similar moral judgments. This viewpoint is that of 'the judicious spectator'. 'So, on Hume's view, then, what makes agreement on moral judgment possible is our being able to take up and to imagine ourselves into the point of view of the judicious spectator' (Rawls, 2007, p. 186).

Put more forcefully, Rawls (2000, pp. 90–1) argues:

> I take Hume to think, then, that the only psychological mechanism that can explain our agreement in moral judgment is that of sympathy, as called into operation and adjusted by the point of view of the judicious spectator. No other passion of our constitution has the features necessary to give rise to our moral sentiments and to secure general agreement among persons scattered in space and time, and in different societies with different cultures.

However, the capacity to form considered moral judgments, from the viewpoint of the judicious spectator, does not necessarily *ensure* that they will be generally embraced in thought or deed. Localized considerations of self-interest and the interests of others in close relation of family, ethnicity and so on may – and often will – trump the moral imperatives of distanced reflection. Hume is only claiming that people *would* commit to the generally held moral judgments *if* people assumed the viewpoint of the judicious spectator. It is only by dint of the development through time of conventions and norms that people in society are likely to take on the generalized moral positions that emanate from that viewpoint. In stable societies the sphere of operation of the judicious spectator gradually expands, reinforcing the conventions and social order in a virtuous circle. Rawls (2000, p. 91) concludes:

> The general appetite to good connects the interests of our self from the present into the future; while sympathy transmuted by the point of view of the judicious spectator arouses our concern impartially for the interests of persons everywhere. So transmuted, sympathy in union with the general appetite to good, lays down lines of judgment that can hold together the social world.[5]

Barry (1989) argues that Hume developed two theories of justice, the first focused on mutual self-interest, and the second on the role of impartiality (the viewpoint of the judicious spectator). Both imply a proto-utilitarianism, most particularly the second. 'The generalization of sympathy is general benevolence – a concern for the public good. The implication of impartiality is, therefore for Hume, some sort of utilitarianism' (Barry, 1989, p.168).

Many of Hume's concerns were prominent in the work of other eighteenth-century political economists and moral philosophers, notably his Scottish compatriot and friend, Adam Smith.

> Eighteenth-century political thought, as it is expressed in Smith's and Condorcet's economic writings, is concerned with individual diversity, with conflicts of interest and conflicts between different principles, with vexation, with history, with personal and public oppression (Rothschild, 2002, p. 219).

Adam Smith is today best remembered for his book, *An Inquiry into the Nature and Causes of the Wealth of Nations*, published in 1776. His other great book, *The Theory of Moral Sentiments*, was published earlier and went through six editions during his lifetime. Sen (2009a) has argued that the subsequent eclipse of the second book by the first has impoverished our understanding of *The Wealth of Nations* and to its implications for economics as a whole.

> The neglect applies, among other issues, to the appreciation of the demands of rationality, the need for recognizing the plurality of human motivations, the connections between ethics and economics, and the co-dependent – rather than free-standing – role of institutions in general and free markets in particular in the functioning of the economy (Sen, 2009a, p. viii).

Sen criticizes 'the fanciful belief' in an inconsistency between Smith's accounts of the role played by 'sympathy' in *Moral Sentiments* and self-interest in *Wealth of Nations*. Both motives for action, sympathy and self-love, figure prominently in both books.

> If self-love is of special relevance in seeking some particular explanation – for example, why people seek trade – then other motivations have important roles in explaining other types of [economic] choices – for example, work discipline and a commitment to obeying good rules and to treating others with respect and honor. The role of self-love in explaining particular economic phenomena does nothing to reduce the relevance of different motivations in the understanding of other economic regularities (ibid. p. ix).

This reading of Smith's account of human motivation underscores the role of sympathy, benevolence and so on in explaining *some* economic processes and outcomes. It also suggests that the very operation of markets that satisfy the facility to 'truck and barter' depends in part on the generalized existence and potency of these other institutionally imposed, morally based factors – to wit, trust, reciprocity and respect for the law. It also supports the arguments of the contemporary political philosopher Michael Sandel (2013) that there are some things 'money can't buy'. In other words, Smith (and Hume) does not seek to understand the economy as a separate sphere of human society governed by distinct laws grounded only in the selfish desires of individuals. Nevertheless, this is precisely how generations of later economists and other commentators have chosen to interpret Smith (as Sen notes). Duncan Foley (2006) has coined the phrase 'Adam's Fallacy' in a book of the same title to underline this tradition. It has empowered economists ever after to focus only on – namely to build models specified by – the consequences of the independently given, aggregated self-interested actions of individuals, to the exclusion of other individual and collective causal factors. Wells (2014, p. 90) makes a similar argument:

> . . . the popular view of Smith among economists that has resulted from this emphasis is twice distorted. Firstly, it is based on the narrow foundations of a few select quotations from *The Wealth of Nations* (WN) that are taken in isolation as summing up his work (Smith only mentions the 'all important' invisible hand once); and secondly, these quotations have been analyzed in a particularly narrow way. Both selection and interpretation have been driven by contemporary mainstream economists' interest in justifying orthodox economic methodology and their peculiar (Mandevillian not Smithian) assumption of the selfish utility-maximizing *homo economicus*.[6]

Smith, writing after Hume's second thoughts (see note 5), took the plurality of human motivations as a basic axiom of human nature, rather than grounded in a supporting theory of moral psychology: '(t)hat we often derive sorrow from the sorrow of others, is a matter of fact too obvious to require any instances to prove it' (Smith, 2009/1790, p. 13). Not only do markets express and integrate the mutual strivings of individuals seeking their self-advantage, they are also energized by the other-regarding sentiments of compassion, sympathy and fairness, while expressing what Smith called 'prudence'. Humans act prudently by joining reason to self-love, checked by 'self-command'. If all or most people act prudently, the worst conflicts of interest can be contained. If, in addition, all or most express a degree of other-regarding concern – by, for example, keeping promises, paying their debts, treating each other with respect – everyone will benefit over the long run. Good behaviour breeds good behaviour, solidified through institutional convention in the form of social norms backed by sanctions, formal and informal, religious and secular.

Like Hume, Smith introduced a hypothetical viewpoint allowing humans to make disinterested moral judgments and to orient, in part, their actual behaviour to prudently achieve their many ends in a stable, well-functioning society. 'The impartial spectator', like Hume's 'judicious spectator', is meant to distance an individual from the immediate fog of self-focused consideration, to provide 'space' to see the world as others might and thus to act as a check on hasty or imprudent judgment that might express rationalizations rather than reasoned outcomes. The main difference is that Hume's spectator is historically bound to the society under review, an aid for people in that society to jointly recognize and establish the institutions, values and norms that will deliver an overlapping common interest though time. Smith's spectator is a device to bring to the individual's consciousness, knowledge of values and interests of others, both within her society and beyond in societies of other cultures, places and times. This, according to Sen (2009a, p. xviii), satisfies two aims: it ensures that we each have an opportunity to take the interests of those in other, even distant, places into account in our actions; and second, it broadens our perspectives and options, opening opportunities that would otherwise never have been available. This second pay-off is particularly important because it can encourage a progressive, outward-looking entrepreneurial society that delivers increasing prosperity thereby improving the material lives of its citizens – the overriding aim of *The Wealth of Nations* that is not achievable or even comprehensible without the ethical groundwork provided by *The Theory of Moral Sentiments.*[7]

Albert Hirschman in his book *The Passions and the Interests* (1977), having shorn the concept of 'interest' of its negative connotations, also refused to sever it from Smith's moral theory. As Hirschman's biographer comments:

> If there was one man who would set the stage for a great ideological struggle over how to think about markets and politics, private pursuits and public well-being, it was Adam Smith. And Hirschman, anticipating the fight, struggled to create a bridge between the sides by positioning Smith as a man who championed private self-interest but never lost his public moral bearings. Not unlike Hirschman himself (Adelman, 2013, p. 512).[8]

Smith's search for a universalist ethic via the device of the impartial spectator implies an *ethical orientation* in favour of equality and social inclusion and, in public policy terms, for an active interventionist state: '(t)he difference between the most dissimilar characters, between a philosopher and a common street porter, for example, seems to arise not so much from nature as from habit, custom and education' (quoted in Sen, 2009a, p. xxii).

> The global reach of Smith's moral and political reasoning is, of course, quite a distinctive feature of his thought, but it is strongly supplemented by his belief that all humans are born with similar potential and – most importantly for policymaking – that the inequalities in the world reflect socially generated, rather than natural, disparities (ibid. p. xxii).

CONCLUSION

The importance of considering the thought of long-dead eighteenth-century political economists – as Hirschman (1977), Sen (1987) and Rothschild (2002) have argued – is to recognize the complex interrelations between the passions and the interests that existed before modern economics collapsed the distinction into a reductionist theory of rational choice that rules out the explanatory and policy pay-off resulting from an approach that embraces the pluralistic structure of human nature. The end result 200 years later was an economic science trapped in a market fundamentalism that failed to recognize the possibility, still less imminence, of systemic crises to the capitalist society who's nascent outlines were just emerging as the giants of the Scottish Enlightenment penned their magisterial works.

Contrary to the one-sided view of Smith as a gung-ho proponent of laissez-faire, he was all too aware of the existence of entrenched multiple cases of what later economists would call market failure. Consequently, government is called upon to intervene in ways that far transcend Locke's ideal nightwatchman state and the libertarian stance of later political philosophers like Robert Nozick. Public policy is thus cast as a fit subject for the focus of political economy – but not as a set of interventions cut off from the pervasive relevance of ethical factors. Those who came later engineered this split.

How, it can reasonably be asked, did the nuanced, positive, humane and global vision of writers like Smith and Hume – and Turgot, Condorcet, Godwin and Mary Wollstonecraft – morph into the dismal science of the mid-nineteenth century? It is to this question we turn in the next two chapters.

NOTES

1. The first part of this chapter draws heavily on the interpretation of Hume's work by the American philosopher John Rawls, particularly in his lectures on the history of moral and political philosophy, published as Rawls (2000) and Rawls (2007). Not surprisingly, with a philosopher as complex as Hume, other interpretations are possible.

2. '. . . Hume believes that rules of justice could only arise out of mutual self-interest. Hume adds that once rules of justice are in existence, respecting the rules comes to be seen as a virtue. When we adopt an impartial standpoint, we can all approve of justice because we all see how it is conducive to general utility' (Barry, 1989, p.153).
3. Hume's characterization here of 'the double relation of impressions and ideas' draws on his celebrated epistemological account of perception and causality presented in Book I of the *Treatise of Human Nature*.
4. Hume's analysis of causality as constant conjunction of impressions, presented earlier on in the *Treatise*, is presupposed.
5. Rawls (2000, p.101) also notes that Hume had second thoughts and in later writings substituted for sympathy as the basis of fellow feeling, an axiomatic 'Principle of Humanity'. Nevertheless, he still held that human beings are capable of other than purely self-interested motives and behaviour, in all realms of life.
6. 'Smith's defense of capitalism (or, in his terminology, "commercial society") is unambiguous but qualified. There is no inconsistency here. Smith's commitment to a realistic liberalism led him to endorse commercial society over any previous socio-economic system as a social order in which the most people possible could live decent lives. But he was not the blind zealot for the market he is now sometimes portrayed as. Smith was acutely aware of the possible ethical shortcomings of commercial society and, for example, carefully read and responded to Rousseau's powerful critiques of its materialism, inequality, and inauthenticity . . .' (Wells, 2014, p.91).
7. Smith's externalized scope for the operation of our other-regarding sentiments differentiates him not only from Hume's narrower, historically grounded moral focus but also – as Sen (2009a, p.xviii) claims – from the contractarian approach of Rawls's liberal theory of justice. The contrast lies in Smith's espousal of an 'open (as opposed to a closed) impartiality'. It is also the case that *The Wealth of Nations* highlights the negative consequences of the emergence of a commercial society, notably in the physical and morally stunting effects on workers of the growing detail division of labour in industry (this claim is the focus of Well's paper quoted earlier).
8. Adelman (2013, p.520) comments that Hirschman's pioneering humanistic reading of Smith was further developed by Donald Winch (1971) and Emma Rothschild (2002). Sen's interpretation has been noted earlier.

3. Bentham's legacy

Utility is the great idol of the time, to which all powers do homage and all subjects are subservient (Friedrich Schiller).

All other principles than that of utility must be wrong (Jeremy Bentham).

INTRODUCTION

Jeremy Bentham was an English philosopher and lawyer whose long life spanned the early stages of the industrial revolution and who died shortly before the passing of the great Reform Bill of 1832 – legislation that his writings and the agitation of his supporters did much to bring about. As a legal scholar he sought to develop an objective, universalistic theory of morals on which to base both individual human behaviour and (in particular) the acts of government. All acts of individuals and their legislators were to be evaluated and justified on the basis of a single principle, that of utility. The principle is simply stated but its interpretation and application much more problematic as generations of commentators have since found. Bentham himself held back publication of his most important book on the subject – *An Introduction to the Principles of Morals and Legislation* – for a decade as he wrestled with thorny problems that left him '. . . unexpectedly entangled in an unsuspected corner of the metaphysical maze.'

Once out of the maze he famously described the Principle of Utility as follows:

> Nature has placed mankind under the governance of two sovereign masters, pain and pleasure. It is for them alone to point out what we ought to do, *as well as to determine what we shall do*. On the one hand, the standard of right and wrong, *on the other the chain of causes and effects, are fastened to that throne* (Bentham, 1961/1789, p. 17; italics added).

There are two critical implications of Bentham's definition. First, it echoes the late Hume's position by simply claiming as axiomatic that human beings have a particular moral nature, though Bentham collapses the former's two moral drivers into a single one, to seek pleasure and avoid pain. Second, as the italicized sections of the passage above suggests, Bentham asserts that people actually act under the sovereign weight of pleasure and pain, that the 'is' and 'ought' distinguished by Hume can (and *should*) be transcended. Both these implications came to have great impact on the subsequent development of economics.

The rest of Bentham's *Introduction* was devoted to explicating the types of pleasures and pains and the manner in which, conceptually, they could be aggregated, along with the motives driving action towards maximizing the pleasures and minimizing the pains gained. Actions would and should be undertaken by citizens and their governments that maximized the net gains, pleasures less pain, for all sentient beings.[1] In the classical Benthamite canon, it is *total utility* that must be maximized, regardless of the diverse nature of the causes and forms of pleasures and pain and of their distribution across the population.

It is the job of the legislator to ascertain – that is, measure – the value of the pleasures and pains that any proposed act or policy would cause. How is this to be done? First, take an individual to be directly affected and calculate for each pleasure and pain, its intensity, duration, certainty and propinquity. Second, check that the list is complete by considering the 'fecundity' of the act – that is, the probability that the first pleasure will be followed by another – and its 'purity', the probability that a pleasure will not be associated with a pain. The utility of an act for that person will be greater the greater the intensity, duration, certainty and propinquity of the pleasures caused; likewise for the pains inflicted.[2] Thus, taking all this into account:

> Sum up all the values of all the pleasures on the one hand, and those of all the pains on the other. The balance if it be on the side of pleasure, will give the good tendency of the act upon the whole, with respect to the interests of that individual person, if on the side of pain, the bad tendency of it on the whole (ibid. p. 39).

Third, carry out the same calculation for every individual person (sentient being) likely to be affected by the act and sum the net values across the group. Fourth, put into effect all acts that deliver a positive net balance of pleasures or, where resources are limited, rank the acts from highest to lowest net positives and move down the list until resources are exhausted.

Even before considering what summing values means and the units of value to be summed across diverse effects and different people, it is clear that the Principle of Utility, if seriously applied by governments, would tax the informational capacities of legislators armed with a room full of super computers.

The great attraction of classical utilitarianism resides in its bold collapse of all consequences of individual and government action into a single, seemingly unassailable ethical precept. Act so as to create the greatest (net) happiness for the greatest number. Don't worry about the motives behind acts: 'Nothing can act of itself as a motive but the idea of pleasure and pain' (ibid. p. 100). Put all your efforts into measuring and summing the pleasures and pains. Be aware of human motives, intentionality, consciousness and so on – but only in order to more exhaustively grasp their effects on the generation of pleasures and pains; later economists like Mises and Hayek would criticize this level of active intervention of the state in social affairs.

Although Bentham's ethical precepts have been widely interpreted as applying to individual morality in a universal sense, he was writing at a time and in a society that was profoundly unequal, one in which the vast majority of people were poor, illiterate and disenfranchised. Bentham's main goal was to establish firm principles for good government, a solid framework for public policy. This did not rely on all or most people acting morally – that is, consciously acting to maximize their happiness – since most people were not sufficiently enlightened to know how to do so and their sphere of attainable happiness was so limited that simply getting by on a day-by-day basis captured their waking hours. His aim was to convince Britain's ruling class, those wielding real political power to so arrange the affairs of state that the result would be the greatest good for the greatest number of their subjects. Viner (1948 [1973], p. 197; italics in the original) has produced an impressive list of achievements in this endeavour:

> The list of reforms in England which derive largely from Bentham is a truly impressive one, and I present it here only in part: fundamental law reform in many of its branches; prison reform; adult popular suffrage, including woman suffrage; free trade; reform in colonial government; legalization of trade unions; general education at public expense; free speech and free press; the secret ballot; a civil service appointed and promoted on merit; repeal of the usury laws; general registration of titles to property; reform of local government; a safety code for merchant shipping; sanitary reform and preventive medicine at public expense; systematic collection of statistics; free justice for the poor. Bentham was the first person to propose birth control, and this *before* Malthus had published his first *Essay on the Principles of Population* . . . The Ministry of Health which he proposed would be made responsible not only for the sanitation and routine public health work, but also for smoke prevention, local health-museums, and the policing of the medical profession to prevent their formation of monopolies.

Bentham and (especially) his later followers hoped that through public education and stable government the moral characters of the majority would be raised so that the principle of utility would come to direct their behaviours, reinforcing the maximization of total utility. However, this was not to be assumed; it was a work in progress. Bentham for most of his long life was a cautious reformer, conservative to the extent that he believed that maintaining social stability – that is, protecting existing institutions like private property and the rule of English law as a bulwark against the chaos of revolutionary fervor in France – offered the best prospect of maximizing utility in the long run. Towards the end of his life Bentham came around to accept the arguments of his friend James Mill that such a society would, eventually, be democratic but that too would take time and only on the grounds that democratic government was the most likely political vehicle for utility maximization.

DEVELOPMENTS

Over the next 70 or 80 years Bentham's austere theory was developed by a number of philosophers. Important contributions, extensions and corrections were made early in the nineteenth century by Bentham's friend James Mill – and most critically by Mill's son, as we will see in the next chapter – and later by the philosopher and political economist Henry Sidgwick and Francis Edgeworth. Sidgwick in the *Method of Ethics* sought to establish rational principles of practical reason that would maximize the likelihood of achieving the felicific Benthamite outcome. In ethics, he held, there is always one right answer for all those who rationally seek it. 'There is always *one right or best answer*, and this answer is the *same* for all rational minds' (Rawls, 2007, p. 381). He wants to focus on establishing the method or way rational enquiry reaches principles of right action that all will agree to. In doing so he derived a principle of utility that maximized the balance of 'agreeable over disagreeable consciousness'. There was no question for Sidgwick that this principle justified maximizing anything but *total* – rather than, say *average* – utility.[3]

According to Rawls (2007, p. 379), Sidgwick succeeded in demonstrating by systematic comparative argument the superiority of hedonism over intuitionism but could not prove universalistic hedonism (Sidgwick's preferred position) superior to egoistic hedonism. Individuals were acting in ethically acceptable ways by selfishly and exclusively seeking their own utility concerns and did not require their utilities to depend on that of others, though of course they may well do so. Sidgwick's statement of utilitarianism was neutral between selfishness and altruism and could encompass all combinations in between. This went some way to softening the earlier interpretation of Bentham's principle as positing an irredeemably self-centred conception of human nature; it allows but does not assume a position of psychological egoism. However, it was the egoistic, self-centred view of the human actor that passed into the mainstream of economics over the following century and still inhabits the discipline.

Each individual was assumed to warrant having his or her (or its) utility (balance of agreeable consciousness) maximized across m periods of time as:

$$\text{Max } \Sigma U = a_1U_1 + a_2U_2 + \ldots + a_mU_m \tag{3.1}$$

For periods 1, 2, . . ., m

Where a_i are weightings representing *when* they achieve agreeable consciousness across m time periods – that is, the extent to which they enjoy instant rather than deferred gratification.[4]

In applying the calculus to society at large, the principle in its broadest form, called for governments to aggregate the utility of all people (and other sentient beings) over their lives, as stated by equation 3.1.

$$\text{MaxU} = \Sigma\, b_iU_i \tag{3.2}$$

For individuals 1, 2, . . ., n

Where b_i represent the relative weightings of the utility of individuals 1, 2, . . ., n.

This calculus assumes that all individuals know all outcomes and values with certainty. The weights do not express probability judgments.

In classical utilitarianism for all i, $b_i = 1$ (that is, all count equally; Paul is as good as Paula).

It is this latter presumption of equality, that each person's utility counts equally that made utilitarianism so attractive to social reformers and philosophical radicals in the nineteenth century, and down to the present day, resulting in the impressive list of social policies listed by Viner and carried on in the twentieth century with the rise of the welfare state. It is also controversial because it can imply that individuals should treat the utility or welfare of *all* other people equally – that is, that they shouldn't give preference to their family members or close friends or fellow members of tribe, class or caste. Though such a neutral stance might be conceivable in the case of public policy imposed by a disinterested governing elite – indeed, many modern economists in their day-to-day role as advisers seem to assume that this is self-evident (notwithstanding the stinging critique of public choice theorists) – it is demonstrably nonsense at the level of ordinary life in all real existing societies. Also controversial was the implication that anything that gave pleasure to any individual was to be counted on a par with any other pleasure and likewise for pains; the only differentiating factor was quantitative as to relative intensity, duration, certainty and propinquity, though allowance was made for compound pleasures like love and patriotism, as well as simple pleasures of the flesh. It is in this context that Bentham made his famous claim that 'push-pin is as good as poetry' that so enraged the guardians of good taste in the aristocratic Britain of his day. If devoting government resources to expanding the sport of greyhound racing generated more net happiness (after accounting for the disutility of the dogs and rabbits) than supporting the opera and ballet, then the dogs have it. It is easy, even today, to understand why this position is problematic. It was, as we will see, one of the main points that caused John Stuart Mill to substantially modify classical utilitarianism. The mass provision of bread and circuses may contribute to social order and entrench the power of a ruling class but the members of that class are unlikely to be satisfied with a strictly utilitarian justification for their power and privilege. Although an indirect utilitarian argument could be mounted to the effect that maintaining social order where everyone 'knows his place' is preferable to anarchy or the mass pain suffered when revolution against the ruling class ensues (a favoured position of conservatives – and political philosophers like Thomas Hobbes and John Locke), the argument applies only to the transition period and not necessarily to the bright dawn of a new era once the chaos subsides. Breaking eggs may be a justifiably necessary part of historical baking (a favoured position of radicals).

However, as noted earlier and returned to further on, the strictly classical tradition has nothing substantive to say about the distribution of total utility. Paul may be rich in happiness and Paula poor but any increase in Paul's happiness is justified by Bentham's moral arithmetic if it exceeds any loss of Paula's.

Sidgwick's utilitarianism brings into sharp relief the attractions and limitations of this ethical tradition. The idea and aim of calculating and then maximizing the sum total of agreeable consciousness across an entire society over the life of that society makes explicit the impossibility of finding a common measure of what is being maximized. The seeming simplicity of the term 'utility' – measured in 'utils'(?) – collapses when individual consciousness enters the frame; how does one compare still less quantify the state of consciousness of an individual over time, still less compare consciousness between people now or over time?

Nevertheless, Edgeworth (1881 [1932]), in particular looked forward to a future in which it would be possible to measure, within an acceptable statistical range of probabilities, the happiness and pain experienced psycho-physically by and among individuals sufficiently well to inform governments as to the policies most likely to maximize total utility. Colander (2007) provides an account of Edgeworth's notion of a 'hedonimeter' (or 'hedonometer') that would directly capture the individual's agreeable consciousness on the basic of the emerging science of psycho-physics being developed by German experimental psychologists, Ernst Weber and G.T. Fechner; the latter's law seemed to Edgeworth to promise just such a breakthrough. Edgeworth thought that by casting the net over a sufficiently large population aggregating individual pleasures would be worth pursuing. 'We have only to add another dimension expressing the number of sentients, and to integrate through all time and over all sentience, to constitute the end of pure utilitarianism' (quoted in Colander, 2007, p. 217). Thus, Edgeworth expressed in words the intent of equation 3.2, above. Colander claims that Edgeworth:

> . . . further argued that this machine would, in principle, offer reconciliation between egoism and altruism, since the pleasure that people take in the happiness of others would be measurable, or as Edgeworth . . . put it, the hedonimeter would integrate into utility 'the psychical side of a physical change in what may be dimly discerned as a sort of hedonico-magnetic field.'

Edgeworth's excursion into mumbo-jumbo land, represented in this last quote, looks a little less fantastical in the period since the 1970s when once again psychology provided a spur to economic studies of happiness. The efforts by neuroscientists to physically map sites of brain activity and relate them to emotional perceptions at least take up Edgeworth's challenge at the level of the individual.[5]

In spite of Edgeworth's unrealized hopes, classical utilitarianism and its generalized form ran into a dead end by the close of the nineteenth century, unable to conjure up an acceptable interpersonal and intertemporal *cardinal* measure of utility. Nevertheless, it initiated a search for a rational basis for public policy from the viewpoint of the consequences for individual citizens of the alternative actions of government. 'In sum: classical utilitarianism was the first tradition to develop a systematic moral conception under the assumption of a secular society under modern conditions' (Rawls, 2007, p. 395).

Other forms of utilitarianism can be cast more widely to include maximizing non-hedonistic and/or 'rational' human interests, however, constraints are required so that no competing moral principles are introduced. 'Rational' must not imply a moral imperative separate from maximizing 'rational human interests'.

Whatever variant of utilitarianism is proposed it must imply a definition of the good that is:

- independent of and prior to the right
- subjectively related to (a) agreeable feelings or (b) rational individual interests (with 'rational' suitably limited)

- focused on the individual; no *moral* significance is given to relations between individuals
- maximized.

Hence, permissible variations to classical utilitarianism, then, share several characteristics:

- priority of the good over the right
- the good is defined in relation to the individual human agent
- the capacity of pleasure and pain (happiness or some other concept of 'welfare'[6]) is experienced (and measured) at any time by actual individuals at that time and in the circumstances they find themselves. 'We start at each moment in our deliberations from those aspects of people as they are or can be foreseen to be. Practical reason is based upon *given* propensities and desires' (ibid. p. 399).

We can note that the comment in the last sentence has been taken up axiomatically by economics in the form of the exogenous status of consumer and worker preferences.

The difficulties that utilitarianism raises, both conceptually and practically are legion. The ruthlessly individualist cast of the felicific calculus seems to rule out behaviour and policies motivated by communitarian sentiments. Should not governments weigh in the balance the effects of their policies on the strength of social cohesion, cooperation and patriotism? For example, would outlawing private gun ownership increase the sum of human happiness by reducing random killings, increasing a shared sense of security, reducing defensive expenditures on millions of weapons that live their lives in drawers or under beds? To demur by citing the infringement on the right of individuals to bear arms would cut no ice with utilitarians for whom no other moral imperative but good consequences for individuals counts. Instead a gun-toting utilitarian might argue that the level of chaos and unrestrained violence that would ensue if guns were widely banned – when 'only the criminals had guns' – would result in a net negative impact on total utility. The pain caused gun lovers by being denied their weapons of choice would also need to be included in the balance. But is it not also open to argue, from an ethic of community, that the effects of restricting guns are good not in themselves but because they express and reinforce a shared sense of togetherness and mutual trust, in each other and in the institutions that are there to guarantee safety and security? Even this situation could be recast in a utilitarian form if it happened that the utility functions of all, or at least most, people prioritized the achievement and maintenance of social solidarity. In this case the policy of gun control would be morally sanctioned on both utilitarian and communitarian grounds.

Utilitarianism runs up against more difficult headwinds when forced to confront tricky trade-offs. For example, should governments (or private vigilantes) kill a suspected terrorist before any overt action on the latter's part? If the act of terror goes ahead and succeeds, then hundreds of people may die or be injured. Isn't one life lost preferable to many (potentially) saved? Most observers – an impartial spectator – would probably agree but only if (a) the level of probability of the act was very high, (b) the probability of the success of the act was high and (c) other preventive actions were unlikely to succeed. However, it is rational for a pacifist to disagree on the basis of an absolutely firm commitment to the sanctity of all human life, including terrorists, operating from a deontological viewpoint in which Right is prior to the Good. Even a utilitarian may have qualms in this instance; the trickiness relates to the 'probabilities' and 'potential' terms in the stated trade-off earlier. How high must the probabilities be, how successful alternative preemptive action?[7]

Regardless of the form that utility assumes, whether in terms of net happiness, agreeable consciousness, welfare or some other synonym and putting aside for the moment the issue of measurement, the critical issue that most concerns critics is that of who gets what. *What about the distribution of utility across society?* This is irrelevant to a strictly utilitarian position, *unless it is clear that some redistribution would increase or decrease total utility*. Total utility may be increased by taking resources and hence the capacity for happiness away from poor people and giving those resources to rich people to use to increase their happiness. As long as the net change is positive, the act is morally acceptable, indeed mandatory; conversely, a shift from rich to poor is morally binding if total utility is enhanced. Likewise, total utility may increase if the population of poor people increases, as long as the marginal increase in net happiness of the newcomers exceeds any marginal loss of utility by the existing poor and richer people inconvenienced by the expanded strata of the poor. A similar implication arises if average rather than total utility is the maximand. Whatever average measure is used, an increase can go along with increasing inequality of outcomes. Thus average utility increases if an increase in the utility of the rich outweighs any loss by the poor. Recent debates on the increasing wealth of the 'top 1 per cent' relative to the remaining 99 per cent illustrate this point (Piketty, 2013; Dorling, 2014). In short, classical utilitarianism can cover situations marked by all degrees of inequality, from complete inequality to complete equality. I will return to these and related issues in later chapters.

MODERN UTILITY THEORY

The classical utilitarian school petered out late in the nineteenth century. We might well say, with the early nineteenth century critic and essayist William Hazlitt: 'Mr. Bentham, perhaps, overrates the importance of his own theories' (Hazlitt, 1825 [2004]), p. 91). However, the qualitative influence of the doctrine in a number of variants lives on in contemporary philosophical debates (see for example, Sen and Williams, 1982; Smart and Williams, 1973; Brandt, 1979; Hare, 1981).[8] Economists have been faced with major difficulties, namely how to rescue a sense of human welfare maximization dependent on the consequences of the allocation of scarce resources among competing uses. It is the *idea* of maximizing *the good* that modern economics derives from the utilitarian tradition and which underlies the discipline's ethical foundation. Ways would have to be found to operationalize the concept of utility.

Two broad traditions emerged early in the twentieth century, generally called the 'old' and 'new' welfare economics (see Chapter 7 for a discussion). At this point it is useful to focus on the way in which utility came to be first turned into a theory of individual choice or *preference* under conditions of both certainty and uncertainty (more accurately, risk).

One option is to ditch the attempt to find a cardinal measure of utility, to focus, instead, on how individuals *would* act – that is, choose between alternatives – *if* they are rational. In effect, this approach turns moral action into rational choice. Considerations of comparative desire or happiness – should one do A or B – are replaced by the notion of preference satisfaction – would one choose/prefer A or B. The theory of rational choice is based on a small set of key axioms, namely (Gaus, 2008, pp. 36–40):

1. An individual X has a *complete* set of preferences over the options or actions facing him or her. Thus, for any pair of options a and b, X prefers a to b, or X prefers b to a, or X is indifferent between a and b.
2. If X prefers a to b, then X cannot prefer b to a; the preference relation is strictly speaking, *asymmetric*. In contrast if X is indifferent between a and b, X must be indifferent between b and a; this preference relation is *symmetrical*.
3. For all options a, X must prefer a to a or at least be indifferent between a and a; this relation of *reflexivity* is necessary for logical consistency, only.
4. X's preferences must be *transitive*. For any set of options a, b and c, if X prefers a to b and b to c, then X must prefer a to c.

On the basis of these four axioms it is possible to construct an *ordinal utility function* for X that orders (ranks) all his or her preferences consistently. That is, over any set of options a,b,c, . . .,n a non-unique set of numbers can be attached that reflects X's *ranking* of those options. For example, a numerical function that represents X's ranking of a preferred to b preferred to c and so on down to n could be: 3, 2.7, 1.8, . . . 1 *or* 14, 11, 10.9, . . . 6 *or* 1 000 000, 64, 11,. . .,10 *or* any other set of n numbers in strictly descending order. Where two options express a relation of indifference, they receive the same numerical value. There exist an infinite number of specific ordinal functions that consistently rank the set of preferences. Ordinal utility is said to be 'unique up to a monotonic transformation'.

The key point is that no significance can be given to the intervals between the numbers on any of the functions, any one of which could suffice to express X's n preferences.

> It is, then, an error to say (as is all-too-often said) that a person prefers x to y because x gives him more utility. Utility does not explain the preference: utility is simply a representation of the preference. Utility is not something apart from, or additional to, preference satisfaction: it is a numerical function that represents the degree to which a person's preferences are satisfied. Ordinal utility functions map preferences over outcomes on to numbers . . . The size of the differences or the ratios between the numbers, provide no additional information. A person's preference ranking can generate an infinite number of ordinal utility measures . . . All the ordinal utility function tells us is that, for a specific person, a higher-numbered outcome is preferred to a lower-numbered one (Gaus, 2008, p. 37).

> Although the utility language was inherited from the utilitarians – some of whom thought of utility as sensation with a certain intensity, duration, purity or 'propinquity' . . . – there is no such implication in contemporary [utility] theory. To speak of individuals as 'aiming to maximize' utility or as 'seeking more' utility may misleadingly suggest that utility is an object of choice, some good thing that people want in addition to healthy children, lower taxes, or kiwi fruit. But the theory of rational choice says nothing about *what* people want (Hausman and McPherson, 2006, p. 49).

It thus makes no sense to add together an individual's ordinal utilities (numbers) for different outcomes and periods; adding ordinal utilities for the same outcomes for different people is also nonsensical. All that has happened is that utility has been re-engineered as a short hand term for rational choice, *as defined by a minimal set of axioms*. Nevertheless, the older sense of 'something' tangible like weight persists; it is all too easy to slip between the technical sense in which individuals are assumed to be choosing rationally – that is, satisfying their preferences in ways specified by the axioms of choice outlined earlier – to a situation in which they are maximizing utility defined as satisfaction of desires, happiness, welfare and so on. This slipperiness is a marked feature of modern economics and policy debates.

Further slippage is rife. Utility theory does *not* imply that preferences are universally selfish. *What* people want, the content of preferences a, b, c, . . ., n, is an open matter, as far as the theory of rational choice is concerned:

> Someone who ranks the wellbeing of others very highly is no less a utility maximizer than is the individual who is indifferent to the welfare of others. When economic theories treat individuals as self-interested, as they often do, they must add substantive claims concerning what people want to the standard theory of rationality (ibid. p. 49).

A final act of slippage occurs when proponents of rational choice theory imply that so acting is morally good: '(t)o define what rational preference and choice are, is ipso facto to say how one ought rationally to prefer and to choose' (ibid. p. 49). Gaus (2008) attempts a spirited defence of the moral imperative to act according to the axioms of rational choice theory but concludes: '(r)ather than trying to provide instrumental or pragmatic justifications for the axioms of ordinal utility, it is better, I think, to see them as constitutive of our conception of a fully rational agent' (Gaus, 2008, p. 39). Moral content will need to be added!

Although ordinal utility theory has not answered the questions originally posed by utilitarianism, it has, as we will see, influenced greatly both the 'positive' and 'normative' branches of economics and the application of tools drawn from both to inform public policy. It enabled analytical attention to focus on the process of individual choice – recast as 'revealed preference' – rather than the value content of actions by and outcomes for individuals. Having established an ordinal account of individual rational choice, attention later turned to the question of whether a consistent theory of *collective choice* based on a similarly parsimonious set of axioms can be developed. In other words, can an aggregate utility function be constructed for society as a whole? If so, what axioms are required *and* do they carry moral as well as logical weight?[9]

The second way out of Bentham's maze created by the challenge of measuring the utility outcomes of different acts or choices by an individual resulted in the 1950s in a novel solution.[10] The problem with an ordinal measure of utility is that it says nothing about *how much* X prefers a to b compared to c. He or she may just prefer a to b by a whisker but choose either over c by a large margin. For example, a might be a chocolate ice cream, b a vanilla ice cream and c a trip to the dentist; if X has a morbid fear of dentists and/or a sweet tooth then the difference between either a or b, on the one hand and c on the other may be huge.

The approach involves confronting an individual with a series of risky outcomes or 'lotteries' based on his or her ordinal preferences and infer – based on an expanded set of axioms – a cardinal scale of numbers. In addition to the axioms of completeness, transitivity and so on, for ordinal utility, others include the independence of outcomes and technical requirements for handling 'compound lotteries' (see Gaus, 2008, pp. 40–4). The resulting utility function (set of numbers) possesses the 'expected utility' property, that is, the utility of an act X with n possible outcomes is the simple sum of the outcomes multiplied by their respective probabilities or:

$$U(X_i) = p_1X_1 + p_2X_2 +. . . +p_nX_n \tag{3.3}$$

The (expected) utility numbers so derived for outcomes a, b, c, . . . n now enable judgments of relative preference to be made. 'This is an incredibly powerful idea: it generates a cardinal utility measure from a series of ordinal preferences' (Gaus, 2008, p. 41).

The other property of this approach is that the individual's utility function derived is unique up to a linear transformation. This means that there are a number of sets of numbers that will represent the relative scales of preference of the individual in the same way but none that do not have the expected utility property can do so. Purely ordinal functions (without the expected utility property), to repeat, are not unique in this manner and offer no basis for relative scale judgments of outcomes.

Although expected utility theory provides a way of consistently representing the relative strength of preferences for any individual choosing rationally – that is, in ways constrained by the axioms – it does *not* allow comparison between individuals in the way that classical utilitarianism requires. For example, if X's preferences over a, b and c are represented cardinally by the numbers 40, 34 and 3 and Y's preferences over the same set as 35, 25 and 10, this does not mean that X values a and b more than Y and c less than Y. Hence, there is no common scale that allows direct interpersonal comparisons of utility. It does, however, imply that X and Y in this example each individually prefer a to b, moderately and both to c by a long way. This might suggest considerable scope for agreement and cooperation between the two individuals to bring about a or b and/or to rule out c arising. Consider, though, if Y's utility function produced the following numbers: a = 10, b = 12 and c = 50. The two cardinal utility functions are now radically antagonistic and something other than simple agreement would be needed to reach a definite social outcome. The alternative processes could include force, persuasion, tossing a coin, bargaining, fraud, bribery or some form of compensation. Alternatively, government authority – a form of legitimate force – could intervene to impose by way of policy, direct outcomes or rules of the game (procedures) that determine social outcomes. In other cases, market forces or the intervention of civil society institutions can mediate outcomes across different spheres of social interaction.

'Expected utility theory demands more than does utility theory under certainty, and it is much more controversial' Hausman and McPherson (2006, p. 55). In particular, proponents of this approach tend to subscribe to a narrow or thin substantive theory of rationality that implicitly assumes that some individual preferences are 'irrational' (see Hausman and McPherson (2006, pp. 55–9) and Broome (1989). By implication, 'irrational' is bad and 'rational' – based on consistent preferences and 'true belief' – is good. The implications of all this for the development of economics and its grip on public policy occupy Parts II and III of this book.

CONCLUSION

To summarize, the utilitarian tradition failed to provide a universal measuring stick for individual and government action, as intended by its founder, Jeremy Bentham. The modern turn that transforms the notion of utility into a theory of individual (and social) rational choice empties the concept of moral content – *except* to the extent that it implies that human actions and interactions that are not rational are morally impermissible. This claim has made heavy weather against recent attacks. In part this critique is based on experimental findings that real individuals do not choose in ways consistent with rational choice theory (a new heterodox school of behavioural economics has grown since the 1970s to develop this critique).[11] Not only is there a range of cognitive limits and biases that bend actual decision making, also some of these (and other) factors have explicit moral content. Before tracing how the development of a nineteenth-century economic science coped with the ambiguous legacy of its utilitarian origins, we turn to consider an important diversion in utilitarianism, the deviationist contribution of John Stuart Mill.

NOTES

1. Bentham explicitly included the effects on 'lower animals' in applying 'the felicific calculus'. 'The day may come, when the rest of the animal creation may acquire those rights which never could have been withholden from them but by the hand of tyranny

(Bentham, 1789 [1961], p. 381).' In this respect Bentham equates the rights of animals to the rights of all humans regardless of the 'villosity of their skin'. This even-handed approach greatly influenced the fight against slavery in the nineteenth century and the animal rights movement to this day. Peter Singer is the best-known contemporary ethicist working in this tradition.

2. The fecundity and purity of the act are not seen to be properties of the pleasures and pains but only of the act 'and accordingly are only to be taken into the account of the tendency of such act or such event' (ibid. p. 38).
3. The two maximands can diverge, unless the size of the population whose utility is to be maximized remains constant. With changing populations, the switch to average (that is, per capita) utility matters and raises difficult moral questions (see Hausman and McPherson, 2006, pp. 102–3).
4. This, it is important to note, does not refer to the later theory of time preference based on discounting the future to the present; it simply acknowledges that individuals differ when in time they experience given quanta of utility.
5. Colander contrasts Edgeworth's view to that of his contemporary, American economist Irving Fisher. The latter dismissed the task of measuring utility on the basis of psychological laws and chose to measure (infer) it indirectly from the choices individuals make, giving up any attempt at interpersonal comparisons. It was Fisher's approach that prevailed.
6. The complications surrounding a utilitarian concept of 'welfare' are taken up in Chapter 6.
7. There are – in the age of terror – an endless number of similar hypothetical situations that can be advanced to test the moral robustness of utilitarianism; for example, is it justifiable to torture terror suspects to extract information that would prevent an attack and save lives. Torturers through the centuries have answered in the affirmative. When it's not a case of imposing punishment or exacting revenge, utilitarian reasons tend to carry weight for many people. However, the same strictures apply for utilitarians – how reliable and timely will the information extracted be? Will a society that accepts torture lose its moral compass over time? Are there more effective (and less painful) ways of detecting terror plots and nipping them in the bud?
8. Variants include 'restricted utilitarianism', already noted and 'rule utilitarianism'. Interested readers are directed to the references in the text and Hausman and McPherson (2006, pp. 99–109).
9. These questions are taken up in Chapter 10.
10. The key references are von Neumann and Morgenstern (1944), Fleming (1952), Harsanyi (1955). However, the approach stems back to the work of eighteenth-century mathematician Daniel Bernoulli.
11. In fact this line of attack goes back earlier to the work of decision theorists and psychologists in the 1950s – see Edwards (1954).

4. J.S. Mill's apostasy

> In the golden rule of Jesus of Nazareth, we read the complete spirit of the ethics of utility. To do as you would be done by, and to love your neighbor as yourself, constitute the ideal perfection of utilitarian morality (J.S. Mill).

John Stuart Mill was the son of the austere James Mill, Bentham's bulldog. How could the son stray so far from the father and still claim to be a utilitarian warrior? The path was indeed a long and torturous one. Mill *fils*' relationship with utilitarianism can best be described as a love-hate one. Brought up strictly and schooled by his father in classical and modern philosophy and political economy, Mill had imbibed the Benthamite doctrine, along with the Ricardian, by the time he reached his teens. His early essays on philosophical and social matters displayed a deep understanding and commitment to the master. However, following a severe mental breakdown – famously described in his later autobiography – Mill turned on his mentors and began publishing a stream of thoughts highly critical of classical utilitarianism. Rawls (2007) notes Mill's later depiction of Bentham as a 'half-thinker'.

Mill diplomatically waited until after the deaths of Bentham and his father before unloading on them. This he accomplished under the influence of the Saint-Simonians and especially Comte with whom he corresponded. Although flirting with socialism and subscribing for the rest of his life to a progressive social philosophy of progress, he could never jettison the individualist focus of English liberalism and the imperative to ground morality in a universal principle that would guide both individual and government action. Likewise, following the empiricist cast of British philosophy, he insisted that his reading of utilitarianism was based on experience of the social world and not philosophical intuition. However, both the 'intuitive' and 'inductive' approaches he identifies in the first chapter of *Utilitarianism* require general law or laws to be applied to particular cases. 'The intuitive, no less than what may be termed the inductive, school of ethics, insists on the necessity of general laws. They both agree that the morality of an individual action is not a question of direct perception, but of the application of a law to an individual case' (Mill, 1863 [1961], pp. 402–403).[1] Where moralists sought to advance several ethical principles, then the task was to establish an order of precedence:

> Yet to support their pretensions there ought either to be some one general principle or law at the root of all morality, or if there be several, there should be a determinate order of precedence among them; and the one principle or the rule for deciding between the various principles when they conflict, ought to be self-evident (ibid. p. 403).

Most of the book represents Mill's attempts to establish *his* principle of utility as that dominant law. Mill is convinced that *all* systems of ethics, including Aristotle's, are based on the principle of utility properly conceived, but that – regrettably – other moral philosophers are unaware of the fact.

This is a large claim, indeed. How can the age-old arguments about virtue and nobility and sacrifice in a larger cause be reconciled with a principle that seemingly reduces everything to the grubby pursuit of happiness? Mill answers that this is a false characterization of the 'greatest happiness principle'. He dismisses Bentham's psychological hedonism as a misreading of the principle; this is an unwarranted slur, as Sidgwick was later to demonstrate, since the classical principle can easily embrace a generalized hedonism not focused on individual self-interest. More tellingly, Mill takes issue with Bentham's qualitative equalization of the sources of happiness. Push-pin is nowhere near as good as poetry!

For Mill, utilitarian ethics requires actions that maximize happiness conceived as a desired 'mode of existence', as deriving from the satisfaction of realizing one's life's aims – not as mere enjoyable feelings or avoidance of pain. Happiness is achieved by employing one's faculties and resources resulting in enjoyable activity. Here Mill famously distinguishes the higher and lower faculties:

> It is quite compatible with the principle of utility to recognize the fact that some *kinds* of pleasure are more desirable and more valuable than others. It would be absurd that while, in estimating all other things, quality is considered as well as quantity, the estimation of pleasure should be supposed to depend on quantity alone (ibid. p. 408; italics in original).

The higher faculties consist in the enjoyable use of intellect, imagination and moral sentiments; the lower entail meeting bodily needs giving rise to mere pleasurable sensations. A well-ordered life consists of being able to exercise both higher and lower faculties in 'appropriate' measure and order. The ordering of activities generates satisfaction of the higher qualities first. A quality of experience is higher when a person has a 'decided preference' for it over others independent of any feeling of moral obligation or circumstantial advantage. To judge of relative qualities of pleasure, the person must have experienced the whole range to be judged and have a developed capacity of self-awareness. 'To say that there are higher versus lower pleasures is just to say that we decidedly prefer a way of life the special structure of which gives the central focus and priority to those activities that call upon the higher faculties' (Rawls, 2007, p. 263). No amount of the lower-ranked pleasure can compensate for giving up the higher pleasure. Here Mill parts company radically with Bentham for whom the source and quality of pleasure is irrelevant; other things being equal, equal quantities of pleasures are equally good no matter how caused or of what character. Eventually, the amount of pleasure from reading more and more poetry will decline so that it is good to switch to push-pin. Here Bentham is implicitly invoking the law of diminishing marginal utility. Mill, however, can never allow any amount of push-pin to displace the pleasures derived from exercising the higher faculties in reading poetry. Mill does allow that a minimum of pleasures secured by the lower faculties is vital for human beings to live in order to then move onto employing the higher faculties to enjoy the higher quality of pleasures. The latter qualities and activities giving rise to them dominate the life plans (schedule of activities) of those who have been able to develop suitable character; *the role of good policy is to create the institutions, values and attitudes necessary to develop suitable character throughout society.* The more people are able and enabled to develop the higher faculties, the greater their happiness and the greater the total happiness in society.

This is Mill's ethical argument for what *should* happen. The fact that he urges public policies to form character in tune with this ethic, suggests that real existing societies of his day are not producing people with the motivation or ability to so order their individual life plans. Policy is here proposed as a corrective to the existing viciousness of life as lived in Mill's time. Wicked institutions spawn morally stunted lives; enlightened institutions can nurture morally exalted ones.

> A cultivated mind (I do not mean that of a philosopher, but any mind to which the fountains of knowledge have been opened, and which has been taught, in any tolerable degree, to exercise its faculties) find sources of inexhaustible interest in all that surrounds it; in the objects of nature, the achievements of art, the ways of mankind, past and present, and their prospects in the future (Mill, 1863 [1961], p. 415).

Mill's psychology suggests only that people are inherently *capable* of becoming morally competent individuals able to make a decided preference for the higher over the lower pleasures in the sense noted earlier.[2] This is a social and political task-in-progress. It will take time. Moreover, the process is self-reinforcing. As institutions, legislation and policy emerge to improve the higher faculties of the masses, the masses will support further character-enhancing institutional developments in a virtuous civic cycle. This later led Mill to oppose the immediate granting of universal male franchise (one man, one vote), arguing instead for a system of plural voting weighted in favour of social classes deemed to have already developed the suitable character to support representative government and to orient policy to encourage universal improvement. On the other hand, he did strongly support votes for women – of suitable character. His politics was one based on class not gender.[3]

Mill's psychology is anchored in a concept of human dignity. As our higher faculties develop through appropriate education and acculturation, we realize and become self aware as moral beings and come to derive heightened pleasures from the exercise of our higher faculties and to regard, other than minimally necessary, attention to the objects of our lower faculties as degrading and unworthy. The desire to maintain our dignity becomes the basis of our happiness, even when it entails foregoing substantial lower pleasures. To the charge that people, even of the most refined moral sensibilities, are still likely to choose and act in ways that maximize their happiness regardless of the impact on society overall, Mill is scathing. 'When people who are tolerably fortunate in their outward lot do not find in life sufficient enjoyment to make it valuable to them, the cause generally is, caring for nobody but themselves' (ibid. p. 414).

Likewise, the claim that some people with cultured minds sacrifice their own happiness in nobly furthering the happiness of others does not, Mill retorts, invalidate the principle of utility since it is the outcome for the total utility of society that matters not the happiness of any individual. Moreover, once society has developed to the point where most people are willing to sacrifice or limit their individual happiness the total is likely to be doubly boosted. First, the quantum of outcomes of behaviours satisfying the higher faculties increases all round, and second, the individual happiness of those with 'a cultivated mind' (that is, the majority) increases as they derive satisfaction from living in such a well-ordered world.

Mill's historical, institutionalist stress on the cumulative, self-reinforcing development of the ability of civilized people to express their cultivated faculties in maximizing their total happiness implies an underlying harmony of interests, reminiscent of eighteenth-century moralists like Hume, Smith, Condorcet and even Rousseau. As this process of civility unwinds, more and more people bring their individual behaviours into line with what results in the greatest happiness for all. The sanctions to so act are both internal and external. The former come from the growth in the individual's moral sense of obligation to act according to a developed moral code. External sanctions are thrown up by observing the model of others' behaviours and the general approval and disapproval of others with respect to one's own behaviour.

In the fifth and final chapter of utilitarianism, Mill reflects 'on the connection between justice and utility'. For Mill, our sense of justice derives from the generalization of a basic instinct to 'repel or retaliate a hurt' against us and those we sympathize with to everyone, through an enlarged sympathy and enlightened self-interest. This, he holds, means that the sense of justice is not contrary to the principle of utility but derives from it.[4]

Individuals have rights that are generally respected in order for utility to be maximized. Where a person's right is threatened, sanctions can be imposed by law, moral approbation or conscience up to the point of severity that does not lead to a fall in total utility. A given set of rights is likely to develop to maximize utility over the long run – that is the consequentialist justification for having rights. Particular rights in individual cases can be overridden only when not to do so would lead to a loss in total utility, for example, jailing a suspected terrorist before he or she commits an act of terror – but from a Millian viewpoint, the strong onus of proof is on the jailor and the process should be carefully framed and monitored to prevent abuses by the agency involved (see quote in Rawls, 2007, p. 275).

However, Rawls claims that elsewhere Mill seems to prioritize the general right to justice as a central element in the 'essential groundwork of our existence' in society – without reference to maximizing utility. He holds that the rights of justice cannot be overridden by the aims of policy (ibid. p. 276) pointing to philosopher Ronald Dworkin's distinction between questions of principle and questions of policy. Mill here seems to want it both ways. His focus on individual rights and moral obligations begins to intrude issues of distributive justice contra the neutrality of utilitarianism with respect to whose utility is at stake. As long as total utility is maximized, its distribution is irrelevant; issues of distribution only become relevant when a change would increase utility overall.[5]

The principle of utility may require some people to be systematically denied rights and/or rights to be unequally respected and enforced. Why is Mill convinced that utilitarianism implies equal basic rights in the long run? This returns us to Mill's specific psychology of morality.[6]

The principle of unity with others, Mill argues, is natural rather than artificial in that it does not decline through experience and reflection; rather, bonds of affection and the repeated experience of reciprocity strengthen it. Modern society is an historical project of making people aware that they are mutually dependent and this strengthens the sentiments of unity – the view generally held that we are all in the same boat – so that all of us come to be concerned for the common good. However, Mill does not allow that there may be different views persisting about what the common good is; Mill's liberal individualism is blind to the realities of entrenched class conflict.

> Thus, by Mill's criterion of the artificial v. the natural, the desire to live in unity with others is natural and not undermined by analysis. And it is this conviction (indeed all these convictions and attitudes together) about the desire to be in unity with others that Mill says is the ultimate sanction of the principle of utility, and so the ultimate basis of our willingness to give justice (Rawls, 2007, p. 283).

Although Mill has, late in life, circled back towards a version of utilitarianism, it is a pale and convoluted account, lacking the conciseness and ethical power of the classical canon that is at the same time being developed by Sidgwick and others. On the other hand, Mill's more nuanced analysis has the advantage that it takes seriously the historical and institutional context of real people's lives in their current social condition and, in this aspect, resembles Hume's approach. The individuals whose lives are to be made happier are not atoms randomly colliding but people who have families, jobs and (different) prospects in life – what social scientists would later call different life-chances. Perhaps, understandably, writing in the decade after Darwin and Herbert Spencer's seminal works, there is the flavour of evolution in Mill's characterization of utilitarianism. As such, Mill (like Bentham) looks to good government to act in ways that facilitate the progressive march to a happier world. Unlike Bentham, this is not seen as a series of one-off legislative acts but the gradual creation of a social climate conducive to the formation of good character on an expanding scale.

The basic challenge raised by the central role of government in facilitating maximum utility over the long term had been prefigured by Mill in an earlier book, *On Liberty*. The basic question raised there is: what is the scope and limit of power that government can exert over the individual in a modern society characterized as industrial, democratic and secular? Put another way: how can we control the abuses of democratic government imposed by the tyranny of the majority over the minority? The abuses of monarchs had already been checked in Britain by the emergence of unwritten constitutional conventions and legal processes. Mill, like generations of philosophers before him, stretching back to the ancient Greeks, worried about the power and unruly nature of the *demos*. Democracy was a recent reinvention, a fragile flower, easily – in the view of the ruling classes of Europe – degenerating into mob rule. The French Revolution, the revolutions of 1848 and the wide-ranging social unrest of the post-Napoleonic era were still foremost in the mind of respectable society. Equally, Mill recognizes, modern society was on a trajectory to increase the power over individual views, sentiments and interests of the majority by 'the ascendant class'. However, it is the growing political power of the majority, meaning mass working class, that Mill fears most are not ready to responsibly govern the minority of the educated respectable middle class. Until the latter can expand to absorb more of the former and/or the lower classes can be raised up to civilized standards, caution must be exercised in – for example – extending the franchise.

Mill, thus, presents his 'Principle of Liberty' as the standard from which to judge, monitor and impose limits on government policy in a mass democracy such as that beginning to emerge in Britain in the second half of the nineteenth century. Mill here echoes some of Tocqueville's earlier concerns about American democracy.[7]

The principle of liberty applies to specific individual liberties:

1. Freedom of thought, expression and conscience.
2. The right to frame one's own life plan, to act as one desires, restricted only by the injunction not to injure the interests or abrogate the rights of others.
3. Freedom of assembly, to combine with others to further joint interests in ways that do not injure the legitimate interests of others.

In short, the principle of liberty enjoins government to ensure that all citizens enjoy maximum freedom of thought and conduct in pursuit of their interests and life aims that do not limit or injure the right of others to pursue their interests and aims. Only by reasoned argument can the appropriate limits be specified and applied.

The principle is also proposed as a civic educational strategy for 'improving' the working classes newly coming to the vote, and to provide a check against unthinking, populist policy that would harm the common interest in the long run until the civilizing effects of mass education and refined, rational discourse have done their work. Mill hoped (like Marx) that the results of his philosophic writings would help the working class masses to short circuit their path to a better world (though Mill and Marx had very different views about what that better world would be and how the masses would get there).

The principle applies only to competent adults, excluding children, the mentally deficient and 'backward societies'. It also fails to hold in societies beset by external enemies or serious internal conflict. Thus Mill's principle of liberty is subordinated to the principle of utility. It applies where and when its general observance is conducive to maximizing utility as Mill conceives the latter:

> . . . it is clear [for Mill] that the Principle of Liberty is not a first or supreme principle: it is subordinate to the Principle of Utility and to be justified in terms

> of it. Rather, the Principle of Liberty is a kind of mediate axiom . . . But nevertheless one of great importance: it is a principle of public reason – a political principle to guide the public's discussion in a democratic society (ibid. p. 289).

Many actions of individuals will upset or hurt (cause disutility to) others. In many cases these are unavoidable collateral effects of the broader gains from having an open society in which the basic liberties are protected for all, and are acceptable as long as total utility is maximized. However, some limits on individual liberties are justified. That is, total utility over time would be less if these limits on individual conduct were not legitimately (justly) imposed through law and/or the moral coercion of enlightened public opinion. Mill seems to have in mind here individual actions like incitement to violence and sedition. The onus, however, is on government or other coercive forces to justify the limits placed on individuals by recourse to publicly stated and defended reasons demonstrating the threat to total utility posed by the actions of the individuals or groups in question.[8] Certain types of reason are ruled out by Mill, notably (1) paternalistic reasons (the good of the individual as judged by someone else); (2) reasons of excellence (individuals would be 'better' people, as judged by someone other than the person) and (3) reasons of dislike or disgust (in the view of other people or public opinion/taste).

For Mill, the bigger picture means that in the long run, modern societies would never be better off (generate greater utility) unless his principle of liberty holds without exception. Thus, allowing the majority to interfere with or coerce minorities in some cases might result in short term gains in total utility but by the very fact of allowing an exception, society would be placed on the slippery slope to declining utility, since no one could be guaranteed maximum liberty over the long term. If you lose your liberty today, then others may do so tomorrow. This position is at least arguable. In a society with a stable class structure, existing patterns of privilege and control may mean that continued repression of the rights of minorities may pay off in total utility terms indefinitely. Mill may counter that such societies were not the modern, developed institutional worlds – the advanced nations – to which his principle is to apply. All people in a society have an equal permanent interest in living in a situation where all enjoy equal justice and security to rationally choose their preferred way of life. Thus, all have a permanent interest in securing the social conditions that will (a) achieve the progressive movement towards such an optimal state and (b) preserving the social conditions necessary to maintain that happy state.

> The permanent interests are, then, permanent in two ways. They are permanent as interests in the necessary conditions of continual progress to the best and also

> natural state of society; they are also permanent as interests in the conditions required to remain in that best state, once it is reached (ibid. pp. 301–302).

Mill's idea of the best state of society implies that it is the state which most realizes our nature as social beings – that is, as beings happiest and fulfilled when we fully develop and apply our higher faculties in ways consistent with equal justice and the legitimate interests of others in that society. 'To sum up: the first permanent interest is that in the basic rights of equal justice: it is an interest in the conditions necessary for continual progress to the best state of society as a state of equality, as well as necessary to remain [in] that state once reached' (ibid. p. 302).

The second permanent interest is in securing laws and public attitudes guaranteeing (protecting) individual freedom of thought and conscience – both as desired in themselves and as likely to lead people towards finding the truth on any subject – thus avoiding superstition and being open to manipulation and exploitation by others. Ignorance is not true happiness conducive to maximizing utility.[9] Responsible free speech leads to rational discussion and the emergence of truth by progressive elimination of error. Mill here implicitly assumes that the optimal society towards which we are progressing will necessarily ensure that all people have adequate access to relevant knowledge and sources of information untainted by powerful special interests. As noted earlier, Mill is aware that this does not mean that there are to be no reasonable limits on speech – for example, incitement to violence, slander, sedition and treason in time of war, are to be prohibited in the just society.

The third permanent interest concerns the liberty of individual tastes to devise and carry out our plan of life to suit ourselves – as long as this doesn't prevent others from doing likewise. Rawls calls this the permanent interest in individuality. No one person or institution has the right to override this legitimate interest.

The fourth permanent interest ties the others together and holds that every individual has an interest in acting to entrench institutions and attitudes that achieve a society guaranteeing equal rights to justice and liberty, as expressed in the first three permanent interests. For Mill, according to Rawls, the more society approaches the ideal or natural state, the more everyone seeks to share the benefits of belonging to that society with their fellow citizens. Benevolence based in repeated reciprocity leads towards the ideal or natural society of equality – but equality of what? Not absolute equality of outcome if the permanent interests embedded in the principle of liberty is to be respected.

Rawls argues that Mill's utilitarianism demands a natural society in which the four permanent interests are satisfied, since only in such a social environment can people apply the decided preference criteria that differentiates higher from lower quality pleasures to be maximized. 'This has the striking corollary that in the absence of just and free arrangements, there is simply no way for society to acquire the specific knowledge and information it would need to maximize utility in Mill's sense' (ibid. p. 306). 'The upshot is that to maximize utility in Mill's sense, it is necessary to set up just and free institutions to educate people's abilities' (ibid. p. 307).

Rawls notes that it is only necessary for Mill to make a broad-based distinction between higher and lower pleasures and higher and lower faculties. Mill holds an optimistic view that, given the broad division and lack of fine-grained distinctions, almost all people are educable to the degree necessary to develop the higher faculties necessary to appreciate and value the higher pleasures. The higher pleasures of the most talented or educated are not superior in utility weighting than the higher pleasures of the less talented. There is no aristocracy of refinement. No basis exists on which to rank ways of life in a natural society in which just institutions prevail. Hence, no natural aristocracy of the type clinically dissected by Anthony Trollope in his high Victorian novels.

Mill's utilitarianism therefore calls for substantial government action in the economy and broader society, particularly in policy areas like education, health and social security. It is less unambiguously supportive of economic egalitarianism buried within the bowels of Bentham's (and Sidgwick's) classical doctrine. Mill, having written the basic economic text of mid-century – *Principles of Political Economy* – is well aware of the incentive arguments of the developing discipline. However, his famous distinction between the laws of production which are fixed and immutable, contrasting with the laws of distribution that are malleable, meant that distributional outcomes can be influenced by government and groups in civil society, while leaving the market to determine what is produced.[10]

CONCLUSION

It's clear that when Mill's main mature philosophical works are taken into account, he moved a long way away from the tradition of his father and his father's friends. His primary principle of utility and supporting principle of liberty are proposed as guides to good government judged by the consequentialist ethic of outcome. Public policies must be crafted to satisfy both when in harmony and the former when not, in the historically given context of the time. Mill took for granted that in Britain this would include the continued rise of industrial capitalism. Unlike both Marx and the social Darwinists (the latter who followed Spencer's dictum of the survival of the fittest), he believed that appropriate government policies would and should intervene to raise up the masses to benefit from collective gains in material and cultural well-being.

Writing mid-century, when the gains of industrialization were beginning to filter through to British workers and general living standards for many were on the rise, this seemed a reasonable bet. However, Britain entered into what has been retrospectively called 'the great recession' in the last quarter of the nineteenth century. Intensifying class struggle and social conflict increasingly pitted representatives of the working classes against the 'ascendant class'. The window for a progressive liberal opening that Mill hoped for closed, to be prised open temporarily in the decade before the Great War, before being slammed shut by war, depression and war again. Many of the policies and developments that Mill hoped for surfaced only after World War II as the modern welfare state. However, from the 1970s onward, they too were progressively wound back as the boundaries of class inequality hardened and the age-old political problem of the tyranny of the minority over the majority assumed its normal place. Plutocracy rather than mob rule faces us today.

NOTES

1. *Utilitarianism* was first published as a book in 1863. References here are made to the 1961 reproduction in the same volume as Bentham's *Introduction* and Mill's essay *On Liberty*.
2. This *capacity*, Mill argues, is a basic feature of human nature. 'The present wretched education and wretched social arrangements, are the only real hindrance to its being attainable by almost all' (Mill, 1863 [1961], p. 414).
3. The key texts are: *Representative Government* (originally published in 1866) and *The Subjection of Women* (published in 1869).
4. This discussion of Mill's conception of justice relies on the interpretation of Rawls (2007).
5. For a fuller discussion of Mill's attempt to square his account of rights with his conception of justice, see Rawls (2007, pp. 278–80).
6. Rawls (ibid. pp. 269–70) outlines six principles underlying Mill's psychological account of morality.
7. Economists and political philosophers have what Joseph Schumpeter called semi-conscious 'pre-analytic visions' about how government and policy works that influence their substantive analyses. Mill's internalization of many of the values and norms of class and status stratified Victorian England indelibly influenced his moral and political philosophy.
8. Rawls here sees Mill's argument prefiguring his own concept of 'public reason'.
9. As a member of Britain's upper middle class, Mill is worried about the ability of radicals to lead the masses astray, away from the path to genteel civility.
10. Mill's categorical claim (on the eve of the marginalist revolution) that all the important discoveries in political economy had now been made turned out to be as accurate as the similar claims (a) by classical physicists at the turn of the twentieth century that all the important laws in physics were now in the bag, (b) by the great American economist

Irving Fisher in 1929 that US stock prices were not overvalued and (c) by Nobel Laureate Robert Lucas at the turn of the twenty-first century that capitalist economies had now seen the last of the dreaded (endogenous) business cycle. Fisher at least had the decency to lose his personal fortune backing his claim and then turned his formidable talent to determining why he had been so wrong. Lucas and other 'new classical' economists refuse to admit they were wrong or acknowledge any intellectual complicity in the material losses and mental anguish of countless others.

5. The retreat to the margin

> My father's approach might be said to be derived from Bentham, the founder of the psychological school to which he essentially belonged (H.S. Jevons on his father William Stanley Jevons).

> Menger was one of those men who can claim a single decisive achievement that made scientific history (Joseph Schumpeter).

During the early 1870s, three economists in three countries seemingly independently published what was essentially the same idea. This is not a unique case in the annals of intellectual history. The phenomenon of multiple discovery has occurred from time to time and been variously explained as the culmination of a series of unrelated preconditions brought together by a catalyst, either an act of individual genius or a response to underlying historical-institutional developments possibly brought on by a crisis. In this case, and for whatever reason(s), William Stanley Jevons in England, Carl Menger in Austria and Léon Walras in France (later Switzerland) sought to reconstruct economics on the basis of a focus on the allocation of scarce resources among the competing ends of the representative utility maximizing consumer. Instead of following the classical school of Smith, Ricardo and (J.S.) Mill in identifying the causes and consequences of economic growth (total utility or use values) and its distribution between classes over time, they narrowed their concern to how consumers get the most utility or satisfaction from the given total product produced at a point in time.

This shift of emphasis meant that consumers were constrained to choose between the utility-generating uses of the resources under their control. To consume more of good A meant consuming less of good B. What combination would produce the greatest satisfaction? The law of diminishing marginal utility was first definitively stated by Heinrich Gossen in 1854 but this was not known widely until much later and probably not by Jevons, Menger and Walras, who were each initially unaware of each others' work. For any good, total utility increases with quantity consumed but does so at a decreasing rate (Gossen's first law). As the utility gained from consuming each extra unit of A declines there comes a point where more utility can be gained from switching to consuming units of B. A consumer maximizes her total utility when the ratio of the marginal utility of A to the price of

A is equal to the ratio of the marginal utility of B to the price of B, and the same for all other goods C, D and so on. (Gossen's second law). In this 'equilibrium' it is not possible for the consumer to increase total utility by any other allocation of her given resources.

Jevons published a brief outline of this approach in 1862[1] unaware of Gossen (and others[2]) and was moved to publish his full length version in *The Theory of Political Economy* in 1871, prompted by the publication of papers by the Scottish engineer, Fleeming Jenkin getting at the same idea in the late 1860s. Menger's *Principles of Economics* also came out in 1871. Both insisted on the primacy of the psychological relation between consumer and material consumption as the driver of economic outcomes. This both drew on Bentham's utilitarian principle but sought to narrow its scope to *both* focus on the satisfactions that could be attained through market exchange *and* sever analysis of this process from any explicit ethical stance. Implicitly, however, the ethical charge lingered on; it was somehow 'right' that consumers should get the biggest bang for their buck. Inefficiency in a world of limited resources, defined as not maximizing given consumer wants, was wasteful. By assuming both resources and consumer tastes as given, they ruled out much that was of interest to utilitarians like Mill for whom the 'right' tastes mattered. Sidgwick too hoped for a liberal society in which mass happiness would increasingly entail an improving general character in the population.

Jevons and Menger used their analyses to explain the formation of relative prices through the lens of their marginalist analyses. The former did so in explicitly mathematical form (as did Walras); the search for the maximum is tailor made for the application of the differential calculus. Menger and the Austrian school he initiated eschewed mathematics. Neither theorist had any time for the real cost theory of supply provided by the classical school. Supply was given by factors outside the analysis. In Jevons's pithy summary:

> Cost of production determines supply
> Supply determines final degree of utility
> Final degree of utility determines value [i.e. price].[3]

It is true that Jevons did attempt to apply his felicific calculus to the issue of labour supply, an important component of the production cost. He argued that workers would progressively supply their labour up to the point at which the marginal utility derived from the extra income earned (to pay for extra consumption) just equaled the pain (disutility) of the last hour worked. This idea that work was painful and to be endured has a long history in Western thought; grinding work was God's penalty in being cast out of the Garden of Eden. It came to be reinterpreted as the opportunities foregone in 'leisure', a catchall term for other uses of the worker's limited time. This idea has had an enduring life in modern economics, at least at the level of abstract model building. Institutionalist analyses of labour markets have been more interested in pointing to the multidimensional aspects of work, including the effective constraints imposed on workers to freely choose their work hours in real-life labour markets and the potentially positive utility returns to meaningful work.[4] Menger and Walras simply assumed supply conditions as given.

Within 20 years the one-sided application of the marginalist approach was generalized in the work of economists like Philip Wicksteed, John Bates Clark and, above all, Alfred Marshall:

> The significance of marginal utility theory was that it provided the archetype of the problem of allocating with maximum effect. It was not long before the same approach was extended from the household to the firm, from the theory of consumption to the theory of production. The theory of utility supplied most of the excitement of discovery in the seventies and eighties, but it was the introduction of marginal analysis that marked the true dividing line between classical theory and modern economics (Blaug, 1968, p. 273]).[5]

It was this break that truly defined 'the marginalist revolution' and the supremacy of 'neoclassical economics'. In this move Marshall's *Principles of Economics*, first published in 1890, was decisive. Walras and Menger sidestepped the question of the measurability of utility; the concept was used qualitatively to explain price determination in exchange economies, assuming axiomatically the right form and shape of individual (cardinal) utility functions. Jevons cribbed by suggesting that prices could be used to 'measure' utility by assuming the roughly approximate constant marginal utility of money. Marshall followed this suggestion (somewhat uneasily) – a classic case of:

> *if* **a** exists, then **b**;
> **a** doesn't exist but let's assume it does;
> *then* **b, c, d . . ., n** follow.

By the time the analysis gets to stage **n**, everyone has forgotten that **a** doesn't in fact exist, namely that the critical initial assumption on which the final conclusion rests does not hold. This I shall call 'the Marshallian fudge'.

An ordinal utility function tells the direction of a consumer's preferences (first partial derivative) but only a cardinal function (as described in Chapter 3) gives a clue as to the intensity of those preferences (a negative second derivative in the case of diminishing marginal utility). However, this doesn't provide a basis for calculating total utility from the consumer's preference set. That would require knowledge of not merely the relation between intervals on the scale but between the numbers forming those intervals, expressed in what Edgeworth called the 'third degree of utility' or third partial differential, resulting in a utility function 'unique up to a multiplicative constant' (Blaug, 1996, pp. 315–16). Marshall avoided the problem by assuming the constancy of the marginal utility of money in order to derive demand curves satisfying Gossen's second law. This assumption is intuitively unappealing since it assumes that an extra dollar is worth the same regardless as to how many dollars one already has. Surely, a dollar is worth more to me in utility terms if I am poor than if I am rich.[6]

Although such a (non-achievable) utility function of the third degree would establish a cardinal link between marginal and total utility for an individual it does nothing to aid comparisons *between* individuals in a way required by classical utilitarians. It is still not possible to add up the separate utilities of individuals as required by equation 3.2 in Chapter 3. The constant marginal utility of money as a common measuring rod is even less intuitively convincing when comparing the utility of different people. However, at the qualitative level, it is self-evident to all but Marshall and (some of) his followers that a dollar is 'worth more' to a poor person than a rich person.[7] Who would claim that a given windfall gain would generate more happiness for Rupert Murdoch than an unemployed homeless person. Such would be the case only in the unlikely case that (a) Murdoch was a pathological miser (b) Murdoch believed that the homeless person's gain would destroy the incentive and institutional structure of a functioning capitalist society and hence bring his empire and civilization as we know it tumbling down or (c) the homeless person would 'waste' the windfall, perhaps on alcohol or gambling that leaves him less happy after 'blowing the lot'. Barring these or some similar circumstances, it seems obvious that, within a scale range, more happiness would come from relieving the extreme hardship of the homeless unemployed rather than augmenting the wealth of the wealthy. Rough interpersonal comparisons of welfare are clearly unproblematic in ordinary life and underlie deep-seated moral views about fairness governing the moral universes of most people, including policy makers and economists when the latter are off duty.

In this sense, the theory of marginal utility has more radical implications for public policy than classical utilitarianism (which is distributionally neutral), since it is a short jump from considering the impact of windfall gains to look at redistribution of current wealth. If a dollar is worth more to a poor than a rich person why not take dollars from the latter and give them to the former? We may not be able to compute the actual net increase in happiness across society but we can be reasonably confident that it will be positive. Such a broad calculation lies behind the introduction of progressive taxation and the rise of the welfare state before and after World War I and even more so after world War II. This has not been a politically uncontested process, of course. The case against progressive redistribution has called upon arguments similar to (b) and (c) above, namely some variant of the argument that redistribution destroys work, savings and entrepreneurial incentives so that everyone ends up with less income than before (the total pie shrinks or doesn't grow as quickly as it would have without the changes) or that the poor don't know how to spend their wealth wisely. They might be termed the 'entrepreneurial' and 'paternalistic' arguments against egalitarian redistribution, respectively.

Similar complications arise when considering how to allocate the cost of paying for publicly provided services. 'The optimal theory of taxation' has exercised economists since the days of Smith and Ricardo. The 'optimal' in the term is value laden. Governments have always throughout history been vitally concerned with how to extract resources from their citizens in order to finance wars and public works. However, the driving motive was power seeking not ethics. By assuming a well-behaved income utility curve for all people, rich and poor, with marginal utility declining over the entire range of incomes, a progressive income tax can be justified on the principle of 'equal marginal sacrifice' – so that each individual is taxed in a way that equalizes their loss of marginal utility. That raises two questions. What happens if income utility curves are not well behaved (that is, are concave) or change curvature over the income range? Second, what if tastes or aspirations change with income so that the curve shifts?[8] On the other side of government expenditure, what should determine the 'optimal' consumption of service provision and income transfer?

Even with the basic assumption in place, adding a string of further restrictions does not get over the problem of the under-specification of representative utility functions. Trying to use money prices to represent the utility consequences of government actions inevitably biases outcomes to higher income and wealth holders. Willingness to pay, or some proxy has an implicitly regressive normative impact on policy outcomes. This point will be further argued in Part II.

CONCLUSION

By the beginning of the twentieth century, economics had moved a long way from its utilitarian roots. The recognized inability to give sense to what it means to maximize utility or net happiness caused economists to narrow their gaze to the more tractable issue of explaining how prices (including wages and interest rates) are formed in freely operating market economies. Left behind, however, was an equal sense of something missing. What was the *value* to human actors of freely operating market systems? What *justified* the nature of economic organization and the social consequences resulting? What role *should* government have in monitoring and, perhaps, intervening in market processes? These are all basic ethical or normative questions the answers to which cannot be read off from the utility and cost curves of the new microeconomics. The answers came, historically, with the rise of two variants of what came to be called 'welfare economics', based on different conceptions of how human welfare is to be defined and maximized. However, both subscribed to the basic consequentialist tenet – judge actions (and inactions) by the results of their outcomes with respect to a given Good. 'Consequentialism is the doctrine that one should judge things morally by their intrinsic value and the value of their consequences' (Hausman and McPherson, 2006, p.99). Although recent developments in the philosophy of economics have moved away from a strictly utilitarian ethic, the discipline has stayed broadly within the consequentialist frame, illustrated by the work of economists like Amartya Sen. By delving more deeply into the concept of welfare and the particular, restricted manner in which orthodox economics treats this category it is possible to interrogate the ethical and political efficacy of the orthodox economic evaluation of public policy – the aim of the remainder of this book.

NOTES

1. The paper was presented to Section F of the British Association for the Advancement of Science as 'Brief account of a general mathematical theory of political economy'. It made no impact, to Jevons's dismay.
2. There were other precursors, especially in France and England.
3. Jevons used the term 'final degree of utility' for what would later be termed 'marginal utility'.
4. Marxists and other radical critics stress the asymmetric power relations in labour markets, undermining notions of free individual choice explicit in neoclassical models.
5. In a later edition of his book, Blaug rephrased this passage. 'To become somewhat more explicit, the principle at issue is that of equalizing marginal values: in dividing a fixed quantity of anything among a number of competing uses, efficient allocation implies that each unit of the dividend is apportioned in such a way that the gain of transferring it to one use will just equal the loss involved in withdrawing it from another . . . The whole of neo-classical economics is nothing more than spelling out this principle in ever wider contexts, coupled with the demonstration that perfect competition does under certain conditions produce equimarginal allocations of expenditures and resources' (Blaug, 1996, p.280).
6. In fact, Marshall's notion of a common marginal utility of money applies, strictly

speaking to money income flow not to the level of income, and to the assumption that the consumer's expenditure on any one commodity is a very small proportion of total expenditure. The implication, nevertheless, is that the marginal utility of income is constant in both senses.

7. Marshall's uneasiness at having to make the assumption suggests that he too really knew that a given sum of money meant more to a poor than a rich person. His successor and disciple, Arthur Pigou was even more explicit about this reality (see Chapter 7). Both economists were prepared to employ 'the fudge' in order to make their specific analyses tractable.
8. Assuming, as Marshall (and Sidgwick) did that the optimal tax requires equal absolute sacrifice of *total* utility by all individuals regardless of their level of income, it is not possible to specify the optimal tax regime, since we have no sure knowledge of the precise shape of individual income-utility curves. This seemed not to worry Marshall, who, as noted, avoided the issue by simply assuming a constant marginal utility of money income for all people, regardless of their relative levels of income. His successor Pigou (and Edgeworth) disagreed. For a discussion, see Blaug (1996 pp. 320–2).

PART II

Analysis

6. The concept of economic welfare

> If you are an ethical consequentialist, you would need to decide *whose* outcomes matter, *which* particular outcomes matter most, and *how* to combine and weigh these outcomes across individuals and values (Jonathan Wight).

Economics emerged from its utilitarian womb under the nineteenth-century spell of the rise of industrial capitalism, the triumph of science and the ideology of material progress. Its consequentialism, therefore, was indelibly marked by this fact. Liberal individualism provided a perfect framework within which the doctrines of the discipline developed. The question of *who* matters was seemingly clear – individual people or 'households'? *Which* outcomes proved a little trickier. *How* to combine and weigh relevant outcomes across individuals and values, as we have seen, raises the most difficult ethical questions of all.

The seemingly obvious focus on individual welfare is ethically misleading. This fact is evident in the slippage from individual to household. A household can, in turn, become a family – and there are many types of families, even in contemporary Western societies – as the popular television series *Modern Family* demonstrates. Different individuals within a household came to have different roles, duties and status. In the nineteenth century when economics formed as a distinct discipline, the household was unambiguously patriarchal. In all social classes an adult male was the head. His dominant position in the home and broader society was reinforced by the key institutions of state and civil society, expressed in the laws of the land, the teachings of religion and the general culture of the times. Women and children had circumscribed roles and duties, supportive of the master. In the upper class, households extended to servants of varying status. The material welfare of a particular household depended on the class position of its head but the distribution of welfare within any household was unequal. Indeed, as the even newer discipline of sociology was discovering, the family or household *was* the basic unit of social class in industrializing societies. Social mobility between the generations existed but was strictly limited; privilege and power was both gendered and transmitted inter-generationally. Economics has never sufficiently recognized this reality, even within its narrow conception of welfare. The individual decision agent – *homo economicus* – continues to provide the analytical 'point of entry' (Wolff and Resnick, 2012).

There are many possible dimensions of individual welfare and 'illfare'. Material benefit is one. Everyone values the consumption of adequate food, shelter, clothing, energy and other necessities. In addition, an endless range of luxuries attracts the majority of humanity in the developed world and increasing numbers in 'emerging economies'; only the most dedicated ascetic denies their allure. Most people also seek to avoid diseases, personal injury and other 'bads'. But material welfare defined by the consumption of 'goods' and avoidance of 'bads' covers only some of the desired outcomes we cherish.

People value not only the total quantity of goods but also their distribution across society, based on ethical norms of fairness or justice. One of the major failings of classical utilitarianism, after all, was its neutrality with respect to distributional issues, both within the household and across the broader society, although egalitarian tinges began to creep through the cracks once attention focused on the notion of diminishing marginal rather than total or average utility. Another valued outcome, famously advanced by the philosophers of liberalism, is *freedom* – the capacity for individuals to express their views, freely assemble and pursue their life plans without arbitrary constraints imposed by the state or other institutions. Wight (2015, pp. 24–6) lists other desired outcomes, namely, the reverence for tradition, the benefits gained from a safe and secure environment and the enjoyment of things that have intrinsic value like parenthood, loving relations and citizenship. Whereas many though not all goods can be delivered through well-functioning markets, outcomes of intrinsic or primary value like freedom and national security cannot be. The intrinsic value of having children or being a citizen would be destroyed by buying these 'goods' in the market (see, Sandel, 2013). Thus, economics confines its scope to a limited range of desired outcomes, though (controversially) the boundary is porous and the maximizing calculus inherited from utilitarianism often appears in areas previously immune to its application.[1]

Even within their circumscribed world, economists face the daunting problem of reducing the myriad consequences of human interaction in the economy to manageable analytical proportions. How can the manifold dimensions of human welfare be reduced to a common denominator? The answer, sketched in Chapter 5, focused on the particular manner in which the concept of utility evolved. No longer was utility to be treated as a psychological relation between the subject and the object – still less as an objective property of the latter – but as expressed in or revealed by the actual choices individuals made in the market (and other choice situations). Analysis thus focused on the circumstances and outcomes of choice. Welfare was whatever individuals chose. This slant chimed well with what became the standard definition of the scope of economics: namely as '. . . the science which studies human behavior as a relationship between ends and scarce means which have alternative ends' (Robbins, 1932, p. 15). The focus on allocating limited resources across limitless possible ends – both through and outside the market – directed attention to the process of achieving resource outcomes and away from the need to measure the *stuff* of outcomes, offering what philosophers call a 'formal' theory of well-being:

> 'Formal' theories of well-being specify how one finds out what things are intrinsically good for people, but they do not say what those things are. To maintain that welfare is the satisfaction of preferences is to offer a formal theory of well-being (Hausman and McPherson, 2006, p. 119).

It is simply *assumed* that (a) the choices people make expresses perfectly their preferences, (b) that those preferences obey the basic axioms of rationality defining either an ordinal or cardinal utility function and (c) these preferences perfectly reflect people's individual welfare. Finally, buried within this approach is the implicit assumption, never recognized or interrogated, that it is *good* for people to satisfy their preferences, whatever they happen to be. Preference satisfaction has become a good in itself, rather than (only) a means to the good; this supplies the inherent ethical charge to the economist's concept of *efficiency*, a point taken up in Chapter 8.[2]

Each of these assumptions can and has been challenged. In the first place, actual choices will express not merely what a person wants but (a) what she thinks she wants, (b) what she thinks is available and (c) what she thinks is efficacious. All choices are situational not open ended. For example, someone who cannot read will not choose to buy a book, any book. Even a literate person may likewise ignore the book option if the nearest bookshop is hundreds of miles away. Even if literacy and accessibility do not prove obstacles, the book may not be sought because the person does not *believe* that its consumption will satisfy her quest for knowledge. This last point is critical because it raises the issue of true versus false belief. Beliefs underlie all our behaviours as human agents. Beliefs are social constructions that evolve at the deepest layers of our personalities; they come to form a core of our identity. They emerge and solidify through social interaction, habit formation and local habitat. Beliefs whether true or false are stubbornly held, built up over time and are fiercely defended. Belief that cigarette smoking causes cancer may discourage many people from smoking and prompt some smokers to quit. Others may smoke in the belief, stoked by tobacco industry advice, that there is no definitive proof of any causal connection. In both cases people are acting on the basis of beliefs held with varying degrees of certitude. If smoking causes cancer, then smokers are suffering a (possibly terminal) decline in their welfare. If smoking does *not* cause cancer, then non-smokers are being denied a possible avenue of welfare enhancement.

One response would be to say – so what? Life is a gamble, you make your play and you take your chances. This cavalier attitude seems to appeal to some people, particularly when young; how else can we explain the tendency of young male drivers to kill themselves on the road?[3] For most people, however, there seems to be something *bad* about letting false beliefs destroy lives. Doesn't someone – government, parents, educators, scientists, community leaders – have *some* role in providing the facts or, at least, in cautioning hasty or uninformed decisions? Clearly, in most societies the answer is yes, especially if some people or organizations have a vested interest or self-chosen mission in misleading others. Governments run advertising campaigns advising citizens of the dangers of smoking and reckless driving and heavily tax the former product and fine the latter behaviour. Legislation limits the sale of cigarettes and the conditions under which people drive on the roads. All such acts impose constraints on the way an individual expresses her preferences in allocating her scarce resources. To support such interventions means taking an ethical stance – namely, that it is not *right* to allow poorly informed or misled people to choose freely. The opposite stance also imposes an ethical imperative; people *should* be allowed to go to the devil in their own way. This latter view prioritizes absolute freedom of choice, regardless of how well informed one is, over any empathic or paternalistic attempt to limit that choice or provide relevant information on which choices can be made.

The emphasis on markets expressing the voluntary preferences of parties who must therefore each believe that they gain (otherwise they would not voluntarily engage in market transactions) also runs up against the key qualification: it is only the *effective* preferences of market participants that are satisfied – that is, those preferences backed by the resources required to effect a transaction. This explicitly raises the issue of the distribution of resources as well as their allocation; the manner in which welfare economists and political philosophers have addressed this fact is the subject of the next three chapters.

An equally disturbing possibility haunts the preference satisfaction approach. In highly stratified and stable societies many people will 'learn' their place, will accept through absence of viable choices and prior experiences, how to operate within a restricted universe of thought and action. One becomes acculturated to the familiar. A poor peasant living inland will not have had the opportunity to form preferences over bathing in the sea. Women in many societies and times have been systematically excluded from spheres of life outside the confines of home and family and denied access to information, education, (equally) paid employment and travel. People with disabilities like blindness, birth defects and acquired brain damage likewise face restricted social *capacities* to form and act on their preferences. Sen (1992), for example, proposes that policy makers should take into account the relative effective capacities of different people to transform available resources into desired outcomes, to the extent that preference satisfaction is to be ethically privileged (see the more detailed discussion in Chapter 9). Moreover, dominant economic, political and cultural institutions will form the channels through which unequal preference universes are constructed and imposed in the real world. Policy makers cannot avoid making judgments about where and when to override market-mediated preferences; and the decision *not* to make an explicit judgment implies an ethical stance. By treating individual preferences and resource distribution as exogenously determined, economists filter out most of the policy decisive factors impinging on the welfare of citizens. This is like denying that there is an elephant in the house because one happens to be sipping tea in another room. To rephrase Keynes's (1923 [1971]) famous phrase from another context – 'economists set themselves too easy a task' if they assume that the resource allocations of markets express the *real* preferences, still less the welfare, of participants. Just because it is practically difficult (impossible) to accurately gauge the (changeable) preferences and the limitations constraining their formation, it does not follow that by assuming the market knows best, actual outcomes will necessarily carry ethical justification. Neither is it the case – on either consequentialist or non-consequentialist grounds – that by so ignoring resource distribution, relative capacities and socio-political processes the resulting constricted analysis (and policy recommendations) is 'scientific' and value free.

Whatever the abstract philosophical attractions of the extreme libertarian position, it has had little practical impact on real existing societies. Governments of all persuasions and other institutions intervene in myriad ways to regulate the lives of their citizens. 'The market' itself is a socially constructed institution in part created by government actions (and inactions). Even in societies dominated by neoliberal public policies over the past 40 years, preferences expressed through and outside markets have been constrained, based on widely held moral values, differing capacities and the unequal power of different interests (see Part III). As Reich (2015) has argued persuasively, government sets the rules within which markets operate.[4]

That leaves the issue of the validity of the axioms of rational choice.[5]

This has raised thorny philosophical problems. There may be a number of different concepts of rationality. Since the axioms laid out in Chapter 3 never apply in actual choice situations characterized by radical uncertainty (not just risk), incomplete information and cognitive limits, is there some sense in which 'constrained rationality' can still deliver an ethically convincing defence of preference satisfaction? If so, what is the nature of the constraints on free choice? A consequentialist position would hold that such is the case if allowing (encouraging) preference satisfaction would in most cases enhance the individual's welfare. However, that means that we would need some measure of welfare independent of the actual choices made. Engagement in voluntary trade, as in buying a packet of cigarettes, may not be either necessary or sufficient to increase my welfare, if I am under the illusion that smoking is good for my cool image and does not harm my health. There are other ways that I can project a cool image and relax in company – unless that entails binge drinking and driving home. Smoking and drinking (and gambling) raise another problem with policy implications. Should governments intervene when the issue of *addiction* arises? Can someone be said to *voluntarily* agree to regularly smoke, drink alcohol to excess and gamble the weekly wage away?

The issue of how much and who should intervene raises still further ethical questions. In democratic societies, institutions and norms generally support a distinction between the private and public spheres with government intervention ideally restricted to the latter. This division is itself socially produced and differs between societies and over time. In the latter context, we can note the changing views about and the practice of policy in the area of domestic violence. In most Western societies today, the police and judicial systems intervene (with less than perfect effectiveness) in order to protect the physical and psychological welfare of the more vulnerable members of households. In earlier times and other societies such matters were and are routinely deemed closeted within the private sphere of civil society, the business of family and church authorities. In Saudi Arabia, women are publicly shamed and even beaten by police if they appear in public dressed in what is judged to be inappropriate attire or without male family escort.

Suitably finessed, the concept of rationality can be hedged around to exclude most of the intuitively unappealing cases raised but at the cost of rendering it useless as an ethical guide to policy in the real world. Governments and communities are continually faced with situations that call for judgments as to when, how and where to intervene in the lives of people – for their own good or the good of society (however defined). The political process will bring together the various and competing views as to the scope and targeting of policies that impact on welfare across society, helping to define as well as express the beliefs and desires that drive social interactions that create the mosaic of opportunities and lack thereof between individuals and groups forming that polity. However, there is no convincing sense in which the competing interests can be said to have equal capacities to affect policy outcomes: some are more equal than others.

Since there is unlikely to ever be absolute agreement on what the best (optimal) outcomes are, we are left with a messy, second-best option of outlining some of the possible good outcomes that people in their everyday lives and government framing policies can adhere to.

A GUIDE TO GRASPING WELFARE

The first signpost is to recognize the moral limits to markets, noted earlier. Simply because a market exists, does not mean that this will lead to welfare enhancing outcomes for all market participants.[6] Markets for drugs of addiction, human body parts and slaves are ethically unacceptable to most people in advanced Western societies today. This has not always been the case in other societies and other times.

Some would see the market for some animals (whales, rhinoceroses and other endangered species) as illicit. Animal rights activists go further and would argue, on ethical grounds (utilitarian or otherwise) against the sale of live sheep to the Middle East, greyhound and horse racing and other forms of exploiting animals for human benefit.

Second, economists that advise governments need to widen their view and consider non-consequentialist factors that matter to real people. Chief among these goods, as noted earlier, are certain things that have *intrinsic* rather than (or in addition to instrumental) value. Citizenship that conveys a personal sense of self-worth and dignity certainly has a raft of positive outcomes, material and immaterial. However, most citizens value their civic status as an end in itself, regardless or alongside the benefits. Moreover, most are willing under certain circumstances to sacrifice (trade off) these advantages if required in order to protect their status as citizen and the similar standing of their fellow citizens. How else are we to *fully* comprehend the willingness of people to volunteer to fight in wars in which they face likely death? The emphasis is on 'fully'. It is certainly true that some people enlist in search of personal adventure, excitement, escape from boredom or because they are badly informed about the probability of being killed. But – big 'but' – these factors do not exhaust the motives or moral factors behind enlisting 'to do one's bit'.

This example moves the discussion well beyond the ethic of outcomes to a consideration of duty and/or virtue. If citizenship as a right delivers good outcomes, it also comes with a set of duties; duties are the obverse of rights (Wight, 2015, p. 43). Virtue ethics focus on the right thing to do. Moral value resides in the characteristics of the act or choice; the intention, not the outcome (only) matters. Doing the right thing will often entail sacrificing desired outcomes, even one's life for friend, family member or broader group. This is not – or not only – because of altruistic motives but also because it is morally imperative to so act. It is a case of, following Martin Luther, 'here I stand, I can do no other'.[7]

Whether or not the rights underlying the moral duty to act virtuously – to enshrine the right character by one's actions – are derived from religious or secular traditions, from holy scripture or rational enquiry, the ethical imperative is absolute – in theory! In practice, public policy would prove difficult in some cases impossible to implement, once groups with diametrically opposed conceptions of the right coexisted in society. Something would have to give. Someone would have to restrict or trade off some of her deeply held beliefs and moral commitments. Alternatively, where the stakes were high and the conflicting world views radically divergent, fight or flight would ensue. Civil war or mass exodus has characterized the histories of many societies in which deep divisions existed with respect to basic moral absolutes. In most cases conflict arises from religious sources, witness the current war and refugee flight in Syria and Iraq, a powder keg ignited by US triumphalism following the collapse of communism. In the United States itself the Civil War in the nineteenth century between the North and South turned on basic conflicts over the morality of slavery and the property and civic rights of citizens, as well as a host of material economic interests.[8]

Where deeply opposed moral commitments characterize a society, resolution will normally reflect the existing or emerging unequal division of power, as occurred to end the US civil war. This suggests that where that division changes, where the position of powerful groups is successfully challenged, prevailing moral certitudes will also come under attack. New or resurrected old ethical imperatives will emerge to legitimate the interests and moral sentiments of the rising powers, not necessarily smoothly or immediately. For some time, a babble of competing moralities may confuse matters. Economists do policy makers no favours by forcing their attention to focus on a narrow conception of human welfare, the market mediated outcome of individual preferences, when the real world continually throws up conflicting demands for a range of other outcomes and desires.

Taxation provides a useful case. Economists have long debated the characteristics of an optimal taxation regime. Their conclusions reflect the particular normative analysis of efficiency (discussed in the next two chapters).[9] The policy conclusion in broad terms favours lump sum taxes and taxes on expenditure rather than incomes. However, the former are only efficacious, in terms of the conventional analysis, if totally unexpected and the latter are regressive in impact – that is, if broadly based, they fall proportionately more heavily on lower income people.[10] Both outcomes are likely to cause anger and push back from taxpayers. In the first case, people do not like nasty surprises, especially if they have based their life plans on the conditions of the pre lump sum tax world. In the second case, regressive taxation undermines widely held views about fairness and equal sacrifice in liberal democratic societies. Political salesmanship of a high order is necessary to slip highly regressive taxes past suspicious electorates. Orthodox economists make this job easier when they claim, erroneously, that their policy advice is based on value-free scientific analysis. To see why directs our attention in the next chapter to the manner in which economists developed the normative turn of the discipline in the early twentieth century and then sought to obscure this fact.

NOTES

1. For example, the work of Gary Becker (1981) on marriage and the family, a sphere of intimate personal relations, demonstrates the tendency of economists to extend their methodology to novel fields.
2. Hence, the distinction drawn by Hausman and McPherson between substantive and formal theories of well-being, implicit in the quote above, breaks down in practice; a process – preference satisfaction – has come to attract de facto substantive ethical significance. It is this fact that encourages many economists to slip between choice as process and utility as happiness when analysing policy options. Hausman and McPherson (2006, p. 121) recognize this tendency: 'We guess that many economists do not take the standard definition of welfare [as preference satisfaction] literally. They believe instead that welfare is a desirable mental state, such as happiness.'
3. Road safety researchers and psychologists are well aware of the tendency of young men to overestimate their driving prowess and their bulletproof protection.
4. See discussion in Chapters 10 and 18.
5. Etzioni (1990, Chapter 8) argues that the concept of rationality advanced in neoclassical economics is essentially tautological. Moreover, it carries an implicit ethical commitment by orthodox economists. 'The deeper reason neoclassicists assumed that individuals "must be" rational, "must be" able to form their own judgments, and that their choices must be perceived as basically morally correct, is because neoclassicists believe that any other position would justify a curtailment of individual rights . . . In short, the neoclassical concept of rationality is rooted in a Whiggish concept of society and of liberty' (ibid. p. 137).
6. The belief in the mutual gains from voluntary trade lies at the heart of the conventional approach to economic welfare, expressed as maximizing the sum of consumer and producer surpluses (see Wight, 2015, pp. 65–72.)
7. Whether or not Luther actually physically stood in front of the church in Wittenberg in 1517 and uttered these words as he nailed his 95 theses to the great door is irrelevant; the moral sentiment stands as representative of a coherent moral position. Although the imperative to do the right thing has been historically closely related to various religious traditions, it also arose in the work of one of the greatest moral philosophers, Immanuel

Kant. Kant's categorical imperatives provided the universalistic viewpoint from which to assess an individual's duty to act in ethically imperative ways (Wight, 2015, pp. 40–4. His approach underpinned the famous theory of justice proposed two centuries later by the American philosopher John Rawls (see Chapter 9).

8. From a consequentialist viewpoint, policy *should* consider the likely consequences of taking or not taking into account the existing conflicting moral commitments of groups in their societies. Not to do so – and on occasion to strategically favour some viewpoints over others – would be to deny that real consequences of action and inaction matter ethically.
9. Note that the use of the term 'optimal' carries with it a normative or ethical implication.
10. The conventional analysis also assumes perfect labour markets and that substitution effects outweigh income effects in the behaviour of investors and workers.

7. Cambridge versus Lausanne

> Hence, the range of our inquiry becomes restricted to that part of social welfare that can be brought directly or indirectly into relation with the measuring rod of money. This part of welfare may be called economic welfare.
> (A.C. Pigou)

The previous chapters have traced the emergence and development of the ethical foundations of the new discipline of economics. By the early twentieth century the neoclassical turn imparted by the founders Jevons, Menger, Walras and Marshall had been further developed by their followers, the next generation – Wicksteed, Pigou, J.B. Clark, Fisher, von Wieser, Böhm-Bawerk, Pareto and the Swede Knut Wicksell. The first two generations were in no doubt that economics was about *both* explaining how complex societies went about the 'ordinary business of life', to use Marshall's much quoted opening phrase *and* bringing about the improvement of the material lot of 'ordinary people'. The question of how these two elements – that came to be termed the 'normative' and 'positive' – were to be pursued was taken up by A.C. Pigou and Vilfredo Pareto.

MARSHALL'S FAVOURED SON

Arthur Cecil Pigou was born on the Isle of Wight in 1877. He progressed through Harrow School to Kings College Cambridge where he excelled as a student of history and philosophy. An accomplished poet, he quickly turned to the study and teaching of economics. Appointed to a fellowship at Kings, he succeeded Alfred Marshall as Professor of Political Economy in 1908 and held the chair until 1943. Marshall reputedly vacated the chair early to ensure Pigou's succession. Pigou repaid his mentor by steadfastly maintaining a disciple-like loyalty to the precepts of the master. 'It's all in Marshall' was his stock reply to anyone who sought guidance on a thorny matter of theory or policy. Although eclipsed by Marshall's other brilliant junior colleague, John Maynard Keynes, Pigou stands as one of the giants of the discipline whose collected works are as impressive, if not as voluminous and well known as Keynes's own.

Pigou made major contributions to the study of the business cycle, public finance and the workings of labour markets. However, he is most remembered for his book *The Economics of Welfare* that went through four editions and many reprintings.[1] In the first chapter of the book he laid down the terrain on which economists were to operate. As the quote at the chapter heading implies, the concept of human welfare is to be segmented into the economic and the rest. As a graduate of Cambridge's moral sciences tripos, Pigou was well aware of the main philosophical debates in ethics and aesthetics and of the long tradition of the Aristotelian search for the good life. His aim in Chapter 1 of *The Economics of Welfare* was to delineate the scope of economic inquiry by distinguishing those aspects of the good life that affected the lives of people through the operation of markets and the formation of prices (the 'measuring rod of money') from all other determinants. This, he argued, was not to deny the importance of the non-economic factors, in ordinary life or government policy, but to make tractable and coherent a scientific economics, to clearly distinguish positive arguments about what is from normative claims about what should be. This distinction has ever after served the discipline well to insulate its practitioners from having to face the actual consequences of the uses to which their 'positive' analysis has been put in the public policy arena.

Pigou sees economics as a human science, different in critical ways from the material world of the natural scientist, notably physics. 'Hence, in economics there is not, as in dynamics, one fundamental law of general application, but a great number of laws, all expressible, as it were, in equations of similar form but with different constants' (Pigou, 1920 [1950], p. 9). Economics distinguishes itself from the 'pure' science of physics in other key respects. First, the economist can never isolate particular factors under laboratory-like conditions. Natural experiments in the human sciences are rare and rarely unproblematic. This follows, in part, because there are so many variables and parameters (Pigou says 'constants') at play and the parameters are not stable between people and over time. It is as if the gravitational constant keeps changing.

A pure economics mirroring physics would, in his view, be agnostic between the formal conclusions following logically (mathematically) from any given set of axioms, much like the equal alacrity with which mathematicians approach Euclidian and non-Euclidian geometries. 'Now, if our end is practice, it is obvious that a political economy that did so extend would be for us merely an amusing toy' (ibid. p. 6).

> Contrasted with this pure science stands realistic economics, the interest of which is concentrated upon the world of experience, and in nowise extends to the commercial doings of a community of angels (ibid. p. 6).

Pigou did not live long enough to witness some of his successors get carried away by the attractions of pure economics turning on the commercial doings of a community of angels, rebranded as representative agents. Much of academic economics now takes place in a toy fair. He was clear that the focus must be on 'the actual world of men and women as they are found in experience to be'. He further claims to be driven by two propositions: first that the elements of welfare are states of consciousness and second, that welfare 'can be brought under the category of greater and less', with the implication that more is good and less is bad. The first proposition is an axiomatic nod back to utilitarianism as left by Sidgwick and Edgeworth. The second proposition hints at the salience of ordinal measures of welfare (to be rigorously developed by Pareto and followers), though the immediate introduction of the measuring-rod of money provides a path back to the cardinal concept that underlies the use of metrics like real GDP per capita as an index of standard of living.

Pigou wishes to radically separate the economic and non-economic dimensions of welfare and to stress their non-commensurability.

> There is no guarantee that the effects produced on the part of welfare that can be brought into relation with the measuring-rod of money may not be cancelled by effects of a contrary kind brought about in other parts, or aspects of welfare; and if this happens, the practical usefulness of our conclusions is wholly destroyed (ibid. p. 12)

and again – '(a)ll that this means is that economic welfare will not serve for a *barometer* or *index* of total welfare' (italics in original). This is a large claim and one long forgotten by most modern economists when they come to urge governments to act in certain ways justified by the concept of economic efficiency, derived not from the 'old' welfare economics of Pigou but the unthinking application of Pareto's 'new' welfare economics. It is rarely (never?) acknowledged that the practical usefulness of their conclusions is wholly destroyed.

Pigou seems to have in mind some version of Mill's higher pleasures when contemplating the non-economic expressions and causes of welfare, personified in two ideal types of men (women need not apply[2]). The first is a man attuned to the quiet beauties of nature, to the aesthetic of art and poetry, one who is likely to contribute to the cultural elevation of the nation, indeed world. Perhaps he saw himself and other Cambridge colleagues in the mirror here. The other type was the man of the soil and industry who can adapt knowledge and skills to producing the material means of existence, a can-do individual. At roughly the same time Böhm-Bawerk's student Joseph Schumpeter was casting the industrial entrepreneur at the centre of his dynamic account of capitalism.[3] Economics, Pigou held, could only get to grasp with the activities of the latter type, except to the extent that the cultural productions of the former found market outlets. The division could also be expressed geographically; the south east of England and Scotland versus the north and Wales, and over time, say the Germany of Schiller and Goethe versus the industrial Germany of Bismarck.

As a rule it is only the satisfactions and dissatisfactions of people that can be brought to market. Utility is gained through consumption of material and immaterial goods accessed through income 'earned' by the disutility of labour or the fruits of abstinence (saving) – one's own or one's benefactors. This simple circular flow is qualified by 'environmental' causes that may change elements of the (dis)satisfactions generated. Economic factors may impact for good or ill – 'modified' is Pigou's term – on the non-economic welfare of people. In particular, the nature of work apart from wages may cause an increase or decrease in conscious happiness. Some work is inherently challenging and satisfying – the life of a fellow at Kings College, for example. Other jobs may be dangerous and monotonous or carry stigma. Work is not, after all, a bringer of disutility – for everyone. Moreover, the extent of disutility may vary with the environment (time, place and context) in which the job is carried out. Even today the status of an Oxbridge college servant may not cause the status angst of servants employed in other situations: culture, history, teamwork and *esprit de corps* matter. In pre-industrial times the familial nature of labour expressed and reproduced long-held cultural values that largely defined the satisfactions of life; it was not all a case of 'the idiocy of rural life' to quote Marx and Engels's dismissive view. Even within the bowels of modern urban capitalism, the family farm and business continues to deliver the goods, material and immaterial, to its collective workforce. The non-familial based organization of cooperative endeavours can have similar outcomes, through clubs, interest groups and the like. Positive job satisfaction can even exist in large bureaucratic organizations that inculcate and psychically reward common loyalties and values among its employees. Hence:

> The esprit de corps and interest in the fortunes of the firm, which animate the workpeople in establishments where the personal intercourse of employers and employed is cordial, besides leading to increased production of wealth, is itself an addition to welfare (ibid. p. 16).

This last insight derives from Pigou's close study of the nature of the actual, as opposed to idealized, workings of labour markets and hints at later studies of internal labour markets, industrial participation and incomplete contracts. It also helps explain part of the psychological pain experienced by workers and whole communities when a large local business goes bankrupt. Pigou was not above suggesting that government may sometimes be justified in intervening in order to prevent such pain, that by so doing, it '. . . might increase welfare as a whole, even though they were to leave unchanged, or actually to damage economic welfare' (ibid. p. 17). An example here would be where a government steps in and subsidizes a firm to keep employing its workers rather than let the firm go out of business and its workers become unemployed. This conflict between maximizing growth in GDP and maintaining full employment lies at the heart of many economic and social policy debates (and political conflicts) today in Western economies undergoing deindustrialization.[4] Neoclassical (especially 'new classical') economists simply assume that labour markets work to quickly if not instantaneously re-employ 'freed' workers so obviating the need to protect workers in their current jobs; government interventions – in this view – simply reduce potential output (economic welfare) for no offsetting gain. Keynesians, of course, see the neoclassical model as a special and atypical case and reassert the need for government to be concerned with ensuring adequate effective demand in order to prevent both total output and employment falling below maximum levels. Whatever the long run outcomes of intervention, democratic governments are likely to be focused on short-term effects of their policies on employment, especially in the lead-up to elections. When an economic crisis unexpectedly erupts, everyone rediscovers his inner-Keynes – for a while.

The other main way that the pursuit of economic welfare may affect non-economic welfare concerns the manner in which income is spent; '(o)f different acts of consumption that yield equal satisfactions, one may exercise a debasing, and another an elevating influence' (ibid. p. 17). Pigou here contrasts the differing influences on people of public museums and public houses. He speculates on the wise governor who might reasonably (value-laden?) prefer diverting wealth from the vicious pursuits of the rich – gambling, opium eating and so on – to poor people who are likely to improve their lives by improving their diets and weatherproofing their homes.[5] In other cases it may be the gambling and vice of the lower classes that are to be discouraged, while the beneficial expenditure of the rich on the fine and performing arts are applauded. It is in this context that Pigou is most transparently revealed as a fan of John Stuart Mill's utilitarianism and an unapologetic adherent to the elitist cast of British liberalism. It is here too that he explicitly calls on ethical arguments, widely shared by those in his social milieu, to persuade the reader of the distinction between the economic and non-economic dimensions of welfare. Ethics, however, is reserved for the non-economic. He wishes to preserve for economics a realm of value freedom, while acknowledging the necessity for the legislator and executive to make ethical judgments and trade-offs in real world situations where the total welfare of people is at stake. Many economists have followed his lead and ended up in the same stand-off. To argue for policies on the basis of an unwillingness to take an ethical stance on the policies as acts in themselves and/or their consequences across the board, is to assume a value position by default. This was the broad conclusion of the value freedom debate in the social sciences in the 1960s – a conclusion that has never been accepted by the mainstream practitioners of orthodox economics.[6]

Pigou points to a final complicating or 'modifying' factor in the decision to use the measuring-rod of money as the defining metric for analysis, drawing further back beyond Mill to Adam Smith. Invasion by a foreign power inflicts widespread dissatisfactions on the population at large. Both Smith and Pigou were attracted to the argument, beloved of monarchs and republican governments alike through the ages, that keeping one's enemy poor is a useful insurance policy against just such a catastrophe.[7] This might take the form of erecting tariff barriers against the potential enemy's exports, even though this would reduce domestic economic welfare, as Ricardo had proved a century before. 'Injury to economic welfare may need to be accepted for the sake of defensive strategy' (ibid. p. 19). Pigou gives as a near-contemporary example the pre-World War I German government's policy of building up a domestic grain store rather than exporting it, that allowed Germany to withstand the allied blockade and stay in the war longer than otherwise would have been possible.[8]

The conclusion: '(t)he preceding discussion makes it plain that any rigid inference from effects on economic welfare to effects on total welfare is out of the question' (ibid. p. 20). Having clearly distinguished between economic and non-economic welfare and the often-antagonistic relation between both, Pigou nevertheless reserves the right for economists to rely on a subjective and qualitative probabilistic rule of thumb. When it is clear that some development increases (decreases) economic welfare, *unless there is specific evidence to the contrary*, it can be assumed that total welfare is increased (decreased) in the same direction, though not necessarily by the same amount. This argument – what I would term 'the Pigouvian fudge' – he calls 'a presumption', drawing on Edgeworth's equally vague notion of 'unverified probability'. What Pigou seems to be claiming is, that absent any disconfirming evidence, an increase in net satisfactions expressed though market processes enhances total welfare, though not in any quantitatively exact manner.

There are two troubling implications of this fudge. First, it is all too easy to forget that probable does not mean always. The subsequent history of the discipline and the policy uses to which it has been put amply demonstrate this amnesiac tendency. Economists and politicians often fall for the fallacy of misplaced quantification. Inputs or outputs that cannot be quantified are quietly ignored. Pigou's framing of the challenge puts the onus on finding disconfirming evidence of antagonistic relations between the economic and the non-economic. More subtly, the use of the expression '*non*-economic' imparts a negative value flavour to the comparison. Second, Pigou himself is aware of the doubtful logical foundation of the argument. Looking again to Mill, this time the latter's *Logic*, he acknowledges that '(t)he study of a part of things, he [Mill] points out, cannot in any circumstances be expected to yield more than approximate results' (ibid. p. 21). Pigou thus falls back on a contingent defence of his position. Causal propositions in economics can only be advanced in conditions where the impact of non-economic factors are constant or do not 'vary beyond certain defined [but never specified] limits'. These conditions, he believed, held in the Europe of his day.

Having carved out a sphere for the practice of a scientific analysis of welfare, suitably fenced around, Pigou devotes the rest of Part I of the book to quantifying economic welfare, its change and its distribution across the population. The economic impact on welfare is expressed through the market allocation of resources and the resulting distribution of goods and services to consumers. The critical linking mechanism is via the generation and distribution of incomes, to workers and wealth holders. This flow of goods and services is measured by 'the national dividend' or what is now termed national income.[9] 'The two concepts, economic welfare and the national dividend, are thus coordinate, in such wise that any description of the content of one of them implies a corresponding description of the content of the other' (ibid. p. 31). Pigou provides an impressive conceptual exegesis of the concept of national income that has not been markedly improved upon since. He is careful to closely define and apply his terms, counsel avoiding double-counting, rule out transfer payments via government taxes and subsidies, and notes the special challenges posed by accounting for durable goods. Even more impressively – having raised the measuring-rod of money to the fore – he playfully (for an economist) delights in pointing to the conceptual 'paradoxes' when laying it on. Some unsold services are vital to the delivery of marketed services, while others are 'interwoven' (Pigou's term) with them. For example, donated or gifted services are excluded from the national dividend, while the same services purchased are counted. Farm families that consume part of their harvest have only the marketed residue of their crops included. Indeed, the whole realm of 'housework' is excluded from market-based measures of economic welfare. 'Thus, if a man marries his housekeeper or cook, the national dividend is diminished' (p. 33).

What to do? Pigou offers a choice. We can dispense with any attempt to quantify national income in money terms or we can compromise. Unsurprisingly, Pigou opts for the latter strategy, though he does acknowledge that there is more to be said for ditching the measuring rod of money than is 'sometimes allowed'. With a nod to Marshall, he proposes to take as the definition of the national dividend 'that suggested by the British income tax commissioners'. In addition to the things bought with money income, this includes the estimated value of services provided by a homeowner's dwelling (its imputed rental value). Excluded are gifts, non-money exchanges, the benefits derived from personal property and the services provided by public goods, notably roads and bridges, defence and 'free' public education. Later national statisticians have included public goods by (under)valuing them at the cost of provision in the government budget. However, Pigou establishes an escape route for this narrow definition of national income. 'I reserve full liberty, with proper warning, to use the term in a wider sense on all occasions when the discussion of any problem would be impeded or injured by a pedantic adherence to the standard use' (ibid. p. 34).[10]

Having established, to his satisfaction, a workable concept of national income applied to a given period of time, conventionally a year, Pigou moves on to the difficult task of measuring the change in the national dividend between periods. This is important because he wishes to be able to determine whether economic welfare is increasing or decreasing over time, and by how much; within the terms established by the principle of unverified probability, this would also cast light on the progress of total welfare. Only then can economists make useful, 'practical' contributions to public policy. What usefulness (value) would a realistic economics be if it could tell citizens and their governments what their welfare is today but not whether it is more or less than yesterday? If the national dividend consisted of a single product then there would be no problem, since a physical change in the item would indicate the direction and scale of the change; likewise, if the number and proportions between several or many products remained unchanged. However, in the real world, the provision of some goods and services will be increasing while others decline and new products will come on line while others disappear entirely. 'In these circumstances there is no direct means of determining by a physical reference whether the dividend of one period is greater or less than that of another . . .' (ibid. p. 51). If we have recourse to the measuring-rod of money, the prices people pay for the products purchased in each period, it may be possible to simply add and compare the totals paid each period. This, in fact, governments do when they release annual GNP figures. But, as Pigou noted, this makes conceptual sense only if the tastes and the distribution of purchasing power between people remains constant over time. Unfortunately for the economist, this does not in general hold, even when new products are not being added and existing products removed from the purchasers' palates. Tastes can change significantly from year to year. New technologies can radically alter the distribution of incomes, as can government intervention on both the taxation and expenditure sides. The 'basket of goods and services' consumed changes, both because tastes change and because relative prices of the products making up the basket change.

> We are thus confronted with the awkward fact that there are likely to be certain changes in the constitution of the national dividend, of which it is not possible to say that they are either increases or decreases in an absolute sense. Plainly there is serious objection to a definition that leads to this result' (ibid. p. 53).

Never fear, Pigou plays the escape card or fudge. Between two periods when tastes and distribution changes, the *direction* of the change in total monetary value of the national dividend in the second period will be the same as that viewed from the prices ruling in the first period. 'The defect in our definition is thus not a fatal defect' (ibid. p. 54). Moreover, anticipating Churchill's later defence of democracy as imperfect but better than the alternatives on offer, Pigou claims that his approach is less defective than others. Thus, at the end of Chapter V, Pigou (ibid. p. 54) provides the following exact definition of an increase in the national dividend (that is, economic welfare), worth quoting in full to demonstrate the seriousness with which he approaches his subject and his desperation to escape the logical difficulties thrown up by reliance on the measuring-rod of money:

> From the point of view of period I, an increase in the size of the dividend for a group of given numbers is a change in its content such that, *if* tastes in period II were the same as those prevailing in period I, and *if* the distribution of purchasing power were also the same as prevailed in period I, the economic satisfaction (as measured in money) due to the items added in period II is greater than the economic satisfaction (as measured in money) due to the items taken away in period II. From the point of view of period II, an increase in the dividend is defined in exactly analogous ways. From an absolute point of view an increase in the size of the dividend is a change which constitutes an increase from both the above two points of view. When of the two [calculated] dividends, one is larger from the point of view of one period and the other from that of the other, the two are, from an absolute point of view, incommensurable (italics in original).

Pigou implies that situations of incommensurability, identified for reasons of conceptual completeness, are relatively rare in practice, at least when considering two periods close together in time. The final conceptual brick is added by noting that when the number of people in the group – the population – changes, the correct comparison is between the per capita national dividends of the larger and smaller groups in both periods. However, it is not clear what averaging measure is to apply to the total populations in each – arithmetic mean, median or geometric mean.

Having somewhat exhaustively established and defended a workable *definition* of a change in economic welfare, Pigou must now offer some way of quantifying the *scale or size* of change. This creates a need to construct a series of price index numbers across contiguous time periods. This is – again – a second best or fallback position. As a good Marshallian, Pigou would prefer to add up the consumer surpluses of all consumers to arrive at an accurate measure of the total that each person would be willing and able to pay above what they do in fact pay in each period. Since Marshall had himself ruled such an approach impractical in the real world, all that is left (imbibing the Marshallian fudge) is to deal with actual sets of price data available. This can be broken down into three stages:

1. Establish the measure that would most closely conform to the definition *if* all relevant information about prices and quantities bought were accessible.
2. Make a 'mathematical' attempt to construct a measure *from a sample of actually available* price and quantity data that would most closely fill out that measure.
3. Make a judgment as to how *reliable* the practical measure is as an index of the desired measure.

The final index used can fail in practice on two grounds: first, the available data sampled may be incomplete or biased towards easily captured values; second, the sample biases may change over time, between periods. The more unreliable the measure the more contentious will be comparisons between the national income at increasingly distant periods.

Even with these qualifications, it is not required that the absolute size of the dividend change is significant. It is only required that the index measure reliably tracks relative increases in the monetary value of the dividend. For example, if in period II the dividend is x per cent higher than in period I, rather than y per cent higher (where $x>y$), then the measure would show a higher increase when economic welfare increases by x, than when it increases by y. In the rest of Chapter VI, Pigou provides a brilliant discussion of the challenges and limitations inherent in constructing and applying index numbers to the tracking of growth in national income. Having done so, he applies the fudge – it is not a perfect measure but it is the best we can do – and moves on to consider the vexed issue of the effects on economic welfare of the distribution of the national dividend.[11]

Pigou's major concern here is the key question raised by the rise of modern liberalism in the Anglo-democracies: namely, what is the case for and the consequences of a progressive redistribution of welfare from the rich to the poor? He identifies the various mechanisms by which this can occur:

1. Redistributing income or wealth – that is, redirecting greater purchasing power to the poor.
2. Technological change that cheapens the production of goods and services most heavily consumed by the poor.
3. Government-imposed rationing that increases the consumption of poor people who would otherwise be priced out of the market.

To this list one may add the direct provision of goods and services by government – for example free public schools and hospitals – funded by a proportional income tax, leaving the distribution of resources unchanged. Pigou also notes the contra case. If technological change or the taxation burden favours the consumption of the rich, the national dividend is redistributed in a regressive manner. However, for most practical purposes, when we talk about redistribution, at least in the short run, the emphasis is on improving the relative purchasing power of poorer sections of society; '. . . this sort of transference is the most important, and may be regarded as the typical, means by which changes in distribution favourable to the poor come about' (ibid. p. 89).

Pigou here is attempting to establish a connection between the effects on economic welfare of a progressive change in the *distribution* of the national dividend similar to the link between changes in economic welfare and the *size* of the dividend. In spite of the fact the rich consume a smaller proportion of their current incomes than the poor – that is, they save more, storing up a greater capacity to consume more in the future – the former are still likely to consume in the current period much more than the latter. Moreover:

> . . . it is evident that any transference of income from a relatively rich man to a relatively poor man of similar temperament, since it enables more intense wants to be satisfied at the expense of less intense wants, must increase the aggregate sum of satisfaction. The old 'law of diminishing utility' thus leads securely to the proposition: any cause which increases the aggregate share of real income in the hands of the poor, provided that it does not lead to a contraction in the size of the national dividend from any point of view, will, in general, increase economic welfare (ibid. p. 89).

This is, perhaps, the strongest and most potent statement in favour of egalitarianism ever advanced by a front-line economist. It is the boldest statement following from jettisoning the Marshallian fudge by assuming that money income obeys the law of diminishing marginal utility. It must have all been deeply worrying to the wealthy and powerful of the day, even more so when Pigou argued that the loss of utility (satisfactions) borne by the rich will be less than that caused by the absolute reduction in their incomes, since the happiness of the rich depends on their incomes *relative* to each other. If the incomes of all rich people are cropped by similar amounts, relativities are maintained and their satisfactions are likely to fall by less than the law of diminishing marginal utility would suggest, strengthening the case for progressive redistribution in favour of the poor. This last claim is contentious, even for non-misers, but it does raise an important issue in the light of the recent debate over the emergence of extreme inequality in the form of the 1 per cent thesis (Dorling, 2014). If the super-rich strive not to raise their absolute incomes but in a never-ending arms race to receive the status and power satisfactions by pulling in higher incomes than each other and the merely-rich, then the simple redistribution of the national dividend loses contact with the total economic welfare of the population. National income measured in money terms can rise, fall or stay the same, without impacting consistently on the final net sum of satisfactions enjoyed by rich and poor. Other moral judgments will need to be made to justify limiting the incomes and wealth of the former and bolstering that of the latter.

In fact, Pigou's case for progressive redistribution can and was attacked on a number of fronts, several of which were opened by Pigou himself. First, the last sentence of the quote above, notes the qualifier – the fact of and means by which income is redistributed must not result in a contraction of the total pie. This harks back to the argument noted in preceding chapters that reducing inequality will reduce incentives and productivity and not lead to a permanent increase in the living standards of the poor. Second, if the 'temperaments' of rich and poor are significantly different, all bets are off. Inherited differences in 'mental constitutions' will change the felicific calculus. It should be noted that Pigou rounds out Part I of his book with a chapter on 'the quality of the people' in which he flirts with the eugenic enthusiasms of his time; he is probably the first economist to footnote Mendel's *Principles of Heredity*. Even without inherited differences, as noted earlier, different upbringings and ranges of experience and sensibilities may dampen the welfare-enhancing effects of progressive redistribution. The rich may derive greater dissatisfactions from seeing their disposable incomes decline by a given amount – having to cut back on opera and ballet performances – than the poor who gain the same extra income only to splurge it on 'inappropriate' pursuits:

> For, if anyone accustomed to a given standard of living suddenly finds his income enlarged, he is apt to dissipate the extra income in forms of exciting pleasure, which, when their indirect, as well as direct, effects are taken into account, may even lead to a positive loss of satisfaction (Pigou, 1920 [1950], p. 91).

Pigou's class prejudices are here on show.[12]

Although all this has a modern ring, seemingly prefiguring the special pleading of vested interests in defence of established privilege, it can more reasonably be seen as reflecting Pigou's adherence to Mill's (and Marshall's) belief in the need to gradually improve the living conditions, aspirations and characters of the poor through environmental interventions – good role models, good schools, good health, good working conditions and so on. He was explicit about the temporary nature of any 'foolish expenditure' occasioned by 'suddenly' increasing income, confident that when the living standards of the poor gradually and permanently improves, they will come to acquire the necessary capacities and characters to lift their satisfactions to sustainable levels, foregoing the lower pleasures in favour of Mill's higher ones. 'Thus, in the long run differences in temperament and tastes between rich and poor are overcome by the very fact of a shifting of income between them. Plainly, therefore, they cannot be used as an argument to disprove the benefits of a transference' (ibid. pp. 91–2). His argument can also be read as supporting transfers in kind by government rather than by cash-in-hand – at least until character growth has progressed sufficiently among the lower orders.[13]

Whatever, the scientific claims made by Pigou for his attempts to apply the measuring-rod of money to defining, measuring and distributing what he regards as economic welfare, there are clear ethical elements to his analysis. It is implicitly assumed without consideration that command over more resources in the market is better than commanding less resources. Economic (and total) welfare is equated with satisfying individual desires, however arising. Redistributing resources is justified by reference to maximizing total individual satisfactions and not, say, to expanding life-chances as an end or right in itself. Considerations of duty and obligation, that might colour the moral universe of conservatives, are ignored. Even within a consequentialist framework, there are other outcomes like building community cohesion and banishing extreme deprivation and discrimination, that fall outside Pigou's purview.

At this stage in the book, Pigou might be dismissed as a narrow, albeit subtle utilitarian. This view does him a disservice. Having carefully confined attention to the market-determined nature of welfare, he progresses to a radical analysis of *the failure of market processes* to actually – in the real world of 'men as they are' – maximize welfare as previously treated. To the earlier recognition of the existence of monopoly, going back to Adam Smith, Pigou adds a whole new category of *market failure* – the pervasive existence of external effects, positive and negative. It is this analytic innovation and the policy implications stemming from it that has secured Pigou's fame in the history of economic thought.

Complacent assumptions that 'free markets' automatically result in the maximum economic welfare, as defined, are untenable. As Pigou puts it:

> Certain optimistic followers of the classical economists have suggested that the 'free play of self-interest', if only Government refrains from interference, will automatically cause the land, capital and labour of any country to be so distributed as to yield a larger output and, therefore, more economic welfare than could be attained by any arrangement than that which comes about 'naturally'. There is ground, however, for believing that even Adam Smith had not realized fully the extent to which the System of Natural Liberty needs to be qualified and guarded by special laws before it will promote the most productive employment of a country's resources (ibid. pp. 127–8).

Were the free interactions of individuals driven solely by unrestrained self-interest we would find ourselves in Hobbes's State of Nature – 'and the life of man, solitary, poore, nasty, brutish and short'. It is in everyone's interest to ensure that no one steals or cheats in the market but in everyone's individual interest to do so if he or she can get away with it. Only government-enforced rules backed by widely held moral commitments, he suggests, can prevent what later economists came to term 'free riding' and the terribly compelling logic of 'the prisoner's dilemma'.[14]

Although Pigou recognized these failings in real world economies, and their implications for policy, he focuses instead on a different set of problems – or 'obstacles' – that systematically undermined the pure theory of 'natural liberty' through the market. In passing, it should be noted that contemporary champions of 'free enterprise', particularly politicians, seem to have no cognizance of the existence and importance of externalities and the other obstacles to allocating a country's resources in 'the most effective way'.

Pigou makes the distinction essential to economic understanding between resources as a *stock* of productive capacity and uses of this stock to generate a continuous *flow* of product to purchasers. In order to ensure than the maximum flows are generated from a given stock of resources, attention must focus at the margin, on the impact on net product of adding a little more resource to existing uses or moving that increment from an existing to a new use. Maximum output occurs when the marginal increase (decrease) in output is equalized in each and every productive use, valued by their respective market prices. Otherwise moving resources from the current use could increase total product with the lower marginal net product to the use promising a greater return. In well-functioning markets, industrialists (capitalists) will be driven by competitive forces and the aim/necessity to maximize individual profits to so allocate the resources each has. The total produced, multiplied by their individual market prices forms the (raw) national dividend. However, capitalists are only interested in allocating their resources with an eye to the value accruing to themselves individually. Hence, it is what Pigou terms 'the marginal *net* product' that competition equalizes across the economy courtesy of the benign invisible hand. Contrast this with 'the marginal *social* net product' which '. . . is the total net product of physical things or objective services due to the marginal increment of resources in any given use or place, *no matter to whom any part of the product may accrue*' (ibid. p. 134; italics added).[15] In this context the national dividend should include *all* consequences of economic activity and not just those accruing to the parties directly involved in productive and exchange activities. Pigou gives as an example a railway that showers the woodlands through which it runs with sparks causing damage to property owners along the line. The net revenue earned by the railway company will form part of the national dividend to which should be added or subtracted the external or 'third party' effects on, in this example, owners of the woodlands who suffer losses from burnt logs.

Pigou gives a large number of examples of the externalities, both positive and negative, that he believes characterize the modern urban-industrial society of his day. On the positive side he points to the (market) value accruing to a beekeeper who locates next door to a commercial flower grower, by comparison to returns resulting in locations more distant from pollen-beckoning land uses. On the negative side, people living downstream from a factory that spews chemical pollution into the river suffer the health and blighting consequences ignored by the polluter in deciding what, how and how much to produce. In the former case, the conventional market valued measure of the national dividend understates the true impact on economic welfare; in the latter case, it overstates it. Only in the absence of externalities, positive and negative, will the marginal social and private net products be equal and the market measure of national income accurately reflect the economic welfare of the community.

The social or 'augmented' national dividend will only be maximized if and when the marginal *social* net product is equal across all uses. However, sadly, there is no mechanism that will automatically bring this about. Only the visible hand – occasionally boot – of government can recognize and intervene to move the economy towards more fully utilizing its total resource potential. This led to the worrying implication – for economists and capitalists – that capitalism was not necessarily the best of all possible worlds, in other words that inefficiency was inscribed in its very bones. It took four decades for this claim to be challenged. In 1960 Ronald Coase published a paper, *The Problem of Social Cost*, arguing that, in theory, third parties could negotiate with each other and with the parties creating the externalities to voluntarily compensate the loser – the woodland owner for property damage and the beekeeper for 'free' services provided to the neighbouring flower grower. Moreover, in the case of negative effects like pollution as long as the negotiations are 'voluntary', it doesn't matter if the polluter compensates the pollutee or the other way around. A value judgment backed by bargaining power will decide which direction compensation flows.

'The Coase Theorem' as it became known depends for its validity on strict conditions. In particular, property rights have to be clearly delineated and enforced – leading to the reality that government and market are not alternative and competing ways of organizing the economic process but intimately interconnected. Second, and equally critically, there must be zero transaction costs and adequate information among direct and third parties for meaningful negotiations to result in welfare enhancing outcomes. 'Alas, transaction costs are always positive and, in that sense, the Coase Theorem is another impossibility theorem' (Blaug, 1996, p. 585).[16] The complex task of identifying and coordinating the interest of numerous third parties in many cases simply makes the Coase approach impractical.

Pigou's solution turned on the role of government in levying (indirect) taxes on those agents imposing negative externalities, and paying subsidies to agents creating positive effects, thereby removing the gap between the marginal social and private net products so that resulting market prices could correctly value the flows of goods and services reaching purchasers.[17] Blaug (1996), following John Hicks, notes that many of Pigou's actual examples relate to large-scale, economy-wide interconnections that are not amenable to marginal analysis. Thus, Pigou points to the pervasive externalities imposed by town planning regulations, the escalating negative consequences of industrial accidents, the deleterious physical and moral effects of child labour and the indirect global influences on people of 'bandwagon effects', resulting, for example, in over-consumption of alcohol through peer pressure or (we might add) the rush to consume expensive motor cars and Parisian fashions. In any event, the practical challenges of estimating the *physical* dimensions of these and other external effects are huge. Then comes the problem of *valuing* the physical effects, in order to calculate the required monetary size of the offsetting taxes and subsidies. Actual market prices are not appropriate since, by definition, they exclude the effects to be compensated – that is, they are the *wrong* prices. The right prices would be those that *would* have ruled had the taxes and subsidies been made; this adds another layer to the valuation correction.

All this does not overly concern Pigou, who is diligent in laying down the map of complex interactions and imperfections in how real world markets operate. His is a dynamic economy of moving and interconnected parts. He assumes relatively free but not abstractly perfect markets for land, labour and capital. He accepts the limitations of information inherent in the real world, among producers, consumers and governments. He recognizes the need for judgment by the latter when it comes to deciding where and when to intervene and at what level to set and who to levy taxes on and dispense subsidies to. It is not the case for Pigou that governments have to get it totally right or refrain completely from intervening. Pragmatic, practical policy is the order of the day – but policy in the full knowledge of the complexities involved. The intellectually flabby view, shared by many liberals and conservatives, namely that all governments need to do is leave markets as they exist to allocate society's scarce resources, will not do. This comfortable approach will not make the most efficient use of society's resources if efficiency is conceived as maximizing economic welfare, as defined. In Blaug's (1996, p. 583) succinct words: '(i)ndeed, no one can continue to believe in the spontaneous coordination of private and social interests who has digested Pigou's insistence on the possible interdependence of firms and households.'

Lying at the base of *The Economics of Welfare* is the author's Victorian moral commitment to improving the material lot of the poorer classes in society. In this he faithfully follows the path laid out by the moral compass of his master and mentor, Alfred Marshall. His economics is unabashedly, unashamedly normative, while at the same time claiming 'scientific' status for the discipline, suggesting the illegitimacy of separating the two approaches. He was able to manage this logically dubious approach by sticking to a cardinal conception of utility as adequately captured by market prices suitably adjusted *and* by encouraging economists and policy makers to adopt a pragmatic, probabilistic mindset – close enough is generally good enough.[18]

He could realistically charge government with intervening where appropriate and where the cost of doing so (probably) did not exceed the net benefits to households realized. No starry-eyed socialist, he held that in most circumstances markets worked well enough to improve economic welfare over time but where they demonstrably fell down, government agencies were morally obliged to step in. The practical result would, over time, realize the dreams of modern liberals like J. S. Mill, a new society in which the majority of citizens enjoyed the material and cultural benefits bestowed only on the fortunate minority in earlier times. Pigou, like

Marshall and Mill, was never willing to follow more stringent neo-classicals in dumping the latter's focus on the temporal process of economic change – though he did jettison the more pessimistic prognostications of Ricardo.

This conceptually pragmatic and messy position affronted many economists for whom the creation of a positive science of economics became the end, rather than the less heroic creation of a toolkit designed to reform society along moderately egalitarian ends. Physics envy rather than moral purpose energized economists on both sides of the English Channel and the Atlantic Ocean. What they sought was an analytic framework that delivered a grand concept of efficiency shorn of any explicit value judgments about distribution. In effect, they wanted to refute Mill's claim (in *Principles of Political Economy*) that the laws of production were immutable but the laws of distribution malleable and susceptible to policy intervention. They wished to prove that both were immutable, the consequence of given resources, technologies and consumer tastes processed through perfectly competitive markets. As if in answer to their prayers, along came Walras's successor, the Italian economist Vilfredo Pareto.

THE SHOCK OF THE NEW

Pareto was born in Paris of Italian parents in the year of revolutions, 1848. No revolutionary, he trained and worked as an engineer and developed a robust classical liberalism antithetical to government intervention in the economy. In midlife he took up economics and championed the application of mathematical methods to the discipline. In this he followed and developed the earlier work of the Frenchmen Cournot, Dupuit and Walras. Like fellow railway engineer Jules Dupuit and unlike failed engineer Walras, Pareto's mathematical skills were sufficient to convince many coming to the discipline that this way the future lay. Formal analysis would, it was hoped, lift economics above the ideological fray between liberals, conservatives and socialists, finally severing it from the philosophic and historical roots in classical political economy.

Pareto's key book – *Manual of Political Economy* – was published in 1906, a few years before Pigou's original *Wealth and Welfare*. It was not published in translation in the English-speaking world until 1971, but was widely available in French from 1927 and thereafter exerted a crushing effect on the 'old' welfare economics. Having been dispatched to the wings by Pareto in the twenties and by Keynes a decade later, Arthur Pigou became (unfairly in my view) the 'forgotten man' of economics.

The *Manual* opens with the methodological claim that there are three reasons for studying political economy. The first two refer to the aim of assisting people and governments to more effectively go about their business and 'to do a little good' (echoes of Marshall). Pareto, however, is only interested in the third rationale:

> The writer may intend only to search for the uniformities that phenomena present, that is to say their laws . . . without having any direct practical usefulness in mind, without concerning himself in any way with giving recipes or precepts, without seeking the happiness, the benefit or the wellbeing of humanity or any part of it. In this case, the purpose is exclusively scientific; one wants to *know*, to *understand*, no more (Pareto, 1927/[1971], p. 2; italics in original).

No statement could more eloquently and radically distinguish the new from the old welfare economics, contrasting Pareto's exclusive positivistic focus from the 'realistic economics' of Pigou and the Marshallians.[19] Pareto's economic analysis is entirely *static*, which is to say that it follows the progenitors of the marginalist revolution by concentrating on what he calls the 'general notion of economic equilibrium'. 'The theory of statics is most advanced; we have only a very few notions about the theory of successive equilibria, that of economic crises, nothing is known about dynamic theory' (ibid. p. 105).[20] Following the broad utilitarian tradition Pareto aims to understand how an aggregate of individuals goes about satisfying the wants, desires or tastes of each given the obstacles each faces in terms of knowledge and resources. He also wishes to demonstrate that the underlying law-like uniformities of outcome are explicable through the routine operation of market processes – for goods and services and factors of production.

> The principal subject of our study is economic equilibrium. We will shortly see that this equilibrium results from the opposition between men's tastes and the obstacles to satisfying them. Our study includes, then, three very distinct parts: 1. the study of tastes; 2. the study of obstacles; 3. the study of the way these two elements combine to reach equilibrium (ibid. p. 106).[21]

This reduces to an analysis of choice under constraint. He distinguishes two types of choice situations. The first compares how an individual chooses between actions in terms of how each impact on his or her desires. These desires frequently display self-interest but may also cover altruistic ('if the meaning of that term could be rigorously defined') or mixed motives. 'What does constitute the essential characteristic of this class of theories is that we compare sensations of one man, and not those of different men' (ibid. p. 106). The second theoretical approach seeks to compare the 'sensations of one man with those of another man'. 'This study is one of the most unsatisfactory in social science' (ibid. p. 106). Pareto rules out the second approach, effectively denying the scientific usefulness of any interpersonal comparisons of utility. Indeed, so much baggage had the term utility come to carry that Pareto replaced it with another, namely 'ophelimity', defined as the quantity of pleasure the individual derives from a given quantity of a product. Since, he denies the possibility of quantifying pleasure, even for a single person, he rejects any cardinal notion of ophelimity in favour of an ordinal conception. Ophelimity serves as an index of greater and lesser satisfaction or agreeableness for an individual.[22] Subsequent economists followed his lead, while quietly ignoring his terminology and resurrecting the term utility buttressed by the basic axioms noted in Chapter 3.

Pareto takes the notion of indifference curves, familiar from the earlier work of Edgeworth, to express the map of consumer preferences in purely ordinal form. However, unlike Edgeworth, he assumes indifference curves as given and deduces the process of equilibrium from them 'without resorting to ophelimity' (see footnote 4 on p. 119 of the *Manual*). This provides the base on which later economists came to treat consumer demand as a theory of revealed preference. From this position he offers his famous notion of welfare optimality:

> We will say that the members of a collectivity enjoy maximum ophelimity in a certain position when it is impossible to find a way of moving from that position very slightly in such a manner that the ophelimity enjoyed by each of the individuals of that collectivity increases or decreases. That is, any small displacement in departing from that position has the effect of increasing the ophelimity which certain individuals enjoy, and decreasing that which others enjoy, of being agreeable to some and disagreeable to others' (ibid. p. 261).[23]

By integrating the analyses of production and consumption using a formal mathematical approach, Pareto was able to prove that the outcome in a perfectly competitive economy would be Pareto optimal in the sense just stated. This became known as 'the first fundamental theorem of welfare economics'.[24] His contributions in the 1890s and first decade of the twentieth century came to dominate debates among economists in the 1930s and 1950s, culminating in the work of Bergson (1938), Samuelson (1947), Arrow (1951) and Arrow and Debreu (1954). Chipman (n.d., pp. 8–9) concludes:

> Pareto's influence on modern economic theory has been profound. He was the first to make ordinal utility a systematic part of the subject, in his observation (quite consistently with his use of utility measurement for other purposes, e.g., classification of commodities into substitutes and complements) that all the propositions concerning equilibrium of consumers follow from the ordinal ranking of indifference surfaces, without the need to assume measurability

> of utility . . . Equally profound has been his impact on welfare economics; he turned what in Walras was a tautology into an important theorem which remains today the main justification for the implementation of a system of competitive markets.

What Pareto is widely but wrongly assumed to have achieved is a conception of economic efficiency independent of any value judgment about how the satisfactions produced are distributed among consumers. This claim and the slippery notion of efficiency are interrogated in the next chapter.

NOTES

1. All references here will be to the 1950 reprint of the 1932 fourth edition. The book was originally published, in a more condensed form, in 1912 under the title *Wealth and Welfare*.
2. For much of Pigou's time at Cambridge women were not formally enrolled and did not graduate from the university.
3. In 2012 a 26-year-old Schumpeter (1912/1934) published his book, *The Theory of Economic Development* in German. It was not translated into English for another two decades. Thorstein Veblen (1921) in *The Engineers and the Price System*, explored similar themes.
4. Such developments can have major political consequences, as the outcome of the Brexit vote and 2016 US presidential election dramatically demonstrated.
5. It should be clear that Pigou is not simply making a positive claim based on rational analysis but intruding a moral judgment about what governments should do to bring about the morally elevated society that Mill and other modern liberals promoted.
6. Many economists implicitly accept the nihilistic ethic of Hitler's rocket scientist, Wernher von Braun, who absolved himself from wartime moral responsibility by claiming that he only sent the rockets up, and did not decide where they fell. The critique of value freedom in the social sciences was sparked in America by the broad academic and cultural environment of dissent during the civil rights and Vietnam War movements and the specific fallout from the US Army funded study *Project Camelot* that brought together researchers from across the social sciences to inform counterinsurgency 'black' operations in Latin America (see Horowitz, 1967).
7. It also justified government expenditure on building an adequate defence capacity to be financed by taxation, further impacting on welfare. Today, we are used to the special pleading of what Eisenhower dubbed 'the military-industrial complex'. The arguments have evolved to include the generation of jobs, but the value proposition remains – it is 'good' to prevent enemies, however defined, from threatening our territorial sovereignty. Following Smith and Locke, the primary *duty* of a government is widely held to be guaranteeing 'homeland security', never more so than in the post-9/11 world of the surveillance state. The use of the word 'duty' signals that a moral judgment is being smuggled into the analysis.
8. It is obvious that this policy has ethical implications tied to the age-old arguments as to the nature of a 'just war' and the more recent delineation of 'war crimes'.
9. Strictly speaking, Pigou adheres to Marshall's use of the term by including the current production of capital goods (net of depreciation), as opposed to Irving Fisher's focus on current and future consumption flows. This resembles the modern measure of net national product at market prices. Current policy attention is fixated on *gross* national (actually, domestic) product, since this carries with it a closer value concern with employment levels.

10. One can only marvel at the dexterity with which the Pigouvian fudge is wielded here. It also underscores his determination to use – and not be used by – economic tools to practice a 'realistic economics'. Like Keynes and their common Cambridge master, Pigou saw economics as the task of developing and applying a conceptual 'toolkit' to practical purpose, a practice ideally akin to dentistry, in Keynes's later words.
11. One can only shake one's head at the decline in sophistication of subsequent practice in using national income measures as an indicator of standard of living. All the subtle conceptual and practical difficulties and careful limitations explicitly addressed by Pigou are simply ignored. Economic commentators and politicians follow the trend in real GDP per capita avidly as *the* holy grail of policy assessment.
12. Nevertheless, the 'sad' fate of some people who win large lottery prizes echoes Pigou's argument here, though hardly provides a general case for declining to collect on a winning ticket.
13. Pigou can thus be seen as a link in a chain of progressive liberal thinkers stretching from Adam Smith, through John Stuart Mill to Amartya Sen in our day.
14. The truly terrible nature of this logic – and the moral blinkers economists can be constrained by – is evidenced by the fact that the inventor of game theory, John von Neumann, supposedly advised American military leaders to launch a first-strike on the Soviet Union before the latter was impelled to beat them to the nuclear trigger. In fact, as I will argue later, real people (as opposed to *homo economicus*) develop socially situated moral and other values that limit the problems of interaction between self-interested individuals. Unsurprisingly, America did not unleash nuclear Armageddon in the early-1950s, though nuclear brinkmanship did surface from time to time as in the Cuban missile crisis of the early 1960s.
15. 'The value of the marginal social net product is simply the sum of money which the marginal social net product is worth in the market. In like manner the value of the marginal private net product is the sum of money which the marginal private net product is worth in the market' (ibid. p. 135).
16. Blaug is referring here to Kenneth Arrow's famous impossibility theorem concerning voting, of which more later. Cooter (1987, p. 67), following Arrow (1969), shows that '. . . the Coase Theorem in any of its three interpretations encounter obstacles that suggest that it is probably false or a mere tautology'. The value of the Coase Theorem (a term which Coase himself did not use) was to point out that taxes were not the only way to 'internalize' some externalities. Other mechanisms could draw on markets and extended contracting; this was termed by Cheung (1969) 'the equivalence version' of the theorem. However, as noted earlier, where there are many parties, high transaction costs made Coase's property rights approach inapplicable in terms of Pareto optimal outcomes. Further criticisms hinge on problems of incomplete information and the intricacies of bargaining strategies and perverse incentives among effected parties. See Hahnel and Sheeran (2009) and Halpin (2007) for recent critical discussions.
17. This still leaves open the question of how governments finance any excess of required subsidies over tax receipts in a given period.
18. Pigou's conception of a realistic economic 'science' was of a rigorous analytical pursuit to understand human behaviour in a defined domain, adequately qualified by recognizing when analysis had exhausted the capacity of delivering useful answers.
19. We leave aside the problematic nature of the implication in the last sentence of the quote above that the 'purpose' of anything entails a value proposition; it is *good* to be 'scientific'. It is deeply ironic that despite rejecting any normative cast to his analysis it was to supply the normative underpinnings of orthodox economics ever since first widely known, through the central concept of 'Pareto optimality' (see Chapter 8 for a detailed discussion).
20. The core of Pareto's economics of welfare resides in Chapters III to VIII and his famous (mathematical) Appendix. Other parts of the book are generally ignored. This is a pity since there are many interesting suggestions in the earlier and later chapters, for example his comments on population, market structure and other 'obstacles' to the textbook

workings of markets; here he comes closer to Pigou's realistic discipline. Moreover, the first two chapters demonstrate Pareto's wide knowledge of the philosophical antecedents of political economy and his wider interests in what became the work of his later life, creation of a broad social science or 'general sociology' of which economics is but a part. He looked forward to the (distant) day 'when the laws of social science can be deduced from the principles of psychology'; what, I wonder, would he make of the recent developments in behavioural (and neuro) economics? Schumpeter (1943 [1987]) points to Pareto's book *Mind and Society* as an important source of understanding the role of 'extra-rational' and irrational forces in human social behaviour, a view of which modern-day followers focused on the model of rational choice appear unaware.

21. This clear statement would be instantly recognizable to current economics students.
22. Under restricted assumptions, Pareto demonstrates that such an index or function is constant up to a linear transformation (see the discussion in Chapter 3).
23. Drawing on what became known as the Edgeworth–Bowley Box diagram familiar to undergraduate students, Pareto comments: '(c)onsequently, if we move away from the position of equilibrium a finite distance along a straight line, the ophelimities which the two individuals enjoy can vary in such a way that the one increases while the other decreases [on the contract curve linking the points of tangency of opposed indifference curve sets], or so that they both decrease together, but they cannot increase together [leaving the contract curve completely]' (Pareto, 1927 [1971], p. 263).
24. Chipman (n.d., p. 6) notes that Pareto also got close to deriving 'the second fundamental theorem', of which more is to be said in the next chapter.

8. What *is* efficiency?

> Analysis of efficiency in the context of resource allocation has been a central concern of economic theory from ancient times, and is an essential element of modern microeconomic theory (Stanley Reiter).

> This 'ethics-related view of social achievement' cannot stop the evaluation short at some arbitrary point like satisfying 'efficiency' (Amartya Sen).

UNPICKING PARETO

This chapter concentrates on the treatment of welfare within the Paretian frame of reference. Once economists narrowed their collective gaze from their classical predecessors' concern with the long-run process of economic development to the scarcity problem, the quasi-engineering notion of efficiency – getting the most from given effort or a given outcome from minimum effort – naturally assumed centre stage. The idea of maxima and minima also led naturally to the formalization of the problem in the language of calculus. Given the idea of limited resources and unlimited uses for those resources, economists came to an understanding of 'opportunity cost'. Every possible use of a resource had a cost, all the other uses to which that resource could not be put. The question was – how is that cost to be calculated?

Economic efficiency implied a twofold process. First, available resources had to be employed to maximum effect given the technological knowledge of the time and place; this is a condition familiar to engineers. Second, the outcomes had to satisfy the multifarious given wants of consumers engaged in voluntary exchange through the (competitive) market.

> In this context efficiency means going as far as possible in the satisfaction of wants within resource and technology constraints. This is expressed by the concept of Pareto optimality, which can be stated informally as follows: a state of affairs is Pareto optimal if it is within the given constraints and it is not the case that everyone can be made better off in his own view by changing to another state of affairs that satisfies the applicable constraints (Reiter, 1987, p. 1).[1]

Thus state A is Pareto optimal (an economically efficient outcome) if and only if it is *not* possible to redistribute resources to achieve *any* feasible state B in which everyone is better off in their own individual views. That is, economic welfare is maximized, given the constraints. This leads to a conception of a Pareto improvement in welfare in suboptimal situations. State B is a *Pareto improvement* over state A if and only if *everyone* is better off in B, in his or her own view. To remind the reader of the discussion in Chapters 3 and 5, 'better off' means reflecting the preferences of the individual as expressed in an ordinal utility function satisfying the axioms noted there. Strictly speaking the definition just given has been called 'the weak version of a Pareto improvement'. The strong version of the Pareto principle is more universally and controversially advanced – namely, B is an improvement over A if at least one person is better off and no one worse off.

The strong version brings out the hidden value proposition in the Pareto principle most clearly.[2] For example, it asserts that welfare increases in a society if Donald Trump and Warren Buffett gain a few more millions each while everyone else remains where they are, including the homeless and starving. Some people, extreme libertarians and others enamoured of the 'aspirational society' for example, would willingly concur. Other, more community oriented observers, would not. What would the impartial observer think? On what ethical grounds would one decide? It is possible to argue for both positions from both consequentialist and non-consequentialist approaches. Of course, it is highly unlikely that no one would be worse off in the real world if billionaires enjoy enhanced returns. But putting that important point aside until later, it is significant to note that the claim that (Pareto) efficiency can be divorced from its normative cast is simply untenable.

It might be thought that the weak version of the principle gets over this issue by requiring that everyone benefit from any change in resource allocation. However, reflection indicates that this simply pushes the value proposition back a stage. The ethics resides in the question, what is the morally acceptable division of the total gain? The familiar diagram below allows us to tease out these issues.

This diagram maps the utility space of two individuals, Ella and Brian. Every point in the space bounded by the curve represents a feasible combination of utility outcomes for the two people, given existing resource and technology constraints. The curve is called the utility possibility frontier. No point beyond the frontier is feasible given the constraints at this time.[3] The frontier thus represents the locus of all Pareto optimal outcomes for these individuals. Following Pareto's lead, economists have developed in detail the conditions required for a market economy to find itself somewhere on the frontier.[4]

Assume that we start at suboptimal position A. The segment bounded

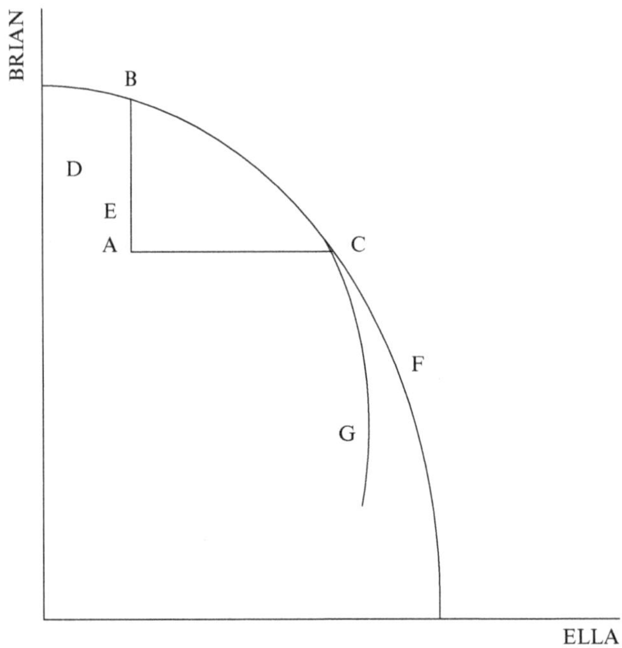

Figure 8.1

by ABC includes all changes that meet the Pareto principle in its strong form. A move, say, from A to E is efficient in that sense. Brian prefers it, while Ella is indifferent between A and E. Any move in a north-east direction satisfies the weak version of the principle; both parties prefer the result to staying at A. The (first) fundamental welfare theorem proves that a perfectly competitive economy will gravitate to a position on the frontier, that is, starting from, say, A, market processes will move Brian and Ella to some point on the frontier between B and C, as long as *all* the conditions for optimality hold (see further on). *Where* exactly, is indeterminate and will reflect the respective tastes and resource endowments, including skills, of the pair. It will also depend on their relative bargaining power. If Brian is in a position to block the move – to prevent the market from working smoothly – the outcome may move north-east-north and end up closer to B than C but short of the frontier, because the optimal marginal conditions have been disrupted. Nevertheless, Brian may be quite happy since he prefers the outcome over A and Ella may have to simply accept the slightly better (from her viewpoint) outcome resulting from picking up the scraps.[5]

This brings us to the 'second fundamental theorem of welfare economics' that demonstrates that *any* initial distribution of resources will, in a perfectly competitive world, lead to a Pareto optimum, to a position on the utility possibility frontier.[6] Thus, if resources could be instantly redistributed away from Brian to Ella without cost, market processes would move the outcome to some point like F where Ella is better off than at A and Brian worse off. It is not possible to say whether this is an increase or decrease in welfare on purely Paretian grounds; that is, because the move fails the strong Paretian principle, though it may be justified on other grounds (see further on). An explicit value judgment is required (as opposed to an implicit value judgment if the move does meet the Pareto principle in its weak or strong forms). Before going on to discuss the implications of this, it is important to note the following points. First, this second or 'separability' theorem seems to support the argument that we can consider efficiency and distribution as distinct issues, with value judgments reserved for the question of getting the initial distribution of resources 'right' and then letting the impersonal market loose to move the economy onto an optimal destination, one from which it is not possible to improve outcomes for some without reducing outcome for others. However, as the earlier discussion noted, if the initial position was A or E, this suggests an initial resource distribution in favour of Brian who may use some of those resources to thwart a significant redistribution in favour of Ella, effectively rendering much of the frontier to the south-east of B unachievable. Starting from an unequal initial distribution of resources, such as at A, there may be in force, politically speaking, a 'power path dependence' dynamic.

Second, even if a significant redistribution of resources is feasible, it may involve significant transition costs. Thus, Samuelson argues: '(t)he essential point now to stress is that we could move people to different points on the utility-possibility function only by *an ideally perfect and unattainable system of absolutely lump sum taxes or subsidies*'(in Phelps, 1973, p. 86; italics in original). Since the only politically feasible means of redistribution, using policy interventions like progressive income taxes or rationing, result in some distortion of the marginal conditions defining the locus of Pareto optima, the utility possibility frontier bends inward below the point C in Figure 8.1, and society may end up at some point G, better for Ella but not as preferable for her as F and significantly worse for Brian.

> We can pick policies which strive to minimize the harmful effects of redistribution but in practice we cannot reduce such effects to zero. A 'feasibility utility function' can conceptually be drawn up which lies more or less far inside the utility-possibility function, depending on how Utopian were our assumptions about legislation, public opinion, etc. (Samuelson, op. cit. p. 87).[7]

Putting these considerations aside and returning to the optimal 'first-best' world, what might determine the superiority of B, C, F or any other

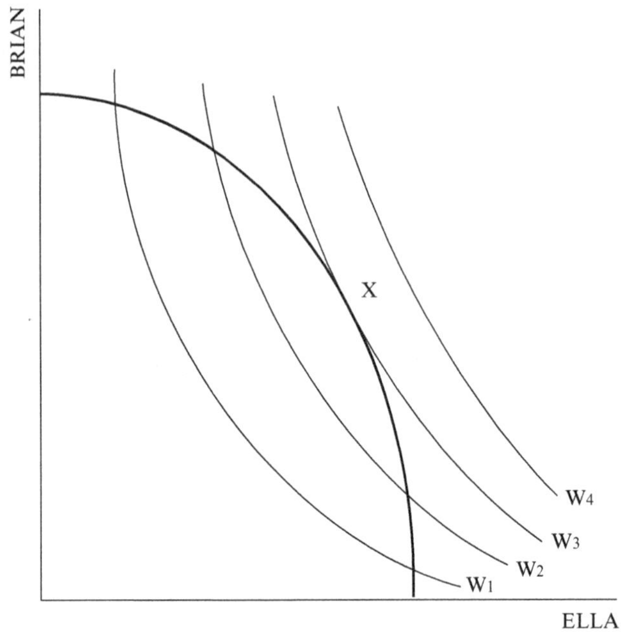

Figure 8.2

point on the frontier drawn in Figure 8.1? The conventional answer is provided by the concept of a 'social welfare function' (SWF) introduced by Bergson (1938).[8] This is an ordinal preference ordering of every possible combination of utility outcomes that can be represented graphically as in Figure 8.2.

The contours represent increasing levels of welfare moving north-east from W_1 to W_4 and beyond. Each contour maps the locus of utility outcomes for Brian and Ella providing a given welfare judgment, according to some given value commitment. In this case, I have assumed a welfare function embodying the Paretian value judgment – namely that welfare increases if one person is better off and the other not worse off.[9] The point X at which the welfare function is tangent to the utility possibility frontier is the 'optimum optima'. It is not possible given the value judgments defining the SWF ordering, to achieve a point on the frontier that is 'better' than X; all other points lie on lower welfare contours. Unsurprisingly, X is normally referred to as 'the bliss point'. It has no practical policy significance, since even if policy makers had an idea as to its rough location (whatever that means in a society of millions of people), then they would have to ensure a situation in which all the conditions of optimality held *and* engineer the appropriate initial distribution of resources from which market processes would move inexorably to the bliss point. It also leaves open the question; what are the value criteria on which the SWF is constructed and who decides the issue? The weak version of the Paretian principle is but one of any number of such criteria. We return to this matter in Chapter 10.

However, the problems posed for the Pareto principle by endemic market failure, including political transaction costs, go well beyond those raised by Samuelson. The very nature of markets as social institutions aggregating *information* that directs the voluntary actions of participants *ensures* (except in the most limited of cases) that 'free' market exchanges will fail to move the economy towards the utility possibility frontier. This follows from the incomplete scope and asymmetric distribution of information across participants. Nobel Prize winners Joseph Stiglitz and George Akerlof have led this work on 'information economics'. Drawing on Greenwald and Stiglitz (1986), Stiglitz (2001, p.505) concludes '. . . whenever markets are incomplete and/or information is imperfect (which are true in virtually all economies), even competitive market allocation is not constrained Pareto efficient.' In his Nobel lecture Stiglitz (2001, p.471–2) commented:

> The set of ideas that I will present here undermined [Adam] Smith's theory and the view of government that rested on it. They have suggested that the reason that the hand may be invisible is that it is simply not there – or at least that if is there, it is palsied.

And again (ibid. p.486): 'Perhaps most importantly, under the standard paradigm, markets are Pareto efficient, except when one of a limited number of market failures occurs. Under the imperfect information paradigm, markets are almost never Pareto efficient.'

This work is devastating for the fundamental theorems of welfare economics, even within the narrow confines of their theoretical specification, and thus, for the policy implications of non-government intervention.[10] The final nail in the coffin was hammered in by the theory of the second best, discussed in the next section.

BACK TO THE REAL WORLD

Recent research in behavioural economics has found pervasive human tendencies to act in ways that confound the axioms of rational choice noted in Chapter 3. In this context, it is the consistent behaviour informed by deeply embedded, morally energized views on fairness that undermines the plausibility of the Paretian principle, particularly in its weak form. Take the move from A to E in Figure 8.1. Analysis backed by experimental data has shown that Ella is likely to regard this change as 'unfair', and may act to block the move if she can. Why, it might be asked, as she is no worse off? In fact, she is worse off if we take into account that the move causes her distress (disutility) by insulting her conception of what Australians call 'a fair go'. Ella's view of the change looks more like a move from A to D. Real people seem to have a culturally etched (and possibly biologically evolved) imperative to demand fair and punish selfish treatment from each other. This after all, is understandable in a species that Aristotle called political animals. Experimental results under controlled conditions suggest that any division of gains less than about 30–70 tends to spark non-compliance by the relative 'loser' (Coyle, 2007; Kahneman and Tversky, 2000; Fehr and Schmidt, 2004; Fehr and Gächter, 2000, 2002). Most people, at least in the controlled experimental conditions of studies in Western democracies, appear to embrace opportunities to punish others who are believed to act unfairly or greedily, to 'cheat' or claim more than they 'deserve', *and* to be willing to suffer costs to themselves for imposing such sanctions. Indeed, as will be argued further on, recent research by psychologists and anthropologists demonstrates that non-Western societies exhibit similar tendencies to punish cheaters, though the nature of the cheating behaviours and the sanctions vary widely according to local cultural mores. Hence, returning to our diagram, even if the perfect market inexorably moves the economy in a northerly direction from A, in what sense can it be said that Ella has voluntarily acceded when she thinks that she is headed north-west?

This raises the thorny problem of how independent and stable the utility functions of the two people are. Hirschman (2013) provides an interesting metaphor to describe a utility function that encompasses both same-regarding and other-regarding dimensions. He recounts his common experience driving though the tunnel from Boston's Logan Airport under the Charles River. Often he finds himself in one of the two lanes that stops to a crawl, while the other lane flows freely. Initially, he is happy because he realizes that some luckier people than he are getting home on time. His happiness is also boosted by the thought that, if one lane is moving, then eventually his lane will start to flow too; the freely flowing lane signals that he too will gain. However, as time passes and he remains stuck, his mood changes. Envy and anger replace his earlier benign response to the cars speeding past in the other lane. Hirschman refers to this parable as 'the tunnel effect'. It suggests not only that utility functions can be interdependent but also unstable, depending on the circumstances (behavioural economists would say, 'framing') of the situation.[11]

This raises the importance of social processes of *reciprocity* that anthropologists have long seen as the necessary 'glue' to holding a society together over time. Alongside and sometimes trumping humanity's propensity to truck and barter, people devise ways of managing exchanges with each other outside explicit market institutions. These social institutions of cooperation and reciprocity are every bit as decisive in constraining individual behaviour in social environments as that refracted through the market. Cicero wrote, '(t)here is no duty more indispensible than returning kindness . . . all men distrust one forgetful of a benefit' (quoted in Gouldner, 1975a, p. 226). Gift-giving and receiving can be as important as buying and selling in cementing relations between people, though in a capitalist society the latter often and perhaps increasingly precedes the former act. The commercialization of giving gifts, especially if it comes in the form of money, can undermine the cohesive purpose of the process. Moreover, there clearly are activities and social interactions that necessarily lose part of their social significance when 'reduced to mere monetary calculation' (Sandel, 2013).

The British sociologist and social policy adviser Richard Titmuss in his 1970 book, *The Gift Relationship*, advanced the most famous argument along these lines. In it he compared the systems of blood donation in the United States and Britain. Donations were 'voluntary' in both countries, in the formal sense that no overt coercion was used, no 'blood tax' levied. However, in the United States, donors were paid for their blood, while in Britain they were not. Titmuss found that on objective outcome grounds, the British system outperforms the American. 'Despite the supposed efficiency of the market, he argued, the American system leads to chronic shortages, wasted blood, higher costs and a greater risk of contaminated blood' (Sandel, 2013, p. 123).

However, Sandel comments, Titmuss finds against the marketization of blood on two explicitly ethical grounds. First, US donors are predominantly poor and black, while recipients are rich and white. In an unequal world the rich can afford to buy blood and the poor cannot afford not to sell it, even to the extent of over-donating, much the same logic that drives poor peasants to over-exploit their meagre land resources. This outcome offends against widely held views of fairness, ethically significant from some consequentialist and rights-based viewpoints, though not from others, such as a strict libertarianism holding that as long as overt coercion is absent, then the poor have every right to exploit their bodies. Similar arguments are advanced in support of the market for organs and prostitution.

Titmuss's second critique centres on the way that commercializing blood donation necessarily undercuts communal bonds of mutual trust and the ethic of altruism. Once the market takes over people feel a lower moral duty to donate. Sandel refers to this as 'the corruption objection' leading to market incentives 'crowding out' non-market social norms. Titmuss's concern was that as the rule of the market gradually extended into more and more spheres of family and community life, the prevalence of market norms would inexorably drive out altruistic and reciprocal motives throughout society, an ethical parallel to Gresham's law, bad values drive out good.

> The case illustrates how people's moral beliefs and preferences influence economic outcomes and also how economic arrangements (in this case, whether there is a market for human blood) can influence what people feel a moral obligation to do. We do not know whether the explanation offered by Titmuss for the dramatic differences between outcomes in the United states and Britain is correct, but there is no way to understand or assess it without attention to systems of moral beliefs, which (according to Titmuss) explain the choices of individuals (Hausman and McPherson (2006, p. 302).

Kenneth Arrow (1972) rejected the corruption charge by the familiar discipline resort to the axiomatic defence – let us *assume* that the introduction of a market does not crowd out non-market norms, *then* in this case, adding a market for blood expands the choices of donors who can freely choose to donate either altruistically or for money. By a neat use of the Marshallian fudge, the problem evaporated. Arrow also supported the blood market by further assuming that altruism and ethical behaviour are scarce goods. In such a world, he suggests, it makes sense to use markets where they are efficient, and reserve the call to moral obligation for situations where they are not – for example, in carrying out the defence of the realm or countering widespread externalities beyond the reach of the Coase solution. Arrow doesn't want to rely too much on ethical behaviour rather than self interest. Individuals caught in the prisoner's dilemma would have cause to disagree; the best way for both parties to avoid bad outcomes is to count on the (blood) brotherhood of thieves, the joint belief that the other will honour his promise to keep quiet, though, of course, the threat of payback may also encourage joint silence.

Arrow's economistic analysis is widely embraced since it accords with the post-1870 fixation on scarcity as the core concept of the discipline. The approach faintly echoes the most selectively quoted passage from *The Wealth of Nations*, to the effect that it is not from the benevolence of the butcher and baker that we reliably get our dinner but from their regard to their self interest.[12]

An alternative view, expressed by Sandel, is that moral values and civic virtue can alter quantitatively and qualitatively depending on how and how often they are called upon. Crowding out and crowding in can, in his view, and that of many moral philosophers (Sandel quotes Aristotle and Rousseau) occur.[13] To some extent, a positive loop exists. The more people believe that others are acting ethically, the more likely that they will too. The reverse holds; the more people believe that others are acting unethically, the less likely that they will act ethically. A form of 'ethical externality' pervades the moral space. Positive reinforcement can make society morally unstable (up and down). 'Use it or lose it' characterizes the moral universe of *homo socialismus*.

> Think of a loving couple. If, over a lifetime, they asked little of one another, in the hopes of hoarding their love, how well would they fare? Wouldn't their love deepen rather then diminish the more they called upon it? Would they do better to treat one another in more calculating fashion, to conserve their love for the times they really needed it? (Sandel, 2012, p. 128).[14]

Or, to put it another way – there is no ethical analogue of the first law of thermodynamics, no principle of the universal conservation of love. On the other hand, there may be moral entropy defined by the downward spiral of ethical disorder in societies where the communal bonds of reciprocity and benevolence decay.

Sandel, contra Arrow, is strongly of the view that markets can and do crowd out moral values that Sandel holds dear, justified implicitly, I would argue, on consequentialist grounds. That is, the numerous examples he gives of money 'spoiling' the party refer to outcomes that he finds morally reprehensible and which he seeks to convince others of this view. What he appears to fear most is the escalating erosion of civic communitarian values as the positive downward loop gathers pace, as more and more spheres of social activity are commercialized. In relation to his examples of professional sport (naming rights, moneyball and so on) one could add the intrusion of sports betting and illicit and potentially dangerous drugs.

Hume's attempt almost 300 years ago to establish a moral psychology, to *explain* moral behaviour in naturalistic rather then religious or ethical terms, has been resurrected recently by social and cognitive psychologists drawing on the experimental work of evolutionary biologists, neuroscientists and social anthropologists. Haidt (2013) has provided a useful review and account of the substantial research carried out in moral psychology in recent decades. He argues that copious experimental and field evidence from a range of different cultures demonstrates the universal tendency of people in those societies to form moral judgments intuitively and that the mechanisms accounting for the tendency are embedded in the evolutionary history of the human species. However, although the *capacity for and general directions* of moral behaviour are innately inscribed, the specific *content* of morality is socially constructed. This means that although all humans have the capacity to express moral disgust, the actions or practices that trigger disgust vary across and within cultures at different times. For example, cannibalism is morally repugnant in some societies and normal practice in others. Other situations instantly trigger moral condemnation. Seeing a group of protestors burning the American flag repulses most Americans, while leading to spontaneous rejoicing in some other parts of the world. Acts of disobedience against elders is viewed as a moral affront in some societies, while accepted positively as a sign of personal autonomy elsewhere. Harming helpless individuals or animals raises the moral temperature in many but not all cases. Finally, actions deemed sacrilegious, as insulting the sanctity of life – whether cast in religious, spiritual or humanistic terms – fires the moral outrage of most of us.

Human evolution may have created these innate moral intuitions and inclinations, the general orientation but not the destination, so to speak. Moral behaviours in all their specificities are not evolved fully formed. Haidt (ibid. p. 153) quotes the neuroscientist Gary Marcus's definition of innateness as 'pre-wiring' rather than hardwiring the brain. 'Nature provides a first draft, which experience then revises . . . "Built-in" does not mean unmalleable; it means "organized in advance of experience".' The mind in this view is 'righteous', pre-programmed to respond to triggers in ways that once had adaptive value in the dim distant past of the human species. The original triggers are long gone but the adaptive mechanism lingers to be activated in the form of moral intuition by a changing cavalcade of later triggers that vary across time, space and cultures and result in the kaleidoscope of moral codes observable in human history continually revising the first draft of our evolutionary past.[15]

> Morality is a *becoming*. It is not fixed, carved in stone, but a situation. It is situated physically and metaphysically along a continuum, and is in itself a situation in which all factors are at play. Different moral judgments are made according to the state of the individual's *moral becoming*. This is the constant and continuous choice process men [*sic*] undertake every conscious and unconscious moment (Honeywill, 2016).

Haidt identifies six 'moral foundations' – termed 'the taste buds of the righteous mind' – pre-wired into the human brain:[16]

1. *The care/harm foundation*. Initially triggered by the adaptive advantage of caring for children during their long dependent maturing, current triggers can be anything that makes us sensitive to the suffering of others. The roots of beneficence, sympathy, empathy and compassion reside here: the wellsprings of conditional or reciprocal altruism.

2. *The fairness/cheating foundation.* Initially triggered by the adaptive advantage of reaping the benefits of social cooperation without being cheated, current triggers make us sensitive to indications that other people are likely to be good (or bad) collaborators, suitable for mutual gain through reciprocal altruism. Emotional responses typically include anger, gratitude and/or guilt.
3. *The loyalty/betrayal foundation.* Initially triggered by the adaptive advantage conferred by stable coalitions, current triggers encourage self-identified membership of and support for groups of all kinds – sporting teams, school or university, one's employment organization, and one's village, town and country. Responses arise in the form of group pride and rage at defectors.
4. *Authority/subversion foundation.* Initially triggered by the adaptive advantage arising from securing a widely recognized position in social hierarchies, current triggers result in respect accorded to (and expected by) those individuals occupying positions of high status – professionals, bosses, sporting champions and celebrities of varying types. Anger (expressed or repressed) is directed towards those challenging the existing status order.
5. *Sanctity/degradation foundation.* Initially triggered by the adaptive advantage of avoiding contamination (for example through infectious diseases) current triggers are sparked by culturally specific taboos. Those breaking taboos are the object of disgust and social rejection.
6. *Liberty/oppression foundation.* Originally triggered by the adaptive advantage of the social group controlling alpha individuals, current triggers include culturally significant perceived threats to widely valued ways of life, making people sensitive to and ready to oppose oppression. In Western democracies it manifests as a suspicion of limits to individual freedom. In more traditional, hierarchical societies, it results in self-imposed limits on the actions of powerful individuals. Expressions of anger, even violence, enforce moral codes drawing on this foundation.

Haidt credits Hume with grasping the naturalistic basis of morality in the historically situated circumstances of social existence, eschewing all rationalist, transcendental accounts, such as those offered by the social contract theorists of his day. Haidt argues that the pre-wiring of morality on the basis of the six moral foundations accounts for the universal tendency of human beings to respond intuitively in terms of emotions of compassion, anger, respect, fear, pride, patriotism, disgust and so on. However, the actual events or circumstances that trigger these emotions and the form the latter takes vary widely over time and place. History and culture are continually revising our moral codes and the behaviours influenced by them.

Haidt uses the metaphor of the elephant and its rider. The former is the moral inclinations and codes that we have each grown up with in our particular social locations. The rider is our reason by which we seek to control and direct the beast. In fact, as Hume famously said, 'reason is the slave of the passions'. The elephant leans towards the intuitively 'known', while the rider's job is to explain and justify why – *after* the lean has occurred. Normally without realizing it, rationalization masquerades as reason. The rider is the elephant's public relations agent. Left alone, our judgment is never wrong. Haidt relates this rationalizing tendency to the substantial body of evidence provided by psychologists and behavioural economists on so-called 'confirmation bias'. Only by interacting with others who question the subtle and not-so-subtle tricks by which we each justify our moral positions can some degree of self-awareness and objectivity be injected into the picture. Social interaction through what some philosophers call 'public reason' offers a potential escape from the inevitable clash of deeply embedded, defended and opposing moral worldviews.

The notion of a pluralistic theory of moral behaviour foundations implies that, in any actual socio-historical situation, the moral intuitions that drive behaviour draw on a palette of primary colours – that is, derive from a particular, historically specific *weighted* combination of the six foundations outlined earlier, progressively overlaid by generations of accumulating cultural influences. Haidt terms the particular palette or combination of moral foundations the 'moral matrix' characterizing a given society at a given time. The moral landscape of Western societies, in this view, is strongly structured by foundations 1, 2 and 6, while traditional and many contemporary non-Western societies are strongly organized according to foundations 3, 4 and 5. In this view, although human nature is 'mixed' by all six foundations, societies and subgroups within society produce pictures of different hues. Even within a society like contemporary USA, different subgroups will embrace and express different moral matrices. For example, Haidt (2013, Chapter 8) provides evidence that progressive political liberals in the USA are strongly grounded in moral foundations 1 and 6, while conservatives draw moral compass from across all six fronts. Libertarians or classical liberals, on the other hand, are driven primarily by moral inclinations emanating from foundation 6 with scant influence by other foundations except a particular version of the fairness/cheating font, where fairness is related to conceptions of 'proportionality'. That is, fairness is seen as receiving in proportion to one's individual contribution, rather than need; a case of from each according to his ability, to each according to his ability. This, he suggests, accounts for the greater electoral success historically of the Republican over the Democratic Party in America, especially at local and state levels; the latter misreads the vast bulk of voters whose moral groundings are multidimensional.[17] Democrats rely overly on the votes of liberals, while Republicans harvest the support of both conservatives and libertarians.[18]

It is important to note that the fact that behaviour is almost certainly influenced by the deeply structured plurality of moral values varying between and within societies does not answer the basic ethical question of what values are right, what behaviours are morally justified and on what ground. One is still left to argue from either a consequentialist or non-consequentialist perspective.[19] In a democracy it would be widely held that governments should try to institute laws and policies that reflect the dominant values of citizens, to embody however contentiously the ethical commitments where a workable 'overlapping consensus' to use John Rawls (1993, Lecture IV) term, exists. This still leaves open the tricky question of *how* overlapping and what happens to the moral beliefs of minorities, especially where they clash with mainstream positions. Examples here are religious or cultural practices – like female circumcision (or genital mutilation or sacred ritual, depending on one's viewpoint) sanctioned in some Muslim communities in Western societies or polygamy preached in some religious sects in America.[20] In a theocracy like Iran, government policies will express and reinforce (moral path dependence) the values and practices of holy writ, regardless of how widely and deeply they are held in the population at large; however, this does not preclude covert acts of resistance to orthodoxy by minorities, as in the case of the regular observance of Zoroastrian rituals in Iran that stretch back to an ancient Persian past.

Let us return to the notion of *reciprocity*. Gouldner (1975a, pp. 232–6) goes on to argue that the implicit treatment of reciprocity as equal exchanges by many sociologists and anthropologists misses the point that stable societies can and do survive on the back of all manner of *unequal* exchanges. Unequal powers establish patterned – that is institutionalized – exploitation where the distribution of collective social exchanges result in unequal gains. Exploitation is rarely if ever total *or* totally absent. In a companion paper Gouldner (1975b) adds that reciprocity is a weak condition for the survival of societies. Justice and fairness expressed by widespread internalization of the norm of reciprocity may be *necessary* for societies to persist but, claims Gouldner, they are not *sufficient* for the purpose. In addition, he argues, social order and stability requires some norm of beneficence or 'goodness':

> This norm requires men [*sic*] to give others such help as they *need*. Rather than making help contingent upon past benefits received or future benefits expected,

> the norm of beneficence calls upon men [*sic*] to aid others without thought of what they have done or can do for them, and solely in terms of a need imputed to the potential recipient (ibid. p. 266; italics in original).

Bowles has collapsed both reciprocity and beneficence into a single 'norm of strong reciprocity':

> Strong reciprocity is a propensity to cooperate and share with others similarly disposed, even at personal cost, and a willingness to punish those who violate cooperative and other social norms, even when punishing is personally costly and cannot be expected to result in net personal gains in the future. Strong reciprocity goes beyond self-interested forms of cooperation, which include tit-for-tat and what biologists call *reciprocal altruism* . . . which is really just self-interest with a long time horizon (Bowles, 2012, p. 131; italics in original).

Bowles summarizes the evidence linking attitudes to political support for redistribution in favour of poorer people underpinned by widespread norm of strong reciprocity in Western capitalism. However, the last sentence of the quote above can be read as effectively ignoring Gouldner's stress on the independent reinforcing role of beneficence in holding societies together. Beneficence for Bowles – and many economists – reduces to a long-term strategy to advance self-interest, a long game of 'tit-for-tat'.

Although Haidt rejects the selfish gene theory of morality, he nevertheless accepts a version of the reciprocal altruism position, ruling out what one might call 'asymmetric altruism'. Haidt (2013, Chapter 9) points to the increasing evidence for the process of group selection in human societies. The moral foundations that favoured group cooperation allowed those human collectivities in which these inclinations were strongest to outcompete and out-reproduce less cooperative bands. Central to this evolving outcome were the emergence of social institutions and moral behaviours that entrenched (built upon) the 'groupish' elephant of our natures. Haidt is here subscribing to a theory of biological and cultural co-evolution, where natural selection is occurring at both the levels of the organism and the human group, initially extended family groups, then the tribe, confederation of tribes, nation and empire. The idea that different institutions, values and behaviours change through time and indirectly modify underlying gene pools is not problematic. However, Haidt goes further and claims that the interplay of biological and sociocultural forces changes the genetic pool over a much shorter timescale than most evolutionary biologists accept. Thus Haidt claims that co-evolution exists at a literal organic, rather than metaphorical, level. This is a strong claim indeed, based on a reductionist application of evolutionary psychology tinged with the older sociobiology of biologists like E.O. Wilson (whom he quotes).[21] This interlinkage of biological evolution and cultural change is not sufficient to account for many observable behavioural traits in modern and ancient societies – but it is also not necessary for such explanation. Once extended human groups form, for whatever reason, cooperation through division of labour and technological innovation (including institutional innovation) can rapidly drive social change. War and technological change has been, historically, particularly important in building huge internally differentiated human collectivities that go well beyond kinship and tribal loyalties. The flexibility and complexity of the evolved human brain can and has created many ways in which to express the biologically encoded behavioural proclivities, including the moral intuitions that underlie the emergence of distinctly different human societies. Moreover, it is not obvious that, in all circumstances, societies where a significant proportion of the population act in unconditional – that is asymmetric – altruistic ways will be swept aside by societies whose members are focused only on pursuing advantages for their family, tribe or nation. The rise and fall of nations and empires depend on the interaction of diverse biological, natural environmental, sociocultural, economic, political and contingent factors and are not reducible to a single grand causal narrative. There is plenty of room for stable societies where moral values of genuine benevolence and sympathy crowd in and supplement patterns of kin preference and reciprocal altruism.

The bottom line is that, if the work of moral intuitionists like Haidt is to be taken seriously, something more than self-interest is going on. The six moral foundations Haidt identifies as intuitively powering humanity's moral judgments – fairness, harm prevention, loyalty, authority, liberty and sanctity – provide firm foundations for the institutionalization of robust social norms and patterns of behaviour that cannot be understood by only considering the interplay of self interested individuals. However, this point is vital: as I have already stressed, understanding how people act morally – and with what consequences – does not answer the question as to how they *should* act. But understanding the moral drivers of behaviour in a particular society is critical to devising and implementing policies that 'nudge' outcomes towards what are determined to be ethically desired ends – at least this the case when seen from the consequentialist viewpoint developed in the next chapter and Chapter 11.

Enough has been said here to point to the grounds on which the policy discussion in Part III will be approached.

BACK TO PARETO I – THE PROBLEM OF SECOND BEST

Returning to Figure 8.1, it appears reasonable to assume that, given the assumptions and ignoring the previous section, starting from any suboptimal point like A – satisfaction of one or more of the marginal conditions of optimality not yet holding – must move the outcome north-east towards the utility possibility frontier. That is, towards a Pareto optimum expressing a Pareto improvement in either a strong or weak sense. Unfortunately for Pareto's hopes and those of many of his followers, this has been definitively disproved. A third welfare theorem – 'the theory of the second best' advanced by Lipsey and Lancaster (1956) – upset that particular conceit:[22]

> The basic principle is both simple and devastating. The marginal conditions of the Paretian optimum are not valid criteria of an increase in welfare in a context where they are not all simultaneously satisfied. If one of those conditions cannot be fulfilled somewhere in the economy then a first-best (Paretian optimum) situation cannot be achieved. The best that can be achieved is second best, but this requires violation of the Paretian conditions in context where it would be possible to satisfy them (Winch, 1971, p. 110).

In other words, if pervasive and permanent market imperfections exist, say due to multiple externalities, selective monopolization of industries or incomplete and asymmetric information among market participants, then policies designed to remedy one or a few of these imperfections will not *necessarily* result in a Pareto improvement (move towards the relevant segment of the utility possibility frontier between B and C in Figure 8.1), *unless all such imperfections are simultaneously removed.* Devastating indeed. Put another way, the fundamental theorems of welfare economics become irrelevant in the real world where policy makers must deal with markets as they are not as they could be. Instead of imposing 'competition policies' aimed at reducing monopoly power in particular industries, welfare in the Paretian sense *may* be better served by making some competitive industries more monopolistic (though this will not necessarily be the outcome). Allocative efficiency could be achieved by *not* allowing markets to operate unhindered.[23] 'In general, while the Paretian conditions constitute a simple statement of necessary first-order conditions of a first-best, there is no corresponding set of rules for the achievement of a second-best, or even a better, position in a world where the first-best is unattainable' (ibid. pp. 110–11). It is possible to derive certain formal rules for specific cases but each such exercise depends on the narrow assumptions specified and in no way parallels the first-best general equilibrium solution (see Winch, op. cit. p. 112–16).

BACK TO PARETO II – WHAT ABOUT THE LOSERS?

What is left after the devastation wrought by the theory of the second best? By and large, everything. Economists noted the interruption – rather like a hacking cough in the theatre – and then carried on as though nothing had happened. Both in academic and policy environments, economic efficiency continues to be regarded in first-best Paretian terms and any policy change in the direction of better satisfying one or more of the marginal conditions of optimality is greeted with applause and the claim that welfare has been increased. Enhanced efficiency is its own reward. Only those – it is claimed – who would intrude value judgments could possibly question the objective, value-free improvement resulting.

This is the bold position implicitly advanced when at least a weak version of the Paretian principle holds, when the move in Figure 8.1 is from A towards B, C or points in between B and C. However, it was soon recognized by most economists and everyone else that most changes in market mediated resource allocation results in both winners and losers (and those left untouched). What, ignoring problems of the second-best, can be said of the welfare consequences of a move from A to D? In this case, Ella loses (moves to a less preferred position) while Brian gains. The response came in the 1940s by way of what was termed 'the compensation criterion'.[24] Put simply, the change resulting in a move from A to D in Figure 8.1 is held to represent an increase in 'potential welfare', if the gainer Brian could compensate the loser Ella and still be better off after the change – that is if compensation would, if made, return the pair (say) to point E at which Brian is better off than at A and Ella is as well off as before. Brian might even be able to over-compensate Ella, sharing the gain by returning to a point slightly north-east of A; this would meet the weak version of the Pareto criterion.

It was soon noted that as a potential criterion for a Pareto improvement, something more was needed. Scitovsky (1941) demonstrated situations in which it was possible for the compensation criterion to be satisfied in both directions. That is, having moved to a position like D it may be possible for Ella to compensate Brian to move back to A.[25] This leads to the paradoxical situation that D is both a potential improvement in welfare over A and a potential decrease. The compensation principle was left in a very weak and torturous form as follows: a change in resource allocation represents a potential increase in welfare if and only if (a) it allows the gainers to compensate the losers and still be better off *and* (b) the losers cannot then reverse the change leaving the winners better off than the original change.

All this is beside the point. The unsatisfactory ethical basis of the compensation principle is obvious – unless one assumes an extreme libertarian stance. What does it matter to the losers whether they *could* have been compensated, if – in fact – they are not? Ella is unlikely to cheer a move from A to D on the pure possibility of receiving adequate compensation from Brian. An independent observer of egalitarian bent would decry the change if no compensation is made; indeed, such an observer would favour changes made in exactly the opposite direction, south-east from A in Figure 8.1. This led economists to recognize that, to achieve an increase in economic welfare, any change *must* result in an acceptable distribution of the gains made. Emphasis here is on the value criteria determining what is acceptable. 'If there are any losers, a distributional judgment is still required to the effect that the benefits outweigh the losses *in terms of welfare*' (Little, 2002, p. 23; italics in original).

Sen (1987, p. 33, fn. 4) has neatly summarized the ethical inadequacy of the compensation principle, regardless of the logical inconsistency uncovered by Scitovsky:

> Another – arguably more basic – difficulty relates to the question as to why the mere *possibility* of compensating the losers should be adequate to establish a social improvement even if the compensation is not, *in fact*, to be paid. The losers could include the worst off and the most miserable in society, and it is little consolation to be told that it is possible to compensate them fully, but ('good God!') no actual plan to do so. If, on the other hand, the losers are, *in fact* compensated, then the overall outcome is a Pareto improvement, and then there is no need for the compensation test as a supplement to the Pareto principle. So the compensation criteria are either *unconvincing* or *redundant*. The Pareto principle can scarcely be extended to cover judgments of distribution without actually making interpersonally comparative distributional judgments . . .

Sen has also sensibly noted that although no objective value-free basis for making interpersonal comparisons of welfare is available, judgments based on broad value grounds like favouring increasing resources and opportunities to the most disadvantaged at the expense of the most advantaged is highly likely to increase total welfare however conceived. This, after all, (as noted earlier) is the value proposition underlying the historical emergence of the welfare state in twentieth-century capitalism; only in recent decades has both the welfare state and the values on which it rests been progressively challenged and partially dismantled. The opposition that has sprung up against such neoliberal attempts, most vividly expressed by 'the Occupy movement', is an indication of the deep-seated pervasiveness of norms of reciprocity, benevolence and altruism in many countries.

The debates over potential increases in welfare could safely be left to the gnawing criticism of mice if it was not the case that the substance of this approach has been smuggled back into the public policy arena through the widespread practice of cost–benefit analysis. This familiar tool in the economist's armoury, I will argue, is a spectacular example of what can be called 'the Paretian fudge', resting on its Marshallian foundation.

PARETO AND PIGOU – A REAPPROACHMENT?

Cost–benefit analysis emerged in the United States in the 1930s as the federal government sought to *justify* massive public investments in water and other major infrastructural projects.[26] The approach involves several steps:

1. Identify the range of effects of a project or policy on parties likely to be effected.
2. Quantify the scale of each effect (positive and negative) on each party in terms of a common unit of measurement.
3. Add up the positive numbers and the negative numbers and subtract the latter total from the former, leaving a net total value.
4. If the net total is positive, the project is justified on efficiency (potential Paretian) grounds; if it is negative, the project is an inefficient use of resources.

But what is the common unit of measurement to be? Money, of course! More accurately, the benefits of a project to people can be represented by what they would be willing to pay to receive them and the losses by what they would be willing to receive to accept them. However, in the absence of data on the willingness of people to pay and accept, we are left with what people actually do pay in the market. Where markets do not exist – say, in the case of a toll-free road (a 'freeway') or the value of the services provided by an open public park – economists have devised cunning techniques to impute what people would have paid if they could.

Using money as a unit of value raises the question of the value of money itself. Put baldly, money today is worth more to people than money tomorrow, since, it is assumed, most people prefer the power money gives to consume now over delaying consumption to some future time. Moreover, money in the hand can be used to accumulate more money in the future. *Time preference* is itself a component of individual utility functions. Hence, step 2 above involves a further qualification. The flow of benefits and costs must be discounted over the time period they are expected to eventuate before addition and subtraction occurs in step 3.[27]

However, there are far more basic and problematic concerns raised by this approach than quibbles about the time value of money. Hausman and McPherson (2006) list five implications of the conventional approach to cost–benefit analysis. First, all effects have to be quantified. Second, only people matter. Third, only welfare defined as preference satisfaction matters. Fourth, only welfare as judged by individuals themselves through their expressed preferences matter. Finally, net arithmetical benefits are equated with aggregate welfare consequences.

Each of these implications carries an ethical charge and raises controversial issues. The second, third and fourth points have been discussed in Chapter 6. Welfare is an ethically contested concept. Other 'goods' like rights and duties also matter. People may be misinformed about the consequences of their choices. Some ethicists include the 'welfare' of non-humans in their calculus. And so on.

Focusing on the first point – is some number better than no number (this is the subtitle to a survey article by Diamond and Hausman, 1994)? Why should all effects of a policy or project be reduced to a cardinal number? This, after all, was the spur behind ditching Pigou for Pareto, to avoid having to entertain a cardinal concept of utility and the interpersonal comparisons entailed. Using money as the measuring-rod conflates the new and old welfare economics. Pigou has made a comeback through the back door. Moreover, the potential compensation principle lives! The Paretian fudge is indeed traceable back to Marshall's implicit assumption of the constant utility of money or income.[28]

It is easy to demonstrate ethically dubious outcomes from the application of conventional cost–benefit analysis. In the first place, wealth or resources bias the outcome. Projects with the highest net social present value will tend to be those that favour the wealthy since, by definition, they are in the best position to be willing *and able* to pay the most for outcomes that benefit them and to avoid the costs imposed on them. This is a bias built into the use of money as the common unit of valuation. Economists like to use the metaphor of consumer sovereignty – the consumer is king. Alternatively, consumers are painted as voters and money as votes. The market or its analogue in cost–benefit analysis delivers goods in response to the money votes cast. However, this is no democracy of one person, one vote. It is an oligarchy where the rich have many votes each and the poor few or none. All people are sovereign but some are more sovereign than others!

What about the fact that, depending on the resources, talent and imagination of the analyst, some possible effects will be excluded from the final calculation? It may simply be impossible or undesirable to impute a dollar value to some outcomes. 'One would get very misleading information concerning the relative value of a car and a spouse by investigating how much someone is willing to pay for each!' (Hausman and McPherson, 2006, p. 149).[29] What happens then? Well, those 'difficult' effects are lumped together under the category of 'intangibles'. Present to be sure but more in the form of Banquo's ghost than Macbeth. The headline figure of any cost–benefit analysis is *the* figure – the quantified net present value that is held to reflect the efficient use to which resources should be put. *All effects excluded from the analysis are implicitly zero-valued, when the unit of value is money*. This approach to social evaluation expresses the fallacy of misplaced quantification in an attempt to demonstrate the 'scientific' nature of an efficiency-driven discipline. Many consequences of a policy change or major project are unknown at the time of decision or are likely to result in unintended outcomes. It may be wiser to eschew an overly deterministic approach by focusing more on the intangibles and the limitations of our knowledge, especially of the uncertain future, and give less attention to squeezing every dollar value possible into the picture, regardless of how implausible the basis of valuation in a desperate effort to appear to be 'scientific'.

As it dawned on economists that there are distributional value judgments and biases in favour of the well-off built into the fabric and practice of cost–benefit analysis, it was suggested that the calculation could be modified by explicitly varying the relative weights of benefits and costs of a project felt across the socio-economic landscape. In conventional cost–benefit analysis the consequences are 'equal-valued' across all people affected. Alternatively, the dollar values ascribed to poorer groups could be boosted and the numbers for richer groups discounted before the net calculation is made (Campbell and Brown, 2003). The problem moves back a stage: on what basis should the relative weights be based? Whose values should determine the weights? There are many possible, conflicting answers to these questions, reflecting different ethical stances. Although this approach fails to avoid the quantification fallacy, it has the advantage of restraining the unthinking application of the efficiency narrative in the public policy sphere. It opens up a potential debate about the distributional consequences of policy and does not allow outcomes to automatically reinforce the interests of the already well-off.

This, indeed, is a variant of a normative argument often advanced in favour of standard vanilla cost–benefit analysis – namely, that it serves as a starting point for a fuller discussion of the distributional issues. By having a definite figure in place, people and policy makers have something concrete to argue for and against. This claim is undermined by the tendency of economists and policy makers to cling to the original (unweighted) figure, as a castaway to his raft; economists are just as likely as ordinary folk to be influenced by the process of 'framing'. Any contrary suggestion can be dismissed as 'unscientific' or expressing vested interests, forgetting, if they ever knew, that the vested interest of the well-off are already embedded in their 'unweighted' figure. It is the implicit assumption of the constant marginal utility of income or wealth – the stance that a dollar of benefit or cost is 'worth' the same to Donald Trump as to a poor or disabled person – that lies at the heart of the distributional debate, and the consequences for non-welfare values. The fact that most cost–benefit analysis is (with some exceptions, of course) used in the real world to justify policies that benefit most the well-off means that economists advising on the basis of such techniques are implicitly endorsing the inegalitarian consequences that flow from their analyses. It is unconvincing for them to advance the Von Braun defence. To use cost–benefit analysis to measure changes in welfare is like a carpenter using a ruler that changes length to measure up beams and bearers to build a house.

Before addressing an equally disturbing distributional implication of conventional cost–benefit analysis, it is worth exploring some of the points raised earlier in the guise of an imaginary scenario. Let us assume that there is a coal mine proposed for a particular region of prime agricultural land. Also assume that within the boundary of the mine project there exists the habitat of an endangered species of bird – let us say the orange-bellied parrot. Further assume that another part of the region contains an area of extreme natural beauty visited by thousands of people a year. Should the responsible government agency grant a permit for the mine to go ahead? The private company proposing the project has clearly calculated a positive net private return, otherwise it would not be seeking permission to proceed. Suppose a standard social cost–benefit analysis is presented entailing the private costs and benefits expected plus an enumeration and estimation of some of the externalities, positive and negative. Ignoring disputes over the 'correct' social discount rate and the built-in distributional bias, there are a number of key questions to ask. Who carried out or paid for the analysis? What externalities are included and which ones ignored (implicitly zero valued)? These first two questions are related; the scope for selectively framing the analysis will impact on the bottom line. On what basis are the extra-market social and environmental effects valued? It is likely that techniques like travel time to recreational areas and contingent valuation will be used to price the value of natural landscapes and habitat destroyed by the mine construction and operation. It might seem straightforward to value any loss of agricultural output caused by the mine but even here uncertainty as to the long-run effects of water table changes and the future price of commodities make calculations tentative. In a situation of multiple cross-cutting effects with uncertainty as to outcome to varying degrees, there is a tendency to focus on what can be measured with some degree of confidence.[30]

> By 'uncertain' knowledge, let me explain, I do not mean merely to distinguish what is known for certain from that which is only probable . . . The sense in which I am using the term is that in which the prospect of a European war is uncertain, or the price of copper and the rate of interest twenty year hence, or the obsolescence of a new invention, or the position of private wealth owners in the social system in 1970. About these matters there is no scientific basis on which to form any calculable probability (Keynes, 1937, pp. 113–14).[31]

From the point of view of government making decisions, in this case whether or not to grant the mine permit, having something like a seemingly scientific analysis with a headline quantified conclusion, is a useful prop to justifying whatever decision is made. Since, the analysis is, for the reasons advanced above, likely to reflect the interests and preferences of wealthier citizens, that decision is less likely to spark worrisome (for politicians) political opposition than if the decision favoured the less influential at the expense of the wealthy. The extinction of the orange-bellied parrot and the interests of the poor devotee of Wordsworth's daffodils will count for nothing. Parrots have no (money) votes, only diehard human supporters, some of whom may move beyond tree-hugging to mobilize sufficient political support to defend Polly's habitat. If protest is to occur, however, it is more likely to come from farming interests who believe their future livelihoods will be adversely affected by the mine. It is worth pointing out that in such cases another 'economic' criterion, another number, is often advanced, notably the employment creating effects or number of new jobs created. Various estimates of primary and secondary jobs created are thrown into the mix. This factor is already included in a cost–benefit analysis as a project cost. However, to the people likely to be employed and politicians seeking their votes come election time, it is vital, forming a desired outcome in its own right. In many cases this is the decisive political factor on which the final decision rests, that and the electoral marginality of the region in which the project occurs. Such claims are often inflated by proponents seeking permits and readily accepted by politicians garnering votes.[32] In reality, governments can try to but cannot credibly outsource the decision to economists, however imaginative and technically proficient, on the basis of an ethically limited and politically biased analytical toolkit.

Finally, we come to perhaps the most intractable problem with the use of cost–benefit analysis in public policy. The question posed earlier as to who matters is critically important when it comes to considering intergenerational matters. Thanks to the magic of compound interest, even a modest social discount rate rapidly reduces the value of benefits and costs borne by people in the future, particularly those not yet born. When policies (including the policy to do nothing) impact on far distant generations, the latter's interests (welfare, rights and so on) will be effectively ignored.

In an inter-temporal version of the tragedy of the commons, too much emphasis today will focus on current generations with too little regard for their descendants. Other policy evaluation techniques and guides will be needed, though not forthcoming as long as economists wielding traditional economic evaluation methods monopolize the public debate and deafen the ears of policy makers.[33]

BACK TO PARETO III – THE CHALLENGE OF 'DYNAMIC EFFICIENCY'

To date, the discussion has assumed a static frame; resources, tastes and technologies are given. So too are cultural attitudes and practices and current policy settings. What happens to the Paretian concept of welfare when one or more of these 'exogenous' factors change?[34] The short answer is that, over real time, the utility possibility frontier changes. Figure 8.3 demonstrates a situation in which the frontier U^1_f shifts outward to U^2_f. Such a shift could occur for a number of reasons. First, investment in

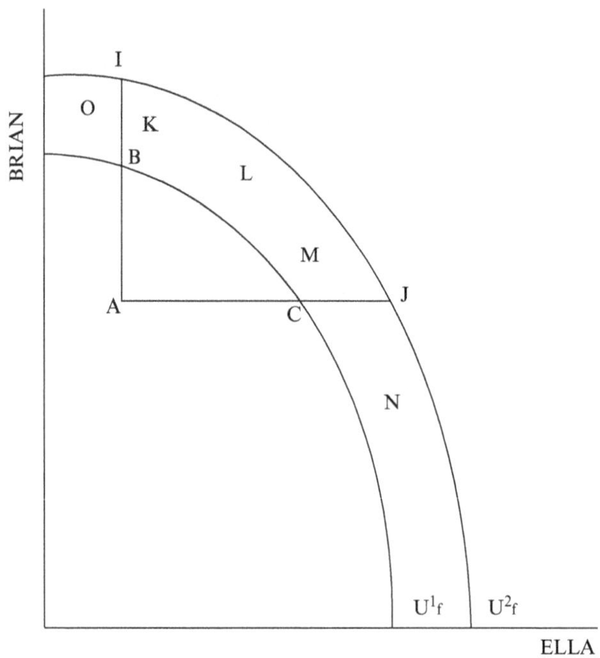

Figure 8.3

productivity enhancing human and material capital could result in the production of more goods and services from current resources. Second, the total quantity of resources can be increased through greater savings, reduced wastage and population growth. Third, tastes may change in ways that favour the application of productive existing technologies (and organizational forms). Fourth, and of great importance practically, technological progress may generate larger outputs from given inputs.[35] Fifth, new and cheaper to exploit natural resources will likewise expand production possibilities on which material welfare depends. Finally, government policies (and non-policies), including changes in regulations, can have a range of intended and unintended outcomes.

These categories do not exhaust the factors conducive to increasing productivity but capture the main types. They often operate interdependently. For example, policies to encourage savings or investment in scientific research can result in significant technological advances. Direct government investment in education has proved critical over the past century in improving labour skills. Likewise spin-offs from government defence spending and major infrastructure investment radically improve technologies throughout the economy; the Internet and US interstate highway system are commonly advanced examples. Government immigration policies also influence the size and, depending on selection criteria, skill composition of the workforce. Public education campaigns can change attitudes, tastes and behaviour with respect to smoking, health and car driving behaviours. It may also happen, of course, that major shocks like war, famine, natural disasters or civil unrest will shift the utility possibility frontier *inwards*. War can result in the physical destruction of material capital and infrastructure and the decimation of the most productive section of the population.

Figure 8.3 shows an outward shift in the frontier.[36] Starting from point A, the zone of potential Pareto improvements has expanded from area ABC to area AIJ. For example, the strong criterion is met at points K, L and M, though the distributional outcomes differ. Three points should be stressed here. First, there is no guarantee that either market- or state-driven processes will result in the achievement of any of these points. Second, the end result may lie outside the expanded zone, say at point N or O. The interplay of market and political forces will determine where the economy 'ends up'.[37] Attempts to reach say, M, may end up at N. Third, dynamic analysis renders the concept of a utility possibility frontier irrelevant, even without considering the force of second-best arguments. A frontier that is continually changing and which can never be reached, even at the moment of stasis, still less clung to as it shifts through time, offers no realistic target for policy or moral evaluation.

It is not clear, a priori, whether greater competition in an industry or sector encourages innovation or not. Schumpeter (1943) for example, argued that improved dynamic efficiency normally requires a degree of monopolization to generate the expectation and reality of excess profits that provides the incentive for capitalists to innovate. This view contrasts with the orthodox stance (also stressed by Karl Marx) that competition delivers the negative spur forcing capitalists to innovate (accumulate) or perish.

Putting those arguments aside, Bowles (2012) offers one argument for at least *attempting* to keep roughly within the expanding Paretian zone of improvement, to the extent that this can be achieved. 'Hard redistribution' resulting in actual losers may encounter effective resistance, while 'soft redistribution' within the expanded zone is more likely but not guaranteed to achieve general support. 'The fundamental point is not that all changes should be strictly Pareto improving (no losers) but that egalitarian redistributions should be productivity-enhancing' (Bowles, 2012, p. 28). Bowles goes on to introduce a direct interlinkage between the distribution of welfare and its level, the latter still conceived within a Paretian frame. He argues that there are cogent reasons for why 'excessive' inequality retards productivity growth and expanding utility possibilities. Put another way, reducing inequality may increase productivity and the potential for all parties to gain, in their own terms. Why might *increasing* equality payoff in enhanced productivity? Bowles offers the following reasons.

First, incentive structures in highly unequal societies can undermine the productive effort of some agents. Bowles gives the example of workers on fixed wages who have no material incentive to work beyond a minimum acceptable level of effort in the workplace. The employer has limited surveillance and sanctioning tools to recognize and rectify sandbagging by workers, following from the twin problems of incomplete contracting and asymmetric information. No contract, however closely worded, can anticipate all circumstances in which workers can 'go slow'. Even if they could, workers have better information than their employer about how hard and well they are working. This implied power relation in the workplace will be more in favour of the employees when labour markets are tight or particular skill sets are scarce; workers will also be in a strong position if they are well organized and represented by trade unions protected by pro-labour industrial laws. Employers, in turn can and do push back through sourcing labour elsewhere – or threatening to – pushing governments to pass and implement anti-union laws and by switching to piece rate pay systems, subcontracting or labour-saving technologies. Alternatively, they can offer workers the chance to share in the profits of the firm through bonus, equity or similar means, linking total worker remuneration to the firm's commercial success. By reducing inequality, labour productivity and firm profitability can be increased, a move north-east in utility space as workers, shareholders (and managers) all gain.

The idea that the limited liability company is a vehicle for meeting the interests of a range of stakeholders – share (equity) holders, creditors, workers and taxpayers – was popular in the first decades after World War II. However, with the rise of modern finance theory and neoliberal ideologies from the 1970s onward, the range of interests represented has shrunk to one (two if bonus-harvesting senior executives are included) – the common stockholder. Maximizing shareholder value has trumped older value positions. Industrial relations have taken on a harsher and more confrontational hue. The countervailing power of unions and other social institutions has wilted under the relentless neoliberal project.[38] Inequality, far from declining has intensified during this period. At the same time, most measures indicate declining productivity in those economies embracing neoliberal imperatives (Galbraith, 2012; Stiglitz, 2012; Reich, 2015). Establishing the counterfactual – what productivity and growth levels would have been like if inequality had declined instead of increasing over the past 40 years – is not possible. However, if Bowles's argument is sound, then the loss in *potential* welfare in the wake of increasing inequality is considerable and the *actual* change would represent a pronounce shift northward in Figure 8.3, with the vast majority of people in Ella's position with a few Brians (the 1 per cent?) just loving it. No matter how far and fast the utility possibility frontier is pushing outward, the powerful minority will monopolize the gain and the possibility of even faster and further expansion of the frontier that could be achieved through redistribution will be foregone.

A second reason that greater equality may increase productivity concerns the role that trust and loyalty plays in overcoming the coordination problems posed by incomplete contracts. Where it is impossible to adequately identify and facilitate joint actions that achieve mutual gains (as in the prisoner's dilemma), this outcome may evolve through norms underpinned by mutual trust and commitment.[39] In well-managed companies, employee pride in and loyalty to the company can be a powerful motivator to productive effort independent of material incentives and sanctions. This fact partly explains the grief, anger and resistance evinced en masse by workers when a long-established company is taken over by new owners and managers who proceed to slash jobs and strip assets to enrich shareholders and, most of all, themselves. Government policy through the provision of a social wage or safety net can contribute to the building of a cultural environment in which the necessary values of trust and mutual concern flourish. 'In addition to the invisible hand of competition and the fist of command, a well-governed society must also rely on the handshake of trust' (Bowles, 2012, p. 8). Stiglitz (2015) has nicely summarized the point in the title to his short essay 'In No One We Trust'.

The third argument against inequality and in favour of greater equality focuses on the costs of defending an unequal status quo. An excessive commitment of resources may be needed to protect the property and persons of wealthy elites, by way of costly expenditure on police, security and justice systems, resources that could be used productively in other areas that would expand productivity. The large-scale use of 'guard labour' – police officers, security contractors and prison staff – is essentially 'defensive spending' and has an opportunity cost in foregone productivity growth. Unlike real defence spending, doubling prison warders is unlikely to spawn an Internet revolution. When the mob get unruly, when the state and private sector forces of repression lose control, the security of property rights underpinning the existence of markets comes into question, reducing the incentive of domestic and foreign investors to commit to long term projects; indeed, capital flight will occur when social order breaks down.

> These three reasons why inequality may be bad for productivity by – diluting incentives, discouraging trust and diverting resources from productive uses to enforcing the rules of the game or driving a harder bargain – suggest that the nature and distribution of property rights critically affect the performance of the economy . . . *In particular, there exist a class of distributions that are both more egalitarian and more efficient than the concentrated asset-holding observed in most capitalist economies*' (Bowles, 2012, p. 15; italics in original).

In terms of Figure 8.3, this suggests that some egalitarian resource redistributions will expand the frontier faster than otherwise and result in significant welfare gains for both Brian and Ella. There is, of course, no way of determining just how radical the redistribution should be, even in terms of the ethical imperatives embedded in the Paretian moral frame. There is no way of identifying still less achieving the 'Goldilocks' level of (in)equality. However, the key policy point is that in many current advanced capitalist economies, the trend is towards increasing inequality and insecurity and that *some* reversal is highly likely to enhance productivity and growth, as well as satisfying some of the non-monetary values of some citizens relating to self-esteem and autonomy.

A final perspective on the dynamic dimension of the efficiency question has been offered by the so-called 'new growth theory' of Paul Romer.[40] Romer demonstrated that in situations where increasing returns hold, increasing productivity and economic growth result, systematically rendering irrelevant the static marginal conditions of optimal allocation (based on the pervasive existence of diminishing returns in production).

To achieve robust growth will often require government policies favouring investment in goods and services that are 'non-rival' in consumption – that is, goods and services the consumption of which by one person does not reduce the ability of others to consume them.[41] Public roads and the Internet up to the point of congestion are examples. The provision of public education is also party non-rival in the sense that up to the limits of school classrooms and educational methods and technologies of the day, improved education for some does not prevent fellow classmates from also benefitting and developing skills. The provision of such basic infrastructural and enabling underpinnings has been partly responsible for the impressive growth of real world economies over the past two centuries and the catch-up growth of many emerging economies today. The key point of this (contested) approach is that economic growth is largely caused by endogenous factors, through positive spillovers from investment in human capital, research and innovation and policy support for 'the knowledge' (or 'new') economy. The values attached to such developments can be judged from a number of alternative ethical viewpoints – the outcomes in terms of various conceptions of the good, and implications for the honouring of rights and obligations, and virtuous behaviours.

CONCLUSION

The twentieth-century emergence of Paretian welfare economics seemed to herald the arrival of a scientific value-free distinction between the positive and normative dimensions of the discipline. In reality, however, the Pareto principle defining efficient resource allocation enshrined a distributional value judgment within its core.[42] Even in a perfectly competitive market economy there is no value-free way of deciding which 'optimal' outcome (position on the utility possibility frontier) is truly the best. Once the theory of the second-best appeared it meant that in any real world suboptimal situation it was not possible to determine, *inter alia*, if a change results in a (Pareto) improvement in economic welfare or not. It is clear that, not only do normative (ethical) values impact on the positive outcomes of real world market processes, but also the reverse is true; positive economic analysis implies and reinforces normative values. This latter point is most apparent in the application to public policy of the economist's favoured tool of economic evaluation – to whit, social cost–benefit analysis. Policies justified by use of this technique inherently benefit those with the most dollar votes. Moreover, many effects of projects evaluated thus are effectively zero-valued, left to the footnotes of technical reports that count angels on the head of Adam Smith's pin. The temporal myopia of analysis effectively disenfranchises future generations and imparts a spurious certainty to situations of immense complexity and uncertainty in the sense used by John Maynard Keynes and Chicago School founder Frank Knight.

Perhaps the greatest irony of the prevalence of cost–benefit analysis in the policy realm is that by choosing money as the common unit of measurement, including when estimating Pigouvian externalities, the escape route from cardinal utility promised by Pareto collapses.[43] Value judgments as to the distributional impact of policy – entailing interpersonal comparisons – are there but hidden. Efficiency is a moral fig leaf behind which economists cover up their scientific credentials. The most deleterious consequence of this effort at concealment is that it licenses wealthy elites and their political representatives to justify the egregious inequalities that emerge in contemporary society. The inequality question has been to date sidelined by economics but calls for explicit consideration in its own right, pushing moral factors to the fore. This we return to in later chapters.

The next chapter extends the discussion to explicitly address theories of social justice, widening the ethical frame well beyond the economists' focus on 'efficiency'. If the efficiency calculus does not drive public policy, what should? There are, as we will see, a number of answers to this basic question.

NOTES

1. Reiter provides, for the mathematically adventurous, a detailed technical treatment of the concept of efficiency in both 'classical' and 'non-classical' conditions, where the latter refers to the existence of 'imperfections' like indivisibilities, externalities and 'non-convexities' in production and consumption. The discussion in this chapter uses the familiar two-dimensional device to explore the conceptual issues. The results are generalizable to n-person situations.
2. For an insightful discussion of how the interpretation of the different versions of the Pareto principle and how they relate to the weaker concept of 'minimal benevolence', see Hausman and McPherson (2006, pp. 64–72 and pp. 136–40).
3. Over time, of course, the frontier can shift due to changes in technologies, resources, external shocks and government policies. This, as we will see, raises questions of 'dynamic efficiency', for the moment ignored.
4. The set of marginal conditions was comprehensively specified by I.M.D. Little (1957). Other standard presentations appear in Graaff (1957), Winch (1971) and Ng (1983).
5. Barry (1989, Chapter II) provides a useful discussion of the issue of fair division of a cooperative gain, raising the moral implications of the notion of a 'threat potential'.
6. I use the term redistribution of resources rather than income (or wealth) because the non-monetary 'assets' of people, like their skills, abilities and attitudes, are often relevant to preference (utility) outcomes, as well as other concepts of welfare. For this reason, Sen (1992, 2009b) uses the concept of 'capabilities'. Sen's analysis makes the idea of redistributing the capacity to satisfy individual preferences even more complex and problematic than discussed in this chapter.

7. Graaff (1957, p. 80) comments dismissively: '(i)ndeed, the whole concept of political feasibility is itself so flexible that there is not much point in retaining the feasibility locus as a tool of analysis'. In this manner Graaff is able to save the 'pure' analysis that is tractable mathematically by denying the existence of the real world, which is not.
8. Graaff (1957, pp. 48–52) provides a useful discussion of how the SWF can be derived from as the contour of a set of 'community indifference curves'.
9. There are many other value judgments that can order a social welfare function – for example a social ranking that expresses the ethical values and/or preferences of a ruling priestly class (see Chapter 10 for a further discussion and exposition).
10. Stiglitz and Greenwald go on to prove that government taxes can, in the face of pervasive externalities, often if not always result in a Pareto improvement, a better late-than-never nod to Pigou.
11. Formally, the analysis can encompass interdependent utility functions, moving the analysis to a non-neoclassical world, but the result is of little practical interest and cannot be demonstrated using the heuristic device in Figures 8.1 and 8.2. (Even in formal terms, it is not possible to rule out the existence of multiple bliss points.) Its relevance breaks down completely when we consider the subsequent discussion in this chapter.
12. The relevant passage is quoted in Hausman and McPherson (2006, p. 303).
13. Frey and Oberholzer-Gee (1997) present a case study demonstrating 'base motives driving out noble ones' (see Dutt and Wilbur, 2013, p. 108 for a discussion). Sandel and others argue that properly functioning markets require a hefty dose of mutual trust and transparency. 'A paradox arises to the extent that it is true that the market is dependent on normative underpinnings (to provide the pre-contractual foundations such as trust, cooperation and honesty) which all contractual relations require. *The more a people accept the neoclassical paradigm as a guide for their behavior, the more the ability to sustain a market economy is undermined*' (Etzioni, 1990, p. 250; italics in original); the more, it can also be added, that the defensive activities of monitoring and enforcing contracts will cost the society to keep markets functioning at least at some suboptimal level.
14. At least one Nobel Prize in Economic Science has been awarded to an economist who answered 'yes' to that last question.
15. The model of evolution Haidt relies upon explicitly rejects 'the selfish gene' version of natural selection, popularized by Richard Dawkins. Dawkins's hard-wired neo-Darwinism has fallen out of favour. There are too many biological processes that just cannot be explained by that reductionist route. The phenotype rather than genotype is seen as the basic unit of evolution. Stephen Jay Gould (2002, Chapter 8) provided a devastating blow to neo-Darwinism that has been hammered home since by biologists studying the surprising evolutionary strategies of viruses and other organisms. The field of epigenetics traces the varying ways that gene expression is triggered at the level of the organism by environmental rather than DNA mechanisms. The old 'nature-nurture' paradigm is old hat. (See also the contributions of the collection of sceptical Darwinians in Mazur, 2015.)
16. Haidt (2013, pp. 116–18) explains that he developed his theory of moral foundations on the basis of the 'three ethics' theory of the anthropologist Richard Shweder (see Shweder et. al. 1997) who argued that societies developed varied patterns of moral values depending on whether they had institutionalized an ethic of autonomy, an ethic of community or an ethic of sanctity.
17. A further source of political advantage for the Republican Party, he suggests, comes from the way in which 'fairness' (foundation 2) is defined by many to align with 'proportionality' or desert rather than equality. Hence, conservatives rail against those – welfare recipients, the unemployed and so on – who are deemed to take more than they give, more than their due. 'Fairness' is seen as getting what you put in – by hard work, determination, doing it yourself; 'cheating' is freeloading, expecting other, hard-working people to look after you.
18. This argument was advanced before the dramatic resurgence of populism in European

and American electorates, culminating in the British Brexit and US Presidential polls of 2016; more on this in the final two chapters.

19. In Chapter 11 I outline a consequentialist account based on the likely effects of morally oriented behaviour on actual government policies.
20. It was this concern that led John Stuart Mill to hang back on radical democratic reform in nineteenth-century Britain, fearful of the tyranny of the majority (lower classes) over the minority (people like himself). The position of pacifists during wartime nicely expresses the moral and political challenge.
21. Haidt (ibid. p. 247), for example, criticizes Stephen Jay Gould for arguing that the human genome was set down many millennia in the past and has not changed over the past 40000 or 50000 years.
22. For a graphical demonstration, see Winch (1971, pp. 110–16).
23. The second best critique applies within the static world of given resources, tastes and technologies. It has nothing to do with arguments in favour of monopoly around notions of dynamic efficiency, innovation or so called X-efficiency.
24. This argument was first put forward by Kaldor (1939) and Hicks (1939).
25. For an explanation see Little (1957), Mishan (1964) and Winch (1971, pp. 143–50).
26. Basic references include: Campbell and Brown (2003); Layard and Glaister (1994); Mishan and Quah (2007).
27. There is a huge literature on the 'right' discount rate to use in *social* cost–benefit analysis. In general, as a rough rule of thumb (emphasis on the 'rough') the discount rate for projects with significant public good or positive externalities is held to be lower than for projects carried out privately through the market. That is, the social discount rate is lower than the private discount rate established in the capital market, implicitly reducing the extent to which benefits and costs to future generations are discounted. However, the fact that the welfare of future generations is discounted – that is, 'worth' less than for people today – remains in the frame.
28. The key concept, utilized by Pigou, is Marshall's notion of 'consumer surplus'. See Winch (1971, Chapter 8) for a useful discussion.
29. This raises all the ethical considerations addressed by Sandel in *What Money Can't Buy* (2013). Walzer (1983) also identifies a range of areas of human interaction where market logic rarely if ever intrudes; he terms these 'blocked exchanges'.
30. Keynes's notion of investors operating under chronic uncertainty relying on rules of thumb applies equally to governments facing the need to make decisions with multiple objectives and constraints.
31. Keynes (1937, p. 115) went on to attack his colleagues thus: 'I accuse the classical economic theory of being itself one of these pretty, polite techniques which tries to deal with the present by abstracting from the fact that we know very little about the future.'
32. Ironically, when such directly political factors determine policy, any economic analysis that comes up with a negative net present value is quietly consigned to oblivion.
33. Nowhere is this more germane than in the area of climate change, where the status of 'loser' is potentially universal and terminal.
34. The issue of whether some of these changes are in fact exogenous is contested and has implications for ethical evaluation.
35. Joseph Schumpeter (1934) in *The Theory of Economic Development* (originally published in German in 1911) like Karl Marx stressed the disequilibrium-causing impacts of waves of innovation in new products and forms of business organization, as well as new technologies.
36. It is worth reminding the reader that the utility space in Figures 8.1 to 8.3 are defined by *ordinal* utility functions. The units on each axis are independent. Any comment on 'division' of the total gain from a move in that space has to be read in that context.
37. 'Ends up' is used metaphorically here. The whole point of dynamic analysis is to recognize that nothing stands still in real time. Conceptually speaking, the static utility possibility frontier is a construct in perpetual motion, in, out and round about.
38. Berry (2013), Reich (2015).

39. Bowles (2012) quotes the earlier work of Arrow (1971) here, who argued that ethical norms underlie social behaviour that makes up for market failures.
40. Romer (1986), Beinhocker (2006).
41. Only so-called 'positional goods' are purely rival. Few, if any, goods are totally non-rival. Most goods and services lie somewhere on a spectrum from low to high degrees of 'rivalry'.
42. 'Efficiency is necessarily a value laden concept and cannot be freed from the notion that efficiency is somehow more desirable than inefficiency' (Blaug, 1996, p. 592).
43. As we have argued earlier, the new welfare economics, like the old, implicitly accepts Pigou's demarcation and isolation of the material dimension of welfare, tying the latter to the consumption of goods and services, ignoring the 'non-economic goods' that people actually value in life – love, compassion, loyalty, trust, reciprocity, benevolence, citizenship, belonging, service, respect, autonomy, liberty.

9. Social justice and economic policy

> The difficult conceptual issue that has to be addressed is the determination of how justice and injustice in the world has to be examined and scrutinized. This is where we need political philosophy in general and a theory of justice in particular (Amartya Sen).

Previous chapters have outlined how orthodox economics developed an explicitly normative cast in the early part of the twentieth century. Social values were derived from the interaction of individual agents each attempting to maximize their utility through voluntary choice in the market. The old welfare economics associated with Alfred Marshall and Arthur Pigou sought to reduce the utilitarian aim of maximizing total utility to maximizing the national income measured in monetary units. However, they did so with an eye to its distribution aimed at raising the material living standards and moral character of the poorest sections of society. The new welfare economics trumped the old by eschewing the cardinal concept of utility and therefore sidestepped the problem of interpersonal comparisons by adopting an ordinal measure and intruding a particular value proposition defining an increase in social welfare at the societal level. Consequently, as Dutt and Wilber (2015, p. 55) argue, '. . . the theory of ethics implicit in mainstream economics is a very limited and partial one which follows a consequentialism that is related to a particular variant of utilitarianism based on the Pareto principle and the social welfare function.'

FROM THE INDIVIDUAL TO THE POLIS

Theories of social justice attempt to establish an ethical analogue to individuals at the level of society as a whole. Like its utilitarian roots, mainstream economics falls into that category of social justice theories that justify social arrangements and policies resulting in the maximization of some social good, in this case resulting from the most efficient allocation of resources depicted by location on society's utility possibility frontier. Over time, the metric of per capita GNP provides a one-stop indication of how economic welfare is progressing. Of course, other maximands are conceivable. For example, it can be argued that societies should be so arranged in order to maximize freedom or individual liberty, not as a matter of individual right but as an outcome desirable in its own terms. Problems would arise in determining what maximizing liberty means; for example, is some degree of trade-off – more freedom for most but less for some – allowable? No trade-off in liberty is acceptable to those for whom it is a basic, inalienable individual right. A theocratic society may morally exhort its citizens to act in ways that maximize adherence to the revealed preferences of the Gods (revealed, that is, by His earthly Ministers). An atheistic conception of social justice – revolutionary France under the Jacobins or Cuba after the revolution – can focus on the maximization of social virtue as citizen or comrade. Public policies and institutional arrangements will follow. Thus, for example, in Cuba, the government has prioritized the universal provision of high quality health care, while limiting political freedom and the consumption of many other goods and services, the reverse of priorities of its near neighbor, the United States of America. The key point of this and other conceptions of social justice is that they operate at the societal level and focus on the institutional arrangements that define and constrain the legitimate actions of government.

The problem with stretching the maximizing approach to social justice is that it starts to run into alternative conceptions. Thus, the French Revolution expressed a triple concern with equality and fraternity, as well as liberty. Cuba also adheres to an ethic of equality and a particular view of fraternity or community. Following the Enlightenment, equality has assumed a central role in many theories of social justice. It has been *inequality* that has required stronger justification (Tawney, 1931). Miller (1982) identifies several ways in which a commitment to equality reflects an intrinsic connection to morally persuasive aims such as fairness (Scanlon, 2003). As noted in Chapter 8, there is significant evidence across societies and cultures pointing to the moral force of notions of fairness and reciprocity in human interactions. Also noted there was the impact of unequal resources on political influence over government enactment and enforcement of legislation affecting the life-chances of citizens. Miller also stresses the importance of equality – or more to the point, the absence of significant inequalities – to the widely desired objective of self-respect. Extreme inequalities in wealth and social status, undermines the self-respect of those standing lowest in the hierarchy, regardless of their formal equality before the law as citizens. Related to this is the fact that inequality of condition and status prevents everyone from showing *equal respect for others*. A situation in which some people feel and act as superior to fellow citizens results in the decay of social solidarity, in the loosening of communal bonds – in short, in the decay of *fraternity* as a moral objective and cohesion as a social fact.[1]

The key question is – how equal? What degree of inequality over which areas of social intercourse are to be deemed dangerous to social solidarity? Only extreme egalitarians propose social arrangements that would guarantee absolute equality of status, resources and power. It is difficult to even imagine such a world outside the literary genre of dystopias. Argument legitimately revolves around the degree and focus of spheres of inequality. In capitalist democracies equality manifests as a generally held commitment to equal treatment in the legal system, equal voting rights and equal protection of property rights, though real world democracies seldom live up to these ideals in practice, due to underlying and pre-existing inequalities of resources and power. Equality of opportunity is particularly difficult to achieve in societies riven by entrenched class, ethnic and gender inequalities.

However, equality of both outcome and opportunity has been attacked as morally irrelevant by theories concerned with either *need* or *desert*. Significant inequalities of outcome may result from widely differing needs over the life course. Thus, children may reasonably expect the societies into which they are born to provide a high level of care until maturity, regardless of the resources, abilities and opportunities of their parents. Universal state education and policies targeted at infant health follow such injunctions. Likewise, elderly people can expect their final years to be without privation and provide a degree of autonomy and self-respect. Policies with respect to age pensions and health benefits follow naturally in this view. Other people may be prevented by accidental or inherited disabilities from effectively taking up the opportunities available or be denied access through inadequate policy supports or social discrimination. Policies mandating adequate physical access to public transport and buildings seek to offset the inherent disadvantages facing people so affected. However, simply by making all positions and roles in society nominally open to everyone may mask barriers that require compensating policies to reduce if not negate them. The number and diversity of barriers to equal opportunity are so great and many are submerged as to make the effort to redress the balance in total impossible; the best that can be hoped for is that some of the most obvious and egregious barriers – like Jim Crow practices in America's South – can be wound back.

Alternatively, it may be argued, attempts to reduce inequalities of opportunity will fail in the face of inherited or acquired talent, which should be suitably celebrated and rewarded. No amount of government intervention will equalize the chances of everyone to sing at the Milan Opera House, race Usain Bolt at the Olympics or win the Nobel Prize for Physics. Natural inequality should, in this view, be reflected in social inequalities; the bell curve will out. This is a congenial doctrine for those in the top tail and reassuring to the majority who believe themselves (often incorrectly) to be clustered around the median. After all, aren't we (mostly) all middle class? Well, no! As I will argue in Chapter 13, recent research has amply demonstrated the phenomenon of 'the disappearing middle' in many contemporary societies.

Buchanan (1988) argues that inequalities that arise from individual birth, effort, choice or luck are morally justifiable and beyond the legitimate scope of government redress. He is, however, somewhat uneasy about the claims of birth or inheritance. But what is *morally deserving* about inheriting wealth or fortunate genes, or being in the right place at the right time or putting in great effort at work? This question is especially relevant when we reflect that the capacity to work hard or be in the right place is partly dependent on the accident of birth and inheritance. Beyond these considerations, a natural aristocracy of merit, however defined (and by whom) is as morally questionable as a social aristocracy of birth, especially from the viewpoint of the moral claims of self-respect, social cohesion and communal life.[2]

Neoclassical economics developed an implicit moral theory of just desert, to complement its explicit commitment to the Pareto principle. In perfectly competitive markets factors of production will be rewarded just up to the value of their respective marginal products. In the absence of externalities of all kinds – a truly heroic assumption – marginal private and social net products will coincide. This mathematically elegant symmetry delighted early proponents of the theory of marginal productivity, John Bates Clark and Philip Wicksteed. It convinced the Fabian socialists like George Bernard Shaw to turn away from Marxism in their quest to civilize capitalism. In retrospect, it is difficult to get excited about the theory. What is so special, morally speaking, about owners of productive resources receiving the value of their marginal 'contribution', even if we can give a meaning to 'contribution'? Why should we celebrate if workers receive a wage based on the contribution of the least productive member of their group? The answer resides in the morally charged notion of 'contribution'. All owners of 'factors of production' are placed on an even footing. Owners of capital resources come together harmoniously with their hired workers and landowners to jointly produce output whose total revenue is divided up among them according to the market-mediated marginalist calculus. Even assuming away most externalities, this picture of harmonious and voluntary cooperation ignores the obvious fact that not all owners of factors of production meet on equal terms. Coercion has ever characterized real world labour markets, while insider trading (Stiglitz's incomplete and asymmetric information) makes financial markets opaque and inefficient.[3]

JOHN RAWLS'S *THEORY OF JUSTICE*

In 1971 Harvard philosopher John Rawls published his monumental book, *A Theory of Justice*. Rawls (1971) challenged utilitarianism front on, drawing on his deep knowledge of and commitment to Kant's rationalist ethic, the categorical imperative. Rawls believed that under suitable circumstances, individuals could and should 'act only according to the maxim whereby you can at the same time will that it should become a universal law'. He accepts the Humean view that self-interested individuals can all benefit by mutually agreeing to cooperate.[4] Whereas Hume explicitly rejected the historical reality of an actual contract or agreement as fanciful, Rawls constructs an imaginary or hypothetical choice situation where, he claims, everyone will reach the same position as regards 'the basic structure' of a just society. In some respects this echoes Rousseau's bold claim in *The Social Contract* that virtuous citizens, unsullied by the degradations of post-state of nature society, will be moved to all individually will the 'general will' in the interests of all. However, Rawls's citizens are each denizens of an acquisitive liberal capitalist society, uninterested in being virtuous, just desirous of ensuring an acceptable life in real-world capitalist democracies.

The challenge of achieving universal agreement as to the basic institutional set-up of a society of determinedly self-interested individuals with cross-cutting and often antagonistic interests is met by positing an 'original position' located behind 'a veil of ignorance'. No one in the original position knows what position he or she will occupy in the just society, not even what generation, gender, religion or ethnicity they will inhabit. Each is to make a simple choice of the basic principles that will order society, a once and for all choice that establishes the economic, social and legal institutions that cannot later be challenged or changed. Since no one knows their position in that society, once they step out from behind the veil, each is likely, Rawls argues, to be careful and take proper account of the possibility that he or she may come to occupy a very lowly position with respect to inherited and culturally determined resources, opportunities and status.

In such a contrived situation Rawls argues that everyone will gravitate to the same set of principles, namely:

1. Each person is to enjoy an equal right to equal basic liberties, compatible with a like set of liberties for all.
2. Social and economic inequalities are permitted only to the extent that:
   (a) they attach to positions in society equally open to all, and
   (b) they must be of greatest benefit to the least well-off in society.

The first principle is the familiar liberal commitment to individual autonomy, freedom of expression, a free press, and so on. Principle 2(a) expresses the equality of opportunity condition. Rawls calls Principle 2(b) 'the difference principle', which requires that social arrangements and policies should only countenance inequalities in the distribution of 'primary goods' to the extent that they maximize the life-chances of the most disadvantaged citizens. Primary goods are generalized resources, like wealth and basic rights that are necessary for an individual to pursue any personal plan of the good life. Rawls further argues that in the original position an individual will be risk averse enough to pursue what game theorists call a 'minimax' strategy – choosing in a way that minimizes the maximum loss – that is the situation if he or she happens to end up at the bottom of the social ladder with respect to inherited and other primary resources. Moreover, since basic liberties are the most primary of primary goods, Principle 1 will be 'lexically' ranked over Principle 2. No one would choose a basic structure that allowed the possibility of anyone's basic liberties to be traded off in favour of meeting the demands of Principle 2(a) or 2(b). Rawls sought to distance people from the immediate consideration of what is in their individual interests in order to stimulate agreement over a fair ordering of society in which each person has a reasonable chance of carving out a materially and morally satisfactory life. 'Fairness' is the ultimate test of a just society, not any particular set of outcomes.

Rawls's theory has generated an avalanche of critical responses, both negative and positive (for example, Hart, 1973; Barry, 1973; Blocker and Smith, 1980; Peffer, 1990). Rawls has attempted to address many of the criticisms, particularly with respect to the game-theoretic nature of choice under radical uncertainty, the lexical priority of equal liberties and the under-specification of primary goods (for his 'reappraisal', see Rawls, 2001). Readers can be forgiven for being bamboozled by the complexities and changes of emphasis in the Rawlsian approach and debate.[5] In answer to the question 'is Rawls right?', an early commentator concluded:

> I find it extraordinarily difficult to get a grip on this question, despite the care with which Rawls develops subsidiary themes in his theory. The problem, in part, stems from the fact that Rawls says little or nothing about the concrete facts of social, economic and political reality . . . *A Theory of Justice* can be placed historically in the tradition of utopian liberal political economy of the late nineteenth and early twentieth centuries. One could characterize it briefly, even brusquely, as a philosophical *apologia* for an egalitarian brand of liberal welfare-state capitalism. And yet the device of the bargaining game and the veil of ignorance, while preserving the political, psychological and moral presuppositions of such a doctrine, raise the discussion to so high a level of abstraction that the empirical specificity needed to lend any plausibility to it are drained

> away. What remains, it seems to me, is ideology, which is to say prescription masquerading as value-neutral analysis (Wolff, 1977, p. 195).

What Rawls appears to be seeking is the a priori banishment of politics from the practical realm of political action. Since the rules have been agreed in advance, no correspondence can be entered into. Regardless of the actual outcomes of policies in real world situations, everyone is bound by their common prior hypothetical agreement to accept them, come what may. What happens if actual outcomes subvert the principles of justice, say by not improving the lot of the least well-off? Who and by what means will substance be given to determining when the least well-off have *adequately* benefitted from particular policies? What redress will individual citizens have if Rawls's ideological confidence in the benign workings of liberal capitalist economic and political institutions proves unfounded, say by the path-dependent institutionalized polarization of power and privileges? Rawls's commonwealth grants citizens the right to express dissent but not the means of making that dissent effective in changing the institutional structures that affect their capacity to realize their individual life-plans.

Most difficult of all for Rawls's original conception of justice is his insistence that it applies to 'a well-ordered society' defined as one in which there is a strong consensus of basic moral beliefs or intuitions. He later modified his position (see Rawls, 1993) to allow the existence in society of multiple and conflicting moral belief systems. His well-ordered society now supports and celebrates a plurality of moral traditions that form 'an overlapping consensus of reasonable comprehensive doctrines'. Justice as fairness now forms 'a political conception of justice' in which the two basic principles are supported or endorsed by the main religious, philosophical and ethical doctrines that characterize a well-ordered society such as the liberal capitalist constitutional democracies of the West. Rawls clearly wrote before the rise to political prominence of fundamentalist religious political movements in both America and elsewhere, though some inkling of the difficulties raised for his theory on this score should have been evident in the rise of the religious right in America during the 1980s. Such moral-religious-political conceptions hardly qualify as 'reasonable comprehensive doctrines' in the liberal sense intended by Rawls. Perhaps he would accept that in such circumstances his blind agents in the original position, cognizant of the possibility that such deep divisions are probable, would be unlikely to all choose the two principles in their original form but would be more inclined to opt for institutional arrangements protecting the rights of individual citizens to pursue whatever moral system they found themselves committed to. This might result in a pluralistic liberal regime protecting and promoting a project of *modus vivendi* or mutual toleration, as Gray (2000) argues the future way of liberalism lies. Alternatively, individuals in the original position, worried about where they could end up – a Muslim in a Christian majority society or vice versa – might choose a basic structure more akin to Apartheid supplemented by strong rights to bear and use arms. Clearly, even Rawls came to accept that his theory of justice had limits with respect to the coexistence of mutually antagonistic moral traditions.[6]

Rawls's theory of social justice is an audacious attempt to provide a deontological argument for the priority of right action over good consequences, to ground government policy and political obligation or duty in mutual agreement among citizens of a political community.[7] It is in the words of another prominent political philosopher, Ronald Dworkin (2011), a case of 'justice for hedgehogs' rather than foxes. The fox, according to the ancient Greeks, knew many things but the hedgehog knows only one big thing. For Rawls the big thing is *fairness* that trumps other bases for the just society. Dworkin agrees that there must be – in the apt title of his book – justice for hedgehogs. Dworkin's one big thing, the rationalistic core from which *his* two principles of justice derive, is the unity of truth and value. Dworkin (2011, p. 1) argues for the unity of ethical and moral values in all spheres of individual and public life. 'Value is one big thing. The truth about living well and being good and what is wonderful is not only coherent but mutually supporting: what we think about any one of these must stand up, eventually, to any argument we find compelling about the rest.' Dworkin (ibid. p. 2) goes on to outline the principles of justice that derive from this one big thing, drawing on the traditions of both equality and responsibility or autonomy.

> No government is legitimate unless it subscribes to two reigning principles. First, it must show equal concern for the fate of every person over whom it claims dominion. Second it must respect fully the responsibility and right of each to decide for himself [*sic*] how to make something valuable of his life. These guiding principles place boundaries around acceptable theories of distributive justice – theories that stipulate the resources and opportunities a government should make available to the people it governs . . . There is no politically neutral distribution.

Hence:

> (t)he question of distributive justice therefore calls for a solution to simultaneous equations. We must try to find a solution that respects both the reigning principles of equal concern and personal responsibility, and we must try to do this in a way that compromises neither principle but rather finds attractive conceptions that fully satisfy both' (ibid. p. 3).

It is on this basis that Dworkin constructs his conceptions of, for example, liberty and the democratic institutions that he suggests will protect the rights to justice and liberty.

At first glance, Dworkin's principles seem to echo Rawls's. However, this impression is misleading. Dworkin attempts to ground his principles in deeply held moral intuitions that he spends a whole book teasing out to establish their significance across multiple domains of value, with an eye to actual consequences for people differentially situated in real societies.[8] Conversely, Rawls believes that his approach grounds his principles in the quasi-realistic rational choices of self-interested agents, based on their knowledge of quasi-historical developments and assumed socio-economic and political 'facts' in advance of knowing their actual position in society.

BACK TO THE REAL WORLD

Sen (2012, pp. 101–102) has advanced the most influential critique of the contractarian approach of Rawls and others by arguing as follows:

> The principal theories of justice in contemporary political philosophy, coming not only from Rawls but also from Robert Nozick, Ronald Dworkin, David Gauthier and others, share in common, explicitly or by implication, the idea of a social contract that identifies ideal social institutions (even though the substantive contents of their respective theories are different from each other in terms of what exactly the social contract should demand). Dworkin's ideal social institutions are not the same as those of Rawls, nor are the Rawlsian ideal institutions the same as Nozick's, but they all have tended to see the theory of justice as being engaged in identifying a particular set of ideal social institutions. Since these institutions need to be implemented, they all need a sovereign state that does the work in line with the respectively identified social contract.

Sen opts to develop his alternative 'non-transcendental' approach to social justice from within another tradition of enlightenment thinkers. 'These theorists did not erect a fully developed structure of a theory of justice, but the ingredients of a different approach – different from the social contract theory – which they helped to identify, can be developed from their alternative understanding of the demands of justice' (ibid. p. 102). More specifically:

> These theorists (including Adam Smith, the Marquis de Condorcet and Mary Wollstonecraft in the eighteenth century and extended later to John Stuart Mill and Karl Marx, among others) took a variety of approaches that differed from each other, but shared a common interest in making comparisons between different ways in which people's lives may go, jointly influenced by the workings of

> institutions, people's actual behavior, their social interactions and other factors that significantly impact on what actually happens (Sen, ibid. p. 102).

Referring to his own pioneering work, Sen calls this tradition the 'social choice' approach. Like the social contract theorists, Sen pays particular attention to the importance of developing supporting arguments and, where possible, agreement over justice-related positions through processes of public reason – that is, by way of rational discourse in which arguments and evidence are overtly considered, weighed up and pronounced upon in what Sen, following Mill, calls 'democracy as government by discussion'. However, for Sen, the aim is not to reach a once-and-for-all consensus on the ideally just institutional arrangements assumed to ensure 'appropriate' behaviour. The aim is to uncover egregious cases of *injustice* and to guide policies to reduce them; his focus is on actual 'social realizations' or 'comprehensive social outcomes' (Sen, 2009b, pp. 215–21). However:

> The social realizations do not ignore the institutions used and the principles that are invoked as [a] guide to human behavior, since realizations are not just about the ultimate outcomes but also about how these outcomes come about. But this alternative approach, which I am trying to develop, has to take a direct interest in the lives that people are actually able to lead, rather than concentrating only on institutions and principles of behavior (with the hope – explicit or implicit – that they would yield the kind of lives that can reasonably be desired) (Sen, 2012, pp. 102–103).

Sen differentiates his approach to the contractarians on three grounds. First, rather than starting with the quest to find the concept of perfect or ideal justice, he seeks (in step with Smith and company) to identify clear cases of injustice with respect to which reasoned agreement could be reached as to the means of reducing or removing said injustices. He mentions the historic successes in ending slavery in the West and the moral imperative today to end famines, preventable epidemics, the absence of adequate medical care, lack of schooling and torture. On might also add, the abolition of current-day slavery and human trafficking in parts of the world. His approach opposes his 'realization-focused comparison' to Rawls's 'transcendental institutionalism' (Sen, 2009b, pp. 4–6).

Second, he argues that by ignoring how institutional structures and processes play out on the ground, contract theorists assume that people will behave appropriately in ways that both reflect the intent of the rules and reinforce them – that is, that no backsliding, freeriding or cheating will undermine the just society. 'But that presumption is an hypothesis, and if it goes wrong, there is nothing in the procedure to make iterative corrections'

(Sen, 2012, p. 103). Additionally, there is no scope to assess the quality of people's lives, including their freedoms and welfare, however defined, because whatever will be will be; actual social realizations need to be assessed for their moral acceptability. Nevertheless, as Sen concedes, Rawls does make some attempt to consider the behavioural requirements for his well-ordered society, and assumes that every citizen has the moral capacity and motivation to act according to the dictates of the principles of justice; this assumption is buttressed by Rawls's notion of reflective equilibrium by which the principles are iteratively harmonized with people's basic moral intuitions. Sen therefore suggests that *A Theory of Justice* might better be characterized as an 'arrangement-focused', rather than purely institutionalist theory (as might Kant's *Critique of Practical Reason*); 'the people' in Rawls's moral universe are implicitly imbued with the fruits of the European Enlightenment. Hence: '(t)here is, obviously, a radical contrast between an arrangement-focused conception of justice and a realization-focused understanding: the latter must, for example, concentrate on the actual behavior of people, rather than presuming compliance by all with ideal behavior' (Sen, 2009b, p. 7).

Third, because contract theories require a rule-setting and enforcing mechanism, they tend to focus on the dominant means historically to hand – namely, the sovereign nation state. This restricts discussions of institutional structures and processes to those impacting on the citizens of that sovereign state. Sen wishes to extend the scope of social justice to the global level. 'This makes reasoning on "global justice" possible, even in the absence of a global sovereign state, which is essential for addressing such problems as global economic crisis, or global warming, or prevention and management of global pandemics, such as the AIDS epidemic' (Sen, 2012, p. 103). What Sen seems to be asserting here is that conventional international means of reaching global agreements among nation states – treaties, diplomacy, international agencies, Summits, G7/G20 and so on – are not up to the challenges posed by emerging global problems. This claim is at least arguable in the light of some successful international efforts to limit nuclear proliferation, attack the hole in the ozone layer, eradicate smallpox, deliver aid to people suffering natural disasters and protect endangered species. However, it is certainly difficult to see how Rawls's agents in the original position could have sufficient foresight to design a basic structure capable of throwing up appropriate policy responses to as yet unknown potential global catastrophes, or even resolve known wicked problems like climate change.

BRINGING THE COMMUNITY BACK IN

The conceptions of justice considered to date turn on the primacy of the individual derived from the Enlightenment, emanating in the two liberal traditions identified by Sen – the social contract and social choice approaches. The idea of a society of human atoms has always worried moral philosophers and political theorists concerned with the communal context within which stable social relations emerge and are reproduced through time. Conservatives are well represented in this camp, particularly those clothing their analyses in religious garb. The counter-Enlightenment of the eighteenth and nineteenth centuries produced vehement critiques of liberal individualism – for example, the works of Vico and Hamann (Berlin, 2000) – as did the Marxist reading of class into history and politics, though in this case analysis looked to the levers of radical social change. Sandel (1982) has referred to the liberal individualist position as promoting a conception of 'the unencumbered self' – that is, that people are each to be considered moral loners, absolutely free to choose the right way to act and be. He rejects this characterization:

> If we understand ourselves, unbound by moral ties we haven't chosen, we can't make sense of a range of moral and political obligations that we commonly recognize, even prize. These include obligations of solidarity and loyalty, historic memory and religious faith – moral claims that arise from the communities and traditions that shape our identity. Unless we think of ourselves as encumbered slaves, open to moral claims we have not willed, it is difficult to make sense of our moral and political experience (Sandel, 2009, p. 220).

The idea of ourselves as encumbered slaves rather than free-wheeling autonomous moral subjects alarms liberals like Rawls who are convinced that liberty as a set of negative freedoms requires an absence of unwilled moral commitments. The contractarian conception of the individual involves, according to Sandel, two categories of moral responsibility or obligation, first to undertake our common 'natural duties' – to grant equal respect to others, to treat others as ends not means, to respect the dignity of all people – and second, to meet any obligations we voluntarily enter into. Obligations of the first type are universal, what we owe to each other as human beings, and do not require mutual consent. Unlike natural duties, voluntary obligations are specific and do require consent; we are each bound morally only by what we agree to without coercion. 'Liberal justice requires that we respect people's rights (as defined by the neutral framework), not that we advance their good' (ibid. p. 224).

Sandel regards this account of political obligation as 'too thin', failing to account for the many special responsibilities citizens of a political community owe to each other. There are loyalties, ties and responsibilities that people have by virtue of their particular historically situated location – as members of a family, tribe, religious congregation, nation – that define who they are. To sever these particular 'obligations of solidarity' from their socio-historical roots denies the essence of who we are as particular persons: '. . . these identities are not contingencies we should set aside when deliberating about morality and justice; they are part of who we are, and so rightly bear on our moral responsibilities' (ibid. p. 224).[9] Sandel's arguments echo Haidt's analysis (summarized in the preceding chapter) of the moral foundations of behaviour but implicitly shifts the discussion from what is to what ought to be; that is, since real people act in these ways, society should be arranged to allow and encourage them to continue to do so. For Sandel, it is a case of 'let the elephants rule'; this is for Sandel, an ethical imperative not merely an empirical truth.

Sandel's approach grounds his theory of justice in a sociological rather than rationalist mould. Real people in their particular social and historical locations acquire moral precepts through living in a matrix of familial, religious, ethnic, gendered and class defined communities, where they must navigate complex, sometimes conflicting obligations. Like Sen, Sandel rejects the transcendental and constructivist approaches to defining and dealing with justice and injustice. Both stress the need to consider outcomes 'on the ground'. Both reject Rawls's arguments for neutrality in public reasoning about the substance of moral obligations and justice. For Sen, the particularity of realized outcomes matters; while Sandel holds that the moral and religious beliefs of people will and must colour their consideration of both the right and the good. What does all this mean for public policy?

POLICY IMPLICATIONS AND IMPERATIVE

The theories of social justice reviewed in this chapter imply a range of moral grounds for government intervention in the economy and thus a variety of legitimate policy arenas and imperatives. Some broad indications of these grounds and imperatives are presented further on. They are traced out in more detail in Part III.

Neoclassical economics, as noted, stresses the role of markets in allocating resources and places a very high bar on government intervention. Since markets are assumed by default to operate efficiently (in Paretian terms), in most cases policy is restricted to correcting clear cases of market failure on a case-by-case basis. In spite of the logical difficulties posed by the theory of the second best, the normal rather than occasional incidence of market failure due to informational imperfections, and the implicit value judgments inherent in the very concept of efficiency, the faith in the ethical efficacy of markets is all but inviolable. Most economic policy takes place *as if* markets operate efficiently and assume that the values implicit in the distribution of incomes and patterns of behaviour generated are morally justified. Close enough is *good* enough, as Marshall said. Hence, the theory of justice underpinning government:

1. prioritizes prevailing institutions that define and guarantee property rights – that is, the right to possess, use and dispose of resources;
2. justifies institutions that regulate market processes and agents where failures are evident which;
3. imposes policies designed to offset or reverse the negative effects of actual market outcomes if and when detected.

For example, competition policy aims to encourage 'contestability' in situations where large firms are thought to be or capable of abusing monopoly power. It is the spur of competition that is held to flush out operational inefficiencies, drive prices down to marginal costs and spur innovation to reap above normal profits. This policy logic has been extended to public enterprises in the form of privatization programmes (see Chapter 12). Other policies are aimed at ensuring accountability, transparency and informational efficiency; for example, company laws regulating financial reporting, auditing standards, bankruptcy and insider trading. The very partial success of such interventions is apparent in the theories of economists like Stiglitz and the recurrent financial crises and scandals reported by the mass media. Market solutions are the default position in this world, as the various attempts to tackle environmental problems by using Pigouvian taxes or pollution trading schemes attest. The weight of argument is all in favour of 'leaving it to the market', albeit with tinkering at the edges, wherever failings are observed to occur. The latter qualification is important. Market failure that is *not* apparent does not exist for purposes of policy. Since mainstream economists operate with a set of preconceptions favouring market solutions many policy advisers simply *don't see* the need for corrective action. It is not a case of 'build it and they will come' but 'don't look, don't see'.

With respect to distributional justice, as noted earlier, properly functioning markets are held to reward people according to their respective productive contributions and hence their desert. Other desert-related dimensions of virtue are ignored. Large inequalities in income and wealth are justified because the market has spoken. Economic rents extracted by high-income individuals are the self-justifying result of superior talents and, hence, deserved ethically speaking. However, all but the most committed of libertarians would accept the legitimacy, even moral imperative, of government intervention to offset the incidence of poverty and individual catastrophes in life, through some combination of taxation, social service provision and social insurance. The policy debates then centre on who 'deserves' to be assisted, in what ways, at what levels and who pays – in short how 'generous' should the social safety net be and how 'progressive' will be the impost on the rest of the society.

The key point to note is that institutional design and policy implementation are determined within a universe of discourse confined by market logic. The values implicit in or underlying the social outcomes for people are 'encumbered' by the metaphor of the market, the virtue attributed to voluntary exchange between judicially equal participants. The possibility that people routinely cast into market exchanges might be *systematically unequal* in their respective powers is simply ignored, ruling out of consideration many of the moral issues that exercise political philosophers operating with different conceptions of social justice. The analytical and value frame of mainstream economists fuels a naive political theory that encourages a distanced political stance; namely, the role of disinterested policy adviser who 'points the way and they will go'. In fact, the conventional nostrums of economists confine the policy agenda and help to legitimate the directions and absences determined by the ruling powers. The popular idea of 'a level playing field' is a nonsense, economically and socially, in a deeply divided, unequal society. Nevertheless, this myth has delivered a potent ideological charge in Western societies ascribing to liberal values.

What about the other approaches outlined above? Taking John Rawls first, only those institutions that satisfy the difference principle by maximally improving the lot in life of the worst-off are morally justified. This would suggest the necessity to impose taxation that is 'reasonably' progressive to fund policies supporting a 'fairly generous' safety net. Policies would also be needed to improve the capacity of people to hold a range of offices and positions (to use Rawls's words) in order to satisfy the equal opportunity principle. Rawls is happy to let political forces in his ideal democracy figure out the details of *how* progressive and *how* generous. He is not interested in the actual outcomes on the ground, as long as the basic structure is sound.

There are many similarities here with the implications of neoclassical economics. Indeed, Rawls explicitly endorses the sway of orthodox markets as the key economic institution in the make-up of his basic structure. His approach relies on a narrowly pluralistic political theory of liberal (capitalist) democracy, and a highly optimistic view of the moral nature of humanity. In real existing capitalist societies, unequal wealth feeds unequal power that, in turn, is highly likely to undermine the operation of both divisions of the second principle of justice. Attempts to square the circle – by for example claiming that actual inequalities of income and wealth are necessary to lift up the lowest of the low – quickly assume the cast of ideological self-justification, if not self-delusion. Unequal wealth and power is also likely to undermine the first and lexically primary principle of equal liberties, when defending and extending the position of the powerful requires restrictions on basic liberties faux-justified, not with respect to a trade-off favouring Principle 2 (ruled out of court by Rawls), but on national security grounds.[10] Sen's critique that when things go wrong Rawls provides no guidance on what to do (other than philosophical hand-wringing) is germane here.

Nevertheless, Rawls's theory diverges sharply from the laissez-faire, market-rules approach since it rejects the full-blown 'whatever will be, will be' logic and allows for – even requires – policies that remove barriers to equal opportunity, including policies of affirmative action or reverse discrimination and various forms of social insurance against inherited or acquired disadvantages. However, it is not clear that the basic institutions that allocate primary goods will be up to achieving these aims.

It is also reasonable to question what we might call Rawls's *moral sociology*. He argues that citizens in the just society have the capacity and motivation to act according to the rules and procedures laid down by the institutional structures. However, the *capacity* to act morally also enables citizens to act otherwise – that is the *ability*, thanks to the extensive individual freedoms guaranteed, to subvert the intent of government laws and civil society sanctioned norms. For example, living in a real world capitalist society that encourages individuals to maximize their wants through market exchange may incubate values and ways of seeing and being that 'crowd out' the very civic-minded morality necessary to maintain mass adherence to just behaviours and support for the institutions of the just basic structure. The creeping commercialization of culture poses an ever-present threat to Rawlsian justice, a case of bad values chasing out good.

Moving onto Dworkin's rights-based principles, what do the twin imperatives on governments of equal concern and equal responsibility imply? 'What political settlement, seeking what distribution of resources, fits our two principles taken together?' (Dworkin, 2011, p. 356). His response is to construct 'an envy test' based on a 'fantasy answer'. Assume people are shipwrecked on a desert island.[11] The available supply of clamshells serves as a token of value and exchange. The real resources of the island – the building materials, food sources and so on are auctioned off in return for payment in shells. Exchanges occur until everyone is satisfied in the sense that no one envies the bundle of resources, including unspent shells, held by anyone else. Through time as a result of good and bad management, good and bad luck and numerous unintended and unforeseen contingencies, some people end up with more resources than others; some people are reduced to penury due in part to their free choices and partly to uncontrollable events. Should government step in to redress the inequalities? Using a more familiar metaphor, everyone has stepped up to the starting line of the race on equal terms but Usain Bolt streets the field and most people miss out on the medals, while some fail to finish, falling to the track clutching their hamstrings. Dworkin here distinguishes *ex ante* from *ex post* equality. Getting everyone to the starting post on time satisfies Dworkin's concept of equal concern without compromising the second principle of equal individual responsibility, to try one's hardest. To go further and compensate 'losers' for losing denies their obligation to act responsibly – and accept the consequences.[12] Equality of primary resources before, not after, the event is paramount:

> . . . ex post compensation would not be a reasonable goal, even if restricted to noninvestment luck. . .. It remains wrong even if we apply it to erase the consequences, not of bad luck as ordinarily understood, but only the bad genetic luck of not having talents prized in the contemporary market. If the community restores people to a condition of equal wealth, no matter what choices they make about work and consumption, then, as I have said, it destroys rather than respects this dimension of responsibility. But there is no way *fully to erase the consequences of differences in talen*t without adopting that foolish remedy. It is impossible in principle, not simply practically impossible, to distinguish the consequences of choice and capacity across the range of economic decision, because preferences and capacity interact in both directions. Our preferences both shape the talents we are disposed to develop and are shaped by the talents we believe we have. So we cannot separate choice from genetic luck in what might seem the most direct way; by making sure, ex post, that people's wealth reflects only the former and no tinge of the latter (ibid. p. 359; italics added).

Before picking up the policy implications of the argument, three comments on the passage above are in order. First, Dworkin's island fantasy starts with equal resources, ignoring the more familiar economic argument against *ex post* equality – namely, that it removes the incentive to grow the total of resources, to seek out as yet undiscovered or exploited clamshells. Second, note the italics added to the quote above. Dworkin refers to the impossibility in principle or practice of 'fully' erasing inherited differences in talent. Sen's key point of departure from the contractarians is that the aim is *not* to focus only on the ideal but also to develop institutions and policies that at least reduce injustices and prevent their accumulation over time. This leads to a third point; ignoring the build up of *ex post* inequalities can be self-reinforcing as the resource wealthy reorganize structures and policies to further favour their interests. One consequence of winning the race will be to ensure that more races of the same kind will be run.[13]

Returning to the thrust of Dworkin's argument, he clearly dismisses the ethical underpinnings of and government's political duty to deliver equality of opportunity in an *ex post* sense – Rawls's Principle 2(a). Nor does Dworkin subscribe to the difference principle in its rigid form. However, the principle of equal concern does require government to take into account the needs of those people who by lack of talent, bad luck and bad choices, are at risk of not making the starting line, by implementing policies designed to establish *ex ante* equality of resources in probabilistic terms. This is to be achieved in an 'actuarial' sense, by allowing both private and government social insurance to cover people for a range of eventualities – sickness, unemployment, high risk employment, accident and so on.[14] Perfect coverage is not required.

> We can try to identify a top coverage level at which we can sensibly assume that most people in our community would have chosen to insure, given what we know about their needs and preferences, and given the premium structure that that coverage would require . . . We can then insist that our [government] officials use at least that coverage level as a guide to redistributive programs of different kinds. We might aim to collect from the community, through taxes, an amount equal to the aggregate premium that would have been paid for universal coverage at that level and then distribute, to those who need it, services, goods, or funds that match what that coverage would have provided them in virtue of their bad luck (ibid. p. 361).

The vague nature of this quoted passage and use of phrases like 'we can try', 'we might aim', 'we can sensibly assume', 'most people', and so on indicates the qualitative nature of the argument being advanced. In reality, the stuff of politics will focus on the quantitative dimension, the dollars of tax and spending entailed and the incidence on both sides of the equation. Dworkin is comfortable with this, content to provide the guiding principles – in this case the need to harmonize the imperatives of equal concern and equal respect, without seriously considering how actual outcomes will depend on the unequal distribution of power.

It is Dworkin's concern with equal respect that contrasts to Rawls's rather cavalier and implausible claim that the difference principle reflects the traditional liberal notion of fraternity.[15] 'The difference principle, however, does seem to correspond to a natural meaning of fraternity: namely, to the idea of not wanting to have greater advantages unless this is to the benefit of others who are less well off' (Rawls, 1971, p. 105). Looked at in another way, the difference principle is better tagged as 'paternalism', likely to encourage deference and servility, rather than fraternal fellow feelings, among both the better and less well off; a case of the 'Chavs' and 'Chav Nots'.[16] Dworkin (2011, pp. 361–2) is keen to defend his own insurance-based concept of fraternity from the charge of 'paternalism', not to my mind persuasively, since he admits that the social insurance programme would be mandatory, the very target for the vehement opposition to 'Obamacare' in America, for example.

Nevertheless, his reliance on market processes sidesteps issues of market failure, including the absence of markets for many of the contingencies Dworkin (and Shiller, 2013) would like to see covered. Arrow (1963) long ago pointed to the problem of incomplete (that is, absent) markets and, along with others, the classic insurance problems of asymmetric information, adverse selection and moral hazard. The task of Dworkin's wise officials is Herculean if they are indeed required to guesstimate 'the top level of coverage' that most people would have chosen had they had the chance and the resources – and the right information. One does not have to subscribe to Hayek's extreme view of the informational inadequacies of centralized government intervention to be doubtful about the counterfactual task set by Dworkin in devising and implementing policy.

The comments above underscore Sen's thoroughgoing critique of constructivist theories of justice – namely, that they provide a shaky foundation for dealing with and reducing actual instances of injustice through appropriately detailed policy interventions by government *and* civil society organizations. Social contract theories are – in this sense – radically under-specified. Sen calls instead for a direct focus on 'outcomes' – but 'comprehensive' rather than 'culmination' outcomes. His is a process-infused consequentialism:

> There is no particular reason to insist on an impoverished account of a state of affairs in evaluating it. In particular, the state of affairs, or the outcome in the context of the choice under examination, can incorporate processes of choice, and not merely the narrowly defined ultimate result. The content of outcomes can also be seen as including all the agency information that may be relevant and all the personal and impersonal relations that may be seen as important in the decision problem at hand (Sen, 2009b, p. 215).

Sen is concerned with what might be called the production line of end states, as well as the product in isolation. An exclusive focus on the latter leaves traditional consequentialist moral philosophy – including various variants of utilitarianism – open to a range of criticisms. 'Indeed, part of the problem with what are taken to be "consequentialist" theories of practical reason lies in the tendency to focus on culmination [i.e. end-state] outcomes only' (ibid. p. 215 fn.). For Sen, consequences – say, of the manner and content of government policy intervention and the behaviours of and relations between individuals impacted – are 'more than just the aftermath'. Consequence-sensitive reasoning includes the comprehensive social realizations encompassing the total state of affairs under analysis. According to Sen, it also makes room for considerations of personal responsibility (Dworkin's focus) in a way that narrow consequentialist (especially utilitarian) analysis does not.[17] This broader ethical frame allows for differences in the way people assess comprehensive outcomes. The utilitarian insistence on universal adherence to a single metric of culmination outcomes is inappropriate. 'To insist on the same requirement in the evaluation of comprehensive outcomes, even when we are concerned with agencies and relations and processes, would seem to be entirely arbitrary, and indeed motivationally contradictory' (Sen, 2009b, p. 220).

In contrast to the utilitarian focus on aggregate individual happiness and the economists' (and Rawls's) resources-based approach, Sen (1985, 1992, 2009b) proposes a freedom-based capability theory in which justice resides in policies and institutional processes that reduce the inequalities in the effective capacities of citizens to pursue their aims in life – 'to do things he or she has reason to value' (Sen, 2009b, p. 231).[18] The central idea of 'capacity' means the *effective* ability or '*real* opportunity' to live one's life as one wishes, given the actual circumstances existing in society at the time. He developed this concept by way of criticizing the inadequacy of Rawls's means-oriented notion of 'primary goods', notably the importance given by Rawls to income and wealth in determining whether social arrangements are just. Thus, increasing the level of primary goods to disadvantaged people, beyond a relatively basic level, and leaving them to parlay those resources into lives worth living may be neither necessary nor sufficient to realize these aims:

> The capability approach focuses on human life, and not just on some detached objects of convenience, such as incomes or commodities that an individual may possess, which are often taken, especially in economic analysis, to be the main criteria of human success. Indeed, it proposes a serious departure from concentrating on the means of living to the actual opportunities of living' (ibid. p. 233).[19]

An individual's capabilities will depend on his or her genetic inheritance – for example, susceptibility to chronic debilitating disabilities and advantages like being born blind or with a high probability of contracting cancer or Multiple sclerosis or, alternatively with superior athletic or musical talents – and socially acquired abilities and disabilities like a good education, good nutrition and acquired brain damage. These capabilities both enable and constrain people from a range of 'functionings' in society. People differ with respect to their overall capabilities and hence real opportunity to convert resources in order to carry out the functions necessary to achieve their desired quality of life. A single defined set of means or primary goods will not, in the light of diverse capabilities and life goals, adequately assist everyone to attain their desired ends. Greater income may indeed help, say, homeless people acquire a degree of permanent shelter, an anchor or base to achieve other valued ends. But that alone is insufficient to remove the stigma associated with the class or caste into which that person has been socially ascribed, nor circumvent socially imposed controls on individual behaviour. A woman in a traditionally patriarchal society may have her freedom of movement and circle of acquaintances tightly constrained, denying her the opportunity to, for example, work outside the home, own property, gain a higher education, control her fertility, leave abusive relationships and so on.

Sen's just society is a set of social arrangements that improve the lives as lived of people with currently restricted capabilities, limits imposed by both genetic inheritance and the real history of their social locations. The ethical imperative driving evaluation of existing conditions and possibilities requires collective action aimed at removing the most restrictive constraints on the freedom of those unable to function according to their freely chosen aims. This includes, crucially, the removal of informational deficits that hide the nature and impact of the restrictions from both the afflicted and the government agencies implicated, giving substance to the idea of freedom to choose. The fact that blind people 'learn' to navigate in a sighted world or the wheelchair-bound avoid steps is no justification for not acting to make their environments more conducive to living a broader range of experiences. Illiterate and innumerate people may get by and not realize what they are missing but access to these resources are primary in the sense that their possession opens up a whole new world of possible functionings – that is, abilities to convert resources into desired outcomes. It is these considerations that point Sen to the 'big' injustices stalking the world – famine, pandemics, treatable illnesses like malaria, global environmental crises, global illiteracy – as well as those closer to home in the West, like discrimination against minorities and chronic unemployment. In general, Sen redefines poverty as 'capability deprivation'.

Sen identifies four main categories of factors that cause variations in the relative potential for individuals to convert income and other primary goods into desired functionings that allow them to achieve 'the kind of freedom valued in human life' (Sen, 2009b, p. 254).

In the first place, individuals differ among themselves according to personal characteristics – age, gender, disability, proneness to illness and so on – creating wide divergence of needs and the ability to satisfy them among people with the same level of income. Those with severe intellectual or physical disabilities will require higher income and other supports to access lives worth living than fully abled people.

Second, diversities in physical environments place greater barriers to be overcome for some people – for example, the need for higher energy resources and higher quality, more expensive housing in regions of extreme cold. Environmental conditions can be altered to offset the barriers through collective civic action and government policy. However, for an individual such conditions are given over the medium term. Problems created by environmental deficits are particularly important in denying opportunities to children whose physical and cognitive development may be harmed by prolonged exposure to harsh and niggardly climates at critical stages in their growth. Naturally occurring famines, flooding, wildfires and other interruptions to food supplies are potent killers of capability.

Third, variations in social environments mean that people who live in stable, affluent societies can benefit from the 'social inheritance' of past government and civic investments in public health, educational services, control of crime and violence. Even individuals with low incomes may be better able to survive and even (to a degree) thrive in these societies compared to poor people in places where chronic under-provision and social disorder prevail; indeed, it may be more empowering to be poor in rich countries than moderately wealthier people in poor countries, though only with respect to cross-national comparisons.[20] Of course, some socio-political regimes may have the incentive and ability to deliberately impoverish particular groups under their dominion, including by imposing policies of massacre and starvation that amount to genocide.

Fourth, relational social position may vary the level of income necessary to achieve the same basic functionings in different societies. Cultural and legal prohibitions may prevent some individuals effectively participating in ways that achieve basic functionings. For example, constraints, partly self-imposed, on women from appearing in public without appropriate escorts and clothing impose extra costs to overcome. Similarly, socially imposed constraints may also dissuade people with particular disabilities or physical disfigurements from full social engagement regardless of income. Such disadvantages can also attack the wellsprings of self-respect and self-confidence.

The various sources of variation in resource conversion potential often interact. Thus environments that generate income and wealth inequalities reinforce status distinctions and power relations, poor nutrition and impoverished social services, which in turn reinforce existing inequalities of income and wealth in a positive (self-reinforcing) feedback loop.

Sen pays particular attention to the issues of reducing capability deprivation caused by the multifarious sources of disability. He quotes studies that estimate about one-tenth of the world's population suffer from disabilities of one kind or another, 400 million of whom live in developing countries.

> If the demands of justice have to give priority to the removal of manifest injustice . . . rather than concentrating on the long-distance search for the perfectly just society, then the prevention and alleviation of disability cannot but be fairly central in the enterprise of advancing justice (ibid. p. 259).[21]

He differentiates between a disabled person's 'earnings handicap' and 'conversion handicap'. The former refers to entrenched disadvantages in accessing income through employment, due to previous barriers to acquiring marketable skills, intellectual and physical impairments, employer discrimination, physical barriers to movement and so on. The latter includes the extra costs that must be met to function effectively, for example, the cost of providing wheelchairs for paraplegics, guide dogs for the blind, in-house carers for the intellectually disabled. 'Thus, real poverty (in terms of capability deprivation) can easily be more intense than we can deduce from income data' (ibid. p. 256). The two forms of 'handicap' often interact in a vicious circle: low income limits opportunities which limits income. 'The 600 million handicapped people in the world are not just plagued by low income. Their freedom to lead a good life is blighted in many different ways, which act individually and together, to place these people in jeopardy' (ibid. p. 260).[22]

The upshot of this approach is that good policy has the good result of expanding the 'conversion opportunities' of those with the most restricted effective capacities to benefit from adequate public health, education, satisfying employment and so on. This does not necessarily mean that everyone will achieve their most desired outcomes, 'merely', that they have the effective opportunity to achieve, given the real barriers, social and inherited, that define their existence. But what is to stop subtle and hidden barriers in the social environments of some people from effectively preventing their effective opportunities to achieve? This, after all, is the most insidious generator of impoverished lives. Sen's answer is to place heavy emphasis on the rule of public reason in well-functioning *democracies* that guarantee the traditional liberal liberties. We return to this matter in the next chapter.

Unsurprisingly, Sen's approach implies strongly interventionist policy interventions to improve the opportunities of people to overcome, should they choose to, barriers to employment, decent housing, healthy lifestyles and environments. This grants government a broad range of legitimate interventions in the way people go about 'the ordinary business of life'. It warrants policies that go well beyond establishing and maintaining the basic institutions of a functioning market economy – that is, beyond enforcing private property rights and the piecemeal targeting of identified market failures. Extensive public service provision and social benefit schemes in areas like public schooling and hospitals, mental health, disability support, housing, education and training and so on will require extensive revenue raising policies that impact directly and indirectly on economic outcomes across society. His approach also calls for policy makers to monitor and adjust policies and the institutional mechanisms for delivering them in light of the actual outcomes for different people and groups in order to test whether and to what extent those policies and processes do in fact reduce existing inequalities in conversion opportunities. What people choose, how they individually and collectively behave, will feed back into revised capability sets, not always in foreseen and progressive ways. That is, unintended consequences of government intervention can unintentionally *increase* inequalities in conversion opportunities, calling for rethinking by policy makers and legislators. A critical rider: Sen is *not* tying government policy to the *actual* outcomes of the institutional-policy interface *but* to ensuring over time that the *opportunities* to develop functionings necessary to pursue the good life are substantially less unequal within and between societies.

This last rider is important and controversial. To pick up the point made earlier, if the criterion for justice focuses on opportunities to achieve, not on actual, (comprehensive) outcomes, how can governments be sure that the 'choice' a person makes not to take up an opportunity is a genuine exercise of her freedom and not the result of 'giving up' in the face of apparently insurmountable obstacles or lack of relevant information or poor self-esteem and self-confidence or, ominously, the deliberate opposition of powerful forces? In cases that are difficult to decide, policy processes and outcomes may be substantially underdone. The informational conditions facing both citizens and government are likely to be most onerous in precisely those cases that are most problematic when it comes to sorting out whether or not a free choice has been made. Sen's answer, I think, would be that by at least recognizing this possibility the task of reducing capability inequalities in the messy real world is on the agenda; forewarned is forearmed.

Finally, what might Sandel's approach herald for the government policy process-outcome complex? Having identified the importance of what Edmund Burke called 'small platoons', the loci of affinity, loyalty and solidarity that command our moral judgments and intuitions, Sandel is keen to tie political obligation and government policy to strengthening or, at least not weakening, the communal links that give real content and meaning to living Aristotle's good life. Many of the policies and policy mechanisms that he would champion will be similar to those promoted by Sen and, indeed, Rawls and Dworkin. For example, loyalty to one's immediate family – in the form of agitating for policies favouring their well-being – may be perfectly consistent with the liberal duties of respecting the rights and opportunities of people more distant from us. However, it may often be the case that loyalties and duties to one's close relatives clash with those broader moral imperatives. Thus, I may push for policies beneficial to my own team with the result of undermining the rights and conversion capabilities of other fellow human beings. The more 'distant' the relationship, the less likely am I to be troubled ethically by this outcome. People starving on my doorstep may move me to support an expanded food stamp programme in the neighbourhood, while starving millions in Africa escape my attention, concern and action. Of course, this seeming double standard could be due to ignorance of situations far away – though the global reach of mainstream and social media make this unlikely for people in the advanced nations. It is also likely that ignoring the plight of far distant peoples can be rationalized away: my help is a drop in a bucket; any aid I give will be diverted or wasted; other people and governments are better placed to improve matters. The potential list of rationalizations is endless. Sandel argues that it is morally permissible for a parent to save her own child rather than that of a stranger if only one can be saved. However, it is not permissible to let the stranger's child die in order to avoid being late for a meeting of the local car rally club. Sandel goes further, however, and argues that it is also morally wrong to save your child by driving over and killing the other child if this is the only rescue action possible. This is not to claim that many if not most people faced with an instantaneous choice like that would let their child die; merely, that so acting would be immoral by breaching our natural duty to all human beings.

This last point is highly contentious. If 'Sophie's choice' can happen within a family, when only one child can be saved by sacrificing the other, then the inclination to save one's child by sacrificing another outside the family or group is even more compelling and less open to moral opprobrium. Rather, sentiments of compassion for the loss of the child is a more likely and justifiable response, along with feelings of regret that such a situation eventuated.[23] As noted in Chapter 8, the moral intuitions that Haidt stresses in *The Righteous Mind* are likely to be the result of the complex interplay between genetic and sociocultural forces that emerge historically in actually functioning communities. To give precedence to the well-being of one's own is both deemed 'natural' and culturally admired, the everyday test of acting morally. This does not mean that people have a moral licence to act without taking into account the rights and opportunities of other people but that we will order our obligations and duties according to the historically given situations we find ourselves part of.[24]

> What we admire is the disposition to see and bear one's life circumstances as a reflectively situated being – claimed by the history that implicates me in a particular life, but self-conscious of its particularity, and so alive to competing claims and wider horizons. To have [moral] character is to live in recognition of one's (sometime conflicting) encumbrances' (Sandel, 2009, p. 237).

But as Haidt (2013) reminds us, it is the elephant of moral intuition that is normally in control and reason the rider justifying the consequences of acting on intuitive, historically crafted moral sentiments. Policy makers and those who would advise them need to be aware of the complex ways in which moral values influence actual behaviour *if* they are concerned more with the goodness rather than rightness of outcomes – that is, if subscribing to a comprehensive consequentialist rather than deontological ethical position. For ethicists of the latter persuasion, the influence of moral values on behaviour and policy are relevant only to the extent that they must (that is, imperatively) be modified, overcome or negated in order for right to triumph.

CONCLUSION

This chapter has moved the focus of attention to the issue of how society is to be organized in order to achieve social justice. Inevitably, basic ethical issues that relate to the conduct of individuals have salience when we come to consider how a whole society should function. We first looked at a range of the theories of justice that have concentrated the attention of contemporary political philosophers, theories that focus on maximizing some defined good like utility, achieving some desired state like equality, rewarding contribution or desert, constructing an institutional order to guarantee rights or alternatively of reducing observable injustices, and the communitarian ideal of a commonwealth of virtuous citizens. Different theories of justice privilege different approaches to and content of public policy.

It became clear that orthodox economics provides a very limited normative case for a particular desert-based ordering of society and intervention by government, based on the inadequacies of evaluative tools expressing the value-laden Paretian notion of efficiency. Before offering in Part III an account of how the influence of this approach has undermined socially just outcomes, and what an alternative approach can offer, the following two chapters develop the ideas raised by Sen's analysis of justice. Chapter 10 takes up the question – is democracy possible? To answer this question, we need to be clear about what democracy is or should be; there are conflicting views here. In particular, what are the implications of inequalities of power and wealth for the realization of the dictates of justice, defined as reducing injustices? Chapter 11 pulls together a revised consequentialist framework, based on the preceding two chapters, for considering how governments should act in order to achieve good social outcomes defined in the comprehensive terms suggested by Sen.

NOTES

1. 'Equality bears more than a causal connection to fairness, self-respect, equal respect, fraternity and freedom from domination. Equality in distribution is not merely a means to fairness, equal respect or fraternity; under many circumstances it manifests these values. Though equality is arguably only a means to self-respect and freedom from domination, the concern for the individuals it manifests is linked to these values' (Hausman and McPherson, 2006, p. 183).
2. Robert Nozick (1974) also offered a rights-based theory of social justice in which the right trumps the good. For Nozick, governments should not intervene to change the outcomes determined by individuals' rightfully entitled resources. In other words, 'good' outcomes however conceived cannot undercut the right of individuals to use and dispose of resources or 'holdings' to which they hold legitimate ownership. Unsurprisingly, Nozick opts for (John Locke's) minimalist or 'nightwatchman' state.
3. Debates in the 1960s – the so-called Cambridge capital controversies – demolished the conceptual basis of an aggregate production function for the economy and the very possibility of measuring 'capital's' contribution to production. For a comparison of the different 'entry points' of the neoclassical theory of marginal productivity and Marxist exploitation theory, see Wolff and Resnick (2012, Chapters 2 and 4).
4. Hume argues and Rawls accepts that 'the circumstances of justice' expressing potentially conflicting interests in society can be overcome by institutional arrangements designed to realize the common interests of all, particularly with respect to the enjoyment of security, order and prosperity.
5. Where conclusions drawn from his theory appear to collide with deeply held moral intuitions, Rawls proposes a back-and-forth dance between theory and intuition until both are brought back into some sort of balance. This notion of 'reflective equilibrium' is itself intuitively appealing but at the expense of weakening the overall coherence and 'bite' of his basic theory. What happens if reflection emerges after people come out into the real world that the basic structure creates?
6. He later made a valiant attempt to establish a social contract between peoples within and across nation states who hold opposing liberal and non-liberal moral doctrines – 'the law of peoples' (Rawls, 1999) – but the attempt hardly deals adequately with the new realities of developments like the Islamic State.
7. Other theories of justice based on mutual agreement and bargaining have been proposed that do not depend on devices like the veil of ignorance and extreme risk-aversion; for example, Gauthier, 1986; Barry, 1989; Binmore, 1994).
8. Although Dworkin's moral theory, into which his theory of social justice slots, draws heavily on Kant (as one would expect of an author whose earlier book bore the title, *Taking Rights Seriously*), he also has an eye to the consequences of social and political arrangements that makes it difficult to place him entirely in the deontological ethical camp: nevertheless, in his extended discussion of justice in Part Five of *Justice for Hedgehogs*, he advances the idea of rights as trumps to identify the subset of political rights that must not under any circumstances be traded off for other values. Rawls's

'transcendental' approach removes his analysis from a direct concern with actual outcomes; as long as the basic structure obeys his two principles of justice, then 'whatever will be, will be'. This 'Doris Day doctrine' raises objections such as those noted above and developed by other political philosophers like Sen (1992, 2009b). The original position presents a narrative that could be called 'the man who knew too little'. See following discussion.

9. Sandel explicitly draws on the Aristotelian virtue ethical tradition as resurrected by Alisdair MacIntyre (1981).
10. Basic liberties like free speech can also be undermined by the threat of expensive litigation through the legal system.
11. It was the ahistorical, transcendental feature of what we would now call social constructivist theories of justice that so annoyed David Hume. It is difficult not to sympathize with him on this score. If one has an eye to the many current examples of injustice in the real world, such flights of fancy are difficult to swallow.
12. The temptation to quote President Jimmy Carter is too great: 'Show me a good loser and I'll show you a loser.'
13. Sen (2009b, p.267; italics in original) summarizes his critique as follows. 'There is, I am afraid, some institutional fundamentalism in Dworkin's approach, and some innocence in his presumption that once we have agreed on some rules for insurance-based resource redistribution, we would be able to forget about the actual outcomes and the actual capabilities that different people enjoy. It is assumed that the actual freedoms and outcomes can be left in the secure hands of institutional choice through *as if* markets, without ever having to second-guess the correspondence between what people expected and what actually happened.'
14. Shiller (2013) has argued that financial markets have the capacity to cover a range of such risks, for those who can and are willing to pay the premiums.
15. Rawls also claims that the other two liberal ideals neatly attach to his principles of justice: liberty to Principle I and equality to Principle 2(a).
16. For a discussion of how elitist notions of meritocracy reinforce relations of deference and undermine self-respect, see Dorling (2015) and Jones (2011, 2014).
17. He also suggests (Sen, 2009b, p.216 fn) that Kant's *Critique of Practical Reason* relies on comprehensive social realizations in articulating his deontological position, a similar point I made earlier regarding Dworkin's approach. Hence, it is not sensible to maintain the traditional sharp division between consequentialist and deontological theories of social justice, at least when extending the scope of both the outcomes and rights concerned.
18. Sen is pointing again to the need for comparative analysis, to the idea of reducing existing injustices defined by differential capabilities determining the scope of functionings achievable: '. . . contrary to an often-articulated interpretation, the use of the capability approach does not demand that we sign up to social policies aimed entirely at equating everyone's capabilities, no matter what the other consequences of such policies might be' (ibid. p.232). The evaluative frame must be aware of the *comprehensive* consequences of possible policies – comprehensive in terms of both processes and first, second and higher degree outcomes, to the extent that they can be foreseen. Good policies may require difficult judgments as to which outcomes matter most, to whom and on what grounds, especially if mutually exclusive goals are in play and power inequalities are entrenched.
19. Sen has been prominent among economists and other social scientists in criticizing the single metric use of per capita GDP as *the* dominant evaluative tool for policy success, having been joined by Stiglitz and others, at the request of French President Sarkozy to find better measures (see Stiglitz et al. 2010). He has also contributed substantially to the set of social and economic indicators in the United Nations Development Program's Human Development Report. These contributions follow naturally from his rejection of the resources approach that underlies traditional economic approaches to development.

20. This would appear to be the case for many of the millions of refugees driven by civil and religious persecution to flee to other countries, especially in the West.
21. Sen (2009b, p. 261) accepts that Rawls's second thoughts do make room for the need to consider 'special needs' of particular groups in particular circumstances but that this is to occur at a second 'legislative stage' – that is, *after* the basic constitutional structure has been established using primary goods as the universal metric of opportunity. Sen (ibid. pp. 264–8) also differentiates his capability approach from Dworkin's version of the equal resources imperative.
22. Sen might also have noted that use of the term 'handicap' in society, the economy and government, is itself considered a material barrier to more equal conversion opportunities. The socio-political consequences of language are well appreciated by many disabled people and advocacy groups, though conservative critics often denigrated this as mere 'political correctness'.
23. Sandel might still argue that regret on the part of the reluctant killer could invoke feelings of remorse and self-guilt, indications that the person knew at some level of consciousness (fuelled by Haidt's moral taste buds) that he had acted immorally.
24. Some utilitarians would disagree and deny the moral case for letting the other child die; Singer's quote on page ii of this book suggests as much (Also see, Singer, 2010).

10. Is democracy possible?

The concept of Democracy is an interpretative and much contested concept (Ronald Dworkin).

INTRODUCTION

The various liberal approaches to social justice discussed in the preceding chapter are (at least implicitly) cast within a discourse assuming that government policies are implemented within a democratic political framework, that is, through institutional means that have evolved over the past two centuries in lockstep with economies organized by markets in Western nation states. Modern democracies have, because of their size and complexity, necessarily developed as representative systems of government. Direct participation in politics has been limited to local jurisdictions and interest groups that seek to influence policies and agendas managed by elected and appointed representatives. Voting, in some accounts, has become the defining feature distinguishing democratic from undemocratic systems. Who votes and how has focused attention of political philosophers, political scientists and political pundits. Over time, the franchise – who votes – has progressively widened from a very narrow group of propertied men to include all adults (with a few exceptions) holding citizenship within the nation. Many voting systems, such as first past the post, proportional representation, preferential voting (also called 'instant-runoff voting'), to name some, have been tried. In most cases 'one person, one vote' and some version of the majoritarian principle have prevailed.

Of course, history has provided ample evidence of the inadequacy of the existence of the popular vote as a marker of democracy, since every self-respecting dictator ensures that he (always he) frequently holds elections and secures thumping majorities against shadow alternatives or no alternatives at all. It is the nature of the supporting institutions and values defined by a liberal culture that determines whether democracy rules. In particular, the existence of freedom of expression, a free press, the rule of law, an educated and well informed citizenry and other effective means of monitoring and holding political representatives and public officials to account are necessary but not sufficient conditions for democracy considered as delivering, in some sense, 'rule by the people'.

Before looking at how justice and democracy might be mutually reinforcing, it is useful to pose the question – is democracy based on majority voting possible? More specifically, given certain axioms of 'reasonableness' concerning how individual preferences are to determine collective outcomes (policies, office bearers, constitutions), is the result indeterminate in some cases?

ARROW'S IMPOSSIBILITY THEOREM

As we saw in Chapter 8, modern welfare economics established the conditions for the locus of Pareto efficient allocation of resources, in the form of the utility possibility frontier. The optimum optima – the bliss point – lying along that frontier could only be conceptually determined by overlaying a social welfare function (SWF, illustrated in Figure 8.2) that ranked every conceivable state of the world – that is, every combination of preferences of every citizen. Economists believed, without much thought, that the SWF would necessarily reflect the preferences of the majority of citizens in a consistent manner. The whole would faithfully represent the sum of the parts, providing a further normative prop for free market systems, complementing the Paretian value judgment of efficient allocation.

Unfortunately, a young Kenneth Arrow (1951) quashed this hope. Much to his own surprise, he established that a SWF satisfying a set of five rather weak axioms or conditions for democratic collective outcomes was a logical impossibility; Arrow referred to any set of axioms or rules for collective decision making as a 'constitution'. At least one of his axioms, he argued, would be breached; it was not possible for all five axioms to hold simultaneously. The five axioms can be summarized as follows:

1. If everyone prefers state A to state B, then the SWF ranks A above B, for all possible pairwise comparisons of states of the world. This is the weak Pareto principle.
2. Whether A is socially preferred to B should never depend on the preferences of any single individual. This is the non-dictatorship axiom.
3. Whether A is socially preferred to B depends only on how individuals rank A and B and not on the presence or absence of any other alternatives. This is the 'independence of irrelevant alternatives' axiom.
4. Regardless of the specific content of individual preferences, the SWF must determine a social ranking of A and B. This is the 'universal domain' axiom that requires a social choice mechanism to always

Table 10.1

	A	B	C
Brian	1	2	3
Ella	3	1	2
Jenny	2	3	1

generate an outcome, regardless of how unusual or idiosyncratic the preferences of individuals.

5. The SWF (pairwise) ranking of alternatives must be complete and transitive. If A ranks above B and B above or equal to C, then A must rank higher than C. All possible alternatives must be ranked. This is the 'collective rationality' axiom.

Arrow makes a further critical assumption: the preferences of all individuals are strictly ordinal; no interpersonal comparisons of utility are allowed.

Arrow's proof holds for any social choice situation involving at least three alternatives and three individuals. It is normally demonstrated in the three by three case, as in Table 10.1, in the form of a voting paradox but the proof generalizes to n-by-n cases.[1]

Options A, B and C can be policies, rules, candidates or any other mutually exclusive set of choices. The ordinal rankings of individuals Brian, Ella and Jenny are transitive for each individual. However, this is not the case when attempting to derive an overall ranking based on majority preference. Thus, Brian and Jenny both prefer A to B, while Brian and Ella prefer B to C; but C is preferred to A by Ella and Jenny. There is no way to rule out any of the three options on majority preferences. The result cycles endlessly, leading to what has been termed 'a Condorcet cycle'.[2] The SWF interpreted as a social decision mechanism fails to deliver a logically consistent (transitive) outcome, breaching axiom 5. A decision could only be reached if one of the people was able to impose his or her dominant preference. Brian would choose A, Ella would opt for B and Jenny would impose C. This, of course, would breach axiom 2 ruling out dictatorship. In many real world cases there will be enough overlap of preferences to generate a majoritarian outcome that satisfies the axiom of collective rationality. For example if X and Y were members of the same family, club or religious group, their preferences may be similar enough to dominate voting outcomes. To see this, swap Ella's rankings of A and C in Table 10.1 as in Table 10.2.

The resulting majority votes expressing a fully transitive social outcome would be: A>B; B>C; A>C. This might occur if, for instance, Brian and

Table 10.2

	A	B	C
Brian	1	2	3
Ella	2	1	3
Jenny	2	3	1

Ella are Christians of varying degrees of commitment and Jenny an atheist. Outcome C is to ban all religious instruction in schools; B is to mandate such instruction in all schools, while A leaves the decision to each school. Although Brian's first preference A is selected and this is not atheist Jenny's first preference, Jenny still prefers a situation where some schools can choose to hold religious classes to option B that forces all schools to do so. Atheist Jenny's first preference is denied but at least she is comforted by the fact that A is better than B. Jenny might still be said to personify John Stuart Mill's fear of the tyranny of the majority over the minority. The options A, B and C are more often used to represent individuals standing for elected office but the logic applies to any set of choices greater than two facing more than two voters.

As a workable voting system, a one person, one vote majoritarian rule can and in reality has arisen in most modern representative democracies, though the exact details vary widely. For example, in the normal situation where a Condorcet cycle does not exist, 'Condorcet winners' can be easily calculated by exhaustively going through every pairwise ranking and determining the option which is most preferred over the second placed runner (option A in Table 10.2). However, in strictly logical terms, close enough is not good enough. The fact of the *possibility* of social outcomes that breach collective rationality cannot be ignored as unlikely outliers, without breaching axiom 4, universal domain.

In fact, most criticism has focused on axiom 3, the independence of irrelevant alternatives. It requires the social ranking of any two alternatives to only depend on their rankings by each individual and nothing else. Even if most people preferred A to B would it be necessary to hold to a SWF that preferred A if A also systematically denied basic rights to some section of the population?[3]

What about the intensity of peoples' preferences? Table 10.3 places cardinal values (as per Chapter 3) on the preferences of the three people; the rankings are the same as in Table 10.1. To remind the reader, these numbers reflect more than an ordinal ranking, indicating the relative preference between the options for each individual, but saying nothing about the relative strength of preferences between individuals. This time

Table 10.3

	A	B	C
Brian	30	2	1
Ella	2	99	10
Jenny	4	3	5

assume that B involves doubling the unemployment benefit, C is to leave the benefit at the same level and A is to abolish it altogether. Unemployed Ella is much more in favour of having her benefit doubled than maintained at its current paltry level and likewise prefers maintaining the benefit to having it scrapped completely. Brian, on the other hand, would greatly prefer to see the benefit scrapped (to force Ella and her kind to get a job), though if this cannot be achieved he is (just) willing to see the benefit doubled (to prevent Ella starving) rather than left at its current pitiful level. Jenny is relatively indifferent to the options though, if pushed, would opt for cutting the benefit completely rather than doubling it.

The SWF still breaches the transitivity axiom of collective rationality; there is no consistent majority choice.[4] However, although the set of numbers in Table 10.3 tells us nothing about how the three alternatives matter between the three people – that is, they do not entail a common metric that would enable interpersonal comparisons of intensity of preference – it does suggest that for Ella the stakes are very high, while Jenny is relatively indifferent about the outcome. It does not take a very strong indicator of interpersonal comparisons of welfare (however defined) to provide some moral grounds based on sentiments of benevolence for preferring the social outcome B. 'We may, for example, have no great difficulty in accepting that Emperor Nero's utility gain from the burning of Rome was smaller then the sum total of the utility loss of all the other Romans who suffered from the fire' (Sen, 1998, pp. 188–9). Sen and other social choice theorists have demonstrated that 'partial comparability' of people's utility may be enough to generate coherent social outcomes.

> There may, thus, be room for demanding 'partial comparability' – denying both the extremes: full comparability or no comparability at all. The different extents of partial comparability can be given mathematically exact forms (precisely articulating the exact extent of inexactness). It can also be shown that there may be no general need for terribly refined interpersonal comparisons for arriving at definite social decisions. Quite often, rather limited levels of partial comparability will be adequate for making social decisions. Thus the empirical exercise need not be as ambitious as it is sometimes feared (ibid. p. 189).

Arrow's impossibility theorem led to what Sen described as a 'big bang' in formal analyses of aggregated decision making. Numerous theorems have been derived based on different sets of axioms that enable consistent collective outcomes to emerge and which identify a range of unintended paradoxes that can guide the introduction of robust voting systems by indicating the need for 'cycle-busting' mechanisms in those relatively rare cases. For example, the work on partial interpersonal comparability overcomes Arrow's impossibility result. Logically consistent social decisions based on aggregating individual preferences can be derived, though the practical applicability of these theorems will depend on the chosen measures of relative advantage and deprivation utilized. The classical utilitarian focus on interpersonal comparisons of mental states can be replaced by empirically operationalized metrics of happiness or well-being, based on particular ethical foundations. Sen's capability approach or Rawls's resource-based theory of primary goods, outlined in the preceding chapter, can provide the degree of partial comparability needed to negate Arrovian impossibility outcomes. Practical policies can be crafted by using the techniques and metrics that are being developed, guided by the analytical models of social choice. At least, this is the case for theories of social justice like Sen's that focus on identifying and reducing actually existing injustices.

Condorcet's contemporary, another French mathematician, Jean-Charles de Borda, devised a simple system for choosing between options. The logic can be grasped by adding the rankings in each column of Table 10.2 giving a weighted ranking for each voter. Lowest score wins. Thus A 'wins' with a total of 5, composed of one first ranking and two seconds; B scores 6 and C 7.[5] In this case both the Condorcet and Borda systems select A as the winner. Perusal of Table 10.1 shows that Borda's method, like Condorcet's fails to break the cycle – all options score a 6.

Other voting methods have been proposed and are in operation around the world in various collective organizations including nation states. For example, the single transferable vote (STV), also called the instant-runoff vote (IRV) provides for the second and, if necessary, lower preferences of voters to figure in the final count. The candidate with the lowest number of first preference votes is eliminated and those votes transferred to the remaining candidates according to the individual second preferences of each of the voters for the eliminated candidate. This process continues until one candidate has a simple majority of overall votes. For example, this system is used to elect single-member representatives to the Lower House of the Australian Parliament and forms the basis for the system of proportional representation to elect senators to the multimember state-wide constituencies forming the Upper House. Note that the IRV/STV approach does not resolve the indeterminacy of preference outcomes represented in Tables 10.1 and 10.2.

First past the post voting is the simplest system devised to select that candidate receiving the largest number of single votes in a single electorate. When more than two candidates contest an election, the winner will often fail to secure a majority of overall votes cast. For example, in a three-candidate race, the winner only needs to secure one third plus one of the votes. The result will depend heavily on factors like how concentrated or dispersed the supporters of the candidates are and how high the voter turnout across electorates. Multi-stage runoff elections can also draw on first past the post counts to finally select a candidate with an overall majority of votes, as is the case with the election of the French President.

Lurking within Arrow's analysis is a further basic assumption – namely, that individuals honestly express their individual preferences. In fact, the vast body of work on voting sparked by Arrow's impossibility theorem and the rediscovery of earlier versions has established the pessimistic conclusion that virtually every system dreamt of is open to problems caused by strategic voting, where some or all individuals have an incentive to misrepresent their true preferences or do deals with each other to exploit anomalies (see Poundstone, 2008, for an accessible survey).

Assume that the true preferences of our three voters are expressed in Table 10.2 but that Brian and Ella are each determined to get their policy up. Both see the other's first preference as the biggest threat to their own winning and so vote by putting the other's first choice last and of course retaining top ranking for their own fiercely desired preference. The result would turn out as depicted in Table 10.4.

The Borda winner is C, a bizarre result since it represents a bad outcome for Brian and Ella, who have unintentionally shot themselves in the foot, since neither have got their first choice up. The Condorcet winner is also C, an equally implausible result. The result, however, meets the collective rationality axiom: C>A; A>B; C>B. Borda is supposed to have priggishly commented – 'my scheme is intended only for honest men'. This form of 'vote rigging' can deliver unintended and unwanted outcomes, and is a recipe for a mediocre or worse candidate triumphing. Even more worrying,

Table 10.4

	A	B	C
Brian	1	3	2
Ella	3	1	2
Jenny	2	3	1

it appears that the most dishonest strategizing works best. If above only Brian 'cheats' by putting Ella's option last and Ella and Jenny vote their true preferences (as per Table 10.2), then A is the Borda (and Condorcet) winner and the axiom of collective rationality is met.[6] It pays to cheat, if you can get away with it, as countless discussions of 'the prisoners' dilemma' have stressed when assuming the universal reach of self-interest in decision making.

The practice known as 'vote splitting' can affect the outcome in first past the post systems. The result of a number of US Presidential elections have arguably been influenced by minor third candidates attracting votes away from one of the two major candidates. Ross Perot in 1992 and Ralph Nader in 2000 are held to have cost George H. W. Bush and Al Gore victory, respectively. Neither victor, Bill Clinton or George W. Bush won a majority of the popular vote, though this outcome can occur through other factors like the variable voter turnout, the peculiarities of the electoral college system and the role of the courts.

Strategic voting can also bedevil proportional representation systems. Voting for the Australian Senate in the 2013 Federal Election is a case in point. A large number of minor and single-interest candidates clogged a very large list of candidates. Deals were struck between a number of minor candidates to 'swap' and bunch second and lower preferences, in such a way that some of them had a chance of winning the final seat in some of the state jurisdictions. As it happened, preference flows cascaded so as to elect several previously unknown candidates representing obscure interests. One candidate famously was elected with less than 1 per cent of first preference votes. Not surprisingly, the major parties subsequently agreed to change the voting system in an attempt to make 'preference harvesting' by independents more difficult. As it turned out, the subsequent general election in 2016 saw more independent senators elected, though not as the result of preference harvesting but because a significant minority of voters directed their first preferences away from the two major parties in a populist move apparent in many democracies in recent times.[7]

The potential for strategic voting has spawned a large industry of political advisers devoted to 'gaming the vote' in favour of their clients. Techniques used include focus groups, push-polling, trawling big data and, of course, political advertising (both positive and negative). Analytically, it has involved the application of game theory, which has also been applied more widely to the questions of moral and political philosophy (see Hausman and McPherson, 2006, Chapter 14; Gaus, 2013; Wight, 2015).

In conclusion, Arrow's original theory is not an invitation to dismiss democratic politics in favour of some form of oligarchy. His analysis and its extensions, instead, force us to consider what are the ethical aims of social decision making and what social, economic and political institutions are required to give substance to their impact in real world situations where paradoxically unintended outcomes *may* arise.

IS DEMOCRACY EFFICIENT?

Sen (1970b) has famously proposed a further paradox that demonstrates 'the impossibility of a Paretian liberal'. On some minimal requirements for individual liberty, and other side conditions, it is not possible for them and the Pareto principle to simultaneously be met. It seems that either (Paretian) efficiency or freedom must be compromised. This contention has generated a deal of debate (see Hausman and McPherson, 2006, pp. 225–8). However, to the extent that the critique of the Pareto principle on ethical grounds discussed in Chapter 8 is accepted, such a result is not problematic – freedom wins hands down, regardless of which theory of social justice discussed in Chapter 9 is drawn upon.

Social choice theory has focused attention on how effectively representative political systems respond to the interests and preferences of citizens who collectively delegate legislative and executive powers to decision makers. A powerful metaphor has been used to demonstrate both the benefits and limitations of such systems.[8] Consider a beach along which bathers are uniformly distributed, left to right. The sun is hot. Two ice cream sellers are deciding where to locate their stands in order to maximize their individual sales. Harold Hotelling (1929), the economist who introduced this metaphor to illustrate his theory of spatial duopoly, demonstrated that wherever each seller started on the beach, competition would push each to gravitate towards the centre of the beach. In the end, they would locate their stands slap up against each other. Why? The implicit assumption is that every beachgoer would like to buy an ice cream but to do so by expending the least energy by walking to the stand nearest him or her. If each seller started at opposite ends of the beach, then each would attract the half of the customers closest to them. People at either end of the beach would have short distances to walk to buy an ice cream, while those nearer the middle would have to walk longer to get their ice creams. However, each seller has an incentive to move location closer to the other end of the beach since he will continue to attract custom from people sitting between him and his initial location at the beach extreme while attracting half the customers sitting between his new location and the other seller – *provided that the other seller remains at the other end of the beach.* Our first seller (say) A located at the left end of the beach can monopolize trade by continuing to march up the beach until locating right up against the other stationary seller B at the right end. Almost everyone will be forced to walk to A, saving an extra step to and ignoring the other seller B. However, this is not a stable situation. B can leapfrog A to the left and secure all the custom coming from the beach to his left, restricting A to the few customers at the very right extreme near B's original location. This leapfrogging process will continue as each seeks to position his stand between the other seller and the (reducing) majority of customers to the left, until both are up against each other right in the centre of the beach where those to the left walk to (say) A and those to the right walk to B. This is the profit maximizing equilibrium for each seller. However, it is not the ideal situation for the beachgoers, who collectively have to walk further than if, for example, A and B had located at locations one quarter of the distance along the beach from each end. The average walk in equilibrium would be equal to a quarter of the length of the beach. The average distance walked in the second configuration would be one-eighth the length of the beach (or double those distances if everyone returns to his or her original spot on the beach). The market equilibrium outcome turns out not to be the most efficient solution in terms of minimizing the total use of resources (that is, energy and time used in accessing ice creams).[9]

Hotelling made the observation that the same logic applied to two political parties each seeking to attract maximum votes in a polity where voters are spread along a political or ideological spectrum from left to right, leading to the familiar situation where two dominant parties offer very similar sets of policies targeted squarely at the voters in the political centre, ignoring the preferences of voters with moderate and extreme left wing or right wing views. The 'median voter' has his or her interests and views count while the remainder of the electorate is effectively disenfranchised, assuming that only two parties contest the election.[10] This centralizing tendency is magnified where voters themselves cluster towards the political centre, reducing (but not eliminating) the degree of exclusion at the diminishing tails of the distribution. To see this, think of beachgoers clustering in the centre of the beach to swim under the watchful eyes of the lifeguards. Nevertheless, the analysis suggests that in two-party representative democracies the one person, one vote majoritarian electoral system is likely to ineffectively represent the views and interests of at least a substantial minority of the electorate. We are once more back to Mill's concerns about the tyranny of the majority.

Although this analysis has yielded interesting insights into the pattern of election outcomes and policy making in mature Western democracies, the theory fails to capture all the important observable features of real-world politics. This is not surprising because the theory rests on strong and restrictive assumptions. In the first place, the theory requires that voters can be ranged along a single ideological political spectrum with respect to the policy 'menus' offered by the parties. Individual voters may, in fact, locate themselves at different points along a variety of issue spectrums, more liberal on some, more conservative on others. Citizens may vote for the menu not (usually) on single issues, weighing up each party's offers on their issues of concern. Second, voter choices will depend on the completeness, relevance and accuracy of the information concerning party policies. Political messaging by parties (more specifically, their political strategists), including the deliberate misrepresentation of one's own and one's opponent's positions, plays a central role in mature democracies like that of the USA. Negative campaign advertisements have become a familiar feature of elections in America and elsewhere. Returning to the beach, consider what happens if a belief spreads that a shark has been sighted at one end of the beach; beachgoers tend to migrate towards the other end, followed (or anticipated) by the ice cream vendors, one of whom may have started the rumour. Fear can be a potent electoral stimulant. During uncertain times, as during an economic recession or war, the electorate tends to swing decidedly to the right.

Third, new parties may enter the lists, locating to the right and left of the main centre parties. Suppose C set up his stand one quarter of the way along from the left end of the beach. He would attract three-eighths of the customers, the quarter located to his left and the one-eighth located to the right of his stand and the midpoint between C and A in the centre. Likewise seller D could locate one quarter of the distance from the right end of the beach and capture another three-eighths of the custom. This would leave sellers A and B with reduced shares of one-eighth each.[11] Depending on the ease of entering the ice cream market, further vendors could set up shop, resulting in a proliferation of small businesses each catering to strictly localized markets.[12] This metaphorically speaking suggests the evolution of two-party duopolies into a multiparty system. Such electoral systems exist, particularly in Europe, leading to the prevalence of coalition or minority governments, and as in Italy, to a significant turnover of governments. Third parties often arise based on regional interests and support; this is the case in the British dominions of Canada and Australia, for example. Similarly, single-issue groups can carve out electoral niches, a vendor selling one particular type or flavour of ice cream that attracts customers from along the beach. Green parties and those supporting animal rights or opposing abortion often start small, though in the case of the Greens, many such parties have sought to broaden their appeal and move towards the centre attempting to capture votes from the main centre-left party. Centre-right parties have come under attack from further right nationalist parties. Political developments in the neoliberal era and especially post-2008 have witnessed a partial fracturing of stable two-party systems in the West, marked by the shift of votes away from the centre, pushing the major parties right towards the 'extreme centre' (Ali, 2015). Once capturing 90 per cent of the vote, the Labour and Conservative parties in the UK now barely attract two-thirds. A similar trend is apparent in Australia, which has had a stable two-party system since early in Federation at the beginning of the twentieth century.[13]

The ease of entry to the political arena is critically dependent on the precise nature of the electoral system, its legitimacy and transparency. Many nominal democratic two-party and multiparty systems are, in fact, effective one-party states presided over by dictators. Election fraud, political violence and corruption undermine democratic institutions; mafia democracy is an oxymoron. Multiparty outcomes and coalition governments are more likely to arise when voting is based on multi-member proportional representation, rather than on single electorate first past the post or preferential methods. The grasp and stability of two-party systems can also be influenced by whether voting is compulsory or voluntary. In latter cases, the voter turnout can fluctuate in unpredictable ways and result in unexpected outcomes. Parties often have a vested interest in encouraging or discouraging high turnouts.

However, the main limitation of the ice cream sellers' metaphor is that it assumes a universal human motive – that is, the desire to consume an homogenous product, ice cream. Voters in democratic political systems will behave in ways that reflect their particular interests and values with respect to the policy offerings of parties competing for their votes. Underlying these values will be moral foundations grounded in moral intuitions created by evolutionary and sociocultural forces that incline voters one way or the other. As discussed in Chapter 8, there is evidence to show that conservative parties in America tend to be more successful than liberal parties since the former are able to resonate the moral sentiments of voters across the full range of moral foundations; at least this is likely to be so in societies with a broad degree of social cohesion. However, where there are deep and wide social cleavages in society – on class, ethnic or religious lines – it may be difficult for democratic elections to result in stable governments.[14] Social polarization leads to political polarization, a 'twin peak' distribution that carries the possibility of policy stalemate, and in the extreme, can cause major civil strife and even civil war or secession. Stable liberal democratic government seems to require what Rawls terms a workable overlapping consensus on the basic institutions of government and values legitimating those 'rules of the game' (See Rawls, 2001, pp. 32–8). Both major parties in America have developed schizoid tendencies of late, represented by the rise of the libertarian right in the Republican Party and the re-emergence of a left wing populist surge in the Democratic Party (as also occurred in Britain with the election of Jeremy Corbyn as Labour leader after the 2015 UK election and the lead up to Brexit). The election of Donald Trump as US President in 2016 radically undermined normal politics in America. His victory seemed to signal a mass rejection of the rules of the political game as normally played and a craving for change – any change – in those rules. It is as if Trump promised beachgoers not a new ice cream but a new beach.

The political stresses, amounting to constitutional crisis that can afflict a polarized democratic polity were amply demonstrated in the two disruptions to politics as usual in the UK in 2014 and 2016. In the former case, Scottish voters decided by a small majority to stay in the United Kingdom but to quote the Duke of Wellington, it was a close-run thing. In the general election the following year the Scottish Nationalist Party won all but one of the Scottish seats in the British Parliament, leaving open the question of Scottish independence. Matters have been further complicated by the referendum to leave the European Union held in 2016. By an even smaller majority UK voters opted to 'leave' rather than 'remain'. 'Brexit' has divided the nation along class, regional and demographic lines of cleavage. It appears that the leave campaign successfully played to the moral foundations and deep sentiments of tribal loyalty and a particular conception of 'fairness', while upper and middle class voters in the south and especially in London regarded remaining in the EU as necessary for economic prosperity (particularly their own); for others, the question became 'whose' prosperity.[15] It may also have been the case that some people made what they believed would be a symbolic vote to leave thinking that the late opinion polls were right and that the result would be to remain. The same factor may have discouraged some remain supporters from voting. Whatever the causes the result poses major political and constitutional issues for the new British government of Theresa May, David Cameron's successor. Scotland and Northern Ireland voted solidly to remain and may seek some way of doing so, fracturing the UK union.

THE INSTITUTIONAL FRAMEWORK

The discussion so far implicitly accepts the pluralistic cast of public choice theory and mainstream political science that has drawn heavily on the model of rational decision making. Rawls, for example, quite explicitly subscribes to the pluralism associated with political scientists like Robert Dahl and the welfarist framework of orthodox economics. The separation and opposition of government and the market holds that each sphere of human endeavour operates according to a similar maximizing logic but that the market *should* prevail and government intervention *should* be strictly limited. The economy and polity, in this view, are and should remain separate spheres of social action. Policy should merely seek to remove whatever barriers there are to competitive market forces. This view rests on a simplistic and unrealistic idealization of 'the free market' and a narrative that opposes the government to the market.

The idea that markets are somehow independent of government policy is a wildly inaccurate depiction of any real world society. Karl Polanyi (1944) in *The Great Transformation* argued persuasively that markets and governments developed together in Western capitalism and form an intricate set of interrelationships that he termed market societies (not economies). Reich (2015, p. 4) more recently elaborated on this theme by stating baldly: 'There can be no "free market" without government'. More specifically: 'A market – any market – requires that governments make and enforce the rules of the game. In modern democracies, such rules emanate from legislatures, administrative agencies, and courts. Government doesn't "intrude" on the "free market". It creates the market' (ibid. p. 5). He argues that concentrating on the myth of the free market diverts attention away from the political-economic forces that determine the rules that constitute real-world market societies and structure the material and other outcomes for citizens. Instead, he claims, we *should* – an ethical imperative – focus on how the rules are set, how they change and with what consequences. This lifts analysis to a meta-level above the everyday concern with specific policies in isolation from how they are systematically determined. It raises the key question – who rules?

> The 'free market' is a myth that prevents us from examining these rule changes and asking whom they serve. The myth is therefore highly useful to those who do not wish such an examination to be undertaken. It is no accident that those with disproportionate influence over those rules, who are the largest beneficiaries of how those rules have been designed and adapted, are the most vehement supporters of the 'free market' and the most ardent advocates of the relative superiority of the market over the government (ibid. p. 6).

Reich identifies five 'building blocks of contemporary capitalism'; five arenas within which the institutional reality of market structures and processes are currently determined. These arenas are characterized by novel transformations in the nature of capitalism driven by the interlinked processes of globalization, technological innovation and 'dematerialization' or the rise of the services economy.

1. *The New Property*. Capitalism can't exist without private property rights that only legitimate governments can create and protect. To the

historically developed rights in material resources and commodities like land, physical capital and consumer products, new forms of intellectual property are changing the face of the economy and everyday life. In existing industries like chemicals and pharmaceuticals the value created and the profits appropriated increasingly depend on the ideas that drive innovation. The digital revolution has changed forever the delivery of a whole range of services from medical diagnosis and procedures to home pizza delivery. It has also spawned disruptive technologies in established industries like tourism and travel; witness the success of Uber and Airbnb. The rules established by national governments and international agreements concerning intellectual property in new and existing commodities are constantly changing as new technologies and business models point up gaps and anomalies in existing regimes.

The rules establish what can be owned, on what terms, by whom and for how long. The decisions as to these issues involve basic moral and political factors. Slavery, for example, has been outlawed in all Western democracies (including America) since the US Civil War, as a result of moral crusades empowering political campaigns. The de facto legal ownership of human beings still persists in some places and has existed *de jure* in many places since pre-classical times up to the present. In general, governments have developed elaborate legal patent processes to define what, who and for how long intellectual property is owned. Important normative debates now inform policy over what biological life forms and basic building blocks of life can be patented. The corporation as the dominant economic institution in capitalism has been progressively created by government rulings and regulations as a separate legal entity, enjoying the basic property rights of ownership, including the right to sue for breach of those rights and – in the USA – the civil right of free speech that allows unlimited political donations to favoured candidates and causes. Large multinational corporations now dominate the global economy and wield enormous power over how the property rights of the new economy unfold.

> In sum, property – the most basic building block of the market economy – turns on political decisions about what can be owned and under what circumstances. Due to the increasing wealth and political influence of large corporations, as well as the subtlety of the contours of intellectual property, these policy decisions have tended to enlarge and entrench that wealth and power. The winners are adept at playing the game. The rest of us, lacking such influence and unaware of its consequences, often lose out (ibid. p.28).

2. *The New Monopoly*. Competition is held to drive innovation and efficiency. However, firms do not compete in a vacuum. The effective degree of competition, including potential competition, is influenced by the nature of the product, the technologies available and the ease or otherwise of entering the market. Natural monopolies have long been seen to pose problems for consumers by allowing the seller to raise prices well above costs due to excessive barriers to entry stemming from economies of scale and scope and the way that networks form and operate. Government ownership or regulation is seen as a necessary antidote. As one monopoly is challenged and supplanted by another – for example, fibre optics outcompeting copper cable communications – political and legal resources are deployed to prosecute the challenger's cause against resources levied by those defending their entrenched position. This is not a neutral game played with fixed rules. The rules are part of the competitive struggle. Political lobbying and legal clashes are part of the process. The level and forms of morally acceptable and politically feasible competition are endogenously determined.

   The increasing role of intellectual property in the new economy has ratcheted up the competitive dynamics of socially constructed market power. First mover advantage, lock-in and network effects, backed by aggressive, strategic use of the patent laws grant the new monopolist with a licence to reap super-profits in the communications, biotech and agri-chemical sectors. Patented herbicides allow Monsanto to bind growers to the use of their patented genetically engineered seeds. Global monoliths like Microsoft, Apple, Google and Facebook lock users into their commercial environments, as a new market ecology displaces long existing ones. The competition is fierce, fought out in courtrooms and legislative chambers. Common tactics include threatening to sue for patent breaches and defamation, tying would-be competitors and critics up in expensive legal proceedings in which smaller parties are at an immense disadvantage against the limitless resources of their persecutors. It is far from an even battle. The major players spend as much if not more resources on advancing and defending their monopoly power as on researching and developing new and technically improved products. Much of this is wasted from the broader social viewpoint, a deadweight cost on society at large. It also marginalizes smaller enterprises, serving mainly to decide the distribution of super-profits among the giant corporations that is, among their senior executives and major shareholders, lawyers and lobbyists.
3. *The New Contracts*. Market exchanges occur through contracts – that is, by nominal agreement between parties. To function well, indeed

at all, rules must be established and enforced that determine what can and can't be exchanged, and what safeguards need to be met to prevent coercion, fraud and deceit. These rules and limits are decided by government agencies. We have already noted (in Chapter 8) Sandel's (2013) discussion of the moral limits to markets, what shouldn't be bought and sold. New technologies have created the possibility of transplanting body parts from live and dead donors to recipients. Most governments have legislated to prevent the legal offer and sale of human organs but as in many cases, an illegal market flourishes.

Animal rights activists have extended the moral arguments against markets for people to other species. In 2012 the Australian government banned the live export of cattle to Indonesia after an undercover investigation by an NGO, Animals Australia, demonstrated the existence of cruel and degrading slaughter practices in some Indonesian abattoirs. The ban was later lifted, ostensibly because the industry in both countries had (inadequately, as it turned out) reformed the management and monitoring of the supply chain. However, other factors – notably the power of vested interests and the rural lobby in parliament and the always thorny arena of relations between the two national governments – were also important. In 2016, the New South Wales state government indicated its intention to ban greyhound racing in its state after more documented revelations of animal cruelty at home and abroad was produced by Animals Australia. Within months, the government was forced to back down and effectively reverse its decision under intense lobbying from the industry and interests adversely affected by the ban. Senior members of the government also lost their cabinet posts.

The power of vested interests to defend their markets in the face of seemingly sound arguments and moral judgments for their restriction is nowhere more blatant than in America's gun industry. The National Rifle Association (NRA) has used its immense resources and political influence to stymie any effective controls over gun sales and ownership in spite of repeated mass gun killings like the Sandy Hook tragedy in which 20 children at an elementary school were shot. The NRA is arguably America's most effective lobbyist and strategic political donor, though this prize might equally be claimed by the global banks that have managed since the global credit crunch of 2008 to pass the cost of repeated bailouts to national government balance sheets and the taxpayers standing behind them.

New digital technologies dominated by giant corporations are locking consumers into markets where asymmetric information between parties makes a mockery of the notion of voluntary exchange.

The concentration of information about purchasing behaviour, mobility and communication interactions allows sellers to tweak offerings in ways designed to anticipate and direct consumer preferences. Possible alternatives are screened out. In short: 'when large corporations have disproportionate power – not only over what's sold, but also over the rules for deciding what contracts are permissible and enforceable by law – those who are relatively powerless have no choice. The "free market" is not, in this sense, free. It offers no alternative' (Reich, 2015, p. 58).[16]

4. *The New Bankruptcy*. Corporate capitalism has evolved institutions to regulate the orderly unwinding of unsuccessful ventures and rules for allocating the costs of business failure among shareholders, creditors (including the government) and customers. Just as investment and innovation would be stymied without clear rules protecting intellectual property, risk taking would atrophy without some way of cauterizing insolvent firms; and as with intellectual property, the rules covering bankruptcy have become heavily biased towards protecting the interests of the wealthy and powerful. 'Bankruptcy was designed so people could start over. But these days, the only ones starting over with ease are big corporations, wealthy moguls, and Wall Street, who have enough political clout to shape the bankruptcy laws to their needs' (Reich, 2015, p. 59).

   Bankruptcy is pre-eminently the domain of government. Legislation establishes the grounds for declaring bankruptcy, the triggers for doing so, along with the processes and safeguards involved in sorting out who can participate and what the outcome with respect to liabilities will be. The courts oversee the application of the rules and arbitrate when they are not transparently observed. Reich notes the wave of bankruptcies that now washes up against the American economy. Airlines, banks and car companies head the queue. In the case of the automobile producers, following the 2008 crisis, they were able to parlay the threat of bankruptcy and the knock-on effects to the economy of mass unemployment into securing a multi-billion dollar 'bail out' from the Federal government. Reich also argues that bankruptcy is becoming normalized, one of a string of corporate strategies for reneging on labour contracts and workers' pension entitlements.

   Arguably, the most egregious example of corporate malfeasance in recent times was the Enron saga. In this case, senior management systematically plundered the firm's assets for personal gain while propping up the semblance of solvency by raiding worker's entitlements and mining creditor gullibility, aided and abetted by shoddy accounting standards and auditing oversight. When the inevitable crash came and the bankruptcy experts arrived to clear up the mess, shareholders and creditors were wiped out and workers in the far-flung conglomerate lost their pensions and future retirement lifestyles. Although the CEO went to jail and the company Chairman died prematurely before following him, most of the cost was borne by others. The same was true of an even more outrageous fraud, the Ponzi scheme of Bernie Madoff (Henriques, 2011). These are extreme and criminal cases. Much more insidious is the way that the bankruptcy rules quietly and routinely protect the privileged in the corporate economy thanks to the institutional environment that has evolved through public policy dominated by powerful interests.

5. *The Enforcement Mechanism*. Bankruptcy regulation is only one, albeit a critical, foundation for the relatively smooth operation of a capitalist economy. Protecting property rights is the most basic foundation of the same structure. The legal enforcement rules are the continual subject of challenge and change through legislative initiative, amendment and reinterpretation. 'Every juncture in this process offers opportunities for vested interests to exert influence. And they do, continuously. They also exert influence on how all this is enforced' (ibid. p. 67). Reich presents the 'progress' of gun legislation as a paradigm case. In response to a successful suit against gun sellers and manufacturers following a mass shooting, the National Rifle Association lobbied Congress to pass the *Protection of Lawful Commerce in Arms Act (2005)* that effectively shielded the dealers and manufacturers from liability for the harm caused by their deadly products.

   Much of the routine enforcement process occurs below the surface of everyday life, beyond the radar of most people. The determinants of what is being enforced, in favour of whom and whose interests are being ignored is of little interest to people unless and until they are caught up in some way. But for the wealthy and powerful interests these issues are of prime importance to their privileged position and the object of constant attention through their legions of lawyers, lobbyists and image consultants. They are well primed to react to any development that threatens their vital interests. Keeping certain threatening issues and information out of the public domain and enforcement system is often as important to these interests as pushing for specific positive outcomes. For example, pushing regulators and the media to avoid scrutiny of unsafe plant and equipment – as in the case of outdated and dangerous nuclear power reactors – boosts corporate profits at the potential cost of disastrous future accidents (witness the Fukushima Daiichi tragedy). The BP-Halliburton oil well blow out in the Gulf of Mexico caused immense economic and environmental damage, while the torturous legal wrangling over liability drags on. Whatever compensation is finally paid out, it will only cover a fraction of the damage caused and flow to a minority of people and businesses affected; the legal and lobbying resources of the major corporate parties will see to that. Bankruptcy delivers the final threat that limits the extent to which a large company can be held commercially accountable for the harm it causes; any negotiated financial compensation will reflect the reality that past a certain point it pays the business to go bust. The rarity of senior executives being jailed is a further check on the efficacy of enforcement in the public interest.

The bias in enforcement arises from a number of sources in addition to the immense resources of large corporations, including the compliance of the mass media, the election of judges in many lower and mid-level courts (in the USA), the cozy relations (capture) built up between regulators and regulated and – most critically – the systematic and deliberate underfunding of public agencies charged with monitoring and prosecuting corporate misbehaviour and malfeasance. All these tactics were implicated in the perfect storm that led up to the global financial crisis of 2008.

James Galbraith (2009) makes a similar and, in some respects, even stronger argument for the institutional capture of what he terms 'The Predator State' by corporate and other conservative forces, aided and abetted by orthodox economics:

> Thus, the profession of an immutable and pristine faith in markets is the hallmark of conservative idealism. The market is the guarantor of freedom, while the state is its nemesis: markets good, government bad. And this perspective is more than just the position held by a handful of zealots. The achievement of conservative economics . . . has been to make it the ticket of entry into reputable political discussion, a rite of passage for anyone who wants to be taken seriously on the public stage (Galbraith, 2009, p. 21).

Galbraith goes on to argue that the increasing freedom grasped by the managerial elite to bend the organizational form of the large corporation to their own personal benefit – at the expense of shareholders, workers and everyone else – led to their capture of the state over the past 40 years. In this project they were joined and assisted by the major financial services firms – the Wall Street banks, hedge funds and mutual funds. The latter trend was buttressed by the congenial theorems of modern finance theory, notably the efficient markets hypothesis, the theory of the market for managerial control and the theology of shareholder value. These developments swamped the much broader corporate commitment of business leaders to 'the public purpose' that characterized American capitalism during the middle third of the twentieth century, a period when the large corporation embraced a multiple stakeholder rather than exclusively shareholder focus. 'This is the predatory state. It is a coalition of relentless opponents of the regulatory framework on which public purpose depends, with enterprises whose major lines of business compete with or encroach on the principal public functions of the enduring New Deal' (ibid. p. 131). Galbraith sees this powerful coalition as a self-serving class that seeks to control the state in order to, first, wind back those state functions that previously delivered the progressive social and economic reforms of the New Deal and, second, to open up those areas to extend their range of profitable activity. The conservative putsch, Galbraith claims, long ago gave up any real belief in the free market and placed their bets on controlling how markets are constituted and operate. They have no interest in shrinking the state as such, only in controlling it.[17]

In summary, it is clear from the diverse arguments presented in this chapter that representative democracies, based on one person, one vote majority rule, however institutionalized, raise questions as to who is represented, whose interests are advanced and who misses out. The question is still left hanging – provided we have some workable notion of democracy, is it worth the effort? This returns us to the basic ethical challenge.

IS DEMOCRACY DESIRABLE?

Before addressing this question directly it is worth clarifying what it is we are talking about. I have been careful to date to restrict discussion to the concept of representative democracy, since over the past two centuries this is what the term has come to mean. In fact, through history there have been many and various ideas and experiments in democracy (Keane, 2009; Sen, 2009b). The historical roots of Western democracy lie in the ancient world, the city states (more accurately, 'citizen-states') of Greece during pre-Christian times. As Paul Cartledge (2016) argues, although ancient Athens during the fifth and fourth centuries BCE is put forward as the paradigm, democracies flourished from time to time throughout the Hellenistic region, waxing and waning as the geopolitical situation varied. Cartledge also stressed the literal meaning of democracy as emanating from *demos* (the people) and *kratia* (grasp or rule). Democracy meant rule by 'the people' – that is by the poor against the wealthy. Democracy was a system of government in a class divided society of wealthy and poor citizens;[18] as such its natural opposite was oligarchy, the rule of the rich over the poor. Following Aristotle, Cartledge (ibid. p. 17; italics in original) argues:

> The real, essential distinction is not mere numbers but poverty and wealth: that is to say, democracy *is* the rule of the poor, oligarchy *is* the rule of the rich, and so much is that the case that even in a situation where the rich were *per impossible* the majority of a city's or state's citizens, Aristotle would still classify and label it an oligarchy and vice versa.

The difference between the modern and classical forms is usually cast in terms of direct or participatory versus representative democracy, and hence the attention is focused on the mechanisms of representation in the latter. It is true that social choice theory can cover collective decisions made directly at the small scale of clubs and town hall meetings but has mostly been scaled up to deal with larger polities. However, as Cartledge (and Aristotle stress), the 'real essential difference' is structural (and not purely institutional), the underlying class division between rich and poor. It is this basic fault line that has made philosophers and politicians uneasy over the past 2500 years. Aristotle was one of the first to worry about the dangers of democracy, the prospect of 'mob rule', government by the unenlightened leading to the destruction of culture. This was essentially the same worry that John Stuart Mill expressed 2000 years later and both philosophers sought to water down the pure form of the heady drink to temper the excessive zeal of the mob, to create a system of government that married aspects of both democracy and oligarchy in order to preserve the best features of both.

The classical class-based concept of democracy has disappeared in the modern era to be replaced by an exclusive concern with political equality defined by citizenship that, in turn, rests on the extension of the vote and the formal freedom to participate in the choice of government representatives and collective efforts to influence their deliberations, actions and inaction. As already noted, political theorists like John Rawls simply assume that this will occur in ways that routinely express and reinforce his meta-level principles of social justice. It is this uncritical view of real-existing liberal democracies that encourages some critics to cast Rawls as an unwitting apologist for capitalism – that is, for the underlying oligarchic rule of the relatively wealthy over the relatively poor. Even where the difference principle holds, liberal democracies are (in this view) still a cover for oligarchic inequality involving the subjection (exploitation) of the mass of the population.[19] How can this be squared with a concern for equal human dignity?

This question moves the discussion onto territory marked out by Dworkin. As discussed, in the preceding chapter, Dworkin held that the principle of dignity requires that every individual be independent from the coercive power of government in order to form his or her ethical choices; this must underlie any acceptable theory of negative liberty. But Dworkin recognizes that citizens must also accept collective decisions through their governments in other matters of justice and morality. 'That sets the stage for the question of positive liberty. I cannot be free from coercive control in matters of justice and morality, but my dignity requires that I be allowed a role in the collective decisions that exercise that control. What role might that be?' (Dworkin, 2011, p. 379).

Dworkin's answer is to oppose two models of self government. The 'majoritarian conception of democracy' – the one that we have been implicitly considering throughout this chapter – holds that self government exists when the great majority, rather than any minority, wields 'fundamental political power'. 'It therefore insists that the structures of representative government should be designed to enhance the likelihood that the community's laws and policies will be those that the largest number of citizens, after due discussion and reflection, prefer' (ibid. p. 383). The alternative 'partnership conception of democracy' requires that people act as partners in a common undertaking. This does not mean everyone having or coming to the same view on policy – as in some Rousseau-like instantiation of 'the general will' – but acting as '. . . if each accepts a standing obligation not only to obey the community's law but to try to make that law consistent with his [*sic*] good-faith understanding of what every citizen's dignity requires' (ibid. p. 284).

Dworkin argues that the majoritarian model fails to guarantee equal respect for everyone's dignity as a human being. Unequal power and influence is, within limits, compatible with the principle of dignity: '. . . arithmetic equality of influence is neither possible nor desirable, and arithmetic equality of impact is essential only so far as deviation means insult [to human dignity]' (ibid. p. 391). Further, majority rule has no special value in itself; it is not necessarily superior to other institutional arrangements. If an alternative arrangement creates greater inequality of impact (outcome) but does not attack the dignity of those who lose out, he suggests, it would be 'perverse' to rule such changes out. Inequalities of impact or outcome are legitimate if they (a) do not flow from any aristocracy of birth, gender, race or wealth and (b) do (plausibly) improve the mutual regard for the dignity of other citizens. The partnership model, he suggests, is more likely to meet these two requirements by severing the legitimate structures of representative democracy from the simple criterion of the arithmetical or aggregative calculus of individual preferences. 'Reasonable people and politicians will disagree about which structures improve the chance that the community will show equal respect and concern for all and each. But that is the test that the partnership conception offers, not the cruder mathematics of majority rule' (ibid. p. 394). Read one way, Dworkin's plea for a partnership model of other-respecting citizens signals a desire to minimize the likelihood of majority mob rule stamping on the rights (dignity) of minorities.[20]

Dworkin's bar is set very high. What happens when (some) people and politicians are not reasonable in his sense of having a well-developed moral sensibility? After all, we live in a democratic world governed by some form of majority rule. His criteria of legitimate democracy cut out precisely when they are most needed – that is when the entrenched inequalities of power and impact threaten the interests and dignity of one section of the population, either particular minorities or the majority of non-wealthy ('the poor'), both manifestations arising in liberal democratic capitalist societies. He appears to rest his hopes on a mixed constitution that formally recognizes a host of civil rights and the separation of powers, as in the United States of America – though he specifically denies that institutions such as an independent judiciary *necessarily* guarantee an acceptable outcome. Dworkin's (like Rawls's) deontological approach prioritizes right action over good outcomes in situations where right action is *not* forthcoming by some citizens.

Dworkin, Rawls and most theorists of democracy tie the concept to the rule of the nation state. Sen (2009b, Part IV), operating from a position of 'open impartiality' argues, instead that democracy and justice are intimately related through the deliberative channel of public reason that can and should be international in scope. He wishes to identify institutional and cultural barriers to the just equality of opportunity (as discussed in Chapter 9) wherever it exists and to encourage institution building and policies that reduce those barriers. Actual democratic arrangements will differ according to history, geography and culture but wherever they encourage genuine public discussion, deliberation and participation the result will likely lead to reducing injustices. Democracies are far from perfect vehicles for social justice but they are, on balance, Sen suggests, more likely than oligarchy to lessen injustice in the world.[21]

CONCLUSION

What all the theorists of justice – whether or not they operate from a social contract or social choice perspective – miss in my view, is the systematic structuring of unacceptably large inequalities of power and impact that effectively render nominally democratic societies into effective oligarchies, in the original classical sense. The way in which the rules of liberal democracies like America's are bent to favour corporate and other elites – in the ways noted by critical economists like Reich and Galbraith – raise extremely high barriers to the reduction of injustice. Nevertheless, the very inefficiencies and inadequacies of democracies in the real world open some opportunities to attack specific injustices in the spirit suggested by Sen, Reich and Galbraith. This point is followed up in Part III, after reprising the arguments to date in the next chapter.

NOTES

1. Eighteenth-century French mathematicians, notably the Enlightenment philosopher and political economists the Marquis de Condorcet, first pointed this paradox out in 1785.
2. Oxford mathematician Charles Dodson, better known under his non de plume, Lewis Carroll, coined the term 'cycle'. Dodson unknowingly rediscovered Condorcet's voting paradox and wrote a number of privately published papers on the subject of voting systems and (appropriately for the creator of *Alice in Wonderland*) their paradoxes.
3. Hausman and McPherson (2006, pp. 220–5) note that Arrow's axioms are more plausible when related to (majority) preference-based decisions. In cases where judgment-based evaluations are called for, fewer or other axioms are arguably more applicable. 'The relevance of social choice theorems to morality depends on exactly what is being aggregated, and for what purpose' (ibid. p. 223).
4. Sen (1970a) formally proves Arrow's impossibility theorem holds in cases where cardinal utility functions *without* interpersonal comparisons – that is, utilizing the techniques of modern utility theory outlined in Chapter 3 – are used instead of purely ordinal ones.
5. Borda, in fact, used tally marks to indicate preferences, so the highest score indicated the winner.
6. Substitute Ella's rankings for A and C in Table 10.2 and do the Borda count. Social transitivity holds: A>C; C>B; A>B.
7. A further factor was the halving of the quota of votes required for election due to the special circumstances of a 'Double Dissolution' of both houses of the Commonwealth Parliament.
8. I apologize in advance to the reader for including this well-worn metaphor and in particular for pushing it well beyond its normal usage. I do so because it remains a simple device for getting across a range of political phenomena without becoming bogged down in mathematical complexities that interested readers can follow up in the voluminous literature.
9. Note that if one seller unilaterally located at a point one quarter along the beach he would lose customers, since those located just over three-eights of the distance along the beach on the side of the relocating seller would switch custom to the seller remaining at the centre location. Even if A and B colluded to each locate at the quarter locations, neither would gain any more market share and each would have an incentive to 'cheat' by edging back towards the centre. As Hotelling demonstrated, cheek-by-jowl central location is both a unique and stable equilibrium.
10. Duncan Black (1948) gave a formal statement of what has been termed the 'median voter theorem', and identified its key assumptions and limitations, some of which are mentioned in what follows. Anthony Downs (1957), in his book, *An Economic Theory of Democracy* extended this analysis sparking lively debate in the emerging field of public choice theory. See also, Buchanan and Tollison (1984), Congleton (2002), Krehbiel (2004).
11. Note, however, that both sellers C and D would have an individual incentive to edge back towards the centre, squeezing A and B until the latter were forced to leapfrog C and D to the left and right in order to recapture market share. This dance would then cycle endlessly, complicated by the opportunistic efforts of new small vendors to join the fun. In fact, the chequered history of the British Liberal Party's decline since its high point

during World War I provides a clear case of being squeezed out by the Conservatives to the right and the Labour Party to the left. Despite various reincarnations and fancy-dance steps, the Liberal Party (currently known as the Liberal Democrats) – apart from its brief, recent and ill-fated coalition with the Cameron Conservative government – has once again been reduced to an irrelevant rump in the British Parliament. However, the two major parties cannot rest easily as new, more extreme elements circle seeking a foothold. Alternatively, A could move left up against C and B right against D, leaving all four with one-quarter of customers and no one in the middle. Empirically this has rarely happened suggesting that some clustering around the centre is at work in most democratic electorates. The 'apathy' or non-willingness of those to the extreme right and left to vote (walk to the nearest faraway vendor) may also entrench central tendencies.

12. It is easy to construct situations where the vendors/parties cycle with those caught in the middle are squeezed out by those to the right and left, suggesting that Hotelling's 'stability in competition depends on very high barriers to entry'.
13. Albeit that the conservative side is (normally) represented by a coalition of the dominant Liberal Party of Australia and a minor, rural and regional based National Party.
14. There may be attractive waves at both ends of the beach and poor swimming conditions in between, so that beachgoers divide themselves into two camps clustered at each end.
15. 'Remainers' or 'cosmopolites' might also be said to adhere to a broader sentiment of tribal loyalty on a European scale.
16. I discuss the layered dimensions of power in my book *The Affluent Society Revisited* (Berry, 2013, Chapter 12).
17. This suggests that the debates over 'privatization' and 'deregulation' are largely misplaced, as will be elaborated in Chapter 12.
18. Of course, the status of 'citizen' in Athens excluded most people, including women, slaves and foreigners (the definition of which changed from time to time).
19. However, Sen has argued that Rawls's discussion of 'public reason' does provide a somewhat 'thicker' concept of 'deliberative democracy' (see Sen, 2009b, pp. 324–7 for a discussion and comparison of the analysis of public reason by Rawls and Habermas).
20. Dworkin uses the telling phrase 'to protect individual rights from dangerous swings in public opinion', in the context of denying the requirement to put fundamental issues to public referenda. This is, as noted, a lasting fear in ranks of ruling elites stretching back to classical times.
21. One is here reminded of Winston Churchill's famous utterance to the British House of Commons in 1947: 'Democracy is the worst form of government, except for all those other forms that have been tried from time to time.'

11. Building a consequentialist framework

> We must be clear about the fact that all ethically oriented conduct may be guided by one of two fundamentally differing and irreconcilably opposed maxims: conduct can be oriented to an 'ethic of ultimate ends' or to an 'ethic of responsibility' (Max Weber).

PROLOGUE

Weber (1919 [1970]) penned these words in his influential essay, 'Politics as a Vocation'.[1] In it he explores the differences between political actors who espouse (or claim to espouse) a deontological commitment to action and policies judged to be 'right' in themselves regardless of the consequences for themselves and others, on the one hand, and actions and policies crafted in the belief (true or not) that certain valued outcomes will eventuate, on the other hand. In the first case politics is driven by righteous intention. In the second case, by the calculation or at least expectation of particular outcomes.

Weber was writing in the disastrous aftermath of World War I, when a defeated and starving Germany faced revolutionary upheaval and violent reaction. He was, understandably, impatient with the ideological extremes expressed by revolutionary socialists and right wing nationalists, each energized by an opposing conception of the right, a chaotic political situation in which each faction focused on (violent) means to progress their vision of a vaguely desired future. Weber's concern was that neither faction seemed to care about what the likely consequences of their rhetoric and actions would be in the actual historical circumstances that existed at the time. This he saw as an extreme example of an ever present danger in politics – the possibility that the logic of the situation in which opposing views of the right clashed would lead unintentionally to unforeseen and unwanted outcomes. He criticized politicians (and their experts and advisers) for prioritizing means over ends, believing that the latter would take care of themselves as long as the former were ethically grounded in a deontological sense, and called for those who would make politics their life work to profess their vocation in the cool light of awareness of the complex outcomes their actions (and inactions) would contribute to.

He gave as an example of an intransigent actor, the syndicalist whose violent acts can be shown unambiguously to lead to consequences the very opposite of their intended outcome.

> You may demonstrate to a convinced syndicalist, believing in an ethic of ultimate ends, that his action will result in increasing the opportunities of reaction, in increasing the oppression of his class, and obstructing its ascent – and you will not make the slightest impression upon him. If an action of good intent leads to bad results, then, in the actor's eyes, not he but the world, or the stupidity of other men, or God's will who made them thus, is responsible for the evil. (Weber, 1919 [1970] p.125).

The person who subscribes to an ethic of responsibility, on the other hand does not seek to pass responsibility for what occurs to someone or something else but in so far as he or she can foresee the consequences as resulting from his or her actions will accept the fact. To have acted intentionally according to a particular set of values does not for the latter actor release him or her from ethical responsibility for the actual outcomes to which those actions contributed, whether or not those consequences were foreseen or (un)intended.

Weber, however, is aware that power in the hands of mortals corrupts. Leaders are beset by vanity and hubris. This is dangerous to citizens because government officials hold the reins of legitimate force; they operate with the legitimate means of violence at their elbows. Ideally, successful leaders must be cognizant of both the antagonistic ethics of ultimate ends and responsibility, to lead by recognizing the normative and affective currents in human nature that influence the behaviour of their subjects, colleagues and themselves, while implementing policies that can, on sober reflection, achieve desired ends. He or she must also recognize the inconsistencies and 'paradoxes' thrown up by the ethical antagonisms faced in real life politics – powerfully stated in the following long passage:

> Whoever wants to engage in politics at all, and especially in politics as a vocation, has to realize these ethical paradoxes. He must know that he is responsible for what may become of himself under the impact of these paradoxes. I repeat, he lets himself in for the diabolic forces lurking in all violence . . . Surely, politics is made with the head, but it is certainly not made with the head alone. In this the proponents of an ethic of ultimate ends are right. One cannot prescribe to anyone whether he should follow an ethic of absolute ends or an ethic of responsibility, or when the one and when the other. One can say only this much: If in these times, which, in your opinion, are not times of 'sterile' excitation – excitation is not, after all, genuine passion – if now suddenly the *Weltanschauungs* politicians crop up *en masse* and pass the watchword, 'The

> world is stupid and base, not I,' 'The responsibility for the consequences does not fall upon me but upon the others whom I serve and whose stupidity or baseness I shall eradicate,' then I declare frankly that I would first inquire into the degree of inner poise backing this ethic of ultimate ends. I am under the impression that in nine out of ten cases I deal with windbags who do not fully realize what they take upon themselves but who intoxicate themselves with romantic sensations. From a human point of view this is not very interesting to me, nor does it move me profoundly. However, it is immensely moving when a *mature* man – no matter whether old or young in years – is aware of a responsibility for the consequences of his conduct and really feels such responsibility with heart and soul. He then acts by following an ethic of responsibility and somewhere he reaches the point where he says: 'Here I stand; I can do no other.' That is something genuinely human and moving. And every one of us who is not spiritually dead must realize the possibility of finding himself at some time in that position. In so far as this is true, an ethic of ultimate ends and an ethic of responsibility are not absolute contrasts (but rather supplements) which only in unison constitute a genuine man – a man who *can* have the 'calling for politics.' (Weber, 1919 [1970] pp. 125–7).

Weber, delivering this lecture-essay in 1919, looked ahead ten years and pessimistically foresaw a period of political turmoil and reaction. This was prescient. The future was to become reality with devastating consequences for Germany and the world, sweeping away the moderate liberal polity that Weber hoped for.

Weber's contemporary, Émile Durkheim, also stressed the affective/normative basis to social action and, in particular, the role of religious belief and practice in creating social solidarity. Leaders drew on their society's dominant religious and ethical values to impose their rule. Modern capitalist societies in which mass populations and a pronounced division of labour predominated posed special political challenges. Social institutions, norms and policies reinforcing common citizenship were necessary to offset the fracturing tendency for individuals to seek belongingness in smaller familial, tribal or ethnic collectivities. Politics necessarily had to bridge the conflicting ethical and religious schisms that were 'social facts', Durkheim's term for a collective or macro-reality that was more than the simple aggregation of individual behavioural (choice) situations.

The third founder of sociology, Karl Marx, offered a radically different perspective. Social divisions were structurally embedded via broad class location. The values and beliefs of people in subservient classes were conditioned by the material interests and power of those in the dominant or ruling class, in capitalist as in earlier societies (modes of production). Like Durkheim and unlike Weber, Marx eschewed methodological individualism. But contra Durkheim, he saw class divisions as unbridgeable, social peace and solidarity as temporary lulls between revolutionary storms. Subject classes could only achieve their real interests and realize their authentic values by politically overthrowing their oppressors. Public policies for Marx meant organizing and deploying politically the means for revolutionary action. In part, this required throwing off the ruling values and norms and intellectual rationales that propped up the ruling class hegemony. In the capitalism of the day, Marx saw classical political economy as a prime culprit in normalizing the class power and position of capitalists.[2]

In their very different ways, the three founders of sociology raised the opposition of morality and power, questioning the role of ethics and political action in public policy. The next section reviews how modern economics that, as noted in Part I, emerged at roughly the same time, addressed this problematic, drawing on arguments presented in Part II. The remainder of the chapter then develops an alternative consequentialist framework for evaluating policy in the light of power.

ORTHODOX ECONOMICS AND THE VALUE/POWER QUESTION

It was pointed out in Chapter 1 and detailed in Chapters 5, 6 and 7 that neoclassical economics confined its analytic gaze to exploring the aggregated consequences of the resource use of individuals acting rationally – that is, according to the austere axioms of modern utility theory. In employing an 'engineering' approach that separated positive from normative analysis, economists believed themselves to be adopting a technical role devoid of ethical content. Such would be the case if and only if the ethic they subscribed to was one of ultimate ends – the end here being to honour at all costs (that is, regardless of outcomes) their status of independent professional expert.[3] Like an engineer designing a bridge but not concerned with where it crosses the river and who it serves, the professional economist's role would be to inform government decision makers as to the most efficient means of achieving ends determined by others, both through markets and where markets fail by way of government intervention.[4] It is sometimes difficult to determine whether academic economists are interested in anything other than demonstrating their technical command of the common tools of their trade. However, even the most 'pure' proponents of their craft feel fully entitled to add their voices in support of particular policies that have demonstrable outcomes at odds with their models' predictions. If, as Milton Friedman (1953) famously claimed, the proof of the pudding is not in the ingredients but in the cake's taste, the economist's larder is indeed bare.[5]

This hard division between positive and normative analysis has not withstood the multiple critiques levelled over recent decades by (some) economists, philosophers and those from other social sciences. The division has been attacked on both positive and normative grounds. First, as Sen and others have argued, the tendency to reduce individual decision makers to calculating machines concerned primarily if not exclusively to further/maximize their own interests misses the avalanche of empirical evidence that real people do not normally act in this way, even when engaging in basic economic activities like buying goods and services and turning up for work. Second, as stressed in Chapter 8, the concept of allocative efficiency drawn upon smuggles in ethical precepts implicitly justifying particular (that is, inegalitarian) consequences. Moreover, by courtesy of a variant of the Marshallian fudge, the policy advice of economists follows an 'as if' path; 'markets are not perfect but policy should be cast as if they were'. In most cases this means recommending policies that 'deregulate' real world markets or seek to mimic what markets would have been, in spite of the value biases built into tools like cost–benefit analysis and the internal theoretical incoherence uncovered by the theory of the second best. More will be said further on about these key points.

THE ONTOLOGICAL AND METHODOLOGICAL LIMITATIONS OF NEOCLASSICAL ECONOMICS

It is clear from the arguments presented in Chapter 8 that the decisions, including the economic decisions, of individuals are materially affected by the values and other normative judgments held.[6] Those values and judgments have deep evolutionary roots in human nature according to moral psychologists like Jonathan Haidt. Behavioural and other heterodox economists have also stressed the cognitive limits to super-rational decision making required by the orthodox paradigm. Other social scientists stress the need to break the bonds of an extreme methodological individualism and situate the decisions making of individuals within the collective institutional contexts that condition the resulting behaviours and the values underpinning them.

Etzioni (1990) has developed what he terms an 'I-We' paradigm to move towards a 'bi-utility' framework in which people seek utility defined as 'pleasure' (Sidgwick's 'agreeable consciousness'?) *and* 'satisfaction' derived by acting according to (driven by) moral conviction, a deeply felt commitment to what is right. The two motives to act can be antagonistic; acting according to moral commitment can result in personally unpleasurable outcomes, which is why the term 'satisfaction' in the preceding sentence is problematic. Moral commitment and utility as pleasure or satisfaction are seemingly contradictory states, at least when the former values are genuinely felt and encapsulated in the individual's actions (rather than being an unreflective nod to conformity with dominant values). Etzioni refers to two moral psychologies of behaviour: neoclassical psychology stresses the role of external stimuli in orienting individuals to act in 'expected' ways in order to be rewarded by social approval; 'deontological' psychology assumes that in some circumstances people will act because they are compelled to by their moral convictions, regardless of whether or not this sparks external approval. He argues that an adequate 'socio-economics' must encompass both psychological fonts of human action, moving away from the formalistic idealization of rationality prevalent in the models of neoclassical economics. 'Hence, a technically precise formulation is: People systematically and significantly behave differently to the extent that their behavior is motivated by moral commitments rather than pleasure' (Etzioni, 1990, p. 67).

Once attention is directed to the determination of *both* the ends and means of action, the role of institutions in influencing both cannot be hived off as someone else's object of study. Both the ends to which resources are directed and the means chosen to reach them are socially constructed. They are co-determined in specific social contexts. The familial, neighbourhood, and broader social collectivities to which he or she belongs – the evolving product of 'the intersection of biography and history', in the words of the sociologist C. Wright Mills – will influence each person's goal-directed actions. Etzioni argues that '. . . people seek a *balance* between their moral commitments and their pleasures (a judicious 'mix') rather than seeking to 'maximize' either' (ibid. p. 67; italics in original). At the individual psychological level, this balance seeking is both ongoing and, to the extent that the requirements of pleasure and duty collide, conflict generating.[7] Various strategies for resolving such conflicts are perfected, on the basis of both inherited human traits and socially acquired skills. These strategies operate at varying levels of consciousness and include various biases, heuristics or rules of thumb identified by behavioural economists. They often entail the deployment of defence mechanisms, false consciousness and cognitive dissonance.

The idea of a precarious balance and judicious mix of motives for human behaviour is uncontroversial for most social scientists – indeed, most people. It sits well with the Weberian notion of an ethical mix of ultimate ends and responsibility directing the work of the 'mature' political participant. However, it clashes with the insistence of an austere, formalistic, atomistic view of the individual presenting in rational choice theory. The latter, narrowly defined, does offer a clear explanation of economic behaviour, albeit a manifestly inadequate one. To assume that all actors are rigorously self-interested in their own pleasures or utility, allows one to derive non-trivial conclusions, even if they are wrong. By progressively expanding the individuals' sources of utility to include other people's pleasures moves the analysis towards reality but at the expense of emptying it of explanatory value. In the extreme – the world of revealed preference theory – when no attention is paid to the differentiating subjective drivers of choice, theory loses all explanatory content.[8] It is what it is (so there!). Utility has become a formal, empty black box. 'From a methodological viewpoint, the all-inclusive expansion of the concept of utility violates the rules of sound conceptualization. Once a concept is defined so that it encompasses *all* the incidents that are members of a given category (in the case at hand, the motives for all human activity), it ceases to enhance one's ability to explain' (ibid. p. 27; italics in original).[9]

By expanding the model of decision making to include normative and affective factors, Etzioni is able to move away from the individualist cast of neoclassical economics and to increase the explanatory reach of the analysis. He specifically rejects the implicit reductionism of accounts (like Haidt's, described in Chapter 8) that ground the evolution of moral foundations at the level of individual and group selection. Following the work of anthropologists and sociologists like Durkheim, he stresses the role of 'genuine altruism' (what I previously called 'asymmetric altruism') in influencing the manner and consequences of social interaction and cohesion. The idea that genuine altruism and other forms of other-directed moral actions are, in the last resort, only explicable in tit-for-tat terms is either an act of faith or, dependent on an evolutionary rationale and, thus, subject to what has been termed 'the adaptationist fallacy' (Gould, 2002, pp. 42–4). Moreover, such reductionist conclusions have both implied ethical force and express the power of dominant interests – whatever exists is natural (could not have been otherwise) and thus good. During the Thatcher government in Britain this crude rationale was termed TINA – there is no alternative. Etzioni's moral economic philosophy (and that of Smith, Sen and others) opens the analysis of social and economic questions and policy to serious ethical and political consideration.

> The neoclassical position that preferences are revealed in behavior and hence there is no need to study how they are formed or changed, introduces a major value judgment into neoclassical economic theory . . . By arguing that the market best serves people's preferences, 'what the individual wants', economists disregard the fact that preferences are to a significant extent socially formed and hence reflect the society's values, culture and power structure . . . (Etzioni, 1990, pp. 246–7).

THE POLITICAL MOMENT

In Chapter 10, I discussed the work of Reich and (James) Galbraith identifying their stress on the systematic use of political power to define the very terms on which 'competition' between producers occurs in contemporary capitalism.[10] The ideology of competition, deriving from the normative charge supplied by the Pareto principle, is, they claim, largely a cover for the efforts of large corporations and their conservative political allies to overcome it, to 'abandon' the rigours and risks of real competition for a pale imitation. By twisting policies to favour their commercial interests and blocking policies that would threaten those interests, corporate capitalism ensures a comfortable environment in which to operate, while all the time professing to champion free markets.

The tendency of large corporate organizations to control or at least deflect the policies of government has been well documented over a long period. In an earlier book, Reich (2008) stressed the enhanced role of political action committees (PAC) and consultant lobbyists, in addition to direct campaign funding, bribery and the promise of future job opportunities, in ensuring compliant government. Gilens (2012) has provided detailed empirical evidence of the strong association of 'affluence and influence'. Hacker and Pierson (2010) note the 'winner-take-all' nature of American politics and, in particular, the built-in tendency for 'policy drift' and stalemate, making it easy for dominant interests to filter out policies that would harm their interests. These filters and blockages were much in evidence during the running stand-off between Republican controlled Congress and the Executive arm of government during the Obama presidency. The significance of 'negative power', the ability to exclude issues from public scrutiny and deliberation, has long been seen to characterize power relations in liberal democratic societies. 'The mobilization of bias' (Schattschneider, 1960) figures as the central theme in the process of 'non decision making', what Lukes (1974) termed 'the second dimension of power'.[11]

Bachrach and Baratz (1970, pp. 43–4) define the mobilization of bias in a political system as:

> . . . a set of predominant values, beliefs, rituals and institutional procedures ('rules of the game') that operate systematically to the benefit of certain persons and groups at the expense of others. Those who benefit are placed in a preferred position to defend and promote their vested interests. More often than not, the 'status quo defenders' are a minority or elite group within the population in question. Elitism, however, is neither foreordained nor omnipresent . . .

In fact, the last sentence is problematic. In societies where privilege and power go hand in hand and are inscribed in the very institutional or class structure, elitism, defined as the *entrenched* dominance of a minority, *is* omnipresent. '. . . the bias of the system is not sustained simply by a series of individual acts, but also, most importantly, by the socially structured and culturally patterned behavior of groups, and practices of institutions, which may indeed be manifested by individuals' inaction' (Lukes, 1974, p. 21–1). This takes the analysis to a third dimension, the power embedded in social structures to routinely and unconsciously mould the views, values and self-perceived interests of the majority of people to support outcomes favouring the privileged minority.[12] Orthodox economics and the policy advice of most economists – focused on the supposed level playing field of free markets – provide part of the moulding or mass socializing processes by which the real interests of the favoured few trump the real interests of the many. The outcomes appear in the growth of inequality and economic insecurity, the increase in social isolation and exclusion, the heightened sense of alienation and disenchantment, the rise in violence, crime and despair, the depreciation of public assets and civility, the despoliation of the natural environment, in other words, the triumph of the 1 per cent (Dorling, 2014, 2015).

Etzioni also addresses the interpenetration of markets and policy, of government and the economy. To the familiar analysis of economic power and market structure – the capacity of large producers to dominate small producers and individual consumers – he argues that we need to understand the 'interventionist power' of economically powerful organizations to bias government policy and how the two loci of power reinforce each other. Thus, not only do oligopolistic corporations influence and benefit from the rules and policies (and inactions or non decisions) of government, but also the latter reinforce or enhance market concentration and power. This dynamic has become even more pronounced in the decades since Etzioni's book was published in the ways noted by Reich, discussed in Chapter 10. Etzioni (ibid. Chapter 13) proposed an interesting typology of economic (market) and interventionist power but leaves it at a 'flat', formalistic level. He makes no attempt to establish which of the forms of interpenetration are primary and which subsidiary. Nor does he move beyond the business firm (large and small) as the organizational vehicle for the expression of market and political power.[13] In short, he ignores Lukes's second and third dimensions of power, implicitly adopting the pluralist paradigm that dominated American political science of his day. Since then, the unevenness of the playing field has become even more obvious and the sources of 'countervailing power' – in trade unions, small business and trade associations, consumer groups and community groups – have atrophied to a significant degree.[14]

AN ETHICAL FRAME FOR A 'COMPREHENSIVE CONSEQUENTIALISM'

This final section attempts to outline a framework for ethically assessing the roles of government and the policy process, where 'process' refers to both the means by which policies are determined, and implemented, and the outcomes arising. I draw here on Amartya Sen's conceptualization of an extended or comprehensive consequentialist ethic (previously discussed), one that does not directly oppose consequentialist and deontological views of how individuals should act either directly or through collective/institutional avenues. In other words, people in ordinary life, officials in government and economists and others advising them have moral commitments that influence their behaviours with various consequences that can impact on ethical judgments about how each should act. To repeat:

> There is no particular reason to insist on an impoverished account of a state of affairs in evaluating it. In particular, the state of affairs, or the outcome in the context of the choice under examination, can incorporate processes of choice, and not merely the narrowly defined ultimate result. The content of outcomes can also be seen as including all the personal and impersonal relations that may be seen as important in the decision problem at hand (Sen, 2009b, p. 215).

Sen, as noted, distinguishes between 'culmination' and 'comprehensive' outcomes. The former refer only to the ultimate results of choices, actions or decisions; the latter encompass the entirety of the social process by which ultimate outcomes occur – namely, with what Sen terms 'social realizations'. Utilitarianism provides an extreme example of an unmediated concern with ultimate outcomes and leaves itself open to deontological critiques about rights transgressions in getting there. 'Anything goes' strikes most people as an unattractive ethical stance from which to live and evaluate life. Other narrow consequentialist approaches that invoke some notion of 'welfarism' also run up against the issue of insufficient sensitivity to the validity of the means used to achieve it. It is easy to propose examples of trade-offs that outrage the moral intuitions of most people – for example, is it acceptable to eat babies during a famine, if this is the only way for some members of the community to survive?[15]

It is necessary at this point to stress the difference between the role of normative factors in behaviour and ethical judgments about the social realizations resulting. When Etzioni claims to be developing 'a deontological social science',[16] he is in fact arguing for the inclusion of moral and affective factors in *explaining* social outcomes. His book is, in essence, a plea for comprehensive consequentialist enquiry, as opposed to the narrow consequentialist models of neoclassical economics. One is still left with the ethical challenge of justifying *which comprehensive outcomes* are good. Although Etzioni (1990, p. 13) claims to be taking a 'moderate deontological' position with consequences considered as a secondary consideration, his analysis throughout reverses the order. Explanation in the light of a realistic account of human decision making, including the salience of power relations, assumes centre stage. His is a 'wide' study of human behaviour in and of society. Nowhere does he focus *explicitly* on ethics as opposed to morality. Even after reading the final chapter on 'policy and moral implications' one is left wondering what distinguishes for Etzioni good policy from bad policy, other than realistic from unrealistic explanations of social outcomes. Of course, as with all social scientists it is possible to glean implicit value judgments and ethical commitments in his work; for example, he is sympathetic to communitarian values and political action from a broadly Millian liberalism.[17]

In what follows, I suggest a comprehensive consequentialist framework for evaluating behaviour and policy that includes rights and duties as secondary (instrumental) constraints requiring judgment within the frame in relation to the explicitly stated (if often ambiguous in application) goal of reducing real-existing injustices. In short, contra-Etzioni and pro-Sen, I offer a 'moderate but comprehensive consequentialist' ethical position. Several elements can be distinguished at the outset:

1. Good (and bad) acts and policies emerge in socio-political situations that constrain knowledge of what is happening, to whom and why. Individuals act within the confines of their beliefs, knowledge, interests and contingent social location. Intention and outcome are often dissociated and actions subject to iterative correction.
2. Moral convictions (held with varying degrees of strength) influence actions and can be reinforced or ameliorated through social interaction over time. These convictions both help to define the good to be advanced and to operate as constraints or limits on its pursuit. Thus, for example, societies in which egalitarian values figure prominently, will likely favour sharing behaviours and policies and discourage egoistic ones. Conversely, in societies favouring traditional hierarchical order, behaviours, judgments and policies that express and reinforce duty, deference and respect and deny dissent will persist.
3. It is unnecessary to insist that in evaluating the social realizations of behaviours and policies that everyone must adopt the same ethical position (Sen, 2009b, pp. 219–20). Good overall outcomes are negotiated in the light of the values predominating in the society at hand, as are the means utilized to achieve them. Hence:

4. In a particular situation, some means will be categorically ruled out by some or most people as morally unacceptable because to do so forms part of the good to be realized. For example, a prohibition on murder reflects the individual and social evaluation that a society that allowed or encouraged it would be less good than one in which the practice was denied: some people will internalize the prohibition as an absolute moral imperative entailing a duty to desist from practicing it.[18]
5. The narrow consequentialist (especially utilitarian) injunction to maximize the good is unnecessary, even self-contradictory, when considering comprehensive social realizations. Trading off competing and incommensurate values defining good comprehensive outcomes is the order of the day, both for individuals and policy makers. Hence, to support the ethical force of (some) rights in some situations is not to do so on deontological but instrumental grounds. For example, a collective commitment to the right of free speech will in many if not most circumstances lead to outcomes most people would judge 'good', partly by reducing the opportunities for authoritarian rule. However, under some situations such as wartime emergency, free speech might legitimately be constrained or suspended.[19] Just because we deny the ethical force of absolute rights/duties under *all* circumstances, regardless of the manifold consequences – the deontologists' position – this does not imply that rights-constrained judgments are invalid under *some* (indeed many) circumstances.

Before dealing with the obvious criticism that such an approach collapses the ethical project into some form of relativism, it is worth noting that the approach just outlined has some parallels to the considerations of pragmatist naturalist ethics,[20] especially the views of John Dewey and Hilary Putnam.

> Dewey urged that we make no sharp distinction between moral deliberation and proposals for change in sociopolitical institutions or in education . . . He saw changes in individual attitudes, in public policies and in strategies of acculturation as three interlinked aspects of the gradual development of freer and more democratic communities, and of the better sort of human being who would develop within such communities' (Rorty, 2005, p. 839).

By denying a sharp distinction between fact and value pragmatists like Putnam '. . . holds that our moral judgments are no more and no less "objective" than our scientific theories, and no more and no less rationally adopted' (ibid. p. 840). Like the pragmatists (and against Dworkin and Rawls) I argue against the coherence of an insistence on universalistic truth in ethics. The good and the right are situationally conditional. Good public policy, in particular, must (in this view) result in good overall outcomes taking into account the values, interests and constraints defining the real world-as-we-find-it *and* the real-world-as-we-would-like-it-to-be. The latter is inherently contestable – in both the realms of ethics and social practice – and no guidebook exists by which to get there. However, following Sen (see comments in Chapter 9 and below) I suggest that good policy seeks to reduce the mismatch between the rhetoric of equal opportunities for people to convert primary resources like income into the ability 'to do the things he or she has reason to value' and the reality of unequal capacities to do so. Emphasis is here placed on the imperative to *reduce* inequalities of opportunities to achieve such outcomes, in full recognition of the wide field of consequences specific policies will spark. It is not a case that anything will do or that policy will actually succeed in its aims. Particular means will be found unacceptable in virtually all circumstances, calling for 'strong' value constraints to be propagated and internalized. Unexpected and undesired outcomes will need to be taken into account and policies adjusted as part of the overall policy frame. Nor will it be practically possible to reduce all sources of unequal opportunity in a particular historically specific situation; political choices will need to be made based on judgments as to the relative value of reducing particular inequalities in that situation at that time. Increasing *effective* freedom to choose means and ends is a vital condition for just institutional arrangements and policy interventions; and with freedom comes responsibility:

> Freedom to choose gives us the opportunity to decide what we should do, but with that opportunity comes the responsibility for what we do – to the extent that they are chosen actions. Since a capability is the power to do something, the accountability that emanates from that ability – that power – is a part of the capability perspective, and this can make room for demands of duty – what can be broadly called deontological demands (Sen, 2009b, p. 19).

Sen argued that liberal democracies offered the best chance for accepting the ethical case for moving towards equalizing the people's opportunities to realize their cherished aims in life. This was also, broadly speaking the position of pragmatists like Dewey and Putnam for whom 'human flourishing' was most likely in societies that were free, democratic and tolerant.[21] But likelihood is not a guarantee. As argued at length in Chapter 10, democracies are paradoxical beasts and conflicts and contradictory outcomes are prevalent. More fundamentally, a full and comprehensive focus on social realizations necessarily entails an awareness of inequalities of power in the three dimensions stressed by Lukes, including those anchored in pervasive class and gender structures, and an ethic of responsibility cannot ignore the possibility of reaction leading to widening inequalities of opportunities (and worse), as Weber warned.

CONCLUSION

This chapter has sought to distinguish the role of moral and other normative/affective factors in determining how people behave in society from ethical judgments of the rightness and goodness of that behaviour, by directing attention to the 'wide consequences' resulting. Contra-Etzioni and pro-Sen, I argue that actions and policies must be evaluated (not just explained) by explicitly considering the extent to which they are likely to reduce currently existing inequalities of opportunities for all human beings, alive and not yet born, to flourish.[22] The intellectual hegemony of neoclassical economics in public policy over the past 40 or 50 years has helped create a range of (comprehensive) outcomes that have systematically intensified inequalities of opportunities in liberal democracies like the United States of America, the United Kingdom and elsewhere in the West. In Part III, I focus on developments over this period that demonstrate the degree to which this has happened. Attention is directed to processes of privatization, 'financialization', increasing economic inequality and crises observed in the environment and the forced mass movement of people. Finally, I return to the overarching issue of the 'hollowing out' of our democratic societies as a focal consequence of the developments identified. The approach, following Sen, is comparative rather than transcendental.

NOTES

1. This is, perhaps, the most famous essay in political sociology. In it Weber provides his definition of the state as the holder of a monopoly of the legitimate use of violence and propounds the three bases of a political leader's authority.
2. The so-called 'fourth volume'; of *Capital – Theories of Surplus Value* – published after his death, demonstrates his serious intent in this context. *Capital* itself was an attempt to turn the tools of classical political economy against itself and undermine the society, which, in Marx's view, they legitimated.
3. A similar discipline-blind ethic of ultimate ends is implicit in J. Robert Oppenheimer's retrospective comments about developing the atom bomb to the effect that 'when you see something that is technically sweet, you go ahead and do it and you argue about what to do about it only after you have had your technical success' (quoted in Sen, 2009b, p.211).
4. The problem with this analogy for orthodox economists is that it points up the obvious fact that their models, unlike most bridges, did fall down in 2008 (see next note below).
5. The metaphor is mine. What Friedman actually argued was that economics was not to be overly concerned with the realism of assumptions and, hence with the plausibility of the explanations offered, but should (note the value proposition) focus on the accuracy of the predictions generated by the models developed. It has been pointed out on many occasions that, based on this criterion, orthodox economics continually fails. One has only to recall the confused, totally bewildered looks on the faces of the world's leading economists and economic policy makers on the morning after the collapse of Lehman Brothers to get the point. This pattern would not be so problematic if the collective

voices of orthodoxy were not so dominant in policy making – or if one did not subscribe to an ethic of responsibility.

6. As Sen (1987, p. 19) pithily notes: 'The real issue is whether there is a plurality of motivations, or whether self-interest alone drives human beings'.
7. 'Stress is inherent in the deontological individual, in being a socio-economic person, because the balance between pleasure and moral conduct is not achieved once and for all. Rather as in riding a bicycle, individuals continuously correct tendencies to tilt excessively in one direction or the other' (Etzioni, 1990, p. 85). Etzioni's two-factor model of human nature has strong continuities with the positions of David Hume and Adam Smith outlined in Chapter 2.
8. Etzioni (ibid. p. 29) refers to the formal treatment of utility as 'the great X': 'It is merely a common denominator, an X, into which all other values can be converted or by which a rank-ordering can be achieved'.
9. No invocation of 'Ockham's razor' or the claimed theoretical benefits of parsimony can justify reliance on tautology in analysing complex social reality. There are strong arguments against parsimony in attempting to understand how economies work (see Hirschman, 1984, for a classic argument along these lines).
10. In this, James Galbraith is extending the work of his father who argued in a stream of books, most particularly *The New Industrial State*, that the managers of large corporations are in the driving seat of the modern capitalist economy.
11. The classic political study of non decision making (in relation to policies to control urban air pollution) is presented in Crenson (1971).
12. 'Indeed, is it not the supreme exercise of power to get another or others to have the desires you want them to have – that is, to secure their compliance by controlling their thoughts and desires' (Lukes, 1974, p. 23).
13. An important source of soft power resides in the strategic monopoly of policy advice wielded by neoclassical economists. As James Galbraith (2009, p. 21) notes: 'The achievement of conservative economics . . . has been to make it the ticket of entry into reputable political discussion, a rite of passage for anyone who wants to be taken seriously on the public stage.'
14. Reich (2015, Part III) discusses these developments in detail. See also my discussion of John Kenneth Galbraith's original account of the concept of countervailing power in the context of his later analysis and recent real world developments (Berry, 2013, Chapter 12).
15. Dr Johnston, after all, did mischievously suggest eating babies as a solution to recurrent famines in Ireland.
16. This is explicitly stated in the title to Part I of his book.
17. cf.: 'Suffice it to note here that structural changes, especially toward a more responsive community, require more than knowledge or even consensus; they often entail mobilization of power by those who are keen on change, to overcome the opposition of those committed to the status quo, as reflected in the civil rights, women's and environmentalist and Progressive movements' (Etzioni, 1990, p. 245). However, in the sentences after this glimpse of pink, he retracts by denying that those seeking change are *necessarily right*, harking back to the need for a realistic *explanatory* theory.
18. Language and meaning matter here: what is murder to some will be justifiable homicide to others, and the distinction may vary over time and depending on the specific circumstances. Thus, for conservatives, abortion may be treated ethically as murder and capital punishment as lawful killing, while liberals may reverse the judgment. Tricky conceptual problems arise when discussing notions of killing in self-defence. This latter issue has arisen in America in relation to the spate of killings of black citizens by the police.
19. Of course, the onus would be on those promoting such constraints to consider the prospects for such moves to be prolonged past their necessity.
20. 'The classical pragmatists saw themselves responding to Darwin in the same way as the great philosophers of the seventeenth and eighteenth centuries had responded to Galileo and Newton' (Rorty, 2005, p. 842).

21. 'For Dewey, the pragmatist who speculated most daringly, and developed the greatest historical self-consciousness, the glory of human beings is their ability to become citizens of a liberal-democratic society; of a community which constantly strives to see beyond its own limits – both with an eye to the inclusion of presently excluded or marginalized human beings and with respect to innovative intellectual and artistic initiatives' (Rorty, 2005, p. 843).
22. The inclusion of future generations in the ethical calculus raises a host of conceptual and practical issues for policy makers and advisers, operating with the extended, comprehensive consequentialist approach suggested here. This is even more the case when the ethical scope of evaluation is widened to include non-human species. Intergenerational inequalities of opportunity arise most particularly in considerations of long-term consequences of current natural resource uses and technologies and the impacts on natural environments and eco-systems. They also concern issues around savings and the non-depletion of accumulated capital resources. Concern with consequences for non-humans normally assumes an 'animal rights' perspective that can be dealt with in either deontological or consequentialist terms. Likewise, environmental and animal rights issues can be treated from an anthropological, human-centred or a decentred naturist perspective. These are large and important concerns, deserving of extensive separate treatment. They are not pursued further in this book.

PART III

Outcomes

12. Privatization

> Sometime during the 1980s, a major international political movement was born. Led by Great Britain, scores of nations began – or considered – selling publicly owned enterprises to private corporations or shareholders (Feigenbaum, Henig and Hamnett).

CONTEXT

The post-World War II era ended in August 1971 when President Richard Nixon ordered the suspension of the US dollar into gold at its fixed rate of $35 per ounce. Thus crumbled the cornerstone of the world's international monetary system, set up by the victorious allies in the latter stages of the War. The system had come under increasing strain as the American government fought the war on poverty at home and the North Vietnamese abroad. The massive growth in government spending on defence and social programmes unleashed inflationary forces that rippled through the other advanced economies. France, West Germany and Switzerland, sought to shore up their flailing fortunes by swapping their growing holdings of dollar reserves for gold, the stock of which was running out in America. In the emerging unstable new world of imperfectly floating exchange rates, international geopolitical turmoil and the surprising appearance of 'stagflation', rising unemployment chasing high inflation, the post-war social pacts between capital and labour, and government and the private sector, broke down.

At the political level, conservative forces were gathering and beginning to challenge the liberal, broadly social democratic Keynesian consensus that had underpinned rapid economic growth and prosperity for the middle and working classes through the middle third of the century. In the USA, these political currents had strengthened and come together as the Republican Party recovered after the debacle of the 1964 presidential election, resulting in Nixon's victory in 1968. During that critical four-year period, a combination of lagging living standards, racial tension, vocal anti-war agitation and rising crime drove the electorate to the right. The liberal moment had passed in America. For the next 40 years the two major parties would lurch rightwards towards the 'extreme centre'

(Ali, 2015). As noted in Chapter 10, the institutional and cultural foundations of countervailing power tottered and the class interests of the rich and powerful would prevail, buoyed by the populist disdain for government encouraged by the ideology and economics of free markets, and the individualist culture buttressed by American exceptionalism and the Protestant ascendency.[1]

Government's overall role in the economy did not, in fact decline during this period; it did, however, change its form. The rules determining how markets operated systematically favoured powerful minorities associated with business, the military-industrial complex, bureaucracies and the professions, forming what I will call the dominant and upper middle classes, roughly the wealthiest 10 per cent in the land.[2] The neoliberal project to destroy opposition to 'free markets' was married to the neoconservative concern with traditional social values – support for the nuclear family, church and capital punishment, and opposition to abortion, sexual freedom, women's liberation and gay marriage. All presidents after Johnson, including Bill Clinton, subscribed to variations of the neo-neo platform, and in particular paid obeisance to the imperative to 'shrink the state'. Government, as President Reagan opined to (general applause), became the problem not the solution. Ordinary Americans, those feeling the burdens of falling living standards and the pain in sending their children off to war, responded enthusiastically. If only 'they' – the government – would get off our backs, we could walk tall again. After the global financial shock of 2008, populist forces have arisen to challenge, however, incoherently, the role of government as traditionally understood and practiced. Powerful vested interests have been successful in diverting attention and blame from systematic biases in the political economy – and themselves – to the government.

Privatization covers a range of financial and political practices that unwound from the 1970s onwards.[3] At base it referred to the rush by centre-right governments to transfer (sell) ownership of government businesses to private owners, in particular to large pension and other financial investor organizations. However, to make the move politically palatable, a share of the sale was often reserved for individual 'mums and dads' investors. The reasons (drivers) for this policy switch are discussed in a later section.[4]

The term was widened and soon came to mean 'getting government out of the way of private enterprise'. Hence, governments in the Anglo-democracies – America, Canada, Britain, New Zealand and Australia – moved progressively to 'deregulate' whole industries like airlines and environmental standards, and to 'outsource' government functions to private firms. In most cases policy entailed disbanding or gutting public agencies previously charged with supplying the services or oversight concerned. In some cases, private provision supplemented continued public supply. Thus, private prisons sprang up or existing prisons were taken over, managed by large security firms, to handle the rapid growth in the prison population that followed the growth in crime and a hardening of sentencing philosophies and practices, itself the result of a range of economic, financial, socio-economic and ideological forces characterizing the neo-neo movement, especially in America.

WHAT IS HAPPENING?

Privatization in its various guises happened earliest and most radically in Britain under the Thatcher government and America, during the Reagan years.[5] A string of publicly owned and operated business enterprises (often natural monopolies) were sold off in Britain during the 1980s, including (to name a few):

- British National Oil Corporation originally set up to exploit the North Sea oil deposits.
- British Petroleum, originally set up before World War I as the Anglo-Persian Oil Company to extract oil in Persia (Iran).
- British Gas Corporation, which was 'unbundled' to separate the pipes and sales functions into distinct private companies.
- British Telecom shares were completely sold to private investors in three tranches over the 1984–93 period.
- British Steel Corporation was privatized for the second time (the first was in 1952, reversing the Attlee government's post-war nationalization programme) in 1988, ending up being taken over by India's largest steel producer, Tata Steel Ltd.
- British Leyland, the end line of a proud British motoring history stretching back to the 1890s, was gradually shorn of its marque brands – Jaguar, MG, the Mini, Rover and Land Rover – and was finally wound up in the new century.

From early in the Thatcher years, local governments were effectively pressured into selling off their public housing stock, formalized in the 'Right-to-Buy' legislation granting sitting tenants the opportunity and incentive to buy their dwellings at substantial discount to market values. Over two decades the public housing stock halved from a post-war high of about one-third of total dwellings in the United Kingdom. Management of much of the remaining stock in council ownership was out-sourced to housing associations and for-profit providers or 'arms length management organizations'.

The privatization programme culminated in Britain with the privatization of British Rail in 1993. The functions were radically unbundled on functional and geographic bases. Ownership of the tracks and stations was separated from ownership of the rolling stock that was leased out to operating companies with franchises to operate on particular routes. Ownership of the infrastructure had to be taken back by government when the private company, Railtrack, collapsed in 2001; likewise track maintenance had to be resumed by the government corporation, Network Rail, when it became obvious that the train operating companies were failing in keeping up.

In each case the avowed aim was to increase operational efficiencies, though an underlying anti-state ideology also enlivened debate between neoliberal proponents and their critics. In most of the British cases, especially those involving natural monopolies, privatization did not lead to a shrinking state role, but to a change from owner/provider of services to their regulation. It was not a case of 'deregulation' but 'reregulation'. New institutional arrangements had to be introduced to prevent private operators from exploiting their monopoly position at the expense of consumers. But in an anti-state political climate naive and self-interested views on the superiority of free markets and the need to free entrepreneurs from the 'dead hand' of bureaucracy led to weak, if not captured, regulatory oversight.

The systematic weakening of regulatory rules and agencies was particularly obvious in the United States. In fact, since nationalization had never proceeded there as far as post-war Britain, privatization largely took the form of de- and regulation. The division of functions between the three levels of government and the differentiated mosaic unfolding further complicated the American situation. The absence of a strong social democratic tradition and decline of organized labour had dampened potential opposition to the call for 'smaller government'. The triumph of neoliberalism was implicit in the widespread but simplistic view that government should *neither* row *nor* steer; the market and buccaneering entrepreneurs would manage all. Government should avoid the water completely.

Unsurprisingly, the mantra of privatization echoed through the economies of US allies in Central and South America. As in the Anglo-sphere and Europe, the energy and utility sectors were the main targets and the key financial intermediaries were the large global banks. On the fall of communism, Western experts descended on the newly independent states of Eastern Europe during the 1990s sparking the 'big bang' privatization of public assets, ably assisted by Western banks and Western governments keen to wean those countries away from the grip of mother Russia.

WHY IS IT HAPPENING?

Orthodox economic justifications draw on the familiar benefits claimed for competition and market discipline. Theoretically, most economists accept that it is not all that simple. In addition to the real world complications thrown up by the multiple existence of market failure(s), that vary across time and economies, and the thorny problems associated with the principal-agent dynamic, institutional design and regulatory efficacy introduce practical complexities in getting the terms of what are normally incomplete contracts 'right'. Auction theory provides a guide for government but is no guarantee that both parties to the deal win. The winner's curse can mean that private agents pay 'too much' for the public asset or licence with a short-term budget pay-off to the government agency that may, however, evaporate in the longer term when the private winner fails and has to hand back a depreciated asset to government. In the long run almost everyone can lose – users of basic services, shareholders of failed private providers, taxpayers burdened with picking up the pieces. Alternatively, it is likely that a large private bidder with a phalanx of lawyers, bankers and political lobbyists in tow will outgun underfunded government providers and pay too little for the asset and be able to effectively evade contractual public service provisions. Nevertheless, the impact on public policy of both the theoretically sophisticated models of neoclassical economics, with its implicit normative charge (Chapter 8) and the simplistic nod to free markets have been significant.

The conventional 'official' rationale for privatization was put by the Organisation for Economic Cooperation and Development (OECD, 2003) commenting on the spate of activity during the 1990s. This report noted that collectively, the OECD countries transferred assets to the total sum of about one trillion dollars (US) during this period and identified five factors driving the process:

- The emergence of a tight fiscal environment and need to control government spending and debt.
- Disillusionment with the generally poor performance of state-owned enterprises (SOEs).
- Technological change in sectors like electricity provision and telecommunications undercutting natural monopolies.
- Globalization of financial markets mobilizing capital searching for outlets.
- Ideological shifts regarding the appropriate role of the state in the economy.

These drivers are blandly presented as independent and taken-for-granted 'natural' events. In fact they are closely interwoven, along with factors completely ignored by such official accounts. The tight fiscal climate and disillusionment with SOE performance has been assumed and encouraged by ideologically driven models contrasting perfectly competitive (ideal) alternatives to (real) state provision. Technological change has not necessarily reduced the role of government in ensuring adequate coverage at affordable costs of basic services for all people; in some cases it has accentuated the barriers to access and raised its cost.

The role of large financial intermediaries has been particularly influential in understanding the degree to which governments have embraced privatization in its various forms. They stand to make large immediate profits from arranging deals with no downside risk if these deals later turn bad. As 'coupon-clippers', they move in and out before the results are evident. The fees charged are a deadweight loss to the primary parties, government and private investors. Limited competition between the market leaders in the legal, chartered accounting and investment banking sectors ensures that these fees are substantial.

Stepping back, there were broader drivers to the privatization push associated with the deterioration of the public finances. From the 1970s, the revenue base of governments in countries like the UK and US was undercut by persistent stagflation and the rising costs of the post-war welfare state as populations aged and the trend to greater economic equality reversed (see next chapter). The 'fiscal crisis of the state' (O'Connor, 1973) became a popular topic of discussion, especially in view of dramatic developments like the threatened bankruptcy of New York City. Government everywhere searched for ways of rebalancing their budgets and getting their balance sheets in order. Commercial ratings agencies – Standard & Poor's and Moody's, in particular – came to exert a strong policing role, constraining the willingness of governments to take on new debt necessary to maintain and upgrade basic infrastructure. With strong political limits to raising taxes that were already high in many European countries – but less so in the US, Canada or Australia – this meant reducing or trying to reduce government spending, especially on depreciating public infrastructural assets currently operating at a financial loss (regardless of the broader positive externalities economy-wide). Offloading responsibility for basic services like transport, energy and public housing promised short-term dividends in the form of lower budget deficits and longer-term pay-offs by avoiding the inevitable costs of repairing and upgrading those assets.

A critical prop to the private takeover of public provision and regulation lurks in the rise of modern finance theory. The 'efficient market hypothesis' (EMH) holds that financial markets will quickly (in theory, instantaneously) price financial assets like equities, bonds and various derivatives to reflect their underlying fundamental values. The EMH holds that financial markets operate to allocate an economy's savings in ways that underpin and ensure an efficient allocation of resources in the real economy. Financial assets are continuously valued in markets or exchanges that evolved for the purpose. Financial assets entail claims on the future returns on the real assets deployed in production. The EMH holds that, at any point in time, their price reflects the fundamental (present) value of the future returns on those real assets – for example, share prices reflect overall investor judgments about the size and timing of the future flow of dividends that they will receive.[6]

The 'semi-strong form' of the EMH argues that financial asset prices like company shares faithfully reflects the significance of all *publicly available* market relevant information. As long as regulators ensure the full and free flow of such information, financial markets will generate the 'right' signals to investors to direct their savings to those producers who are making the most returns – that is, maximizing welfare in the economy. *Informationally* efficient financial markets are therefore hand-servants to the real economy, ensuring (in the world of perfectly competitive markets) the *economically* efficient allocation of resources economy-wide.

There is some empirical support for the weak form of EMH, though some analysts still claim to be able to discern and profit from identifying trends or 'momentum' in share prices. There is virtually no support for the strong form. Up until the collapse of the investment bank, Lehman Brothers in 2008 and the subsequent and still lingering crisis unleashed, most economists and economic policy makers subscribed as a matter of conviction to the semi-strong form of the EMH. Financial markets, they believed, worked well enough to guide savings and investment into the right areas, without direct government intervention. Indeed, by intervening or 'picking winners', governments would distort the allocation of resources resulting in a (Pareto) suboptimal outcome and reducing potential welfare. A corollary of the stronger forms of the EMH is that bubbles and busts in asset prices cannot occur; financial markets will quickly bring any divergence of actual prices back to underlying values.

Since the outbreak of the global financial crisis (GFC) the EMH has taken a fearful beating in all but its very weakest form.[7] If the true scientific test of a hypothesis is its ability to predict outcomes and explain the course of actual events in historical time, then the EMH has been a massive failure. Clearly, with hindsight, it is obvious that the share market in countries like the United States experienced a raging bubble during the late 1990s, was punctuated by the dot-com bust early in the new century, resumed its bubble progression, only to be pricked again by the GFC. A similar story unwound in a number of other countries at the same time.

Nevertheless, the theology of efficient financial markets lingers on, hampering policy makers from instituting the institutional reforms necessary to prevent similar disasters from recurring in future, a reality we return to in Chapter 14. The key point to note here is that the large banks and other financial intermediaries, like legal and accounting firms, have managed to collectively construct a rent-appropriating machine fuelled by the 'churn' of public assets. The crude salute to free markets – that is the conflation of private enterprise and individual freedom – buttressed by the arcane models of economic theory, have resulted in a policy regime in which government failure has become a self-fulfilling prophecy. By starving the public sector of an adequate fiscal base and demonizing public officials as self-serving bureaucrats, the financial-legal complex has perpetuated its own privileges and power. Having helped to create the yawning gap, Wall Street has generously offered to step in and fill it.

WHAT ARE THE CONSEQUENCES?

How has the privatization experiment fared? The first point to make is that this is a question rarely asked and even more rarely satisfactorily answered. The test of the grip that privatization has on the theory and practice of public policy resides in a widespread failure to *systematically* assess the actual outcomes of the variety of privatization exercises that were tried in various countries and sectors over the past three decades. One difficulty of making such an assessment stems from the extensive number and diversity of cases. More fundamentally, it is hard to establish a robust counterfactual basis from which to compare actual developments with what could have happened had the assets and services remained in government ownership and control – *assuming adequate financial and administrative resources were applied.*

Despite the difficulties posed by incomplete and incomparable data, and the scarcity of critical studies, the OECD report noted earlier is able to confidently conclude that '. . . there is overwhelming support for the notion that privatization brings about a significant increase in the profitability, real output and efficiency of privatized companies. The results are particularly robust when the firm operates in a competitive market, and that deregulation speeds up convergence to private sector levels' (OECD, 2003, p.9). The tip-off comes when recognizing the use of vague phrases like 'overwhelming support' and 'significant increase'. Elsewhere the report notes the confusion of aims and means of privatization programmes in member countries and the need to 'make trade-offs'. It also stresses that most attempts to gauge outcomes have focused on conventional microeconomic indicators of performance. There is little persuasive evidence advanced concerning the effects on the macroeconomy; the report states '. . . studies have noted a positive link to improvements in the macro-environment. However, the results need to be interpreted cautiously as there is not enough evidence to establish causality' (ibid. p. 10). Nevertheless, the report is willing to concede that privatization has probably been associated with net short-term job losses. However (conveniently), these effects are poorly understood: the '. . . macroeconomic and fiscal impacts have been the focus of less intense scrutiny, and the distributional effects of privatization are only beginning to be studied' (ibid. p. 9).

Reports by semi-government international organizations like the OECD are notoriously difficult to decipher. Their language and – especially conclusions – are often vague and couched around by qualifications, so as not to offend member national governments. It is impossible to read this report without drawing the conclusion that its authors had already reached *their* conclusions before they had started. Every effort was used to accentuate the positive and downplay the negative consequences of privatization experiences in the countries under review, in line with the prevailing official pro market liberalization position.

A more detailed analytical study of the effects of Britain's privatization programme comes up with more nuanced and broadly neutral conclusions, utilizing, it must be said, the conventional approach of applied welfare (Paretian) economics.[8] Florio (2004) finds that the change from public to private ownership, as such, in areas like telecommunications, had no discernable effect on productivity but did have noticeable regressive consequences for income distribution and jobs. Birdsall and Nellis (2006) differentiate the winners and losers in their review of privatization experiences across a range of sectors and countries. They identify major limitations and gaps in the studies. Nevertheless, they confidently conclude: 'We know that Privatization "works", in the sense that divested firms almost always become more efficient, more profitable, and financially healthier, and increase their capital investment spending.' (Ibid. p. 381). Apart from the vagueness of the term 'almost', their bias is implicit in the bunching of the positive terms, 'more efficient, more profitable and financially healthier', which are basically synonyms.

They summarize: 'The question whether Privatization generally costs at least some SOE workers their jobs is still unresolved. The answer is ultimately based on whether sales increases faster than productivity in privatized firms' (ibid. p. 381). And again:

> The second vital area of [future] research is to conclusively document the labor economics of privatization programs. Do most such programs actually cost SOE worker jobs? Are there gender-specific impacts relating to the total commercialization of state-owned enterprises, as might happen if privatization caused SOEs to shut down child care or other social services? Are there worker training/retraining programs, effective methods of dealing with worker redundancies, or should governments emphasize lump-sum severance packages when lay-offs are required? Do privatization programs create more jobs than they destroy? These questions are not only vitally important to policy making, they are inherently interesting in their own right' (ibid. p. 382).

One can only agree and wonder why these questions have not been answered. This last passage points to the broader impacts of policy changes like privatization that are too readily developed and implemented through the narrow lens of economic orthodoxy and short-term fiscal conservatism, and to the fact that they have not been adequately considered *before* the rush to privatize.

Summing up, a number of negative consequences of privatization have been advanced in the literature. First, concerns have been expressed over poor governance and accountability arrangements, leading to falling standards of service provision. Cost-cutting can lead to cutting corners, progressively reducing quality and/or reach of service. Second, and relatedly, the complexities and commercial secrecy surrounding legal agreements between government agencies and private providers opens the possibility of corruption. This outcome is made more likely when government officials responsible for negotiating contracts and asset transfers end up employed by the private provider. Third, government by transferring responsibility for public services to for-profit concerns gives up the option of using the previously responsible public agency to achieve other public policy goals, like regional development and environmental enhancement – or as the quote above suggests – key areas of social policy. Unless these supplementary goals deliver profitable returns themselves, the private provider has no incentive to pursue them and every incentive to drop them, to focus back on core – that is, profitable – business. Fourth, in general the new provider does have an incentive to strip out those parts of the business that do not contribute to overall profit, leading to cuts in service to lower income and more costly to reach users. More often than not, net job losses concentrated in particular areas or regions follow large-scale privatizations, similar to the outcome of aggressive private equity buyouts. Attempts by government to write public service obligations into the contracts are prone to be less than fully effective. Governments face a conflict of goals here. A major driver to privatize public functions is to improve the government's fiscal position; yet the more restrictions and public good requirements governments place on the private provider, the lower the revenue raised by the transfer. Apart from job losses, the wages and conditions of workers who switch to the private provider may be eroded, and made permanent as job turnover replaces them. Union membership and protection is likely to be less in the private sector. The question is not simply the net number of jobs lost or gained but their quality: (a) what kind of jobs, (b) whether full- or part-time and (c) how remunerated (d) how secure. Fifth, government and private investors face, to some extent, a zero-sum game. The major financial gain in the deal will flow to the party with the best negotiating team. The parties may have conflicting interests: for example, government has a narrow financial interest in minimizing use of a service it outsources – say management of aged care facilities – while the private provider has the incentive to build demand, use and revenue (including government subsidy). Moreover, outsourcing to expensive rent-seeking external consultants may end up costing government more to provide and regulate services than when directly provided by its own agencies.[9] Sixth, privatization can have implications for breaches of privacy and civil liberties, especially in areas like health services and social security. Seventh, any cost savings and capacity to innovate may be offset by the higher costs of finance facing private businesses; governments in advanced economies with their taxpayer standing behind them have better credit ratings and are able to borrow at lower interest rates than in the private sector. Finally, it may simply not be possible to introduce effective competition in some areas like utilities where natural monopolies persist, undermining the expectations of government and consumers that 'efficiency gains' will be passed on in lower prices. These are precisely the industries where regulatory capture is most likely and corrupt practices most beneficial to both parties – a cooperative game in which, however, the taxpayer and consumer loses.

A broader negative outcome concerns the way in which privatization has been the carrier of a cultural attack on communitarian values, the anti-individualist view that 'we are all in this together'. If basic services like health, education, shelter, transport, water and energy – once regarded as 'merit goods' provided by elected governments – are seen as the sole responsibility of the citizen as consumer, then those unable to buy in the market are consigned to chronic poverty, their lives made miserable, a fate visited on their children, helping to entrench and extend class and status divisions through society. Privatizing once publicly owned services, reinforces the crowding out of shared, communal values and perspectives, encouraging people to look to their own and their immediate families' interests. The danger is that once started the process is self-reinforcing as self-interest comes to predominate in the lives of citizens. As governments act in ways prescribed by orthodox economic models, people take on more and more the characteristics of the rational economic actor, bringing the abstract picture of that actor into more realistic focus.[10] The related tendency is for people to develop a progressively more callous disregard for their fellow citizens. The very notion of citizenship entails a strong sense of common interest and purpose. The end point of a fully privatized society is the death of citizenship; in that sense Margaret Thatcher's pronouncement would be correct – 'there is no such thing as society'. It was argued in Chapter 8 that such developments run against deeply embedded moral intuitions that influence human social behaviour. Taken to extremes the privatization of culture – rather than Marx's proletariat – sounds the death knell of capitalism as the mutual trust on which market activity depends atrophies.

There are signs that 'peak privatization' has been reached. In the continuing shadow of the global financial crisis, governments are being forced to reassess the continuing failures of conventional economic policies to restart their economies. In the new era of stagnation, 'the new normal' of low or absent growth (Galbraith, 2014a), privatization has not delivered the hoped-for rebound of productivity; neither has fiscal austerity and non-traditional monetary policy. In a world of savings gluts and negative interest rates, even international bodies like the International Monetary Fund (IMF) and central banks are calling for active public investment in productive economic and social infrastructure, rather than policies that encourage the speculative churn of existing assets. The following example indicates this possible trend.

In August 2016, the US Deputy Attorney General instructed federal officials not to renew contracts with private prison operators or to 'substantially reduce' their scope. This directive followed a highly critical report by the Inspector General, Department of Justice into the management and performance of federal prisons. About 12 per cent of federal prisoners were held in private prisons. This report found that there was a substantially higher incidence of safety and security breaches in those prisons by comparison to those run by the Federal Bureau of Prisons. 'For example, the contract prisons confiscated eight times as many contraband cell phones annually on average as the BOP institutions. Contract prisons also had higher rates of assaults, both by inmates on other inmates and by inmates on staff' (Office of the Inspector General, US Department of Justice, 2016). The cost to government under existing contracts had increased from \$562 million in 2011 to \$639 million in 2014. Although the report made a number of specific recommendations aimed at improving oversight and accountability, it is not clear that the interests of the two parties are closely enough aligned to achieve the profit targets of the private operators and the suite of performance goals of the federal government. In particular, where government has a fiscal and social interest in rehabilitation, early release and lower recidivism, the operators have precisely opposite interests on all three counts. Private prison operators are unlikely to go quietly. They have developed a lucrative captive market (so to speak) and will defend it utilizing their heavy lobbying presence in Washington.

To summarize, the experiences of privatization policies to date have been highly varied and in general fail to validate the theoretical advantages claimed. This has not worried its proponents in both the public and private sectors. For them, privatization has delivered lucrative new avenues for profit in the latter case, and electoral and career success, in the former case. Electoral success has accompanied politicians leading the 'redesign of government'. Public officers moving to take up positions in the new private sector organizations have multiplied their remuneration packages. But what of the broader value question – is all this morally justified?

WHAT ARE THE IMPLICATIONS?

Orthodox approaches to justifying privatization focus on the theory/value-embedded tools of cost-efficiency, cost-benefit analysis and various multi-goal techniques like the 'balanced score card' approach and Delphi-like techniques that attempt to marry quantitative and qualitative judgments in order to establish rankings as to preferred outcomes. I have already noted the conceptual and practical difficulties inherent in social choices that attempt to establish coherent overall rankings. The approach outlined in Chapter 11 suggests a different strategy – namely, we should seek to carry out an analysis of the 'comprehensive consequences' of public policies, in this case the various forms of privatization undertaken or proposed. This analysis would have several components and answer a set of key questions.

First, what concrete actions are proposed? Second, how are these actions to be carried out, by whom and over what time frame? Third, what are the consequences or culmination outcomes likely for particular 'interests' – private bidders and their advisers, government agencies, service users differentiated by class, gender, ethnic, regional and other culturally significant dimensions and society at large – that is, the impacts on the strength of communal bonds, social inclusion and cohesion and on the real as opposed to assumed impacts on productivity. The aim would be to arrive at an overall *judgment* as if and to what extent *particular* privatization policies would be likely to lead to a reduction in *currently existing* inequalities of opportunity (in Sen's sense). One clear focus of attention would be the possible employment effects of proposed privatizations, with respect to the number, type and quality impacts and on the implications of the change for community cohesion. Special attention would need to be paid to the question of what happens if the private operator fails or withdraws from provision of the service in future, possibly involving the inclusion of bond or warranty conditions in the original deal.

This analysis would need to be 'even handed' in the sense that it not pre-judge outcomes by privileging use of a value-biased tool like cost–benefit analysis and would avoid the ideologically convenient reliance on the taken-for-given superiority of market solutions. The central thrust of the approach focuses on determining whether and to what extent the policy enhances the effective ability of people, individually and collectively, to convert their capacities into the lives they value. Will, for example, privatizing a childcare service enhance or harm the real ability of single parents to improve their lives and that of their children; if so, how and if not, what might be done differently? Significantly, *which* single parents improve their opportunities and which do not; who has her ability to flourish curtailed, and who enhanced? Answering such questions is a complex task calling on the expertise of analysts with a range of disciplinary skills – in this example, child and development psychologists, social workers and sociologists, as well as economists and accountants. The onus is on those promoting change to demonstrate that the end will culminate in just outcomes. This obviously and necessarily reduces the role and importance of the economist in public policy, a consequence of no small significance to economists and those who train them.

Finally and critically, a pragmatic concern to reduce injustices requires a cool analysis of the political environment, starting with an appreciation of the vested interests ranged against progressive policy solutions and pushing actual outcomes in directions that would increase rather than reduce injustices. It is counterproductive to devise a policy programme that has little chance of making it onto the political agenda; the power to set agendas is a major tool in perpetuating existing injustices. Part of the analysis must uncover the forces that would block progressive policy and suggest ways of breaking down or bypassing dominant power positions. This will entail both strategic and tactical decisions, knowing when and where to strike, when to hold back, when to escalate, when to retreat. It is unlikely that the move to privatize state functions will be derailed by a few individual victories in particular policy areas. The momentum built up over decades, feeding on the actions of powerful interests, legitimized by narrow economic theories, will not be stopped by occasional outbreaks of anti- free market opposition, or short-lived mass movements like 'Occupy'. Although such events help to raise awareness and provide an outlet for popular discontent, they do not effectively challenge the status quo. This suggests that challenging, channelling and changing orthodox public policies like privatization will entail both working through and on the established political institutions, bringing organized pressure to bear at strategic points and moments. One key point to remember is that wherever the market intrudes, the outcome is tilted towards those with more wealth, income and skills, and against those with less. This bias is reinforced by policies justified by advisers wielding evaluative tools like cost–benefit analysis, and further entrenched by the power of the privileged to normalize the outcome. Hence, part of any just policy that utilizes the market to deliver services must also explicitly include mechanisms to offset the unequalizing impacts. This latter redistributive component will often be the most contentious and resisted element in the policy process, since dominant interests will seek to deny its relevance behind the smoke of market fundamentalism. Conservative politicians will also try to avoid diverting attention from their primary focus on 'budget repair', the task of shrinking taxes paid by their supporters by offloading public responsibilities and gutting 'public serve obligations'.

CONCLUSION

This chapter has presented privatization as an exemplar – almost the paradigmatic case – of the triumph of market fundamentalism in the neoliberal era. A critical political economy of this phenomenon has a role to play in first, demystifying the role of neoclassical economics and its applied policy tools in justifying existing inequalities and injustices and second, in suggesting directions for developing a more just division between the complementary roles of state and market in achieving greater social justice. John Kenneth Galbraith (1958) first advanced the idea of 'social balance' of public and private provision in the 1950s in his book, *The Affluent Society*.[11] More recently, his son James Galbraith (2009) has reinforced the idea of the complementarities of state and market, and the central role of government planning in capitalist societies:

> A country that does not have a public planning system simply turns that function over to a network of private enterprise – domestic or foreign – which then becomes the true seat of power . . . To walk away from this problem with a shrug about 'markets' is to disenfranchise the future. But to 'rely on the market' is to guarantee that the interests of the future will never be provided for (Galbraith, 2009, p. 167).

NOTES

1. Cohen (2016) quotes an anonymous political staffer asserting that 'it never stopped being 1968'. The critical political catalyst was the lasting influence of the third candidate in the previous presidential election, George Wallace. Wallace's performance in 1964 showed that fears of racial integration could cause loyal Democrats to turn away from their traditional political home – in the North as well as the South. Wallace was taking 'a wrecking ball' to the liberal consensus.
2. Frank has called the professionals clustered in the 90–99th income/wealth percentiles 'the liberal class'. I prefer the more traditional term, 'upper middle class' because it covers a broader range of those who do well out of the current socio-economic system without occupying the commanding heights, structurally speaking. I expound on this point in the final chapter.
3. Privatization covers a range of developments, including complete transference of public enterprises (assets and liabilities) to private hands, corporatization, outsourcing services, including management and so on. The term has also been used to refer to the practice of private equity partnerships buying up the shares of publicly listed companies as part of the so-called 'market for managerial control', or less politely, 'asset stripping'. This is *not* the sense in which I am addressing the topic here.
4. According to Bel (2006), 'privatization' was coined by *The Economist* magazine in the 1930s to refer to aspects of economic policy in Nazi Germany.
5. Privatization also swept through Russia and its satellites after the fall of the Soviet Union, on the active advice and persuasion of the World Bank and Western governments and economists. The resulting rise of a form of mafia capitalism was the unforeseen consequence, especially in the key energy sector.
6. There are *three* versions of the EMH –weak, semi-strong and strong. It is the semi-strong form that dominates the finance literature – or did before 2008.
7. This should not have been a surprise since economists like Joseph Stiglitz had been arguing for decades that informational factors ensure that financial markets in particular are liable to fail. See his Nobel Prize lecture for details (Stiglitz, 2001).
8. Like a number of other studies, Florio points to the tendency for productivity and profitability gains to accrue in industries where effective competition exists or can be introduced. Whether these 'gains' outweigh the 'losses' depends on the value calculus applied. As noted in Chapter 8, conventional conceptions of efficiency and tools like cost–benefit analysis enshrine particular value positions that predetermine the trade-off.
9. It is often the case that previously employed public officials who taken redundancy packages are re-employed at higher remuneration by the consultants brought in to takeover services from the agencies that they previously worked for. This lands government with a double fiscal burden, namely the cost of redundancy programmes and higher consultancy fees that together outweigh any immediate and medium-term budget savings. Proponents of privatization, drawing on the claims of public choice theory, may point to the tendency of private managers to reduce the 'featherbedding' of public agencies once privatized. However, this argument follows on from the axiomatic construction of that particular brand of rationalist microeconomics; nor does it consider the wider consequences of any jobs that are lost after transferral of public functions.
10. MacKenzie (2006) refers to this tendency as the iterative process of 'performativity' (in the context of the models of modern finance theory and the real world workings of financial markets).
11. See my discussion in Berry (2013, Chapter 10).

13. Inequality

> The history of inequality is shaped by the way economic, social, and political actors view what is just and what is not, as well as by the relative power of those actors and the collective choices that result (Thomas Piketty).[1]

CONTEXT

In 1958 the Harvard University economist John Kenneth Galbraith (JKG) published a justly famous book – *The Affluent Society* – in which he proclaimed the demise of economic inequality in the leading economies of the world, most notably his own. A little over 50 years later his son, James Galbraith (2012) published a book arguing the opposite, claiming that inequality had returned with a vengeance on a global scale, contributing to increasing instabilities in national economies.[2] In a later book the latter (Galbraith, 2014a) argued that capitalism in the twenty-first century, was gravitating to 'a new normal' characterized by low economic growth, stagnating incomes and living standards, and increasing environmental disruption and social unrest. What happened in the intervening period to blow away the father's confident and hopeful prognosis? What implications does all this have for just policy? This chapter attempts an answer to both challenges.

JKG identified the modern growth-oriented ethical defence of inequality as residing in its functional role in providing, first, the necessary incentives to save, invest and work and second, to supply the savings necessary to fund investment and jobs. In seeking to enrich themselves, the successful ones also provided the means of livelihood for the rest. Provided that this circular process unwound at a sufficient rate, the economy would grow and living standards would gradually improve for everyone, or at least the vast majority. Poverty and want, the curse of early industrial capitalism, would wither, increasingly confined to those he termed 'the case poor' whose individual lifestyles were marred by mental or behavioural deficiencies, illness, addiction or chronic indiscipline – in short, those people who social critics and reformers had long dismissed as 'the undeserving poor'. Although these sad cases may resonate our compassion and prompt private charitable aid, there was, he argued, no ethical policy imperative to intervene to improve their lot. On the other hand, he did see a role for government in breaking the vicious circle of 'insular poverty'; situations where whole communities had been bypassed by growth and systematically denied access to education, health and employment opportunities. As such, he was a prominent public supporter of the war on poverty and the civil rights movement of his time. Nevertheless, the general tenor of his argument was that continued economic growth driven by the post-war dynamic of Keynesian welfare capitalism and wise liberal government would gradually erode remaining bastions of poverty; any remaining incorrigible cases could be dealt with by providing an austere safety net and well-meaning charities.

JKG's sanguine approach to economic inequality was coloured by the era that he was living through. The extreme inequality of income and wealth that had characterized the rise of industrial capitalism before World War I had noticeably declined by the late 1950s. The spread of consumer durables like cars, televisions and labour-saving white goods was driven by high employment and rising real incomes for a majority of households in countries like America and the rapidly reviving war-battered economies of Europe. The increasing reach of home ownership was giving a larger share of the population an appreciating asset and secure lifestyle. He saw this as, in part, arising from the changes in the institutional form of capitalism, in particular as a result of the increasing separation of management and control of the large corporation. Senior managers were now in a strategic position to pursue a range of aims in addition to the competition-forced imperative to maximize profits. Corporate capitalism was increasingly evolving as a 'stakeholder society', in which managers balanced the interests of shareholders, their own interest in growing their scale of operations, and the interests of their workers and the communities in which they operated. The various components of what he had earlier termed countervailing power were keeping corporate excesses under control. The seriously wealthy were also learning to be more circumspect, less prone to flouting their fortunes in displays of conspicuous consumption, more inclined to seek status through public good works and charitable contributions.

This last trend seems, even through the lens of the times, to be tendentious. It might be more accurate to say that the wealthy were more strategic in defending their economic and social position, through withdrawing to the new phenomenon of gated communities, exclusive clubs and distant suburbs. Nevertheless, it is undeniable that life was improving for most households whose male head was employed in the thriving manufacturing and service sectors, as well as for family businesses and farms in smaller communities. With steady economic growth, low unemployment and the sinews of countervailing power in place, many economists and other social scientists looked forward, like JKG, to a rosy future in which the constraints of scarcity and inheritance of misery would fade into history. The happy future of Keynes's grandchildren seemed on the verge of arriving. However, as with the often-made millenarian predictions of the Rapture, the future never arrived. As so often before and since, the death of economic crisis was widely celebrated – right up until it burst on the scene again.

Liberal capitalism at the time in its most developed incarnation was undergoing a process of 'embourgeoisement' by which workers were elevated into the middle class. Capitalism was becoming classless. Such an extreme thesis was quickly dismissed[3] but its echo lasted and has proved highly serviceable in the interest of the dominant class into the twenty-first century.[4] Of more substance was an argument put forward by JKG's contemporary, Simon Kuznets, the first economist to systematically draw on government income tax statistics to estimate historical trends in the distribution of income nation wide. In his path breaking paper Kuznets (1955) provided an interpretation of the changing shares of each income decile in America over the period 1913–48. He suggested that the data could be presented as part of a curve, that had first risen as early industrialization in the nineteenth century drew workers from the subsistence agriculture sector to the factory towns creating poles of affluence among capitalists and penury among workers, then declined through the first half of the twentieth century as the benefits of growth percolated down in the towns and radiated out to the countryside. The Kuznets curve thus provided an easily grasped and ideologically appealing narrative of progressive capitalism. Like JKG, Kuznets believed American-style capitalism to be in the process of solving the age-old problem of inequality.

Piketty has pointed to the highly speculative and ideologically driven interpretation Kuznets offered. The latter readily volunteered that his theory (as opposed to his statistical series) was 5 per cent evidence based and 95 per cent speculation (Piketty, 2013, p. 581, endnote 16). Kuznets also admitted that his optimistic account of the transition to greater equality of outcomes was aimed at encouraging developing countries to remain within the orbit of the American-led free world through the emerging years of the cold war. Hence:

> . . . the magical Kuznets curve theory was formulated in large part for the wrong reasons, and its empirical underpinnings were extremely fragile. The sharp reduction in income inequality that we observe in almost all the rich countries between 1913 and 1945 was due above all to the world wars and the violent economic and political shocks they entailed (especially for people with large fortunes). It has little to do with the tranquil process of intersectoral mobility described by Kuznets (Piketty, 2013, p. 15).[5]

By and large income inequality stabilized during the 1960s and then began rising from the recession-prone decade of the 1970s, continuing to do so for the next three decades and shows little sign of abating in the rich countries.[6] For reasons given later, the inequality question has recently assumed central stage in contemporary discussions of social and economic policy. The next section summarizes the main trends in the distribution of income and wealth observable over this period.

WHAT IS HAPPENING?

1. **Income.** Comparing income inequality across the developed economies, the income share of the top 10 per cent of income recipients by 2008 was nine times that of the bottom 10 per cent (OECD, 2011), reaching 45 per cent of total earned income in the USA by 2010 (Piketty, 2013, p. 291). Conventional measures like the Gini coefficient track a consistent pattern of rising inequality from 1986 to 2008. However, broad categories hide an underlying dynamic that is threatening to radically remake contemporary capitalism in the image of the super-rich. Income growth has been strongly concentrated in the top 1 per cent of income recipients in America, Britain and France. Including income from all sources (that is, non-earned income as well as income from work) the top 1 per cent received almost 25 per cent of total income in America on the eve of the global financial crisis in 2007. This figure is similar to that on the eve of the Great Depression in 1929, surely no coincidence.

   US income inequality at the top end is primarily due to the widening in wages and salaries – that is to the 'pre-distribution of earned incomes' prior to taxes and government expenditures. Although the contribution of rentier income is far from insignificant, Piketty argues that the explosive (his term) increase in US inequality is dominated by what is happening in labour markets, especially since 2000:[7] in addition '. . . the facts show quite clearly that the [global] financial crisis as such cannot be counted upon to put an end to the structural increase of inequality in the United States' (Piketty, 2013, p. 296). Longer-term forces are unequalizing the earned incomes of Americans.

   The key fact pointed out by Piketty and others (for example, Reich, 2015; Dorling, 2014; Stiglitz, 2012; Hacker and Pierson, 2010) is that those in the top 1 per cent are overwhelmingly senior business executives – 'the supermanagers' – of large corporations. In America, most are in the non-financial sector, though finance bosses are well represented. In Britain, the latter are much more likely to be harvesting massive remuneration packages, since 'the city' in London is a larger proportion of the national economy than Wall Street in America. According to Reich (2015, p. 97) average remuneration of US CEOs rose by 937 per cent between 1978 and 2013, compared to 10.2 per cent for average workers; the average ratio of CEO compensation to the average pay of the average worker rose from 30 to more than 300 over the same period. In the older developed nations of Britain and France, inherited wealth and rentier incomes appear to play a more important part in the make-up of the top 1 per cent than in the USA, which Piketty argues follows from the return of the capital/income ratio to early twentieth century levels in the former countries. Of course, over the long run, such differences must converge as high current incomes are locked into inherited wealth – unless interrupted by massive shocks like wars or depressions.

Income inequality is also assuming a distinct geographic pattern in many countries. In the case of Britain, a clear North-South dimension has hardened, while Galbraith (2012) notes that most of the US rise in inequality can be accounted for by escalating incomes in counties focused on New York City, Seattle and Silicon Valley.

It is also the case that the distribution of *disposable* income is becoming more unequal in developed nations, especially after the GFC. Redistribution of income by way of government taxes and expenditure is clearly not offsetting its diverging pre-distribution. Hacker and Pierson (2010) quote data showing that US disposable income for the top 1 per cent rose by more than 250 per cent between 1979 and 2006, compared to a rise of 11 per cent for the bottom 20 per cent. Since the introduction of fiscal austerity measures after 2008, this situation is likely to be more pronounced. However, the reality that relative deprivation climbed the income ladder during this period is reflected in the widening gap between the supermanagers and the rest. It is this pervasive feeling of being left behind that is energizing popular discontent and protest in many countries, expressed from time to time in breakout actions like the 'Occupy' movement and in the apparent rise of populist political movements in Europe and the USA. This general malaise is heightened by the realization that the optimistic hope that individuals can rise by their own efforts is a forlorn one. Social mobility has stalled, particularly in America. People do not circulate into and out of the top income earners during their careers. 'In other words, workers at McDonalds or in Detroit's auto plants do not spend a year as top managers of large US firms, any more than professors at the University of

Chicago or middle managers from California do' (Piketty, 2013, p. 300).

The experience of the last four decades hides what came before. From the 1920s to 1970 income inequality fell sharply in the USA, Britain, Canada and Australia (the last named from a lower base).[8] The other countries of northern and southern Europe also experienced significant but lesser decline. However, what distinguished the Anglo-democracies from the rest was the degree of divergence after 1970. Inequality increased everywhere but most sharply in the former, with Australia a middling case.[9] However, America stood out: '. . . we can say that the upper centile's share in the United States increased roughly twice as much as in Britain and Canada and about three times as much as in Australia and New Zealand' (Piketty, 2013, p. 316).

2. **Wealth.** By the time *The Affluent Society* appeared in the late fifties, the trend to greater equality in America that JKG celebrated had run out of steam. It took another decade or so to go into reverse but the Kuznets curve had inflected. Piketty argues that in order to understand why, we need to grasp the prior role of the changing nature of the distribution of wealth in the first half of the twentieth century. The reason that total income inequality declined until 1950 followed from the drop in income from capital due to the destruction of wealth in Europe and America caused by the shocks of war and Depression. At the beginning of the twentieth century, wealth was much more concentrated than income. For example, the wealthiest 10 per cent (decile) in France owned almost 90 per cent of the country's total wealth, about the same as in Britain: the comparable figure for America was about 75 per cent.[10] By 1950, this share had declined to about 70 per cent in France, 75 per cent in Britain and 65 per cent in America. The share of the super-rich 1 per cent was roughly two-thirds of the top decile's in France and Britain and half in America. Hence, income inequality overall declined because income from capital dropped sharply until 1950. The share of the wealthy continued to decline in those countries until about 1970.[11] Thereafter, this trend reversed, reinforcing rising income inequality generated in the labour market that, in turn, fed back into escalating wealth concentration. The winding back of progressive taxes on wealth and income after 1970 also played its part.[12]

In summary, according to the data presented by Piketty, the distributions of income and wealth in the advanced capitalist economies traced a u-shape from the end of the nineteenth into the twenty-first century. The past four decades have witnessed intensifying divergence of incomes and concentrations of wealth in the major Western economies, coinciding with the rise of neoliberal economic orthodoxy among policy makers. Increasingly, inequality has resulted from the rise of a new labour aristocracy, senior managers from both the financial and non-financial sectors able to extract quasi-rents, particularly but not exclusively in the USA.

> To a large extent, we have gone from a society of rentiers to a society of managers, that is from a society in which the top centile is dominated by rentiers (people who own enough capital to live on the annual income from their wealth) to a society in which the top of the income hierarchy, including the upper centile, consists mainly of highly paid individuals who live on income from labor (Piketty, 2013, p. 2678).

It is only among the very top income earners – the top 0.1 per cent (or one-thousandth of income recipients) – that unearned income from wealth predominates; the remaining members of the top centile (and below) receive most of their incomes from labour or a mix of labour and returns on their wealth.

WHY IS IT HAPPENING?

Kuznets's theory of intersectoral structural change provides, at best, a partial account of trends in inequality at certain stages of development, especially when utilizing inequality measures that draw on grouped semi-aggregated data sets.[13] Orthodox economic theory points to the relationship of worker pay to productive contribution. Human capital theory suggests that the education and training of workers complemented by capital investment increases factor incomes over time. At one level, this is true, even trivial. Unfortunately, it does not adequately explain the diversity of income divergence over time or between regions and countries – even ignoring the obvious fact that the conditions for ultra competitive labour markets are never met anywhere in the real world. 'In order to understand the dynamics of wage inequalities, we must introduce other factors, such as the institutions and rules that govern the labor market in each society' (Piketty, 2013, p. 308).

And, as Reich has cogently argued (see Chapter 10), the institutions and rules have and are being systematically biased in favour of the rich and powerful. It is fanciful to suggest that the hyper-incomes and escalating wealth of today's supermanagers can be explained by their marginal contributions to production or their frugal self-investment in building personal human capital. The creation of new forms of intellectual property, and the processes of monopolizing knowledge-intensive products, and defining contracts and bankruptcy protection, while winding back effective regulation has been influenced by disruptive innovations but driven, above all, by the deliberate political efforts of powerful interests.

Piketty's influential book has pivoted current debates to a consideration of long-term secular trends in inequality in Europe and America and, in particular, to wrestling with what he terms as the two linked 'fundamental laws of capitalism', namely:

$$\alpha = r \times \beta \qquad (13.1)$$

$$r > g \qquad (13.2)$$

Where: r is the rate of return on private capital or wealth; β is the ratio of the total capital stock K to annual output (income Y) in the economy – that is society's total capital wealth as a multiple of national income – and g is the annual rate of economic growth.

Law 1 states that the share of profits in national income α is equal to the rate of return on capital multiplied by the capital to income ratio; it is not really a law but a national accounting identity. Law 2 argues that rate of return on wealth will always exceed income growth in the economy, and since wealth is always concentrated in a relatively few hands, a greater share of income will flow to the rich, further concentrating wealth over time. That is β will increase as K increases faster than Y; with a constant r, α must rise.

If, as Piketty claims, the normal dynamic state of capitalism is high and rising inequality, a dynamic inscribed in its structural bones, so to speak, what happened in the first two-thirds of the twentieth century to temporarily offset the underlying laws of motion? At base, he argues that but for the massive external shocks of the two world wars and the Great Depression, twentieth-century capitalism would have continued on its long-term trend towards ever-more polarized societies, with income and wealth increasingly concentrated at the top. By destroying much of the financial (and physical) value of accumulated wealth, these cataclysmic events temporarily disturbed the operation of the fundamental laws by collapsing β and hence α. In response to these disasters, governments in the West intervened aggressively in the economy in the post-World War II period with public investment creating conditions for growth *and* very high taxes on income and wealth (including death duties), offsetting for a time the underlying long term trend to growing inequality. That is, he suggests, r was still greater than g but not enough to offset the redistributive tax and transfer policies of governments. The top marginal income tax rate in Britain was 98 per cent and over 90 per cent in other Western nations during this period. Death duties broke up many of the great landed estates. During this period labour increased its power vis-à-vis capital and much of the increase in post-war growth was captured by middle income workers who began to accumulate some wealth – mainly in the form of housing and pension entitlements. This, Piketty terms the appearance of a form of middle class patrimonial society, alas to be short lived.

Since r remains above g, as soon as governments moved away from progressive tax and expenditure policies from the 1970s onward, inequality resumed its inexorable upward glide. In thrall to neoliberalism, capitalism is on its way to recreating a deeply unequal future – unless the majority can be mobilized to reintroduce a progressive social democratic state. Failing that, the future prospect is a return to levels of inequality that marked the gilded age of the late nineteenth century in Europe and America. 'The general evolution is clear: bubbles aside, what we are witnessing is a strong comeback of private capital in the rich countries since 1970, or, to put it another way, the emergence of a new patrimonial capitalism' (Piketty, 2013, p. 173).

Piketty argues that g was abnormally high in a historical sense, during the Long Boom of the 1950s and 60s, in the range 2–4 per cent. Up until industrialization, the average rate of growth over centuries was between 0.5 and 1 per cent. Since 1980 growth has fallen below 2 per cent; Piketty forecasts g at no more than 1 to 1.5 per cent during the twenty-first century. Since, unlike Marx and Ricardo, he sees no tendency for r to decline, then the trend to greater inequality will persist.

There are several secondary flourishes to his narrative. First, wealthy people will generally derive a higher r on their wealth than others because they have access to better investment advice and smart tax lawyers. Second, as already stressed, they will collectively exert political power on governments to bend policies to favour their interests – 'winner-take-all politics' undergirding the rise of 'The Predator State'. The current phase of globalization offers large multinational corporations considerable scope to minimize tax by shifting their profits to low tax or no-tax jurisdictions, as companies like Apple, Google and Facebook have amply demonstrated. Such strategies leach over into semi and fully illegal tax avoidance activities, particularly for high wealth individuals, as the publication by WikiLeaks of 'the Panama Papers' attests. They also raise the likelihood of corrupt dealings with host government officials. The national governments of the countries in which the corporations and wealthy individuals are or were originally domiciled and in which most of the revenue and profits are extracted will often find it difficult if not impossible to monitor and control the revenue leakage, especially when the companies and individuals involved are powerfully represented in their political systems.[14]

Criticism of Piketty's laws has been intense in the years since publication of the English translation of his book.[15] What has not been disputed is the scope and reach of Piketty's data, nor his role in diverting attention from the micro to the macro view of global forces driving capitalism over the long run. Some criticism has been levelled at his particular definition and valuation of the capital stock. K is comprised of all personal wealth returning an income to the owner – including real assets like housing and business inventories, and financial assets like stocks and bonds; r comprises the annual rate of return on these assets, including rents, interest, dividends, licence fees, royalties and so on, plus eventual realized capital gains. Most attention, however, has focused on the second law and the claim that r stays consistently high while growth fluctuates and is trending down.

Taking the first point, r may well fluctuate with the business cycle and government monetary policy:

> Piketty's r is basically a weighted average of financial rates of return across the yield curve and the risk profile of privately-held capital assets. It is the artifact of current profits and of discounted profit expectations on market values. If the discount rate rises (falls), other things equal, the ratio of current profits to financial values also rises (falls). But if the discount rate is stable, thanks to long-term stability of monetary policy and of social attitudes – or even thanks only to averaging over time – then that r should also be reasonably stable over time is no surprise (Galbraith, 2014b, p. 146).

Nevertheless, Piketty could reply that it is precisely the long run that he is concerned with and that short-term fluctuations in r wash out over time. The key weakness of the second law is that he assumes that r is independent of g.[16] That is, regardless of how poorly the economy is going, wealth owners will continue to receive their constant rate of return. This would only be true if all returns were in the form of say, British government consuls that are based on a perpetual promise by the British government to pay a given annual dividend forever. In reality, if there is a long-term decline in 'trend growth rates' in the Western economies – a new normal or age of stagnation – then it is at least possible that the return on capital assets will also fall, perhaps to levels below g, reversing the secular growth in α. It is also the case that political movements and policies that result in reducing the net returns to the wealthy will once again lower β and hence α. Piketty effectively equates the return on wealth r and the savings rate. Wealthy people, he implies, will save the returns on their current wealth, so accumulating more wealth, whereas the have-nots will consume most or all of their incomes. In fact, the wealthy may consume or give to charity much of their unearned incomes, reducing their otherwise accumulating stock of wealth. It may even be the case that the *net return* from wealth falls below the growth rate, reversing the march back to the gilded age.[17]

If the second law does not, in fact, guarantee the rebirth of patrimonial capitalism – and Piketty himself, spends the last part of his book arguing for measures like a global wealth tax to prevent such an occurrence – what has been responsible for the undoubted increase in inequality since 1970? The answer, of course, lies in politics and the financialization of capitalism, leading to a series of speculative bubbles, punctuated by short-lived busts. At some point high levels of inequality and social imbalance are likely to act as a break on further economic growth and on the returns to the rich. The vicious circle of lagging effective demand resulting from stagnant wages and declining welfare payments, underinvestment by capitalists, and overvalued financial assets raises the spectre of long-term stagnation such as that experienced by Japan since 1990. At this point, policies for progressive redistribution and public investment in economic and social infrastructure may galvanize democratic politics again, as they once did during the New Deal in America.[18]

Other secular forces driving inequality can be seen to stem from the increasing automation of many previously skilled and semi-skilled jobs – in the extreme what Reich (2015, Chapter 22) calls 'when robots take over'. Galbraith (2014a) also stresses the impact of 'the digital storm' in potentially constraining growth and intensifying inequality – that is, a situation where g, s and r are all falling, though not necessarily at the same rate.

In summary, Piketty's attempt to establish long-run laws determining income/wealth shares behind the backs of the human actors must be marked a failure. It smacks of an old-fashioned economic determinism. Human history is (fortunately) more open to human intervention. However, his data rich analysis *has* galvanized serious debate on what factors – short-term and long-term – do account for the demonstrable trend to greater economic inequality in contemporary capitalist societies and – most importantly – what can be done to reverse this state of the world, always assuming that this value judgment is accepted. This last point raises the ethical dimension to social action and public policy. In keeping with the comprehensive consequentialist framework pursued in this book, before we can take up that question we need to consider the range of consequences flowing from the observable march of inequality.[19]

WHAT ARE THE CONSEQUENCES?

This question has sparked lively debate, both in the literature and in political discourse. Criticisms have ranged from the deleterious impact on particular minority groups to claims that the organic bonds of society are being 'torn asunder'. As an example of the latter consider the following comment from a prominent political philosopher. 'In essence, the social pathology of a highly unequal society consists in the destructive effect that inequality has on social solidarity: in the sense that those who live together share a common fate and should work together' (Barry, 2005, p. 183). The first part of the sentence makes an empirical claim, namely, that inequality breaks down the general sense of a common interest. The second part adds an ethical or normative element, namely that people *should* work together, implying the existence of mutual obligations. This section focuses on the first claim and associated impacts, leaving the second normative claim to the next section.

How might growing inequality undercut social solidarity defined as common regard for and commitment to ensure that all share to a reasonable degree in the opportunities and vicissitudes of life? Emphasis here is on what meaning we give to 'reasonable degree'. Is it reasonable, given the society in question, to require everyone to receive an income that allows people to consume the basic necessities, food, shelter and the opportunity to work? The answer to this question will depend in part on the level of economic development of the society in question. However, even in an undeveloped country where the vicissitudes outweigh the opportunities and most people live at or near subsistence, a strong sense of a common fate and mutual assistance can exist, even though this is driven by the challenge of simple survival in the face of extreme scarcity and environmental threats. It is not clear that as economic development proceeds and opportunities open up that the bonds of solidarity will hold unless the fruits of development begin to filter widely through society. This self-reinforcing cycle of rising opportunity and individual aspiration has enlivened the spirit of capitalism, first in the West and more recently globally. The history of liberal democratic societies led, as we have seen, to a reduction in inequality during the first two-thirds of the twentieth century, with rising aspirations and opportunities for a substantial section of the population. This did not necessarily resolve all tensions threatening national social cohesion. In America, rising affluence and opportunities for white males, underscored the remaining inequalities facing Afro-Americans, Hispanics and women. However, by bringing these 'minority' concerns into the light and onto the political agenda, substantial progress could then be made in extending the reach of social inclusion. Even though these battles for inclusion were not won in any comprehensive sense, some progress was made, especially during the 1960s.

Conversely, as economic inequality intensified after 1970, arguably it has become more difficult to sustain the momentum towards inclusion and the sense of a common fate, as society threatens to fracture along traditional class, gender and subcultural lines. As a growing proportion of the population feel that they are going backwards and that the lives of their children will be worse than their own – in terms of living standards and opportunities to pursue their life's aims – the temptation to draw back and focus on themselves and to ignore mutual communal obligations grows. It is in this context that we are witnessing a populist backlash against multiculturalism and a corresponding rise of xenophobia in America, Europe and elsewhere. Right wing politicians and political movements are carefully cultivating this development, which helps to consolidate the existing and growing wealth and power of the dominant class, concentrated in the top 1 per cent.

Beyond issues of solidarity and cohesion, what areas of negative consequence follow and further intensify rising inequality? I have briefly noted some of the claims put forward in this regard further on.

Education

The introduction of comprehensive, compulsory, free state education was one of the most important and effective policy programmes of twentieth-century liberal democracy. It opened up opportunities across class and status divided societies, while providing the skilled work force that drove growth. Preceding and growing alongside the state system, private schools and colleges also flourished, helping to preserve aspects of traditional social privilege. Wealthy parents largely funded the more exclusive private institutions, though many were also effectively subsidized in various ways by government through favourable taxation treatment and, in some countries, direct subsidies. Access to the most prestigious schools that gave graduates favoured access to the best jobs has always been biased towards wealthy families, in spite of scholarship programmes designed to recruit limited numbers of students from poor or minority backgrounds. With increasing income inequality and rising middle class indebtedness, more families fall back on state schooling, increasing pressures on systems already struggling to maintain facilities, staffing and educational quality in the face of governments intent on cutting back public spending. This is likely to intensify inequality as able students from poor backgrounds fail to enter and graduate from the top schools. Even when they do graduate, they are likely to achieve less in income and advancement than the children from wealthy backgrounds (Stiglitz, 2012, p. 19).

Family background matters, both with respect to unequal access to good schools and directly due to the level of domestic support provided within the family. Children in lower income households are more likely than those from wealthier backgrounds to live in single parent situations, be dependent partly or fully on welfare support, and attend poorly resourced, overcrowded state schools. They often lack the adult and peer role models that point the way to educational and career success. Their schooling is more likely to be interrupted or ended by repeated relocation, domestic violence, restricted experiences and narrow aspirations resulting in lower educational achievement. 'Children do better if their parents have higher incomes and more education themselves, and they do better if they come from homes where they have a place to study, where there are reference books and newspapers and where education is valued' (Wilkinson and Pickett, 2010, p. 105).[20]

Unsurprisingly, standardized tests of basic literacy and numeracy skills among school children show a negative correlation between inequality and achievement across the advanced nations. Similar tests display similar associations within countries like America (Wilkinson and Pickett, 2010, pp. 105–10). The Program for International Student Assessment carried out by the Organization for Economic Cooperation and Development (2016) found a wide variation in mathematical skills across 63 countries. Those countries with lower than average scores on numeracy included the USA, Australia, New Zealand, Canada, the United Kingdom and many other European nations. 'The country where the richest 1 per cent takes the most is also the rich country where sixteen-to twenty-four-year-olds are most likely to be innumerate – [namely] the United States of America' (Dorling, 2014, p. 26). In all but one of the countries studied by the OECD (Liechtenstein), there were moderate to large differences in numerical ability between socio-economically advantaged and disadvantaged students. Correlation is not causation. Educational outcomes are affected by multiple factors acting through the basic primary and secondary socialization institutions of society and the basic distribution of resources, material and intangible. Nevertheless, it is clear that whatever the mix of causes, once children grow to adulthood with widely divergent educational attainments, their different life chances are well entrenched. Such inequalities of skill, attitude and aspiration are reinforced by employment and income opportunities, and passed on to subsequent generations. Education can be a ticket out of want for individuals; its lack can also be a one-way ticket to poverty and hopelessness for an increasing majority.

Health

Urbanization and industrialization was initially associated with declining individual health and major problems in public health, resulting in recurrent epidemics sweeping the nineteenth-century city. Typhoid and cholera were no respecters of social class, though the highest death rates were concentrated in the poorest quarters. The public health and sanitation movement of the late nineteenth century did as much or more than factory and mine legislation to improve the lives of ordinary people in the West.

especially where such services are provided at the local level of government, funded by local property taxes. But even when state or federal agencies provide those services, the greater political influence of people in the more affluent suburbs and protected enclaves ensure that they receive the best services and are able to exclude lower socio-economic status residents from other areas.

Of all the basic services, shelter is most completely commodified, provided through imperfectly competitive markets and home, so to speak, to the greatest inequalities of opportunity. This situation has intensified in the decades of neoliberal hegemony, with public housing increasingly marginalized in countries that had developed a large public sector through the first three-quarters of the twentieth century. In Britain, from the Thatcher era onward, the proportion of public housing in the total stock has more than halved as central government policy deliberately and successfully introduced 'right to buy' legislation encouraging sitting public tenants to purchase their dwellings at a substantial discount to market value. At the same time local governments were starved of funds, accelerating declining public housing standards, effectively guaranteeing that tenants would vote to transfer ownership and/or management of public stock to non-profit housing associations. Private lenders whose risks were constrained by a government national housing benefit scheme and close regulation of the housing association sector funded the latter. The end result has been that the worst maintained and located public housing has remained in local government hands, reinforcing the stigma and multiple disadvantages borne by remaining public tenants.

Employment

The ways in which access to education, health services and adequate housing are provided in a society partly determine the types of jobs that people have and their employment careers through life. In return, job location and careers help determine lifetime educational performance, skills development and housing outcomes, through both intra- and intergenerational time frames. Having and keeping a job is the main way the overwhelming majority of people in capitalist societies receive their incomes in adulthood and provide for their retirement after working life ceases. Increasing income inequality not only stunts the lives – collapses the opportunities – of employees in the bottom four quintiles, whose relative position has, as we have argued, declined, it also prevents them from accumulating adequate savings to self-finance their retirement lifestyles. This latter point is increasingly salient in societies whose populations are rapidly ageing.

The nature of employment has changed in line with neoliberal policies to increase 'flexibility' in the job market. The risk of changing market conditions in the macroeconomy has been shifted from employers to employees, instituting what Hacker (2008) referred to as 'the great risk shift'. As the strength of trade unions has waned and direct government regulation of wages and conditions wound back (where they had existed), workers are increasingly at the mercy of employment contracts that heavily favour employers, creating what Standing (2011) has termed 'the Precariat', a new dangerous class. An individual worker's protection against unfair dismissal is weakened when other workers are too fearful of losing their jobs if they complain in support of their colleague. Their ability to demand guaranteed hours of employment, adequate safety rules, time off for illness and so on is also compromised. New contracts that pretend that they are private contractors deny workers the status as workers, and, hence subvert any remnant rights and entitlements that they may have had as full-time employees. Similarly, intermediaries like labour hire companies break the link between employer and worker, with contracts heavily favouring the employer and intermediary.

We have already noted the role of technological change in destroying skilled as well as unskilled manufacturing jobs, with a corresponding rise in low paid jobs in the service sector. This is resulting in university graduates displacing underqualified applicants in jobs that do not use their skills fully, while also increasing unemployment and underemployment rates and wasting resources. Increasing pay inequality is being increasingly expressed in a structurally asymmetrical polarization of labour markets.

Debt

The declining relative position of middle class households has seen them take on increasing levels of personal debt in an effort to maintain their threatened accustomed living standards. This leaves them vulnerable to the increasing risks they face at work and undercuts their ability to finance their children's education and their own retirements. In a world of stagnant wages and creeping indebtedness, households are cast into a sea of perpetual anxiety and escalating anger, leaving them open to the lofty promises of populist politicians and single-issue saviours. And as recent history attests, and will be discussed in the next chapter, this increasing reliance on debt also raises issues of systemic risk at the macroeconomic and international levels.

Public Finance

As income and wealth has become more concentrated, it has become more, not less, difficult for national and lower levels of government to raise adequate revenues to fund their basic functions. The ability of global companies to avoid income tax and their domestic power, in all three dimensions, to influence policies to extract tax and subsidy favours has also been mentioned. More systematically, the neoliberal campaign, waged over decades and instantiated in America by the rise of the Tea Party, has sought to cut government programmes – excluding defence – by denying supply to the executive, in the hope that government will shrink and tax them less. This has led to several political deadlocks that threatened to close down the federal government and even downgraded the nation's credit rating. The attack on government spending is strategic, focusing on welfare benefits, with recipients castigated as 'scroungers', 'bludgers', 'leaners' and 'deadbeats', while avoiding programmes like support for veterans, the aged and a raft of corporate welfare measures.

An important shot fired in this battle by conservatives draws on the mythology of 'debt and deficits'. By use of the fallacy of composition, conservatives compare the government budget to that of a single household. Since, it is argued, that the latter must balance its income and expenditures, so must the former match its revenues with its expenditures. To allow government spending to outrun revenue, leads to rising public debt and an increasing burden on future taxpayers to repay that debt. What this misses, of course, is that to the extent that government borrows to invest in productive economic and social infrastructure, the economy will grow to comfortably meet these repayments while also increasing living standards; if policies are well conceived, the benefits will be widely distributed. This is not the real aim of the conservative argument, however:

> Today . . . the Right advocates a curious combination of supply- and demand-side measures: deficit reduction, it is somehow argued, will restore confidence in the country and its economy, and thus be positive; and tax reductions will improve the efficiency of the economy by putting money in the hands of those who can spend it well. Of course, if deficits are to be reduced at the same time that taxes are being reduced, it means expenditures have to be reduced by a lot. And that's the true agenda – downsizing government. Indeed, since most on the Right want to protect military expenditures, the necessary reductions in education, research, infrastructure – all the non-defense expenditures – would eviscerate these programs (Stiglitz, 2012, p. 216).

Human Dignity

Perhaps the most morally challenging development for citizens of a modern democracy is that increasing inequality is incubating a return to patrician attitudes of contempt of the masses by the new plutocrats. In Britain, the self-regarding elites cluster around a long-established status order at the head of which stands the monarch. New wealth, however vulgar, is eventually incorporated through marriage, club membership, the right schools and strategic political donations. Members of Britain's Establishment (Jones, 2011, 2014) poor scorn on 'the Chavs', the vast mass of working class and underclass Britons who increasingly inhabit a different world. The contempt of the fortunate few – the various hierarchical layers of the Establishment – for the mob is visceral.

> How has hatred of working class people become so socially acceptable? Privately educated, multi-millionaire comedians dress up as chavs for our amusement in popular sitcoms like *Little Britain*. Our newspapers eagerly hunt down horror stories about 'life among the chavs' and pass them off as representative of working-class communities. Internet sites such as 'ChavScum' brim with venom directed at the chav caricature. It seems as though working-class people are the one group in society that you can say practically anything about (Jones, 2011, p. 2).

Casual contempt and dismissal of people previously regarded as the solid core of society masks an even more alarming rejection of 'sub-Chavs' as sub-human. In a society of Chavs and Chav-nots, the non-working poor are not even worthy of contempt; they simply do not exist in the world of the elites. People sleeping rough on the streets of major cities in Britain and America are deftly trod around, when they are not forcibly moved on by police or rendered sleepless by hostile park design.

Modern Western capitalism is evolving a pernicious caste system overlaying its basic class divided nature. In a world dominated by commercial symbols of success and failure, older status distinctions stretching back to ancient Greece have resurfaced. An educated and wealthy class is using its wealth to distance its members, both physically and symbolically, from the plebian majority. And as in the ancient world, wealth and status brings political power that solidifies and normalizes the resulting fracturing of social bonds. In what sense can the ideals of democratic citizenship exist, still less thrive, in such a world? How can the liberal values of human dignity, self-respect and social justice play out? How can the communally constituted resources of trust, reciprocity, generosity and cohesion survive in an increasingly unequal environment? The short answer is – they can't.

The Rule of Law

It is clear that rising inequality will not necessarily result in escalating social protest and violence. For every outburst like the 'Occupy' events, conservative forces can call on the police powers of the state to restore 'law and order'. Moreover, to the extent that inequality is hidden by geographic segregation and ideological justifications, collective opposition tends not to materialize.[22] A basic premise of democracy is that all citizens are equal before the law of the land. Wide acceptance of this normative claim rests on general belief that the law is blind to class, gender, race and religion. When ordinary citizens come to believe that some people are 'more equal' than others, their commitment to obeying individual laws may waver. If some people are believed to be favoured in the administration of the legal system, to avoid or evade prosecution or punishment (or even serious investigation) that would normally hold, then the trust necessary to maintain peaceful order is undermined.

The fact that no senior banking executives implicated in the 2008 global financial crisis and in a series of international banking scandals since have faced criminal proceedings has angered citizens, who as taxpayers have been called upon to bail out the failing institutions. Furthermore, publication of documents like the Panama Papers reinforces public cynicism that there is one law for the rich (too big to jail) and another law for everyone else. The cost of litigation against wealthy corporations and individuals is prohibitive for ordinary citizens and even cash-strapped government law enforcement and regulatory agencies. Increasing inequality reinforces these tendencies and constraints, even if the untouchable nature of miscreants 'too big to fail' is rejected.[23]

WHAT ARE THE IMPLICATIONS?

The problem that rising inequality poses for policy makers in a democracy resides, first, in comprehending the complex interacting forces – economic and social – that are driving the outcomes. The second challenge arises from the diverse, often cross-cutting nature of those outcomes. This has the corollary that there will be more than the usual number of unintended and undesirable consequences to consider. The third and most difficult challenge is posed by the inherent difficulties in implementing policies that run afoul of the dominant interests and against the ruling ideology that legitimates those interests and delegitimates those policies.

Sorting out the interacting causes and the multiple outcomes of rising inequality requires marshalling and interrogating large quantities of data.

In the age of 'big data' the temptation is to rely exclusively on numbers and to forget that (a) some effects are inherently qualitative in substance, (b) most methods of analysis privilege certain causes and (c) all analysis is, by definition, blind to unknown variables. In a transcendental search for perfect justice, all this would be dispiriting. However, if the ethical project is to reduce the most obvious and egregious cases of injustice, the task becomes merely difficult.

Some simple guideposts can be marked out to orient progress along these lines. First, it must be recognized that simply redistributing income and/or wealth by measures like progressive taxation will not necessarily, by itself, have the desired outcomes. This was the heart of Sen's critique of Rawls's 'resourcist' approach. Emphasis must focus on the relative abilities of people with different capacities to convert greater resources into increasing opportunities, given the institutional environment into which they are thrust. Simply leaving it to the market will not necessarily suffice.

As an example, consider a person confined to a wheelchair. The term 'confined' is significant; it connotes that this person has a range of limitations tied to her physical situation. By boosting her income, say by way of a disability pension, she can purchase a better wheelchair. However, this will not improve her access to buildings that have not been fitted with appropriate ramps; nor will it levitate her into public transport services operating on old infrastructures; nor will it allow her to cook or shower in conventionally constructed houses. This last point is instructive. Housing markets are heavily biased towards providing for the mass market. This means conventional house designs assume a fully abled resident. Modifying houses after they are constructed to meet the wants of people with special needs – like wide corridors and doors and low workbenches for people in wheelchairs – is expensive. In other cases, markets simply do not exist. People who wish to improve their health by walking or cycling to work must risk life, limb and lungs on congested roads. If the group effected and/or the level of resource redistribution is insufficiently large, there is no market incentive to provide the desired services. Government regulations concerning public access to buildings and the mandatory use of universal design in new house construction would need to complement redistribution measures in order to achieve the desired policy outcome in this instance. However, further policies aimed at appropriately retrofitting existing dwellings and other buildings would also be required to deal more fully with current injustices. This would increase the cost of providing the services, impacting on the scale of resource redistribution entailed. And this is but one example; other cases may be even more difficult to frame and resolve. It is this complexity that often makes analysts, advisers and policy makers throw up their hands in despair, sit back and leave it to the market. This is a deeply gratifying outcome for the privileged and powerful.

Policy makers must deal with a pervasive problem; what metrics to rely on. If simply reducing everything to a single dollar figure – to cost both inputs and outputs – is inadequate, what about related measures? In the health area discussion has focused on QALYs – quality-adjusted life years. One QALY is a life lived in perfect health for a year. A life lived for a year at less than perfect health is counted as a fraction of one QALY. Particular health interventions – treatments, medical technologies, drugs, research, training, policies – can be assessed and ranked by the total increase in QALYs compared to their cost to attain a dollar per QALY.[24] This measure of cost effectiveness has drawn criticisms for its quasi-utilitarian cast. Although its application removes the inherently regressive bias of standard cost–benefit analysis, other biases are introduced. For example, measures that prolong the life of someone for many years at partial capacity may trump alternative uses of health dollars that deliver someone perfect health for one or two years. Likewise, QALYs can be maximized by concentrating treatment on easily treated cases with the highest success rate or on younger people with greater normal life expectancy. Who is to decide on the trade-offs and on what ethical grounds?[25]

In the case of education, attempts to assess cost effectiveness of government funding have focused on nominated performance indicators like numeracy and literacy benchmarks, such as the measures used by the OECD's PISA study noted earlier. Other indicators like completion rates and employment placement have also been utilized. However, it is difficult to find operational indicators for more qualitative outcomes concerning how education and training services contributes to social cohesion, moral values and civic duty. Government moneys tend to flow to where indicators can be devised and documented. Teachers and schools, not surprisingly, bend curricula and reporting processes to best meet the extant performance indicators. As in the case of QALYs, the measures partly determine the choices of intervention. Methodology trumps, by default, serious ethical debate and decisions over the 'best' policies.

Returning to the third challenge noted earlier, we can distinguish two components. First, how can policies be framed and justified in the actually existing political environment? Second, as a necessary though not sufficient part of answering this challenge, how can the dominant justifications for existing inequalities be defeated?

Dorling (2015) identifies 'five faces of social inequality' that support existing injustices: elitism, exclusion, prejudice, greed and despair. The attitudes, behaviours and values defining each would need to be taken on and demolished before sufficient political opposition is likely to be mobilized to change the current patterns of inequality. These targets are as follows.[26]

Elitism is Efficient

This view, implicit in the economic concept of efficiency, treats human beings as inherently unequal in abilities, as falling along a bell curve. This view has roots in nineteenth-century biological and social Darwinism, explicitly developed through eugenicist doctrine in the twentieth century with disastrous consequences. In recent times the position has softened somewhat but still insists that it is beneficial for everyone in the long term for those with talents to rise to the top; only in a meritocracy can all thrive. This cosy view forgets that 'merit' is not a combination of intelligence (IQ) and hard work but a collective sociocultural achievement of historically located, structurally unequal communities.[27] Elites are all too often self-selected and adept at shoring up their dominant positions against challengers. The myth of the 'supermen' is just that, a myth. Shaw's play, *Man and Superman*, is a creative excursion in popular eugenics.[28] Elitism in fields like education generates self-fulfilling results. The fact that particular measures generate different categories or rankings of people under specific current conditions says nothing definitively about their capabilities to contribute to society under substantially different conditions. There is no natural hierarchy of human beings, though in all known societies people act as if there is. There are, in human kind, however, deep biological tendencies, reinforced by social institutions, to believe that natural hierarchies – supermen and the rest – exist.

Exclusion is Necessary

'The most terrible result of elitism is that it can be used to justify the exclusion of so many people from normal social activity' (Dorling, 2015, p. 7). If all boats rise on the tide, then let's concentrate on decking out the fastest, sleekest boats! Heaping further advantages on already well provided-for elites has, as a flip side, ignoring large numbers of people. They don't count, except as supernumerary extras. This viewpoint quickly degenerates into a status divide: them and us, lifters and leaners, Chavs and Chav-nots, leaders and led, contributors and scroungers. Ancient, feudal and capitalist societies have all developed hierarchies to justify socially constructed patterns of inclusion and exclusion. Slaves, serfs and workers, along with women and ethnic minorities have been denigrated and excluded from full participation in their societies. From the ubiquity of exclusion apologists deduce its necessity. This is a naturalistic fallacy. Current technologies and resources offer the capacity to provide every citizen in the affluent, developed countries with the opportunity to fully participate in socially and individually fulfilling lives.

Prejudice is Natural

As elites prosper and more people are excluded from important spheres of life, prejudice against target groups grow. As the majority experience declining opportunities and crushed aspirations, as they lose what were previously taken for granted entitlements, someone must be to blame. Minorities and marginalized individuals – scroungers, criminals, foreigners, the mentally ill, particular races – are easy targets for popular resentment. To some extent, prejudice defined as a preference for people like oneself is natural, the result of millennia of social structures working on evolved moral intuitions (see Chapter 8). But in situations of manufactured scarcity for the majority favouring privileged elites – the 1 per cent – this dynamic turns ugly. It contributes to the divisions and conflicts within society, from which elites can partly insulate themselves by living in separate worlds, cushioned by their wealth and guarded by private security services and the coercive arm of the state. It is also easy to inflame fears of the 'dangerous class' through media and constant official denigration. This has the double benefit of reinforcing the claimed superiority of the few, while setting the many against each other.

Greed is Good

Ideologies and social theories that laud the beneficial function of selfish accumulation of wealth as both means and the end of social life, undermines cooperation and denies the full range of human needs and aspirations. It is an ethic that emerges from the previously noted justifications of inequality, while reinforcing those justifications by relieving people generally of the moral obligation to even consider the effects of their self-centred actions, still less to do anything concrete about it. The talented will feast, while the rest will at best survive on the scraps, while the unworthy or dangerous will starve. This creed has proved to be a powerful antidote to a more inclusive, communal ethics of responsibility by removing any lingering vestige of duty to look after one's fellow citizens.

Despair is Inevitable

Depression and anxiety are growth industries in advanced economies. This is good news for Big Pharma but bad for everyone else. After lifting the majority of the population out of grinding poverty and despair, Western capitalism is returning to early nineteenth century conditions of despair and unhappiness. Many if not most children, in particular, are at risk of growing up in a world marked by stunted health and hopelessness. The sheer weight of despair, in turn, will undermine the smooth functioning of society, unless current levels of inequality can be reversed. Weber's age of 'disenchantment' is nigh, not due to the increasing bureaucratization and loss of religious groundings, but as the concomitant of an increasingly fragmented and polarized social existence.

In summary, the ideological justifications legitimating increasing inequality must be challenged and defeated if effective political programmes of reform are to succeed. This chicken-and-egg conundrum poses strategic and tactical challenges. The final chapter returns to matters of praxis and policy involved if we are to take up the challenge.

CONCLUSION

There is already copious research detailing both the degree and direction of economic inequality in the advanced economies (and large emerging economies like China). Likewise, there is plentiful data and analysis, both quantitative and qualitative, documenting the deleterious effects of social, economic and political trends leading to the dominance of the 1 per cent. These outcomes are *not* the result of iron laws and *are* amenable to collective human influence. A comprehensive social science approach can deliver reforms but only if the individualist cast of orthodox economics (and behaviouralist psychology) is transcended. It is important to extend the scope of political economy to incorporate the communally determined processes of reproducing everyday life and to situate the limited but still important role of markets in this broader context.

It is clear that the degree of inequality has passed a critical point, rendering ordinary life for the vast majority of citizens and future generations less and less fulfilling. Hence, efforts to redistribute income and wealth will necessarily be required. This can be achieved by a combination of higher, more targeted progressive taxation and selective social and public investment requiring greater government expenditure. However, in order to avoid the mistake of relying on the 'separation argument' (Chapter 8) of Paretian welfare economics, governments will also need to reconsider where markets are failing and how regulatory regimes can be retooled to compensate. Given the complexity of how complex systems like capitalism work, there can never be an overall blueprint for reform. Progress is likely to be piecemeal policy consisting of a degree of muddling through;

whether we like it or not, this is the way representative democracies work. The key point to remember is that social justice, as approached in this book, seeks not the perfect but the better. And an ethically calibrated economics has a role in getting us there.

NOTES

1. Thomas Piketty's book, *Capital in the Twenty-First Century*, is arguably the most famous economics book since *The Affluent Society*. Both books galvanized popular interest in the subject and infuriated fellow professional economists in their day.
2. Throughout this discussion, the father will be referred to as JKG.
3. The industrial sociologist Goldthorpe (1963) performed the classic hatchet job in his book *The Affluent Worker*.
4. Politically, conservative forces are quick to criticize any attempt by opponents to raise class inequalities on the agenda as engaging in 'the politics of envy'.
5. For an alternative and more nuanced interpretation of the Kuznets curve, drawing on a different methodology, see Galbraith (2014a), who argues that the theory fits the experiences of many developing countries (except China) but not advanced economies (like America) at higher levels of development, unless one changes the viewpoint from agricultural transformation to a geographically grounded understanding of intersectoral structural changes in the economy favouring the financial sector and the speculative workings of urban property markets.
6. The turn backup was delayed somewhat in countries with stronger labour movements. Thus, for example, the level of income inequality remained stable in Australia from the early fifties to the early eighties (Berry, 1987).
7. Piketty demonstrates that capital (unearned) income only exceeds earned income for the top 0.1 per cent of income recipients in 2007, as opposed to the top 1 per cent in 1929. Thus, on the eve of the great recession, the highly differentiated labour market was the primary generator of income inequality for 99.9 per cent of American workers, managers and businesses. Reich (2015), however, refers to the rise of the non-working rich as a counterpoint to the increase in the working poor. The former were also likely to be active in financing conservative politics.
8. See Piketty (2013, Chapter 9) for detailed evidence.
9. During the first half of that period, Australia had a Labor federal government that negotiated social wage outcomes with the trade union movement utilizing Australia's long-standing centralized minimum wage arbitration system that successive conservative governments have attempted (with some success) to dismantle.
10. These data are taken from Piketty (2013, Chapter 10).
11. This was in part due to the impact of high taxes on inherited wealth and incomes in the post-World War II era, especially in Britain where estate duties continued to break up the landed estates of the aristocracy and squireocracy.
12. 'After World War I, the tax rates on top incomes, profits, and wealth quickly rose to high levels. Since the 1980s, however, as the ideological climate changed dramatically under the influence of financial globalization and heightened competition between states for capital, these same tax rates have been falling and in some cases have almost entirely disappeared' (Piketty, 2013, p. 355). See also, Scheve and Stasavage (2016) who provide a compelling historical account of the political and economic conditions under which governments in Europe and America have imposed progressive taxes on income and wealth.
13. As does Galbraith (2012) who provides detailed analysis of between and within group inequality outcomes at different geographic levels, including the national.
14. In August 2016, the European Commission issued the Apple corporation with a

demand for 19 billion euros in back taxes on their past profits based on revenues held to have arisen in EU jurisdictions. Apple has indicated their intention to appeal this ruling, which has massive implications for other multinational corporate giants. Apple has also not too subtly suggested that such moves may influence their future investment and location decisions. The scene is set for an interesting battle that will be closely observed by corporate and government actors everywhere.

15. For a useful collection of commentaries, see the special issue number 69 of the *Real-World Economics Review*, October 2014. www.paecon.net/PAEReview/ Accessed on 27 August 2016.
16. See Galbraith (2014b) and Kunkel (2014) for discussion along these lines.
17. Galbraith (2014b) has formally rewritten this possibility as:

$$r > g \text{ but } [r(1-t)-cc] <= g$$

where t is the rate of tax on unearned income and cc is capitalists' consumption (including charitable donations and other gifts).

In other words, the gross rate of return to the rich less their rate of tax and propensity to consume may equal or be less than the growth rate, causing β and hence α to remain constant or fall. However, as noted above, the capacity and willingness of large and profitable businesses to avoid or evade corporate income tax reduces the likely impact of this factor.

18. The general opinion is now that moderate redistribution of wealth has a positive effect on growth over the long term (Quiggin, 2010; Ostry et al., 2014).
19. Kunkel (2014) notes the contrast between Piketty's analysis of the high and constant rate of return on wealth (interchangeably termed capital) and that of Marxists who stress the technologically embedded tendency of the overall rate of profit to fall. 'Whatever the ultimate destiny of profits, Piketty and the Marxists agree on this much: only politics can curb or cancel runaway inequality' Kunkel (2014, p. 20).
20. Wilkinson and Pickett (2010, Chapter 8) provide detailed sources regarding differential educational attainment. See also, relevant studies footnoted by Stiglitz (2012).
21. The authors also note that there is no definite correlation between life expectancy and the amount spent per person on health. However, America is an outlier with much higher expenditure per head and lower life expectancy than other advanced nations. At the other extreme, Japan has high life expectancy and low health expenditure. They quote the editors of the *British Medical Journal* in 1996: 'The big idea is that what matters in determining mortality and health in a society is less the wealth of that society and more how evenly that wealth is distributed' (Wilkinson and Pickett, 2010, p. 81).
22. Galbraith (2012, p. 13) argues that once the concentration of high unearned incomes concentrated in a few parts of America are removed, the level of inequality of income from work did not increase for most Americans in the 1990s, as opposed to the 1980s – and that this is why the Left could not mobilize opposition to its advantage. 'The problem was not that rising inequality, in those prosperous years was unpleasant; on the contrary, it led to better economic outcomes for most workers. The problem was that the mechanism could never be sustained. And you don't observe how things end, until they do.' The mechanism wasn't sustained; developments since 2000 have spread the cold, hard experience of inequality and insecurity more widely.
23. Stiglitz (2012, Chapter 7) provides a useful discussion of this issue.
24. There is a large literature on this subject; as an example, see Prieto and Sacristan (2003).
25. Various techniques can be used to derive particular weightings for individual patients – for example would they prefer a high probability of low quality for a long time or a lower probability of high functioning for a short time – but this still leaves open the question of choosing *between* outcomes for different people; this was the crux of the matter posed by George Bernard Shaw in his play, *The Doctor's Dilemma*.
26. Dorling fleshes out these justificatory dimensions of inequality chapter by chapter, quoting a wealth of supporting evidence. The discussion following merely highlights the main points.

27. The term and the formula (merit = IQ + effort) were introduced in Michael Young's satirical book, *The Rise of the Meritocracy* in the 1950s.
28. Dorling (2015, Chapter 3) points out the role that international league tables like the Nobel Prizes play in perpetuating the myth of the individual genius, while hiding the historical contributions of many unsung accomplices and the underlying social environment and past investments that all contributed to discovery.

14. Financial crisis

> I must start by being honest with myself and with the reader: although I spend my professional life analyzing the world economy and have seen many financial crises, I did not foresee a crisis of such magnitude in the high-income countries (Martin Wolf).[1]

CONTEXT

Wolf was not alone. The financial crisis that burst asunder the complacent assumptions and expectations of economists and policy makers in the major economies in 2008 was shocking in every sense. Its occurrence was all the more terrible because it was not in the universe of possibilities embraced by those who wielded the policy levers, nor by those who guided them in doing so. The business cycle was dead or at least confined permanently to bed. Except in cases of external shocks like war or major natural disasters, mature capitalist economies were, it was held as a matter of faith, bound to move smoothly through space-time driven by freely operating and clearing markets. As long as governments avoided interfering with the self-equilibrating forces of the market, all would be well. Well, all was not well. Most worrying and threatening of all, the disruptive forces were not from without but from within, endogenous rather than exogenous. The economy was not a well-oiled machine; there was a ghost lurking within.

The fact that few economists and politicians were loath to follow Wolf and admit their mistaken faith in the dominant macroeconomic paradigm of the last 30 years is unsurprising. Professional, political and academic careers were at stake. Ironically, economists who had long taught that sunk costs are just that – sunk – and irrelevant to future actions, clung onto their heavy past investment in neo- and new classical economics, refusing to accept that it was these very theories that helped to lull themselves, governments and citizens into the false sense of security that was so rudely exploded.

As it happened, the crisis can be seen in hindsight, to have been sparked in its heartland by both a large external shock and the confluence of internal systemic tendencies. As always, major real world events turn out to be the result of the both structural and conjunctural forces. America suffered two devastating blows in the first decade of the twenty-first century that blew away the triumphal claims of 'the roaring nineties'. The 'end of history' was not just around the corner after all. When two jet airliners crashed into the twin towers of the World Trade Center in New York City on the 11 September 2001, history returned in a medieval religious garb. The new US president, a born-again Christian, vowed to spearhead a new 'Crusade' against the perpetrators, which has resulted in multiple invasions and entrapment in the Middle East, from which subsequent administrations have not been able to escape.

The second blow fell on 15 September 2008 when the investment bank Lehman Brothers filed for bankruptcy. Like the assassination at Sarajevo almost a century before, the shock – this time in the form of the collapse of one of the big five banks – ignited a conflagration that caused a worldwide crisis, more serious that anything experienced since the Great Depression of the 1930s. Almost a decade on, most of the advanced economies, including America, live in a twilight world of sluggish (at best) growth, low inflation, low or even negative interest rates, overvalued financial assets and an inherited debt overhang that saps the confidence of consumers to consume and investors to invest. In short, the world appears to be in a giant global liquidity trap!

It is true that the current era of stagnation was primed by a large external shock. But without the confluence of a series of earlier events – the Russian debt default, Asian economic crisis and the speculative bubble of the dot-com boom – and the maturation of systemically embedded tendencies, the scale, scope and tenacity of the resulting global crisis would not have been as severe or as long lasting.

WHAT HAPPENED?

Many books, reports and post-mortems have traced the genesis, development and outcomes of the global financial crisis (also called 'the great recession' and 'credit crunch') that engulfed the major economies and their satellites, from the panic-ridden days of September and October 2008 until the present.[2] The comments below seek to draw out some of the salient points in the context of the aims of this book.

The panic of black September 2008 in which six major US financial institutions failed or clung to government life-support, was foreseen at least a year earlier (especially by financial sector insiders) as it became clear that many of the sophisticated financial products created in the rush of innovation in US credit markets during the new century were of highly dubious value. However, this did not derail the impending high-speed crash. Market players, particularly the large investment banks and mutual funds were locked in a frantic dance from which no one was willing to leave the floor.

The gestation period roughly followed that of an elephant. In mid-2007 things began to go wrong. Three investment funds managed by the large French bank BNP Paribas failed, about the same time that two mortgage hedge funds owned by the US investment bank Bear Stearns went bankrupt. Later in the year the British bank Northern Rock suffered the first run on a British bank for a century; in response, the UK government was forced to step in and eventually nationalize it. Across the moat, the American Home Mortgage Corporation went bust, along with a series of banks, including IndyMac Bank, sparking at the time the third largest bankruptcy in US history. The crisis was rolling, contagion in the air. In March 2008 Bear Stearns itself foundered and was taken over for a song by J.P. Morgan, with an explicit guarantee from the Federal Reserve acting as saviour of last resort. The proximate source of the escalating disaster was even clearer when Fannie Mae and Freddie Mac, nominally private but in fact government guaranteed insurers of 40 per cent of US residential mortgages faced the prospect of bankruptcy. These organizations were effectively nationalized under the terms of a 'conservatorship' regime. The US Congress reluctantly voted $300 billion to bail out defaulting homeowners in an effort to assist some reschedule their loans as an alternative to repossession.

All this was relatively calm waters compared to what was going on beneath the surface. Wholesale credit markets were beginning to jam. The formal banking and shadow banking systems were joined at the hip, all players relying on the routine operation of the short-term wholesale market. Nobody knew who was solvent and who was not. The avalanche of asset-backed securities used to collateralize rollover transactions could not be confidently valued since they traded 'over-the-counter', rather than on public exchanges. Fear trumped greed as everyone swam for the same small island. Many drowned, while the powerful struck out for Washington. The oldest but one of the smaller investment banks, Lehman Brothers, arrived first but was left in the water. After frantic but futile attempts to orchestrate a buyout like that for Bear Stearns, the Federal Reserve and US Treasury stepped back and let the swimmer drown.

Apparently, Treasury Secretary Paulson and Fed Chair Bernanke thought that the markets would take it all in their stride and a salutary lesson would be taught to other would-be miscreants. In fact, the lesson became clear and the dunces turned out to be Paulson and Bernanke. 'Too interconnected to fail' joined 'too big to fail' as the main lesson quickly learnt. The Lehman's failure served as a sudden reminder that if one part of an interconnected system fails, the whole is at risk of failing. Risk at the micro level was not the same as risk at the macro scale. The sector and the US government were immediately faced with the imminent insolvency of a far bigger and strategically located player, the American International Group. AIG was the world's largest insurance company and major seller of credit default swaps or CDS. The latter instruments insured the various arcane financial derivatives that had blossomed during the boom years of the early 'naughties', particularly the 'collateralized debt obligations' (CDOs) built on a pyramid of sub-prime mortgages taken out by purchasing homeowners who would never normally qualify for a loan. The large banks developed special purpose vehicles financed by short-term wholesale debt to trade the mortgage backed securities, engineered to attract pension and other investors hungry for (apparently) AAA-rated investments.

All was well, as long as everyone believed that the rivers of repayments would continue with only minimal, historically validated defaults occurring. Investors received their risk-adjusted returns. The banks and brokers harvested their fees and made their capital work ever harder, boosting profit rates on the back of escalating debt leverage. People who had never before aspired to own their homes found themselves owners of minimal if any equity but a mountain of personal debt. It had to end badly.

During 2008 the rate of mortgage defaults escalated alarmingly. As low-start mortgages reset to higher interest rates, low income and no-income borrowers fell behind on their repayments. Increasing numbers walked away leaving their houses to be repossessed and sold off at heavy discounts. Housing prices crashed in many cities and regions, including hot spots like California and Florida. The derivatives backed by these mortgages tumbled along with house prices. However, no one could work out how far – how toxic these assets were. All players found themselves over-leveraged with little chance of refinancing their short-term liabilities. Liquidity dried up, the crisis metastasizing from the financial sector to the real economy. Unemployment rose to double figures in America. Consumption fell as households attempted to belatedly rein in their debt and feared job losses to come. Investment fell as companies shelved expansion plans and sought to reduce their variable costs, especially wages and wind back their outstanding debts to banks desperately trying to shore up their own balance sheets. The large car companies faced falling sales, growing inventories and impending bankruptcy. The US economy teetered on the edge of a second great Depression.

Enter the Federal Reserve and the federal government. The former abruptly reversed the Greenspan doctrine of leaving it all to efficient financial markets. Interest rates were driven down and when that failed to revive the economy, increasingly unorthodox monetary measures were progressively introduced alongside, culminating in several variants of 'quantitative easing' – polite talk for printing money – as deflation rather than inflation threatened to lock the economy into what the early twentieth century economist Irving Fisher called 'a debt-deflation depression'. At the same time the Bush administration lowered taxes in an attempt to get aggregate spending up. However, the vast proportion of the cuts ended up in boosting savings rather than consumption or investment. Next, the Congress passed – after heated debate and delay – the 'Troubled Assets Relief Program' or TARP, a $700 billion fund intended initially to buy up swathes of toxic securities in a 'bad bank', so removing them from the balance sheets of financial intermediaries, rendering them solvent in the hope they would start lending again. But agreement could not be secured as to the price the bad bank would pay; too little and the banks would stay insolvent, too much and they would be rewarded at the taxpayers' expense, a massive dose of moral hazard. In the end, TARP was redirected to recapitalizing the banks in order to save the creditors (that is, each other) and ensure that the escalating cost of the bailout would be borne by taxpayers.[3]

With the real economy reeling and the prospect of mass unemployment looming, the federal government finally launched an old-style Keynesian fiscal stimulus intervention, an $800 billion programme of further tax cuts and new infrastructure spending, in addition to direct support for car companies and lukewarm efforts to fund debt restructuring of mortgagors. Gradually the patient showed signs of recovering, but not quickly. Almost ten years on from Lehman, economic growth in the USA is low by the standards of previous periods of recovery and job creation remains volatile. Asset prices are high and debt overhang still constrains a more robust and broad-based bounce-back.

However, American prospects look positively sunny by comparison to the situation in the Eurozone and other European countries. European banks also experienced considerable fallout from the onset of the global financial crisis in America. German, French and British banks dived heavily into the toxic assets served up by Wall Street. Banks in Belgium, Ireland, Iceland and Britain were nationalized. The Royal Bank of Scotland, the world's largest bank by (boom time) assets, ended up majority owned by the UK Treasury. Other British bank takeovers and bailouts were forced before some semblance of order was restored to the financial sector. The liabilities of Iceland's three banks dwarfed the country's GDP several times over and resulted in the collapse of the economy and the swift departure of the elected government. Ireland's banks were forced to rely on a blanket guarantee by the national government and support from the European Central Banks and IMF but only at the cost of a crash programme of fiscal austerity that pushed the Irish economy into a severe and prolonged recession.

But this was only the beginning. The crisis was severest in the countries of the Eurozone. First Greece, then Ireland, Portugal, Spain and even Italy experienced an evolving sovereign debt crisis as ballooning fiscal deficits drove interest rates on public debt higher; thus, the spread between rates on Spanish and Italian public debt and German bonds hit five percentage points in 2012, while it spiked at over 40 per cent for Greek debt and around 10 per cent for Portugal and Ireland. Understandably, GDP fell hardest and recovered weakly in those countries by comparison to Germany, and France (Wolf, 2014, Chapter 2). What started as a debt crisis in the banking system due to the risky behaviour of Europe's big banks morphed into a sovereign debt crisis as their governments sought to prevent escalating failures in their financial sectors from spilling over into full scale domestic depressions. In only a few of the Eurozone countries was the crisis of public finance due to the fiscal recklessness of government and feckless behaviour of their citizens – only Greece and Italy had ratios of gross public debt to GDP over 100 per cent on the eve of the GFC in 2007. The rapid deterioration in their fiscal positions *after* the crisis hit was accentuated mightily by the need to bail out their private banks and satisfy the austerity requirements of the European Union and its central bank. Prior to 2007, the public debt to GDP ratios of other hard-hit Eurozone countries was under (and as in the case of Spain and Ireland, well under) 70 per cent.[4] Like the first two cases, the public debt to GDP ratios of latter countries soared to well over 100 per cent in the years since, in line with the policy and politics of austerity imposed on all (see further comments below). Whereas the primary cause of the subsequent banking and fiscal crises in Ireland and Spain was sparked by runaway property booms, the spark that ignited crisis in other Eurozone countries (and Iceland, France and Britain) were more directly related to lax regulation and the burden of toxic securities on the balance sheets of their banks.

WHY DID IT HAPPEN?

The overall cause of the great recession and its aftermath was the 'financialization' of Western capitalism post-1980, led by political economic developments in the two leading Anglo-democracies, Britain and the USA. This process had a number of interlocking structural components.

First, the Reagan and Thatcher governments actively sought to *deregulate* their countries' economies, starting with industries like airlines and culminating in freeing banks and other financial institutions from traditional prudential controls. It was this latter move that opened up manifold opportunities for the increasingly integrated mega-banks to mobilize and dispose of huge flows of savings in search of high returns. Key legislative actions in America came during the Clinton administration with the repeal of the Glass-Steagall Act (GSA) in 1999 and in Britain with the 'big bang' reforms in Britain during the Thatcher years, reinforced by further financial deregulation in the Blair government's first term. Such actions encouraged and facilitated large banks to take over smaller institutions and under intense competitive pressures to reorient their commercial activities away from traditionally mundane, low risk lending towards increasingly risky, high reward trading operations. 'Gambling with other people's money' had a large upside and little downside for the banks and intermediaries, and generated a self-reinforcing speculative dynamic that was increasingly difficult for any individual bank to walk away from first, especially since doing so would terminate the billion dollar bonuses appropriated by senior executives in the banks, mutual funds and hedge funds (Reich, 2015; Kay, 2015).

Second, in the increasingly deregulated institutional space, *financial innovation* unleashed a competitive scramble to bring to market new financial products to meet the investment mandates of institutional investors like pension and sovereign funds, and the higher risk appetites of mutual funds and private investors. At the same time government policy, especially in Thatcher's Britain and Clinton-Bush America aimed at creating property-owning democracies through pushing home ownership down the socio-economic ladder. The mass production and aggressive marketing of financial products based on residential mortgages met the requirements of both drivers nicely. The regulatory laxness, the mechanics of structured finance, the organizational chain to implement it, the complementary financial incentives and the risk assessment means of pricing were all in place to create and concentrate an expanding volume of debt that drove economic activity and rising house prices in a self-reinforcing, positive feedback spiral – until the spiral reversed direction.

Third, *monetary policy* under Alan Greenspan drove interest rates to record low levels and kept them there long after the economic recovery from the dot-com bust at the beginning of the new century. Private debt levels rose, leading to buoyant consumption and growing balance of payments disequilibria (see further on) in the Western economies, while stoking rapid growth in the emerging economies, especially China. Rising debt fuelled rising housing prices and booming share markets, stimulating further speculative activity. The Greenspan doctrine preached the miracles of efficient markets and held that modern capitalist economies could grow at faster than past-achieved rates of growth without unleashing inflationary forces. This, he held, followed from the productivity gains driven by the digital revolution, leaving markets to work unhindered and the wise decision by government to allow him to run the nation's monetary policy. The book for the maestro's symphony was provided by his successor Ben Bernanke. The narrative of 'the Great Moderation' presented the progress of the three decades leading up to the GFC as a period of relatively smooth growth, with low volatility, marked by shallow dips and quick recoveries.

Fourth, the dominance of market over government was legitimated by *the resurgence of neoclassical economics and the demise of the Keynesian-inflected neoclassical synthesis* of mid-twentieth-century economics. Hegemony over policy makers was embedded in the robust theoretical reach of new classical economics, associated in particular with Nobel laureate Robert Lucas and the centrepiece of modern finance theory, the efficient markets hypothesis, associated with fellow laureate Eugene Fama. The former put the matter succinctly in his presidential address to the American Economic Association. 'The central problem of depression-prevention has been solved, for all practical purposes, and has in fact been solved for many decades' (Lucas, 2003). In short, economic crises were impossible. Lucas's confident assertion went the way of earlier similar declarations – into the dustbin of history. In the aftermath of the 2008 shock, the sage advice of a forgotten economist, Hyman Minsky (1986), surfaced, along with his analysis of financial instability as an essential, endogenous structural feature of the capitalist economy. This rightly reminded everyone that in order to explain and deal with the outbreak of economic crises it is first necessary to develop theories that recognize their possibility.

For a time – roughly until early 2010 – it was, as Keynes's biographer Robert Skidelsky (2009) trumpeted, a case of 'the return of the Master'. However, like Napoleon, Keynes's reappearance was brief. During 2010, orthodox economists and economic policy makers emerged from shock, collected themselves and began to search out reasons for why they had been right after all. Greenspan's *mea culpa* was revoked; like Archbishop Cranmer, the maestro recanted recanting. The problem was not too much market freedom but too little. Government was the culprit by not withdrawing completely from the economy. (Never mind the practice, look at the theory.) Finance Ministers of the G7 countries soon came around to the revisionist view, useful because it neatly let them off the hook. A few bad bankers, at most, as well as blundering governments had been the source of the crisis and were delaying the swift recovery that efficient markets could bring. Policy attention turned to tinkering at the edges to reduce the likelihood of another banking meltdown and, as the crisis was passed forward from the banks to the governments of the weaker states, to the imposition of austerity measures ostensibly intended to discipline the fiscally irresponsible.

In fact, what happened and is still happening is that the public is not buying the revisionist story. As the crisis drags on, approaching its second decade, alternative narratives are gaining strength, both from the edges of the economics profession and serious financial press, and through the articulation of an oppositionist politics that is expressing a highly critical view of orthodox economics and policy. In the former sense, heterodox economic analysis is underlining the ways in which market failures and behavioural biases predispose economies to unintended and undesirable outcomes.[5] Speculative spirals up and down – self-validating periods of irrational exuberance and pessimism – are held to drive asset values away from fundamental financial values for considerable periods, with dire consequences for the real economy (Shiller, 2008). The narrative of the Great Moderation stoked complacency throughout the economics profession and policy community, buttressing the ideological project of neoliberalism, thereby contributing to the defenestration of the public sector's ability to monitor developments in the financial sector that would cumulatively result in disaster. Orthodox economics first denied the possibility of crisis and then sought to argue away its genesis and impacts. This failure stemmed from a basic unwillingness to appreciate the difference between analysis at the micro and macro levels of the economy, as Keynes had long ago demonstrated. The modern discipline was predicated on the injunction to establish macroeconomics on firm microeconomic foundations, with the latter defined by the theory of rational choice. Consequently:

> The economics profession failed. It failed to understand how the economy worked, at the macroeconomic level, because it failed to appreciate the role of financial risks; and it failed to understand the role of financial risks partly because it failed to understand how the economy worked at the macroeconomic level. The work of economists who did understand these sources of fragility was ignored because it did not fall into the imagined world of rational agents, efficient markets and general equilibrium that these professors Pangloss had made up (Wolf, 2014, p. 2).

Put another way, orthodox analysis failed to appreciate the difference between risk at the level of individual actors and risk of the financial system as a whole nor, consequently, how systemic risk could destabilize the real economy. It was not only the case that some financial actors were too big too fail, but also too many were too interrelated to be allowed to fail if the whole economy was to be prevented from crashing into deep depression.

Fifth, agency problems and perverse incentives characterized the manner in which financial innovation occurred. No one in the chain of securitization by which the toxic financial derivatives were devised and traded had an incentive to ensure that the underlying payment streams were sustainable. In fact, the reverse incentive prevailed as each party to the chain of transactions had a strong motive for ignoring any troubling thoughts lest the flows of new transactions on which everyone's profits depended be interrupted. Far better, it was thought, to pass the parcel along the line and avoid being caught when the music stopped. This turned out to be a mistaken belief for most parties. Those with insider information, like some of the large banks and hedge funds, did manage to avoid the crash when it came, and even to benefit from it, by betting against their own clients. By influencing government bailout policies, operators like Goldman Sachs managed to avoid catastrophe and were soon back to the black, unlike many of their clients.

The size and internal organizational structure of the banks was critical to the genesis of the crisis. In a case of the left hand not knowing what the right was doing, senior management left the trading desks to get on with making the massive profits that generated the massive bonuses that they enjoyed. Managers had a strong incentive *not* to ask questions as long as the profits and bonuses kept multiplying. The anthropologist and financial journalist, Gillian Tett (2015), has posited the 'silo effect' as a key feature of large organizations and as one reason why managers were blindsided by the über-risky actions of their subordinates.[6] In short, financial executives allowed the excesses to occur and multiply because they neither had the incentive to see if they were happening nor the organizational capacity to know that they *might* happen.

Sixth, monitoring the credit worthiness of the new financial products was *outsourced to private credit agencies*. Neither originating institutions nor government regulatory agencies kept a weather eye on the tsunami of new and opaque products that issued forth in the decade leading up to the great recession. Key intermediaries negotiated their credit ratings across the counter on a fee-for-service basis. The sellers of those products paid Moody's, Standard & Poor's and Fitch to rate the products they engineered for investors. Unsurprisingly, the sellers got what they paid for, highly rated junk. Gaming the ratings agencies became routine once the rating criteria, risk assessment models and template were widely known. The ratings agencies joined the chain of institutions with an (perverse) incentive to keep the music playing. Ratings arbitrage joined regulatory arbitrage in the game plan of the institutions packaging the new products.

Seventh, *private household debt* accumulated during the consumption-led boom acted as an increasing burden and brake on household consumption, reinforcing the collapse of animal spirits in the economy at large. Total household debt in America doubled to $14 trillion between 2000 and 2007 (Mian and Sufi, 2014). The policy responses of government failed to relieve this roadblock to recovery. Bailouts focused on saving the banks and creditors rather than restructuring the debts of households facing the loss of their jobs and houses. As noted in the preceding chapter, the growth in household inequality underlay this debt build up, as the majority of people facing stagnant or declining real incomes sought to maintain increasingly unsustainable lifestyles and many others borrowed to simply survive.

> The financial crisis (and the world crisis it engendered) thus represented not so much the natural outgrowth of rising inequality as a further phase; it was the consequence of a deliberate effort to sustain a model of economic growth based on inequality that had, in the year 2000, already ended. In pressing this model past all legal and ethical limits, the United States succeeded in prolonging an 'era of good feeling', and in ensuring that when the collapse came, it would utterly destroy the financial sector . . . We continue to try to cope with the consequences of these extraordinary events (James Galbraith, 2012, p. 293).

Mian and Sufi likewise argue that the debt overhang from the speculative boom transfers risk systematically from lenders to borrowers at a time when the latter are least able to bear it, with dire consequences for the real economy.

> As it turns out, we think debt is dangerous. If this is correct, and large increases in household debt really do generate severe recessions, we must fundamentally rethink the financial system . . . A financial system that thrives on the massive use of debt by households does exactly what we don't want it to do – it concentrates risk squarely on the debtor (Mian and Sufi, 2014, p. 12).

Eighth, the journey to and through the global financial crisis has been influenced by and reinforced what could reasonably be called '*a collapse of moral values*' in the economy. The commitment to market rationality has, I would argue, encouraged an acceptance of selfish behaviour that reinforces a narrow short-term focus that ignores values of mutual concern, trust and reciprocity, the very qualities of community that are necessary – as Adam Smith knew – to make market systems work. This leads to patterns of behaviour by business leaders that would once have been roundly castigated by other community leaders. Part of the political backlash against the efforts of governments to save the economy stems from the gut feeling that 'they' got away with it; 'they', in this case are the senior finance executives who did not lose their boom time bonuses and did not personally face criminal or civil charges in a court. Supported by value propositions like the theory of shareholder value, and the investor-forced focus on short-term returns, managers are encouraged to do all in their power to impress stock markets and financial commentators with their steely ability to drive up profits and dividends on a quarter-by-quarter basis. As a series of well-publicized scandals have been uncovered by other segments of the media, the means to achieve the favourable judgment of the markets include undeclared conflicts of interest, insider trading, manipulation of markets, bribery of public officials and outright fraud.

The list of illegal and semi-illegal practices is a long one. Starting soon after the crisis it became clear that those with inside information as to the dubious value of the toxic assets had effectively moved early to offload most of the risk onto unsuspecting investors. When caught, the perpetrators were able to settle with their most determined victims out of court and without admitting liability. Others escaped their liabilities by taking the bankruptcy route. In a few cases the crooks were caught and punished. The Bernie Madoff Ponzi scheme was the most brazen case, due to the size, longevity and scope of his fraudulent activity, and one might surmise, the fame and influence of some of his duped investors. Madoff was convicted and sentenced to more than 100 years in jail. More recently, a number of large banks like Barclays, J.P. Morgan and UBS have been caught manipulating interbank interest rates and foreign exchange markets and fined hundreds of millions of dollars.[7] As I write, the large established institution, Wells Fargo, is under attack for encouraging ('incentivizing') frontline staff to set up bogus and unauthorized bank and credit card accounts without their clients' knowledge. The bank's CEO has offered to scrap the incentives scheme and forego $41 million in salary and bonuses in an attempt to keep his job. This move appears unlikely to satisfy Congress or assuage public outrage at yet another financial scandal.[8] Also in the firing line, Germany's biggest bank, Deutsche Bank, is facing a 'fine' of $14 billion levied by the US Justice Department for mis-selling derivatives during the lead up to the GFC a decade earlier.[9] The bank, the world's leading derivative provider, is reportedly struggling to meet the fine and is attempting to negotiate it down to a manageable level. Failing that a bailout by the German government appears to be its fallback strategy, an unlikely escape route given that 2017 is a German election year and the hard-line, moralistic stance of the Merkel cabinet has taken on bailouts in other Eurozone countries. As the share price of Deutsche drops anxious investors and counterparties are questioning the reliability of other German banks.

These far from infrequent cases of unethical and illegal business practices demonstrate the extent to which ethical values can be 'crowded out' by models and theories that promote self-interest as the motive spring of economic behaviour. Removing traditional community-oriented values from theoretical and business discourse destroys self-imposed limits on destructive actions that can lead to systemic crises such as we are experiencing. The fact that senior corporate executives can hide behind the legal fiction of the corporation and real or feigned ignorance of what their junior staff are doing, in order to escape any personal responsibility for what unfolds, makes it certain that this particular form of moral hazard will endure. Even when eyewatering fines are imposed and paid by transgressing companies, the prophylactic effect is undercut by the even greater prospective returns that such behaviour garners and the low probability of being caught. It simply becomes a cost–benefit calculation and as I have stressed any cost–benefit analysis is replete with implicit ethical undertones.

Finally, *the global context* in which the crisis emerged and persists needs to be acknowledged. In an important sense, a major crisis was bound to happen, not merely because of the various factors discussed earlier but also because of the build-up of structural imbalances in the international economy after the collapse of the Bretton Woods Agreement in 1971. Export-driven growth in Germany, China and the oil rich countries of the Middle East had as the reverse side a build up of chronic balance of payments deficits in the major Western countries. Capital flows from the former fed booming debt-fuelled consumption and speculative investment in the latter. Austerity policies were forced on deficit nations precisely at a time when they were least able to bear them. Keynes's fears expressed at Bretton Woods finally came true. It was not possible, he argued, to stabilize national economies if they were, collectively, in structural international imbalance. Policies needed to be implemented forcing surplus economies to reduce their chronic surpluses so that those in deficit could rebalance their economies.[10]

WHAT ARE THE CONSEQUENCES?

Part of the difficulty of gauging the consequences of the GFC is the manifold nature of the outcomes and the complex interrelationships entailed. Naturally enough, the first response has been to focus on the numbers, more precisely the dollars lost. 'Natural' because that response reflects the extent to which financial metrics and market values have colonized policy thinking and the popular imagination. The International Monetary Fund (2009) forecast that the losses in the value of financial assets in America would be $2.7 trillion between 2007 and 2010, almost twice the annual GDP of the country. Far more seriously, GDP itself was slated for a big fall. US aggregate output fell sharply over that period and had only recovered its pre-crisis level by the end of 2010, to remain 13 per cent below the 1980–2007 trend (Wolf, 2014, p. 31). In round figures, that meant that the US real GDP in 2011 was about two trillion dollars less than it would have been without the output gap sparked by the crisis. Britain endured a similar proportional potential loss. After 2011 the US recovery was anaemic, continuing to fall below trend; by early 2014 it had only increased by 7 per cent on the 2008 level. Apart from an even weaker recovery in Germany, no other major economy, even the UK, had recovered its 2008 level by the beginning of 2014.

Focusing on the figures obscures the full impact. Millions of workers lost their jobs and incomes, many of who also lost their homes. Unemployment rose to double figures in America and worse happened in Europe. Unemployment reached 50 per cent in Greece, the same as *youth* unemployment in Spain. Millions more lived in fear of following in their footsteps. Further millions saw their house values fall below the level of their outstanding mortgage liabilities. Negative equity and falling inflation increased the real burden of their debts, which for many Americans also included consumer and educational loans taken on in the past in the expectation of continuing prosperity and expanded job opportunities. Beyond the official statistics, underemployment marked by the replacement of full-time by part-time and casual jobs consigned the members of once secure middle class households to a lifestyle more reminiscent of Marx's reserve army of unemployed. Inevitably, women and members of minorities suffered most from the forced restructuring in labour markets, avidly supported by the austerity mindset of governments. The retirement savings of the elderly and those about to retire shrank along with interest rates, destroying the carefully crafted futures of prudent households. Educational funds put aside by parents and grandparents were raided to meet the challenge of current survival. The educational and training of many young people was put on hold, a potential time bomb, both in terms of unmet future demand for the skills necessary to drive innovation and productivity growth, and as an incubator of anger and frustration as young people looked towards a future that offered no prospect of emulating the success of the previous generation. Angry and resentful masses of young people with long lives ahead and little to look forward to present a volatile political challenge to peace and social order, as successive dictators from Augustus Caesar onwards have recognized and turned to their advantage.

At the same time, as we saw in the preceding chapter, inequality increased, with the wealthiest protected from the economic misery visited on the vast majority. The persisting economic crisis inevitably exacerbated other social problems arising from hopelessness and anomie, to use the term applied to such major episodes of dislocation noted by the sociologist Émile Durkheim in the late nineteenth century. Depression, heightened anxiety and suicide tend to accompany economic depressions. Homelessness and crime add their own list of problems to the mix. The crisis has brought home to ordinary citizens the precariousness of life in a neoliberal world, and a strong sense of something important lost; that 'something' resonates deeply with the intuitive moral commitment to community. Governments are faced with challenges on multiple fronts precisely at a time when resources and organizational capacity are stretched and further hampered by the intervention of powerful forces aiming to protect their privileged interests.

The very worst response in such situations is a forced programme of austerity, the very response that has prevailed, once the initial shock to the confidence of economists and policy makers had worn off. The decades long neoliberal attack on the state had achieved its purpose. Governments fell back, more in hope than expectation, on the dexterity of the hidden hand. As the crisis lingered on, it became increasingly evident that markets left to themselves would not break out of the collective funk into which the economy had sunk. Increasingly, unorthodox monetary policy was not working. The central banks were running out of ideas. The built-in stabilizers had done as much as they could to moderate the severity of the slide in GDP but could not alone reverse the trajectory.[11] A more aggressive fiscal intervention was required.

Perhaps the most insidious effect of the crisis has been on the general psychology of the population. Anger as well as hopelessness flourishes; politicians, business leaders, even economists feel the sting of the public backlash. This raises problems for the future viability of democratic societies taken up in Chapter 17. At the point of public action, a growing lack of confidence in the ability of government to govern makes it even more difficult to craft and implement coherent policies. If markets cannot deliver the goods and government is helpless or captive to powerful interests, a sense of resignation sets in and is powerfully self-fulfilling.

The key point is to note that although we have plenty of data on and many suggested 'solutions' to the problems unleashed by the crisis, they are fixated on the proximate structural causes of the crisis – like generals fighting the last war – and ignore the catastrophic consequences just noted in qualitative terms earlier. Thus, for example, Wolf (2014, Part Three), Mian and Sufi (2014, Part III) and Kay (2015, Part III) offer sensible suggestions for reforming the banking sector in order to make banks less subject to sparking speculative excesses and Akerlof et al. (2014) summarizes the reconsidered state of thinking on implications for macroeconomic policy 'after the crisis'.[12] In particular, Kay's proposal to make banking boring again merits action, requiring reintroduction of a strong version of the Glass-Steagall Act that would prevent commercial banks from straying beyond the four basic functions for assisting, rather than subverting the real economy; namely, operating the economy's payments system, matching borrowers to lenders, helping people manage personal finances across the life course and between generations, and helping people and businesses manage risks. This, however, is not enough.

WHAT ARE THE IMPLICATIONS?

A moral response to the enormity of the changes wrought by the financialization of modern society needs to pick up on the guidelines noted in Chapter 12. First and foremost, judgment must rest on a clear analysis of what happened and what went wrong. The GFC was not an accidental event, the unforeseeable result of an external shock. Its genesis was, as I have argued, encoded in the DNA of capitalism, an 'accident' waiting to happen. Orthodox economics in its new classical garb was totally oblivious to the cumulative results of financialization for the instability of the real economy. An adequate analysis must include the systemic effects of social interaction, based on a more realistic and holistic conception of how the economy actually works and occasionally fails to work. Just as critical is the need to cast the analytical net wider to catch the corrosive effects on social cohesion and social order – and to develop policies that offset their malign impact. Among the few well-credentialled economists, Stiglitz and Wolf have explicitly recognized the bankruptcy of orthodoxy. But even they are loath to cast off the shackles of methodological individualism that they see as foundational to modern liberalism and freedom. Although they and others have created space for various heterodox approaches to edge (nudge) into the policy field, they do not embrace or even seem to recognize the role of values in the economic actions of real, community-anchored people, replete with their intuitive beliefs and commitments, in the sense dissected by Smith, Sen and Etzioni (see Chapter 11). Likewise, although their personal liberal values shine through, they do not recognize – or at least, sufficiently take into account – that outcomes on the ground will not simply follow from stating those values but by how conflicting ethical injunctions and naked political power constrain and steer (and block) policy processes. By adopting an academic division of labour – falling for 'Adam's fallacy' – economists desert the field when they are most needed.

Keynes's much quoted lines at the end of *The General Theory* that, in the final instance, it is 'the ideas of long dead economists' that drive politicians and policy, is only partly true. As a lifelong liberal and member of the British establishment, Keynes was unable to appreciate that ideas are not simply the neutral inventions of brilliant minds like his own. They reflect and reinforce the particular historical trajectories of the societies they spring from, most notably the moral histories and the power relations that persist. Liberal individualism, especially when confined to the ideal of 'negative freedom', raises barriers to considering policies that progress 'positive freedom' – that is, that enhance the capacities of socially situated individuals to pursue their life plans. Orthodox and most heterodox economics unconsciously plays to the interests of the powerful, by not challenging them, by steering attention to the policy targets and solutions that do not threaten those values and interests.

In the case of reform of the banking system, the large banks and their political supporters inside and outside government have been successful in deflecting and defusing criticism, shifting the blame for the economic and moral breakdown to other actors, or simply as the price (note the term) we the people have to pay for the privilege of living in a neoliberal world. It is in the world of high finance that the ethical tenets of Gordon Gekko prosper. An ultra-commodified culture of selfish acquisition pervades the financial sector and has colonized other sectors of the economy and society and determined policy agendas. Real reform needs to focus directly on changing that culture through a mix of regulatory, judicial, educational and institutional design.[13] In football terms, this will be like kicking against a strong wind.

CONCLUSION

The global financial crisis burst on a world and an economics profession that was blind to its possibility. Although initial responses managed to avoid the main mistakes that turned the Wall Street Crash of 1929 into the Great Depression, an untimely reversion to the policy of enforced austerity prolonged the misery among the majority of the peoples of the advanced economies. Misery knows many faces but policy focuses on misery expressed in monetary form. Success is measured by conventional metrics like GDP and official (un)employment rates. The depreciation of moral capital and the path-dependent nature of social polarization elude scrutiny. Gainful employment is about more than earning income to consume – though this is an important function in a market society in which labour and most goods and services are routinely commodified. Being employed is also about being valued and valuing oneself; the nature of employment, its enabling conditions and scope for developing one's creative abilities, is an essential part of being human, of living a full and fulfilling life. Adam Smith knew this, so did Keynes, so for that matter did Marx. Later economists following Ricardo and Malthus have forgotten this basic truth. Tragically, the changes to labour markets wrought by greater 'flexibility' are reducing the working lives of an increasing fraction of the working age population to the stultifying stereotype of the dismal science. Farcically, the solution proposed calls for more of the same – more flexibility, less power and independence in the workplace, more casual and insecure employment and lower wages in a global race to the bottom.

NOTES

1. Wolf (2014, p. xv).
2. The list of popular books rushed out to explain the disaster to a shocked general audience is huge. As a small example, see: Stiglitz (2010); Krugman (2008); Tett (2009); Lanchester (2010); Reinhart and Rogoff (2009). Subsequent accounts include: Wolf (2014); Rajan (2010); Roubini and Mihm (2011); Blinder (2013).
3. Merrill Lynch, one of the big five investment banks, had been manoeuvred into a forced marriage with Bank of America at a share price barely a third of its pre-boom peak. This left Goldman Sachs and Morgan Stanley standing to be saved by turning themselves into banking companies in order to access support from the Federal Reserve.
4. Wolf (2014, p. 81, Figure 14) provides comparative evidence on this point, both before and after the GFC.
5. See relevant comments in Chapter 11.
6. Among a series of examples of the silo effect in action, Tett looks at the cases of a large investment bank, a hedge fund and the Bank of England. The novelist and financial commentator John Lanchester (2012) has provided a fictional account of the silo effect (and fixation on bonuses) in a financial services firm in his novel, *Capital*.
7. Who can forget 'the fabulous fab'? Goldman Sachs bond salesman Fabrice Tourre was (eventually) found liable for misleading investors in 2008 by selling a package of mortgage-backed securities known (but not by investors) to be likely to default. Only Fab was found personally liable, Goldmans was able to negotiate a no-fault fine of more than half a billion dollars while conducting business as normal. Fab was due to teach an economics course at the University of Chicago – home of free market economics – in 2014, but the university withdrew his commission once his behaviour had become public knowledge. No doubt Fab is far from being alone among the legions of small fry acting badly; perhaps he was just more prone to hubris than others and paid the price. In the wake of the GFC, a number of business schools are believed to be introducing courses on ethics into their programmes. Perhaps one might be permitted a degree of cynicism as to the motive and likely outcome of such moves.
8. Similar scandals surrounding perverse staff incentive schemes and fraudulent misselling of financial products have hit the four major banks in Australia, that together account for more than three-quarters of all residential mortgage and business loans. The largest, the Commonwealth Bank of Australia, is also under investigation for alleged miss-selling of products by its insurance arm.
9. In fact, the penalty is not a fine because the bank is refusing to admit liability for any wrongdoing. It represents an impost intended to reflect the losses incurred by bank customers and a possible fund to compensate losers. The penalty results from litigation in civil not criminal proceedings. Although the losses inflicted on investors by mis-selling vastly outweigh those due to outright fraud (with Madoff a dishonourable exception) the perpetrators of the former have been spared the rigours of the criminal justice system. Even in the case of the most blatant fraudulent behaviour, as has occurred at Wells Fargo, bank executives have avoided jail time.
10. Keynes's solution was an international clearing union that would punish countries if they persisted in running large balance of payments surpluses. However, the weak British bargaining position meant that America's preferred solution, enshrined in the establishment of the International Monetary Fund and World Bank, prevailed until 1971 (see, Steil, 2013; and Skidelsky, 2000, Part II). Wolf (2014) argues that the

persistent export-focused growth strategy of Germany has generated unsustainable structural imbalances within the Eurozone that lies at the heart of the region's continuing problems.

11. This refers to the automatic tendency in a crisis for the government budget balance to move into deficit as tax revenues fall with output and social expenditures on benefits increase in line with rising unemployment.
12. The work of previously ignored or discarded economists, notably Keynes, Minsky and Kindleberger has finally been acknowledged.
13. The complexities involved and likelihood of unintended consequences must be recognized and factored into policy reforms. However, the blanket claim by the banks and their supporters that this is all too hard and that any move to monitor or limit managerial prerogatives will automatically threaten the stability and solvency of the financial sector, must be treated with extreme suspicion. They would say that, wouldn't they?

15. Environmental crisis

> There once was a town in the heart of America where all life seemed to live in harmony with its surroundings . . . Then a strange blight crept over the area and everything began to change. Some evil spell had settled on the community: mysterious maladies swept the flocks of chickens; the cattle and sheep sickened and died. Everywhere was a shadow of death (Rachel Carson).[1]

CONTEXT

In 1962 the American biologist Rachel Carson published *Silent Spring*, a swingeing exposé of the cumulative effects of chemical pollution in the environment. Lakes, seas and rivers were being destroyed by the indiscriminate discharge of industrial effluent, silently killing the flora and fauna that lived in or depended on the environment playing its natural role. Land and air were similarly befouled. Carson documented in a direct and powerfully personal way the negative externalities that Arthur Pigou had identified as the Achilles heel of capitalism half a century before. However, Carson's work had a far larger longer-term impact, presented in a way that most people could recognize and react to. The mysterious shadow was cast well beyond America. Observers in other industrial countries began to note the phenomenon, most infamously in Japan where the cumulative effects of mercury poisoning begat a new condition, Minamata disease. Rather than marginal side effects of industrial production, the deleterious effects were presented as necessary concomitants of business as usual.

As economists began to digest the implications of Carson's critique – and governments moved to regulate industry – it became clear that the basic problem was systemic. The environment as a complex system of natural and organic ecosystems delivered a stream of natural resources to the economy, including clean air, water and virgin land, at a zero price. As 'free' but scarce goods they were over-exploited, a massive tragedy of the commons was building up steam. The environment was treated as an inexhaustible quarry and a sink of infinite absorptive capacity. A new sub-discipline – environmental economics – was born. Economists turned their analytical tools on the problem of taking the environment seriously – but they did so from the standpoint of their core discipline and naturally tended to promote the market mechanism as the primary model of understanding what was happening and as the main means of correcting failures perceived to be arising. This approach increasingly ran up against alternative analytical and prescriptive approaches drawing on insights from other social science disciplines and philosophy.

WHAT HAPPENED?

The 1960s saw the birth of the first wave of environmentalism. Governments responded to the demands for action by introducing legislation like the US Clean Air Act (1963) that authorized the federal Public Health Service to develop techniques to monitor and control air pollution. The Air Quality Act (1967) extended the reach and effectiveness of monitoring and control techniques. In 1970, the Act was amended to grant federal enforcement powers to the newly created Environmental Protection Agency, a body responsible for coordinating research and enforcement at federal and state levels and broadening the scope of pollution sources and effects. Subsequent amendments further expanded the scope and powers of the agency, culminating in 1990 in the introduction of a pollution permit system and a recognition that pollution problems extended beyond national boundaries to include cross-border and macro-environmental issues like depletion of the earth's ozone layer. The Clean Air Act was important because it was the first time that a national government implemented comprehensive policy aimed at controlling the negative environmental impacts of market-driven economic development. The Act was also influential in encouraging many states of the Union and other countries to set up similar agencies and introduce like policies.

In a broader context, the 1960s and 1970s saw the emergence of a broad-based environmentalist movement, comprising elements of the New Left, life and physical scientists, proponents of alternative technologies and dissident economists. In 1972, the Meadows (Donella and Dennis) and colleagues published another defining book, *The Limits to Growth*.[2] Two years earlier, biologist Paul Ehrlich (1968) published his controversial thesis, *The Population Bomb*, claiming that continuing population growth would breed the world to the edge of starvation. Together these books imparted a sense of urgency tinged with doom. Humankind, they claimed, was locked into a path ending in catastrophe, embarked on a one-way trip over the cliff. The current global capitalist model of permanent economic growth was, they suggested, bound to run up against immovable barriers posed by natural resource limits, accelerating environmental desecration and too many mouths to feed. This stream of thinking had a long tradition in economics, stretching back to Malthus at the end of the eighteenth century. In his book, *The Coal Question*, the co-instigator of neoclassical economics, William Stanley Jevons, had agonized over the likelihood that Britain, the world's industrial powerhouse, would run out of coal and so lose its global economic supremacy. The dismal science was not so called by accident.

However, by the beginning of the 1970s, the dismal past was long forgotten and a sense of optimism prevailed, both in government and the economics profession. Economic growth was the saviour, the means by which the age-old problems of scarcity would be resolved. Some even saw continued growth as the golden path to a world in which scarcity and the discipline of economics as we knew it would become redundant. This view echoed that of both Keynes and Marx; eventually the sordid business of grubbing out a profit by depending on the 'disgusting and morbid' commercial motives and values of contemporary capitalism would be superseded. Differences of opinion arose when it came to the question of timing – when would El Dorado arrive? A prominent anti-growth movement arose to argue that we had reached the point at which economic growth was becoming a self-fuelling end in itself and moving the system away from and not towards a *sustainable* future. The term 'sustainability' emerged as the counterpoint to growth. Herman Daly (1973) edited *Toward a Steady-State Economy* that brought together a virtual pantheon of critics sceptical of the conventional commitment to growth; contributors included Ehrlich, Schumacher, Kenneth Boulding and Garrett Harding, the last named the author of the influential 1968 article, 'The Tragedy of the Commons'. Two other contributors published influential heterodox books at around the same time: E.F. Schumacher (1973), *Small is Beautiful*, and Nicholas Georgescu-Roegen (1971), *The Entropy Law and the Economic Process*. Schumacher's book inspired the commune movement in the West left over by the 1960s hippies. Small scale, self-sufficient societies sought to withdraw from the mainstream economy and society. In this ambition, they followed the much earlier nineteenth-century utopian socialist experiments of Robert Owen and the followers of Charles Fourier and Henri Saint-Simon. Like these early forays, few of the later communitarian attempts outlasted the decade. However, Schumacher's basic ideas and values around self-sufficiency continue to influence discussions of sustainability.

The impact of Daly and Georgescu-Roegen have left a greater mark, culminating during the current century in the 'de-growth movement'. Daly argued for a situation in which the flow of energy and other natural resources is just sufficient to maintain a constant stock of capital and constant numbers of people. Georgescu-Roegen argued that this is possible only in the medium term. In the long term exhaustible resources will be exhausted and diminishing returns will throw the economies of the world into a downward spiral, upsetting the steady state, assuming that one can be reached in the first place. Technological and scientific progress will help prolong the good times but, in the end, it is the end. This harks back to Ricardo's gloomy prognosis but over a much (much) longer time frame.

The work of Daly and Georgescu-Roegen and their adherents established a breakaway strand of *ecological economics* and a journal of the same name. In this tradition, the focus is much more on physical rather than financial flows. This sub-discipline has evolved away from the strict 'energetic' and stock-flow paradigms of the two prime movers to look at the social and communal context in which sustainable living can arise. In a sense, the long, long term matters less for twenty-first century peoples than getting to the end of the current century without suffering a catastrophe of fourteenth-century proportions in which more than half the population of Europe died during the Black Death. Pandemics, nuclear war and irreversible climate change induced by the carbon-intensive process of population and economic growth are threats in the lifetime of people born since the year 2000. The last named is an example of a new kind of environmental threat, a truly macro-environmental event unfolding as the unintended cumulative outcome of countless micro decisions in the economy, community and political system. Human induced climate change and its possible consequences form a complex system which is wickedly difficult to comprehend and even harder to challenge through available policy tools and institutional processes.

WHY IS IT HAPPENING?

The end of the post-war long boom and the appearance of the phenomenon of stagflation hampered the emergence of second wave environmentalism during the 1970s. As inflation ravaged the advanced Western economies and unemployment rose sharply at the same time, the idea that government could fine-tune the macroeconomy to engineer a balance between jobs and price stability evaporated. Immediate political attention turned to 'fighting inflation first' and old economic theories were dusted off to explain the failure of Keynesian demand management tools to deal with the problem. Economic growth was now touted as the only route out of the mire of stagflation. Only growth in a regime of relatively stable prices could generate the jobs necessary to sustain life. Moreover, it was claimed that by growing the economy, we could free the resources necessary to deal with the environmental problems faced. This optimistic view assumed, of course, that economic growth would increase the capacity to solve problems faster than the problems themselves increased. The reverse outcome was just as possible; like a rat running faster and faster around a spinning wheel, no progress is made and the apparatus might even slip backwards.

Nevertheless, in the late 1980s a new term – 'sustainable development' – was coined to describe a situation in which growth occurred while maintaining the stock of 'natural capital' intact.[3] Sustainable development was loosely defined as economic activity that meets the needs of current generations without reducing the ability of future generations to meet their needs. This has proved to be a notoriously vague and open-ended definition. It explicitly introduces moral values around inter-generational equity. However, while ruling out gross destruction of environmental resources in pursuit of growth conventionally conceived, it still leaves plenty of room for widely divergent views and policies as to what constitutes threats to the ability of future generations to thrive. Also left vague are the 'needs' to which the concept refers. Ethically speaking, the notion of sustainable development, like conventional notions of development, is also explicitly anthropomorphically centred. The current and future moral value of environmental resources for other species is ignored, except to the extent that those species matter to humankind.

The opening up of debate around what sustainable development means for policy extended the scope of normative analysis to consider the rights and consequences in traditionally 'non-economic' spheres. Thus, the notion of the 'triple bottom line' sought to position the 'environmental' and 'social' dimensions alongside the 'economic' as targets for policy. The implicit assumption was that it was possible to trade off outcomes in economic, social and environmental terms, both within and between generations in a way that would meet the basic intergenerational ethic of responsibility. To assist policy makers achieve this balancing act, new metrics and analytical tools were proposed, of which social and environmental impact assessment was proposed to complement the hegemonic role of social cost–benefit analysis. Other tools and indices, as noted in earlier chapters, also were advanced. Thus, Daly and John Cobb (1989) introduced their 'Index of Sustainable Economic Welfare' (ISEW), comprising personal consumption *plus* government non-defensive expenditures (for example, education) and domestic labour, *minus* private defensive expenditure (for example, private security services and prisons), the costs of environmental degradation and the depreciation of natural capital. This index has been further developed as the Genuine Progress Indicator (GPI) that widens the net of non-marketed values and costs of natural capital depletion, while explicitly weighting the income distributional impacts.[4] Like all composite indices it raises problems of non-commensurability, providing a target for critics (see further on).

A more radical attack on pro-growth proponents seeks to decouple well-being from material production. The 'de-growth' movement argues for policies aimed at negative growth in either traditional (GDP) or sustainable development (GPI, GNH and so on) terms by reducing production, consumption, resource use and population. A shrinking economy (in traditional terms) would also reduce employment, meaning that hours worked would fall and jobs would be shared, freeing people to engage in other creative, non-remunerated activities. Time-poverty would wither. People would have time to engage in social and sharing – rather than individualistically acquisitive – behaviours, breaking down the barriers to expressing their essentially social nature of consumption. In short, people would bowl together. This approach recognizes the socially constructed nature and the hamster-in-a-wheel dynamic by which wants are endlessly manufactured.[5] Concrete policy directions proposed under the de-growth banner include: moneyless transactions; a generous minimum guaranteed income scheme; replacing large scale infrastructures with decentralized local facilities; sharing key goods like housing; promoting small businesses; strong limits on natural resource use; a focus on preserving biodiversity, and; experimenting with greater direct participation in policy making.[6]

Proponents of de-growth project the outcome of continuing the current trend to growing production and consumption in the advanced nations and its 'catch up' spread to the emerging and poor economies of the world. It is not only minerals and other natural resources that will provide a biophysical limit to continuing growth on the current trajectory. Land and water on Spaceship Earth are also in finite supply. The 'ecological footprint' represents the amount of usable land and water needed to support the resources consumed and disposal of wastes generated by current populations. The footprint of average people in the richest countries has been estimated at more than 20 times that in the poorest. If the ecological footprint of the former was stabilized at current levels and that of everyone else increased to match, simple calculations suggest that we would need several more Earth-sized planets to support human life as we know it. De-growthers therefore conclude that in order to avoid a catastrophic reckoning and future crash if current trends continue, humanity needs to manage a controlled cutback in production, consumption and resource use, now before it is too late.

Critics respond to the de-growth approach as they did to David Ricardo's stark warning of the approach of the stationary state. Continuing technological progress will push back the onset of diminishing returns. In particular, more efficient ways of accessing and using natural resources, including managing land and water, can put off the evil day by wringing more out of less for more to exploit. Admittedly, that will not suspend the long-term operation of the law of entropy but we can still look forward to a long run of increasing prosperity; after all, as Keynes so pithily put it – 'in the long run, we're all dead'. The response, in turn, has been to note the likelihood of the short-term gains from increasing resource efficiency being more than offset by 'the rebound effect'. As the cost of resources falls, their demand increases and people consume more than they would have before the improvement. This is also called the Jevons effect as he noted the relevance of improved mining technologies to accentuating the exhaustion of Britain's coal stocks. In short, the de-growth movement holds that the only way to avoid being locked into an ever greater and faster spiral of environmental decline is to switch tracks to a different trajectory that relies on less not more resource exploitation. In essence, this is a strategic policy proposal as to how to manage risk in an environment of chronic uncertainty.

WHAT ARE THE CONSEQUENCES?

Much of the current policy debate over environmental problems and how to deal with them focuses on the range of specific deleterious consequences of industrial development in the various capitalist and penumbra of non-capitalist societies. It's important to grasp that policies designed to tackle issues like climate change are different in scope and scale to those aimed at, for example, controlling run-off into a particular river, since they must encompass a much more complex set of impacts and raise a host of challenges for policy makers located in specific jurisdictions. Local political circumstances will constrain how transparent the consequences are and how effectively they will be addressed. In the case of industrial effluent befouling a local river from which a small fishing community ekes out a traditional livelihood, it makes a huge difference if the source is a small local business or a huge multinational mining company. In the former case, the effects and remedies are likely to be obvious and readily handled at the community level. In the latter case, however, there will be layers of politically constructed protection for the company and compliant domestic politicians who can deny, first, that any problems exist and second, if they do come to light, that it is their fault or responsibility to fix.

In cases where the impacts are huge, and the faults and responsibilities obvious – as in cases like the oil spill in the Mexican Gulf following the explosion and sinking of the Deepwater Horizon oil rig – the multinational company concerned (BP in this case) must be seen to adequately respond. An environmental problem for the people directly impacted turns into a potential public relations disaster for the company and an electoral threat to politicians in the jurisdictions implicated. In a wider context, the occurrence of what might be called mega-environmental events – that is, events so large and potentially devastating that they can't be plausibly denied – provides political fodder for anti-growth or de-growth environmentalist activists. As long as such events are sufficiently irregular, the politics of protest is difficult to maintain and the values underlying a commitment to the growth paradigm reassert their cognitive and normative grasp. The cycle of exploding popular outrage, hasty retreat, charm offensive, behind the scene deals, image management, public apologies and concrete though partial ameliorative action also characterized the unfolding of the global financial crisis, with a similar eventual public acceptance tinged with a lasting suspicion of multinational companies and inadequate politicians, and a vague desire for revenge.

It is worth looking in a little more detail at the Deepwater case, a dead-set certain inclusion in future business school case studies of how *not* to handle an environmental disaster. In addition to loss of life on the rig, the accident resulted in the flow of five million barrels of oil into the Gulf; the largest ever spill in marine environments. It took several attempts and almost five months before the leak was plugged, though doubt remains as to how complete or permanent the efforts have been. The initial efforts to deal with the spill were clearly inadequate. Widespread pollution of estuaries and coastline, the death of unknown numbers of fish and other marine animals, disrupted fishing, farming and tourism businesses, the increasing incidence of disease and ill health and the sheer debilitating impact on whole communities attempting to come terms with the disaster was difficult to gauge and took time to become clear. The tardy and piecemeal response of public agencies and the company added an overlay of burden on those affected. To many locals, this seemed to be a rerun of what had happened earlier during the Hurricane Katrina natural disaster. BP's response was especially ham-fisted. The then CEO made a hash of assuring local communities and the wider world of how and how quickly the problems would be resolved and people's lives returned to some semblance of normality. For this fault he lost his job, so did many others in communities impacted by the disruption to their livelihoods. Subsequent investigations allocated blame for the failure to BP, its operator and its contractor, Halliburton. In 2012 BP settled with the US Department of Justice, pleading guilty to charges of manslaughter for those lives lost on the rig, misdemeanours and a felony charge of lying to Congress. As in the shadow of the GFC, no senior executive was jailed, though some lower level employees faced criminal proceedings. In 2015 BP agreed to pay $18.7 billion in settlement to the Justice Department and has reportedly paid out more than $40 billion in civil settlements as well as a similar amount in clean-up costs.

Several things stand out in this case. First, the scale and reach of such events are massive. Second, responses to their occurrence are piecemeal, poorly organized and partial. Third, compensation is haphazard, incomplete and delayed. Fourth, the company concerned is able to limit and, to a degree, deflect criticism and responsibility. Fifth, government agencies are poorly prepared and resourced to deal with the crisis and at a disadvantage in calling the company to account. Although large, the monetary sums extracted through a lengthy legal process are inadequate, both as a measure of the full impacts of the disaster and as restitution to everyone adversely affected. For very large companies, even fines and other monetary costs in the billions can be seen as the costs – albeit abnormal – of doing business. As such, the remnant spectre of moral hazard ensures that environmental hazards will also hang around. This last point underscores the general thesis of this book, namely that attempts to monetize values associated with human endeavour inevitably miss out important moral elements of what is important to people living in real communities. No amount of compensation or public apologies will make up for the personal and collective losses – the loss of independence and pride, the fracturing of trust, the destruction of shared memories about how things used to be, and the pervasive sense of insecurity about the future – incurred by the people of Mexico and the US Gulf states. The explosion set off a series of ripple effects that still reverberate in the region and will do so for a long time to come, just as they did after the Fukushima meltdown and decades before, the Bhopal disaster.

As problematic as the Deepwater and other mega-events proved to be, they were relatively confined and tractable compared to the myriad unchartered environmental threats posed by climate change. All four categories of Donald Rumsfeld's knowns/unknowns confront humanity and policy makers. There are many *known knowns*, like some of the consequences of rising sea levels leading to increased flooding of coastal settlements leading to uninhabitable houses and disrupted businesses. It then gets more difficult, particularly associated with the science. What are the effects of that flooding on, for example, local ecosystems – just one *known unknown*? Then there are the *unknown knowns* – what is the range of and what are the most probable impacts on, say, house prices in the region? By definition, the most difficult of all consequences to even glimpse are the unknown unknowns, their number, scale and effects. There are wide differences of opinion, within societies and (less so) within the relevant scientific communities that provide scope and ammunition for vested interests to support policies that protect and enhance their preferred positions.

As always, policy inertia works in favour of interests that have already set the political agenda. In areas of contested terrain, forces for change are at a structural disadvantage, especially where the defensive ramparts are embedded deep in a society's basic class structure. This is certainly the case with attempts to introduce policies designed to mitigate or even ameliorate the prospective effects of climate change, given that the costs can be portrayed as widespread and immediate, while the gains appear vague and diffuse. In the case of unknown unknowns current actions can only be seen as a form of insurance premium in a situation where no actuarial basis exists on which to quantify that premium.

IMPLICATIONS

As noted earlier, there are established methods for evaluating the consequences of many environmental impacts; by 'evaluating', I mean both identifying and valuing outcomes in the normative sense. Each approach will tend to carry with it implicit and explicit normative criteria. To the extent that cost–benefit analysis is drawn upon, the value criteria are embedded in the distributionally non-neutral notion of Paretian efficiency and the dangerous fiction of monetary reductionism, the conceit that we can ignore any possible impact to which a dollar value cannot be attached. This latter practice has been described as placing by default a zero dollar value on those outcomes (see Chapter 8). To go down this path is not to avoid making moral choices but to do so without knowing that you have done so.

Because of the complexity of the causes and likely consequences of climate change, including the political dimension of dealing with it, it has become difficult to adequately devise methods for assessing the relative wisdom of doing A, B, C . . . Z, where Z is the non-decision to do nothing. In such situations, a prudent strategy of wait-and-see – a temporary Z – is often adopted. This strategy can also be seen as an example of 'the precautionary principle' at work. This places the burden of proof on proponents of particular policies (A, B and so on) to demonstrate with plausible assurance that the policies do not inflict harm on people or environments. In a policy world dominated by a pro-growth mindset, the reverse burden of proof holds; that is, opponents or potential victims of a policy are required to demonstrate that some harm will befall them as a result of that policy.[7] A prudential approach, in situations of extreme Rumsfeldian uncertainty, may also seek to qualitatively compare the possibilities of Type I and Type II errors. The former refer to situations when actions are taken that turn out not to have been necessary; the latter encompass actions that, with hindsight, should have been taken but were not. There are costs, both quantifiable and unquantifiable. In the case of climate change, the potential costs of a Type II error are likely to be orders of magnitude greater than for Type I, so claimed the *Stern Review on the Economics of Climate Change* (Stern, 2006).

The Stern Review drew an avalanche of critical responses, focused on the quantitative estimates of costs under both scenarios and in particular on the choice of (a low) discount rate used. Criticisms that reject action now because of a claimed lack of scientific consensus on the reality of climate change can be dismissed, since the consensus is well established; a decade later contrarian views are marginal survivals of earlier political opposition. Criticisms that focus on the discount rate are also misdirected since Stern himself argued that traditional cost–benefit analysis is inapplicable to multidimensional systemic problems and that multi-criteria approaches are necessary to properly address growing concerns.[8] Following Stern and subsequent reports from the International Panel on Climate Change, an international agreement on binding emission reduction targets was negotiated at the end of 2015. The Paris Agreement locks 195 countries into committing to actions that would keep global warming below two degrees centigrade (preferably 1.5 degrees) above pre-industrial times. Considerable scope will be given to individual countries as to how they achieve the level of emission reduction and adaptation measures on the path to stabilizing global temperature rise. Clearly, the Paris Agreement is an important step to coordinate a collective response to a collective problem. However, it is likely to be frequently revisited and revised in the light of future developments and unexpected events; this after all is one benefit of adopting at least a weak version of the precautionary principle.[9]

Sitting within the approach initiated by the Paris Agreement and only partly visible, is a set of ethical questions. Who should bear most of the current burden of curbing emissions and changing energy and industrial technologies in order to achieve the better than 2 per cent target? It appears that, against considerable opposition in some advanced counties and industries, emerging and developing economies will face less restrictive controls on their emissions, compared to the constraints on advanced economy countries. This value position reflects well Sen's open-ended approach to reducing currently the most egregious barriers to improving opportunities for people in the former countries, as does a refusal to use high discount rates to effectively marginalize the life chances of future generations.

The climate change challenge has been partly responsible for stoking the de-growth movement discussed earlier. Reducing material production and consumption levels as traditionally measured is about more than recalibrating the economy; it is also about a transformation in values, about what is important to people. '[D]egrowth is not just a quantitative question of doing less of the same, it is also and, more fundamentally, about a paradigmatic re-ordering of values, in particular the (re)affirmation of social and ecological values and a (re) policisation of the economy' (Fournier, 2008, p. 533).

The life chances of non-human species will also be enhanced if human-induced climate change can be minimized along lines set out at Paris. However, this will not be enough in many cases. Even 'moderate' change in climatic conditions in some regions and some ecosystems will spell doom for endangered species. Even when climate change is not a factor, habitat loss caused by humans and other behaviours like illegal poaching can also result in similar outcomes. Whether one takes an animal rights or a consequentialist ethical position on threats to other species – and whether those threats emanate directly or indirectly via climate change from human actions – relevant public policies (including doing nothing) will express particular values that are indelibly inscribed on and inseparable from the resulting state of the world.

The discussion above has taken an anthropomorphic ethic as given. Hence, I have ignored the very large literature on the philosophical approach sometimes called 'deep ecology' that has emerged since the 1960s, the ethical view that the natural world embracing all life has a value in itself, independent of any relationship to humankind. Such thinking has influenced policies with respect to wilderness preservation, as well as animal welfare. For a discussion see, Naess and Rothenberg (1989).

The challenges of climate change for policy makers are obvious when explicitly considering the five elements of 'the moderate but comprehensive consequentialist' framework suggested in Chapter 11. In the first place, political pressures on governments emanate from positions of widely differing beliefs about what is happening and likely to happen, and express divergent and conflicting interests in policy outcomes. The general pro-growth culture has placed a primary value on maintaining current jobs, justified on quasi-egalitarian grounds – 'everyone has a right to meaningful employment'. Although arguments along these lines are often put as a convenient cover for protecting current inegalitarian outcomes, they capture a genuine and widely shared value; in capitalist societies, unemployment means social exclusion, if not starvation. The political strategy of some environmentalist activists attempting to change the trajectory of contemporary capitalism has thus drawn on the employment generating potential of new environmentally efficient technologies as a counter to job losses in current sectors like coal mining. On the other hand, radical critics of capitalism, such as de-growthers, must respond by pointing to mechanisms for sharing a reducing number of paid working hours and a range of non-monetary forms of productive activity. Other radical approaches dismiss money as a means of social cooperation and exchange completely (see Nelson and Timmerman, 2011). Views, morals and beliefs about complex issues like climate change themselves change over time. As the evidence for the deleterious consequences of a changing climate pile up, popular support for international cooperative action intensified. The Paris summit succeeded where the earlier Copenhagen one failed. Part of the push for a binding agreement came from morally infused arguments that gained ground during the intervening period. Paris also showed the way in which negotiation can work to generate outcomes without requiring a full consensus of value positions. One area of strong agreement, achieved against strong initial opposition, was a general recognition that the advanced countries were in a better position than less developed ones or those large emerging economies like China, to carry more of the burden of mitigation. This depended in part on acceptance of moral arguments based on equality of opportunity in the face of long-standing injustices, as well as on the recognition of power asymmetries constraining the negotiating space. Although arguments were also put at Paris phrased in rights-based language, it is evident that the key moral dynamic reflected an awareness of the consequences of not reaching an agreement binding on most nations in the world. It was in this sense that President Obama's invocation of morality in urging acceptance of the agreement should be read. One final note should be sounded. The future success or otherwise of the Paris Agreement and other policies in actually reducing and stabilizing climate outcomes is an open question. The clash of values, interests and power will, as ever, determine outcomes.

CONCLUSION

Over the past 40 years economists have sought to bring the environmental impacts of economic activity into the basic neoclassical model of how a capitalist economy *should* work. Governments, citizens and (most) economists have recognized that markets left to themselves can generate substantial inefficiencies and inequities unless government intervention offsets the most egregious impacts. Environmental economics, growing out of a conventional recognition of market failure and utilizing key elements of the rational economic agent model, has focused on market-related means of redressing those failures. Whether proposing Pigouvian taxes or introducing markets for traded emission permits, the policies assume that, with a little help, markets know best. There are three major limitations to this approach. First, it assumes that the impacts are independent and relatively small, so that specific taxes or permit systems can be designed to correct mal-allocations. In fact, some impacts are interrelated, arise from the unintended and interaction of many factors, and thus require a macro perspective to properly address them. Policies designed from within a partial equilibrium framework work against this imperative.[10] Second, it places heavy informational and organizational demands on policy makers implementing market-based instruments. Third, the instruments are natural targets for the political actions of interested parties, particularly large corporate concerns.

Climate change provides the paradigmatic case where conventional piecemeal policies may fail to set the 'right' signals, both with respect to the level of the tax or total volume of permits to be traded and the incidence or relative burden of changed price signals on citizens. In hindsight and after irreversible developments, market signals may have inadequately changed behaviours to the degree required. Once set, taxes or permit volumes are politically difficult to change given the fact that individuals' decisions, including large infrastructural investments, will have been made on the basis of the levels and rules originally set. In the case of traded permits, an active secondary market in which government intervenes can help smooth out inflexibilities relating to tax regimes. However, once the efficient market hypothesis is rejected, then secondary markets for permits can be seen to develop speculative excesses that threaten the intended role of such instruments. Direct regulation also runs up against informational, organizational and political barriers but will, in some situations, deliver more effective controls over the worst environmental impacts. The tragedy of climate change as a wicked policy problem is that all known means of attacking its many impacts face huge barriers due to the pervasive and irreversible nature of those impacts. However, it is likely that at some point quite draconian legislation will be required if, as expected, other means fail to move national economies sufficiently to meet the targets for carbon emission reduction required to keep warming at levels less than 2 per cent above pre-industrial levels.[11] This situation could then have major negative economic effects as emitting industries face commercially crippling readjustment demands. This is a case of environmental risk turning into policy risk implying an imminent imperative for such industries to manage that policy risk now. Financial institutions, especially insurance companies, are well aware of these risk trajectories and are beginning to take steps to meet the unknown future.

Radical political approaches to the lack of sustainability in the contemporary world are likely to eschew market instruments and, in the extreme, the very nature of generalized market exchange. Attention focuses directly on the nature of human interaction and cooperation, and on the ethical principles that would underpin them. For those favouring de-growth or communitarian solutions to address environmental crisis, political action must trump the central role of profit-driven and acquisitive motives and values – but without undermining the democratic ethos that historically grew up with industrial capitalism in the West![12]

NOTES

1. Carson (1962). She was savagely attacked the year after publication by leaders and political proponents of the chemical industries, who also sought to delay and frustrate legislation designed to control the worst excesses of pollution. Although Carson died young in 1964, American governments introduced a raft of environmental legislation over the following decades targeted at air and water pollution and land degradation. Political battles continue today over micro-environmental issues associated with activities like fracking and nuclear power.
2. Meadows et al. (1972). An update was published 30 years later: Meadows et al. (2004).
3. The term was introduced in the Brundtland Report, *Our Common Future*, set up by the World Commission on Environment and Development (1987), chaired by the Norwegian prime minister, Gro Harlem Brundtland.
4. These indices are based on the logical distinction between current income and capital depletion, or the difference between gross and net measures of welfare, stretching back to the work on John Hicks (1946) and Keynes's appendix on user costs in *The General Theory*.
5. John Kenneth Galbraith famously advanced this particular critique in his book *The Affluent Society*; 'the dependence effect' refers to the way that in modern capitalist economies, 'wants are created by the process by which they are satisfied' (Galbraith, 1958).
6. A key landmark in the de-growth movement was the *Second International Conference on Economic Degrowth for Ecological Sustainability and Social Equity* held in Barcelona in 2010.
7. Arrow and Fischer (1974) argue that the precautionary principle entails a 'quasi-option'. By delaying action more opportunity is available to discover and analyse evidence relevant to the harmful effects of policy. The more uncertain the future looks at present the greater the benefit from waiting for a clearer picture to emerge. Likewise, the greater the stakes – that is, the larger the possible impacts – the wiser to wait and devote resources to developing a clearer picture.
8. For example, see Barker (2008). Stern also later accepted that the traditional economic method used in the report underestimated the costs of doing nothing now.
9. With the election of Donald Trump to the US presidency, the future of the Paris Agreement (and many other environmental and climate change related issues) is uncertain.
10. But see Greenwald and Stiglitz (1986) for suggestions as to how compensating policies might be designed to deal with some situations of imperfect and incomplete markets.
11. The high probability of future regulatory shock stems from the strength of political forces currently allied against the imposition of effective mitigation actions by industry and governments and by the politics of policy drift evident in many democratic political systems.
12. That stricture does not necessarily apply to existing institutions of representative liberal democracy. Various forms of direct democracy on classical lines may provide a better container for the social structures envisaged.

16. Population crisis

> When is an area overpopulated? When its population can't be maintained without rapidly depleting nonrenewable resources (or converting renewable resources into nonrenewable ones) and without degrading the capacity of the environment to support the population. In short, if the long-term carrying capacity of an area is clearly being degraded by its current human occupants, that area is overpopulated (Ehrlich and Ehrlich, 1991, pp. 39–40).

CONTEXT

As far as can be ascertained, modern humans evolved in and moved out of Africa over 100 000 years ago, dispersing north through Europe and Asia and reaching Australia in the south around 50 000 years ago. The world's population grew to about 400 million by the end of the plague dominated fourteenth century, rising to around one and a half billion by 1900 and six billion in 2000. By 2012 the total had passed seven billion and demographic forecasts suggest that it will peak soon after and begin a slow decline – assuming no major catastrophic event.

The Reverend Thomas Malthus was among the first of the moderns to express concern over the capacity of the earth's resources and human ingenuity to support a rapid increase in the number of people on the planet. Neo-Malthusianism has enjoyed a bumpy ride, arising from time to time to warn of imminent disaster. Part of the attraction of this approach consists in the simple arithmetical logic that seems to explain so much and so much of importance, the very survival of the human experiment.[1] From 1000 years before the Christian era until about 1800, average living standards barely changed as population inched towards its first billion, limited by Malthus's negative checks, the four horsemen of the apocalypse – famine, pestilence, war and death. With industrialization, European settlement of the Americas and imperial expansion, economic growth outstripped rapid population growth leading to rising living standards in the West. The Malthusian trap seemed to lock the remainder of the world into stasis. This pattern of uneven development changed after 1950, as the economies of Asia and to a lesser extent Africa began to catch up, to use the title of Nayyar's (2013) book. This coincided with a rapid fall in annual global population growth, from about 2 to 0.5 per cent, reflecting the inverse mutually reinforcing dynamic of economic and population growth.[2] The most dramatic example of this process occurred in the post-Mao period, as China overtook Japan as the world's second largest economy and hundreds of millions of Chinese were lifted out of poverty. The first decade of the twenty-first century saw world poverty decline significantly, though not yet to the extent proposed by the millennial targets agreed by the advanced nations. Extreme poverty remains concentrated in parts of Asia-Pacific, sub-Saharan Africa, and Latin America (Collier, 2007), many of the places where resource exhaustion and the threat of climate change also exist.

The problem of population is thus twofold. What, given the biophysical constraints of the natural environment would be an optimal or at least bearable global population? Second, what can and should be done about the remnant pockets of poverty – the bottom billion – that persist? Buried within these questions are further policy-related ones. What policies *can* governments, supra-national agencies and community organizations implement to deliver population goals and what policies *should* they implement?

WHAT HAPPENED?

The past 50 or 60 years saw the impact of rapid technological developments loosen the terrible grip of Malthusian checks, as 'the Green Revolution' increased food supplies and basic medical and hygiene standards were lifted in large parts of the underdeveloped world. International agencies like the World Bank, World Health Organization and the World Food Program of the United Nation's Food and Agricultural Organization funnelled resources into the projects that together with the efforts of development aid, direct foreign investment and the work of countless non-government organizations, kick-started growth in many though far from all poverty-stricken countries. Much of this activity was driven by the profit-seeking and foreign policy goals of First-World firms and governments. And, in many cases the flow of resources was diverted to the benefit of local elites, bypassing the majority of citizens whose lives were left wretched. Nevertheless, the period since 1950 has seen populations increase to such an extent – due in part to increasing average life expectancy – that population threatens again to overstretch the carrying capacity of the planet. The dynamic expectation in poorer countries that their futures must follow the resource-intensive, consumption centred lifestyles of the West heralds the real possibility of future environmental crises. Human-induced climate change presents, as we saw in the preceding chapter, the major foreseeable threat in this context.

Although the prospect of Malthusian pestilence in the form of pandemics due to the rise of superbugs outgunning the efficacy of modern pharmaceutical science is a real possibility, and wars of annihilation far from out of the question, the death rate is likely to continue to remain low overall.[3] Thus, to the extent that peak global population is reached and decline set in motion, the heavy lifting will have to be done by achieving and maintaining a low birth rate. This has been the experience in developed economies; in some, like Japan, Italy and even Germany, fertility rates have fallen to such an extent that an ageing population is in or about to be in decline. Increasing economic growth in China has seemingly stabilized its huge population, now overtaken by India's. Mass poverty and inequality in the latter country remains, suggesting that population stabilization is some way off there.

The question of population growth, environmental degradation and mass poverty are thus intimately linked. Dealing with one has implications for all. It is this fact and the political difficulties of dealing with multiple political and cultural jurisdictions that renders policy making so challenging. Although population poses problems that are global, their solution entails action through institutions and avenues that are national and regional in scale and reach, as well as through the avenues of international cooperation.

Looking to the present and recent past, the major population development has been the massive flow, forced and semi-forced, of refugees and asylum seekers. Not since the aftermath of World War II has the world experienced the degree and urgency of people displaced by events beyond their control. The relatively orderly flows of migrants that characterized the period from the mid-1950s to the early twenty-first century, as people left war-ravaged Europe and poorer countries in Africa, Asia and Latin America to seek better lives in the West, has been replaced by large-scale evacuations of the Middle East and North Africa. This has had massive consequences for neighbouring and destination countries. The remainder of this chapter will focus on these issues. The larger question of the optimal global population is beyond the scope of this book and this author.

WHY DID IT HAPPEN?

The proximate causes of the flow of refugees in the Middle East and North Africa can be found in the breakout of 'the Arab Spring' in 2010. From a relatively peaceful revolution in Tunisia, resulting in the overthrow of a dictatorial regime and the eventual establishment of a national constitution and democratic republic, popular unrest spread throughout the region. The initial enthusiasm in the West – confident that the post-Cold War predictions of a new democratic dawn was upon us – faded as protests turned violent, repression stepped up and the prospect of virulently anti-Western ideologies and movements flowered. Libya erupted in civil war as long time dictator Muammar Gaddafi was toppled and then killed by rebel forces. Thereafter, Libya descended into chaos as rival rebel groups sought to establish control over local regions. In fact, for those with some knowledge of the country, its fragmentation post-Gaddafi was to be expected. The country was a nation in name only, a disparate collection of tribal lands presided over by warlords. He who controlled the large oil resources had a chance of imposing an overlordship, especially when supported by Western governments and multinational oil companies. Once Gaddafi's control and international support was gone, other foreign forces, including non-state groups like Islamic State, moved into the vacuum. Much the same result occurred in Yemen on the Arabic peninsular, where Saudi Arabia, Iran and various jihadi groups locked horns in an effort to forestall each other from coming out on top.

However, it was in Egypt that developments most serious for stability in the Middle and Near East unwound. President Hosni Mubarak resigned in 2011 in the face of widespread popular revolt, leading to suspension of the Egyptian constitution and interim rule by the armed forces. In 2012 general elections brought the long-time banned Muslim Brotherhood to power, to be in turn overthrown in a military coup that eventually installed ex-general Abdul Fattah el-Sisi as President. This left an uneasy form of military dictatorship operating within a radicalized Islamic country increasingly uncomfortable with Mubarak's accommodation with the West and America in particular. Popular grievances over official corruption and absence of civil rights continue to simmer.

The other major conflict situation that sparked the wholesale outflow of people en masse from the region was the Syrian Civil War, a conflict that shows no sign of easing, six years on from its inception in 2011. Like Libya and its neighbour Iraq, Syria is a polyglot legacy of twentieth-century efforts of Western powers to control the region's oil resources, a faux-nation constructed regardless of age-old ethnic, cultural and religious traditions and loyalties. Held together by the Assad regime (father and son) supported by the Alawite and Christian minorities, Syria was bound to be fertile ground for the uprising of its substantial Sunni Muslim majority. The revolt broke out in mid-2011 with mass street protests and the formation of the Free Syrian Army, quickly supported by the USA as a means of toppling the Assad regime. A Syrian National Council was formed, based in Turkey, bringing together a number of anti-Assad groups. Syrian Kurds in the north joined the revolt and insurgencies surfaced in various parts of the country.

The civil war intensified through 2012 and in 2013 radical jihadist groups, notably the Al-Nusra Front and Islamic State of Iraq and the Levant (ISIL), took over territory contested by government armed forces and the Free Syrian Army. Pro-Iranian Hezbollah fighters also joined the struggle, as did Sunni Lebanese living near the border with Syria. Multiple and deadly struggles within anti-Assad forces complicated the war and increased the casualties on all sides. American and allied Western air strikes were called in to assist rebels fighting both the government and jihadists. Eventually, in September 2015 Russian intervention on the side of the Syrian government lifted the war to a new level. Now the Syrian Civil War assumed a double proxy war: on the one hand, a struggle between Sunni and Shia Islam, promoted by Saudi Arabia and Iran, respectively and; a confrontation between Russia and America over influence in the Middle East. This latter conflict coincided with a return to animosities between the two veto members of the UN Security Council reminiscent of the Cold War, as old quarrels in Eastern Europe erupted over the Russian takeover of the Crimea and (effectively) Eastern Ukraine.

To date more than 200000 Syrians have died and two million been displaced, adding to refugee flows out of Iraq and Afghanistan where separate long-run wars have been in progress, on and off, since the 1990s. As ISIL and other jihadist movements spread their influence through the Arabian peninsula and North Africa, civil wars threaten to create further displaced populations in the millions, caught between the warring forces and forced to flee to neighbouring countries or face the deadly challenges of crossing seas and hostile territories to find refuge, with a range of consequences for themselves, their countries of birth and their destination countries.

WHAT ARE THE CONSEQUENCES?

A major outcome of civil wars in the Middle East and North Africa has been the mass exodus of people from Syria, Iraq, Afghanistan and Eritrea, seeking asylum in European Union countries. According to the Office of the United Nations High Commissioner for Refugees, more than a million migrants will reach Europe by the end of 2016 (*Euronews*, 2016). In 2015 almost two million illegal border crossings by land and sea occurred in Europe (Frontex, 2015).[4] The major destination countries have been Germany and Sweden. Large numbers of migrants seeking asylum have also headed for France and Britain. The main routes traversed have been through Turkey, Greece and the Western Balkans, until transition countries began closing borders in 2015, and across the Mediterranean

Sea from Libya, Tunisia and Algeria via Italy and Spain. Germany initially offered an 'open door' policy[5] to those seeking asylum but the process of registering and resettling an escalating wave of migrants has resulted in long backlogs and people stuck along the chain of movement. This, in turn, has led to countries through which the migrants moved to close their borders, notably Macedonia and Hungary. Britain too has moved, even before Brexit, to stop the movement from France across the Channel by sea, air and train. This led to a build-up of unofficial transit camps in Calais at the entrance to the Eurotunnel.

Hundreds of thousands of migrants are stuck in limbo as they await processing of their applications for asylum. Thousands more have perished on the dangerous journeys, especially those attempting sea crossings from Africa. The sheer scale of the numbers involved has overwhelmed the capacity of European host countries to cope. In spite of pleas by United Nations agencies and the Pope, and attempts at collaborative humanitarian operations like rescuing migrants from capsized boats in the Mediterranean, most European countries have become increasingly less willing to accept asylum seekers.

As desperate as the plight of those fleeing to Europe is and as hard pressed as are European government attempts to deal with the influx, the situation nearer the war zones, especially in neighbouring countries is even worse. In total, almost five million Syrians have been displaced in the near region. There are a million Syrian refugees in Lebanon, massively destabilizing that already vulnerable small country. Jordon, also a small country, is host to hundreds of thousands of refugees, living in large camps in inhospitable climatic conditions. Turkey now has about three million refugees, including those escaping persecution in Bulgaria and Iraq. Refugees have become a bargaining chip in negotiations between Turkey and the EU. In return for EU money, Turkey has agreed a legally dubious Syrian refugee swap deal with Greece. It is not clear if Turkey's nationalistic president Erdogan is using the crisis as a lever to further Turkey's bid for EU membership.

The situation in Turkey presents a picture that can be seen throughout the broad region of destination countries, especially in Europe. Opposition to migrants and asylum seekers is growing among existing citizens along with the numbers. Fear of 'being swamped' by people from other cultures is overtaking initial concerns for their welfare. Instead of being regarded as innocent victims of war and persecution, asylum seekers are demonized as 'economic migrants'. Xenophobic and racist attitudes are growing in a way not seen for more than half a century in Europe. These attitudes and the fears on which they are based has sparked a resurgence of hard right wing movements, including the National Front in France, United Kingdom

Independence Party (UKIP) in the UK and the Party for Freedom in the Netherlands. These parties have attracted growing electoral support largely due to their hard-line policies on border control and anti-migrant stance. In Britain, the unexpected referendum vote to leave the European Union effectively turned into a vote about migration and border control that in turn reflected concern over job losses and declining living standards at home. The result uncovered divisions around class, geography and, above all, age, and fed off anger directed at 'the elites' in the south-east who had, it was believed (with some justification), benefitted most from the cosmopolitan ties with Europe. The claim that 'they were taking our jobs' resonated in a country with high unemployment outside the prosperous south.

In other parts of the world, similar social and political responses to social dislocation and asylum seeker arrivals were occurring. In Australia, for example, the earlier and still current wars in Afghanistan and Iraq had sent migrants fleeing south to Indonesia in an attempt to reach Australia across the short sea distance between the two countries. People smugglers were trafficking thousands of people, almost all of whom were refugees, to Christmas Island, the closest territory under Australian jurisdiction. Australia, as a signatory to the 1951 Refugee Convention was bound to consider all people who arrive and apply for asylum. Inevitably many of the small unseaworthy boats onto which the migrants were crowded capsized and, as in the Mediterranean, many people drowned. In 2004, weeks before a national election, a Dutch ship, the *Tampa*, rescued several hundred refugees from drowning and sought permission to disembark them at Christmas Island. The Australian government refused and sent Australian Navy personnel to board the ship and prevent it discharging the refugees. A stand-off ensued, during which the government (and opposition) maintained a hard-line stance until eventually the boat departed Australian waters. This turned out to be a watershed in Australian politics. Both major political parties locked themselves into a narrative that played to the xenophobic elements in the domestic electorate. The conservative government coined the very effective phrase – 'we shall decide who comes to this country' and effectively blamed the refugees for their plight. An echo of this phrase resurfaced during the Brexit lead-up in the exhortation to 'no voters' to 'take our country back'.

The companion to Australia's harsh boat turnback policy came in the form of indefinite detention for refugees arriving by sea in centres established offshore in Papua New Guinea and Nauru, with a bipartisan promise that those detained would never be resettled in Australia. As a consequence hundreds of refugees languish indefinitely in conditions that human rights groups have repeatedly denounced as dangerous and degrading. Details of suicide, sexual assault and physical abuse have leaked out as the blanket ban by the government on independent observation has failed to maintain the intended news blackout. The arguably illegal actions of the Australian government and its private contractors has been justified by the claim that to change the harsh regime in any way would lead to people smugglers resuming their deadly trade in human beings. In reality, the politicians are responding to what they believe to be the populist views of a majority of the electorate, afraid to put down the dog whistle for fear of losing votes to right wing fringe political groups who have, as of the 2016 federal election, increased their numbers in the Australian Senate.

The current and previous (Labor) governments have consistently justified establishment of the offshore detention centres as necessary to break the people smuggling trade, to deter refugees from boarding boats in Indonesia and risking their lives in the sea crossing to Australia. This argument arose following the death at sea of more than 1000 (the figure that has gained popular acceptance is 1200) people, including many women and children, during initial attempts by the Labor government of 2007–10 to disband detention in favour of community-based orders while asylum applications were being processed. The rapid increase in the numbers of boats at sea and the drownings that followed was a major factor in the eventual return of an Abbott-led conservative government promising to determine 'who comes to this country'. Prior to that the Labor Party had adopted the same policy and the same rationale, establishing the offshore detention centres, leaving it to the Green Party, some independents and a groundswell of civil society groups to oppose the increasingly barbaric outcomes.

Since 2013, the opposition to offshore detention has grown as evidence of the physical and mental harm experienced by detainees has mounted. In order to deflect criticism, the Australian government has adopted a blanket news ban on reporting either naval action at sea or conditions on the two centres, Manus Island and Nauru. The Australian Human Rights Commissioner has been denied access to the centres, though this has not prevented her from presenting stinging criticisms to the parliament – for which she has been remorselessly attacked by government leaders and denied reappointment to the position. A 'cone of silence' has descended, though one continually breeched by investigative journalists and whistle blowers.[6] In October 2016, Amnesty International (2016) released a report on conditions in the centre on Nauru titled, *Island of Despair*. The report details the everyday experience of anxiety, sleep disturbance, physical attacks by local residents and self-harm. Cases of rape were also reported. Detainees are able to move around the island but must run the risk of hostile treatment by locals who do not want them to remain, a view promulgated by Nauru government officials. Medical, especially mental health, facilities are woefully inadequate; serious or chronic cases must be flown to the Australian mainland, though bureaucratic delays can and have caused complications, including death. 'The extent to which child refugees are subjected to abuse on Nauru is chilling' (Amnesty International, 2016, p. 6). Children as well as adults have been the victims of physical and sexual abuse. They have also suffered disproportionately due to the traumatic events witnessed, the despair of their parents, the effective denial of proper educational and health facilities and the hopelessness of not knowing what will happen to them. The Australian government has effectively sought to outsource the problems to a small, undeveloped nation. This is invalid, in fact and law:

> The Government of Nauru is responsible for the violations of human rights occurring on its territory. However, when it comes to refugees and people seeking asylum, Nauru is not the state in control. The authority responsible for the systematic human rights abuses documented in this report is the Government of Australia. It is the Government of Australia that set up the offshore processing system and the Government of Australia that has forcibly transferred people seeking asylum to Nauru. A range of Australian Government officials and contractors – on Nauru and in Australia – are involved with running the Refugee Processing Centre itself and with the management of the refugee population living outside of the centre. The Australian authorities are continuously informed about what is happening on Nauru (ibid. p. 6).

The damning report of the leading human rights group in the world concludes with a chilling summary: 'The conditions on Nauru – refugees' severe mental anguish, the intentional nature of the system, and the fact that the goal of offshore processing is to intimidate or coerce people to achieve a specific outcome – amounts to torture' (ibid. p. 7).[7]

Dog-whistle politics has assumed a prominent part in the political systems of most countries experiencing the increasing flows of refugees displaced from war-torn regions. Indeed, one of the architects of the Australian policy, ex-Prime Minister Tony Abbott has been widely celebrated by right wing forces open to his proffered advice that Britain too should develop similar hard-line policies to control their borders.[8] The key difference, of course, is that Australia is surrounded by a large moat and boat arrivals are relatively easy to spot and forestall. Also relevant to the more intractable problems for European governments is the sheer scale of the numbers of migrants, compared to the relatively small flow to Australia. And neither Europe nor Australia faces the logistical and resource problems confronting governments closer to the source countries.

IMPLICATIONS

The general issue of mass displacement and forced migration presents one of the major current economic, political and moral challenges of the early twenty-first century, just as it did at the cessation of World War II. The earlier events led to the formation of the United Nations and the development of the Refugee Convention. To date, little headway has occurred in recent times. This is an example – a policy field – in which conventional economic models offer little guidance. Attempts to reduce the policy question to some sort of cost–benefit or even cost effectiveness analysis misses the very heart of the matter.

For example, many Australian voters appear to be convinced that it is 'worth' paying over AU$500 000 per year to keep each refugee incarcerated on Manus Island or Nauru in return for the purported benefit of securing their borders. In fact, even a narrow cost accounting approach suggests that there are cheaper ways of preventing illegal boat arrivals. That they have not been actively pursued speaks to the underlying reasons why offshore detention has remained in place. The argument that the centres are necessary to save lives is a convenient rationale for Australians to *avoid* confronting the moral questions raised, to avoid the question faced in the wake of 9/11 – is it justifiable to use torture to defend the homeland? It is based on a hypothetical claim that the centres deter more people from getting on leaky boats and possibly drowning. It uses the past death of refugees to justify the current mistreatment of refugees by claiming to prevent the future death of refugees. It is this subterfuge that delivers the 'benefit' of peace of mind for which the 'cost' seems to be worth it.[9] This is an understandable but morally flabby position. But it is one that has been highly serviceable to conservative politicians and has locked or wedged progressive politicians into a supporting role.

The fact that there are cheaper ways of preventing deaths at sea is hardly a compelling moral argument in itself. Those who profess a deontological rights based viewpoint would stress the prior moral imperative to respect the basic human rights of current refugees regardless of the consequences, actual or hypothetical. This view, after all, generated the moral case for the creation of the UN Convention. Those subscribing to a comprehensive consequentialist approach, however, would want to *seriously* look at the various policies and combinations of policies that could reduce the incidence of deaths at sea but also recognize the just claims that refugees have to be accorded asylum under the existing conventions and laws. Such an approach would also recognize the political and cultural realities facing policy makers in specific situations. That is, policy, as always, needs to operate from what exists in the moral and cultural universe at hand. The fears of people that they are 'being swamped' may be exaggerated by conservative and nationalistic rhetoric but they are, nonetheless, real and reflect the interwoven biological and cultural factors influencing the moral beliefs held, as argued in Chapter 8. Thus, any policy aimed at improving the prospects of refugees attempting to claim asylum in Australia, for example, will need to demonstrate that by doing so, the domestic economy and society will gain in ways that traditionally have occurred over the decades from the large flows of migrants especially since World War II. After all, more than a quarter of Australia's current population is foreign born.

This has not proved possible to date. The politics of refuge in Australia, as in many parts of Europe, remains locked in the straitjacket imposed after the Tampa incident and the disastrous drowning deaths in 2008–2009. The possibility of combining a robust turnback of any people-smuggling boats, commitment of sufficient resources to speeding up the process of resolving asylum applications in Indonesian and other regional centres, increasing refugee quotas and quietly resettling existing refugees currently stuck in the offshore centres before closing the latter, can be morally justified in the terms presented in Chapter 9. Such an approach would clearly reduce current egregious injustices. It might also have the further beneficial effect of raising public awareness as to the existence of other injustices closer to home – namely, the discrimination and multiple disadvantages of Indigenous Australians.

The Australian case is far less complicated and of a much smaller scale than the challenges now facing Europe and the countries of North Africa and the Middle East. Solutions there entail addressing radical cultural differences. In cultures impregnated with the market morality of neoliberalism, implicitly justified by the model of the rational economic agent, it remains a huge cultural and political challenge to shift the moral discourse of social justice onto a new path, one that would effectively reduce the miseries and injustices of the rivers of refugees seeking sanctuary. The history and outcome of the Brexit exercise in Britain and the rise of Donald Trump to seize the 2016 American presidential election clearly indicates the nature and scale of the task.

CONCLUSION

Population has always been a focus for consideration in the human sciences, not least economics. From the dismal prognoses of Parson Malthus and stockjobber David Ricardo to the proponents of the limits to growth, small is beautiful and de-growth, controlling population numbers has been seen as an urgent task. During the two centuries over which these exhortations have been sounded, the timing of the apocalypse, like the Second Coming, has been pushed back in time. In the long, long run the physics tells us that it must all eventually end. Whether the final disaster comes in the shorter long run is an open issue, raising the question as to what level and kinds of risk humanity is willing to take now. As well as these large concerns, Western countries face the imminent challenges of dealing with the huge flows of displaced people driven by war and poverty from their places of birth. The refugee crisis is upon us now and is in large part the result of the foreign policies and military adventures of advanced Western nations whose governments and peoples bear a moral responsibility to help resolve it. An important part of this response must be to explicitly address the moral case for reducing injustices inflicted on the people forced to flee for their lives.

NOTES

1. For a recent example see Clark (2007).
2. This outcome reflected the impact of one of Malthus's positive checks – vice – or in less condemnatory terms, the spread of contraception, abortion and the education of women.
3. This is not to underplay the very high mortality due to disease and war in particular times and locations, nor to ignore the political causes of mass famine identified by Amartya Sen (1981).
4. Frontex is the European Border and Coast Guard Agency.
5. Germany's chancellor, Angela Merkel was widely praised for her humanitarian approach, until the problems caused by the sheer numbers arriving forced a change of government policy. It was also pointed out that part of the initial impulse to accept refugees related to an attempt to forestall Germany's predicted falling population; a similar initial response occurred in Italy for the same reason.
6. In 2015 the Australian government passed the Border Force Act that carries prison sentences of two years for employees or contractors who publicly speak out about conditions at the centre.
7. At the time of writing the Australian government is negotiating a deal with the US government to settle the detainees on Nauru and Manus Island in America in return for accepting an unknown number of migrants from Costa Rica in Australia. From one point of view this looks like the two governments engaging in people trafficking and indicates the extent of Australia's desperation to end the international condemnation focused on the current policy of indefinite detention.
8. Abbott has been quoted in the Australian press as being 'quietly pleased' at the Brexit outcome.
9. Of course, this is not the only argument in bad faith used to support the policy. Demonizing refugees as wealthy migrants seeking to 'jump the queue' instead of applying to migrate through official channels is a case in point. So too is the very notion that refugees fleeing persecution in Afghanistan, Pakistan and Iraq have the resources and effective opportunity to queue anywhere other than unofficial transit refugee camps from which they are trying to leave. In the Australian case it has long been obvious that most illegal migrants who are not refugees do not risk their lives on boats but arrive by air and overstay their tourist, student or business visas.

17. The hollowing of democracy

> When the social contract is abrogated, when the trust between a government and its citizens fails, disillusionment, disengagement or worse follows. In the United States today, and in many other democracies around the world, mistrust is ascendant (Joseph Stiglitz).

This chapter revisits a number of the issues raised in Chapter 10 in the light of the arguments presented in Part III. I argue that developments in the neoliberal era raise threats to the future functioning of liberal democracy as we in the West have come to know it. We see, to use Stiglitz's words – democracy in peril.

CONTEXT

The historical roots of democracy as a form of government go back, as we have seen to ancient times and the outcome has assumed many specific institutional variants. Although there were earlier small-scale democratic experiments, the first modern representative democracies arose in revolutionary fashion in the United States of America towards the end of the eighteenth century and grew gradually and organically in Britain after 'the Glorious Revolution' of 1689. However, in its contemporary form it was not until the twentieth century that this system of 'self government' became truly representative in the formal sense that all adult citizens were legally entitled – as a mark of citizenship – to vote for the people who governed them.[1] Proponents of Anglo-democracy drew on the liberalism of eighteenth-century philosophy, in particular the work of John Locke, David Hume and Immanuel Kant. The contemporary British political philosopher John Gray (1995) has identified four cardinal features of liberalism: it is individualist, egalitarian, universalistic and meliorist. The focus is on individual citizens who all share common rights and entitlements and on the capacity of citizens to change social and political arrangements to improve their lives. In a later book, Gray (2000, p. 2) distinguished 'two faces of liberalism':

> Liberalism has always had two faces. From one side, toleration is the pursuit of an ideal form of life. From the other, it is the search for terms of peace among different ways of life. In the former view, liberal institutions are seen as

> applications of universal principles. In the latter, they are a means to peaceful; coexistence. In the first, liberalism is a prescription for a universal regime. In the second, it is a project of coexistence that can be pursued in many regimes.

Gray argues that Locke and Kant exemplified proponents of the first viewpoint, as do Rawls and Hayek more recently. The second view was put by Hume and before him Thomas Hobbes; more recently Sen and Isaiah Berlin stress the plurality of valued ways of life and the need to allow for different capacities to pursue them. The first rift in the liberal project came with John Stuart Mill's stress on the egalitarian and meliorist programmes of improving the *effective* opportunities of less advantaged citizens to pursue their particular life plans though collective private and public intervention. Although Mill maintained an unshakeable individualistic focus, he inevitably retreated on the front of universalism. He was concerned that democratic government driven by a voting majority would lead to tyranny over minority ways of living, and that enforced consensus would destroy individual freedoms. This led to a split between classical liberalism and modern liberalism, with the latter focused on individual 'improvement' and the former on individual 'freedom'.[2] For classical liberals like Hayek and Milton Friedman, and libertarians like Robert Nozick, it was enough to ensure that negative freedoms were entrenched and all citizens were equal before the law. Following Mill and later modern liberals like Leonard Hobhouse and J.A. Hobson, formal guarantees of citizenship in a representative democracy meant little unless government policy intervened – for example through progressive taxation and redistribution – to effectively equalize the capacities of people to realize their entitlements as citizens.[3] Keynes and Pigou at Cambridge were supporters of this new Liberal Party in Britain. The reformist socialists gathered around the Fabian Society joined them in this project.

Once the possibility of a difference between formal and substantive equality of opportunity is allowed, the internal contradictions of liberalism are impossible to conceal. Throughout the first two-thirds of the twentieth century, social liberalism or more accurately, social democratic movements by whatever political party label took on proponents of modern liberalism in a competition for the votes of a universally enfranchised electorate. During that period the rise of the welfare state financed by progressive taxation gradually eroded the nineteenth-century polarities of class inequality without eradicating them and without substantially altering the underlying divide between the cultural and moral universes of the plurality of social collectivities separated by ethnic, religious and geographic factors. Following major economic and geopolitical crises in the 1970s, the forces of classical liberalism teaming with proponents of a long-established social conservative tradition successfully challenged the social democratic ascendency in Western democracies.[4] The result – neoliberalism – has remained in the driver's seat to the present day.

WHAT IS HAPPENING, WHY AND WHAT IS LIKELY TO EVENTUATE?

It was argued in Chapter 10 that contemporary capitalism is evolving new institutional rules and routines that effectively express the interests and power of large corporations and their senior managers. The importance of intellectual property and the emergence of new monopolies in communications, pharmaceuticals and energy are creating the increasingly unequal distribution of wealth (see, Chapter 13) that underpins the power of dominant interests to bend policy to suit those interests. The emergence of new markets based on new contract arrangements has widened the scope for private investors and large corporations to take over many functions and products previously provided by governments (see, Chapter 12), as part of a strategy to reduce the scope of government – and the future tax burden on the wealthy. Further rules and procedures protect large corporations from their commercial mistakes though liberal bankruptcy regimes and limitations on liability for damage caused to the person, property and prospects of the vast majority of ordinary citizens.

The emergence of a new oligarchy threatens the institutional and moral foundations of democracy as a substantive – rather than formal – system of self-government in which the capacity of ordinary citizens to pursue their particular desired ways of life is enabled. Once a substantial minority of people begins to doubt that their interests and values are being represented by the executive actions of government, a process of delegitimization gathers pace. What Habermas (1975) referred to as 'a legitimation crisis' is self-fulfilling, undermining the willingness of people to participate in the normal democratic political process. Withdrawal from politics and a focus on the immediate sphere of family and local community further divides and fragments potential opposition to the collapse of the public sphere, reinforcing deeply embedded preferences for one's own over 'the other'. In addition to problems of national governability, this has serious implications for the ability of national governments to deal cooperatively with transnational policy challenges like climate change, refugee flows (see, Chapters 15, 16, respectively) and organized crime.

Once substantial numbers of citizens perceive that the political system is not working for but against them, the scene is set for the emergence of radical anti-democratic forces. One of the most troubling and long-lasting consequence of the global financial crisis, I have argued (cf. Chapter 14) has been the lingering suspicion that 'they' got away with it – and will go on getting away with it. A new political rhetoric is resonating today in many democratic countries, none more loudly than in America. 'The system is rigged' became Donald Trump's rallying call to the disaffected, the large numbers of Americans who are angry with the elites' running the beltway and the coterie of cosy links between Washington and Wall Street.

I argued earlier that liberal democracy on a parliamentary model is both possible (though not without occasional unintended outcomes) and desirable in the Churchillian 'least worst of options' sense, since it provided a potential institutional framework for achieving just outcomes in Sen's sense of reducing outstanding injustices. However, in order to provide such a framework, there must be a strong general confidence among most citizens that the system is *not* rigged. There must, in John Rawls's sense be a workable overlapping consensus underpinning the motivational bases of legitimation stressed by Habermas. The key argument of critics like Reich and Hacker and Pierson is that the political system in advanced capitalist societies *is* indeed rigged, that the increasing confluence of wealth and power is leading to mass social exclusion in the interests of the few. With the current political economy attacked from both the left and right, the centre struggles to hold. In electoral terms this has provided fertile ground for radical undemocratic forces to build support. From the right, nationalistic xenophobic activists are stoking the anti-immigrant, isolationist, tribal sentiments of angry and resentful voters. From the left, sporadic public protests, of which the Occupy outbreak is an example, temporarily galvanize opposition to the same 'elites' that are the target of right wing forces. In a general environment of fear, uncertainty and resentment, it is the former that, to date, have had the most success. This is to be expected in view of the arguments put forward in Chapter 8, since the forces of reaction are essentially conservative, anchored in the full range of moral foundations that make up the human species. The populist surge against the system is just that – a reaction, a groundswell of resentment powering a desperate search for a lost world. That world is one in which virtually all adults of working age could confidently expect to work; a world that all but guaranteed rising living standards for the majority; a world where one's children would be better off than oneself and; a world where most people had real choices of a desired way of life. In that remembered receding past, social and economic conditions were so arranged that the realities of class-based inequality and the social exclusion of minorities were rendered invisible. They were there but hidden, like reefs just below the surface of the water. Once the tide recedes far enough, the rocks and shoals emerge and the shipwrecks multiply. Calm and effective evacuation is impossible in a state of panic. As everyone scrambles for the lifeboats, many drown and the remainder looks around for a captain to save them.

I am writing this in the immediate aftermath of the 2016 presidential election. The American political landscape has changed, one expects permanently. It seems incredible that a property developer with a shady business and personal life could have first seized the Republican Party nomination and then after a bizarrely unconventional campaign, won and become president of the most powerful country in history. That a man with no governmental experience, no knowledge of international affairs and no firmly fixed values other than winning whatever race he found himself in, could triumph, is as clear an indicator as possible that the system is not so much rigged as broken.

The most worrying development during the latter stages of the bitterly fought campaign between Clinton and Trump was the latter's implied threat that he would only accept the outcome of the election if he won. Such statements by politicians chasing election can normally be dismissed as overblown rhetoric. But in this case, Donald Trump is not a normal candidate. Moreover, regardless of what he says after the election, it is not clear whether some of his diehard followers will take him at his word. Political violence more familiar in African dictatorships in an election aftermath is not beyond the realm of possibility following a US presidential election that has defied all precedent – *if* he loses. But he won! Now the key question everyone is asking is: what among the plethora of bold populist promises will he follow through on and which ones will he walk away from. What will happen if he fails to follow through on his promises?

It is clear – but only in hindsight, since virtually every commentator, pundit and pollster got it wrong before the fact – that Trump won *because* he refused to play the political game as normal. As an instinctually brilliant salesman, he had correctly discerned and tapped into the enormous groundswell of discontent, anger and the popular desire of anxious middle class and desperate working class voters in most American states to exit that system.[5] For these voters – white men especially – Hillary Clinton represented the political establishment responsible over the decades for the loss of their economic security and social standing. The Democratic Party in its lurch to the extreme centre defined by the tenets and policies of neoliberalism had left its traditional core supporters behind. The struggling farmers and small businesses dependent on them, the discarded manufacturing industry workers unemployed and without prospects of ever again holding down a permanent well-paid, secure job, the majority of the 99 per cent whose living standards had gone backwards and whose children faced an even bleaker future – all these people looked for an alternative to the empty promises of the ruling political class. And they found the answer in the form of a purveyor of dreams who sold them a vision of the future they wanted and an avenue to punish their tormentors. Trump trod a narrow path to victory by regaining Florida for the Republican Party and picking up the rust belt states of Pennsylvania, Ohio, Wisconsin and Michigan. The latter states had borne the brunt of deindustrialization since the 1970s and voted for Obama's 'hope and change' mantra. They didn't get change and lost hope. In his book *Listen Liberal*, Thomas Frank (2016, p. 1) began thus:

> There are consequences to excessive hope, just as there are to other forms of intemperance. One of these is disillusionment, another is anger . . . For a generation, Democratic politicians have talked of 'hope' as though it were their unique selling proposition, a secret ingredient that no other major-party brand could offer. Today those same Democrats express annoyance that anyone could really have taken them seriously on this hope business.

Trump's victory was not inevitable but it was long in the making. If he hadn't existed, someone like him would have been invented. The 2016 US presidential poll will forever be remembered as the 'anyone but (another) Clinton' election. Sexism, racism and a host of cultural factors influenced the outcome; political scientists and pollsters will pore over the entrails for years to come. But underlying all was the repudiation of an economic regime and political system that endorsed growing inequality and desperation bred of hopelessness, creating outcomes that confronted and insulted deeply held moral convictions about what was fair and just. The result sounded the death knell of the rational decision making model of politics. It is as if the new salesman promised beachgoers, not a new exotic brand of ice cream, but a completely different beach to bathe on. By extension, the result also (further) delegitimized orthodox economic analysis justifying neoliberal policies that professed a commitment to free markets while allowing their subordination to the interests of powerful corporate and political elites. The alternative vision that resonated with disaffected voters looks to the past not the future. It conjured up the world of John Kenneth Galbraith's affluent society in which the post-war boom and the institutions of countervailing power were in full gear. What they are likely to get under Trump, however, is more likely to be Kurt Vonnegut's 1952 novel *Player Piano*, a divided society of technocrats and wealthy enclaves on one side and masses of technologically unemployed and poorly paid people on the other. This latter vision is precisely the reality that the voters fled from. Trumpism is a surface phenomenon but with deep material and moral roots.

The outcome of the Brexit referendum in the United Kingdom is also largely explicable in similar terms. A majority of British voters believed that their system was rigged against them. This belief and their actions were based on the same foundational morality that stressed fairness and loyalty to one's own. Given the relative closeness of the vote (52 to 48 per cent) in favour, it may be that the result reflected some unintended consequences associated with misplaced expectations of a successful 'no' vote. Some votes to leave may have been symbolic protests in the expectation that the referendum would fail, while some 'remain' supporters may have remained at home for the same reason. Nevertheless, there was and is in Britain, as in America, a clear sense that the system is not working for most people. The result was a huge shock for the dominant class, the political and urban elites and others who have bought into and do well out of the neoliberal narrative of free markets and limited government. Unwilling to accept the unexpected outcome of the referendum, the result was successfully challenged in the UK High Court, throwing the certainty and timing of Britain's exit awry. The High Court ruled that the decision to leave the European Union had to be decided by a vote in the British Parliament. Regardless of whether the Conservative government's appeal against the court's decision is upheld or the government calls an early election to seek a mandate to proceed to exit the EU, the outcome at this point is uncertain. Both major parties are internally split with respect to the issue. In a new general election, it is possible that neither the Conservatives nor Labour will be able to cobble together a parliamentary majority to stop Britain's exit. Depending on the seat-by-seat outcome, it may be possible for the party or coalition that forms the new government to pull together a cross party majority in favour of remaining, but at the cost of intensifying internal party disunity and further alienating the large body of disaffected voters who are committed to Britain leaving the EU.[6] In the ensuing political turmoil, the grip of the major parties would likely slip further in favour of fringe movements. The electoral fallout in other European countries, notably Germany, the Netherlands and France is also uncertain. Whether Britain stays in or not, the internal structural schisms of the EU will not have gone away.

Trump and Brexit represent the GFC-style moment for political scientists and the political class – they simply didn't see it coming.

Stiglitz is one prominent economist who has identified the primary cause of the loss of legitimacy of democracy as stemming from the rise in economic inequality previously discussed. He then goes on to observe:

> In the aftermath of the Great Recession there is disillusionment not only with the economic system but also with how the political systems in many Western democracies have been working . . . That there are major failures in our economic system is obvious; but it is equally evident that the American political system [for example] has not even begun to fix them (Stiglitz, 2012, p. 119).

Why then, in spite of the 'obvious' and 'evident' failings of the economic and political systems have both systems struggled on? Why haven't people withdrawn from the electoral system and refused to vote? Why haven't they refused to work for declining real wages? And why haven't they revolted and changed things? At one level, the answers are also 'evident'. Most people have no choice; they must scramble to accept whatever jobs and wages are on offer. The choice is not between work and leisure but between work and starvation – that is the essence of a class society. Pushed a little further, most people work and vote because they believe that this is the right thing to do, their values and sense of self dignity and self-esteem drive them to turn up at their employers' behest and at the voting booth. But these normative drivers are not limitless. 'Such civic virtue should not be taken for granted. If the belief takes hold that the political system is stacked, that it's unfair, individuals will feel released from the obligations of civic virtue' (ibid. p. 120). Stiglitz points to the enormous decline in trust in established American institutions in recent years, including banks, the large churches, regulatory agencies, large corporations, Congress and the justice system. Once perceived transgressions reach a critical scale and frequency – publicized in 'scandals' purveyed by the 24-hour news cycle – the resulting decline in trust and reciprocity accelerates. The danger for social order and the dominant position of the wealthy elites – for those who do well out of the status quo – is that the social and normative basis on which economy and society function will atrophy to the point where mass revolt occurs, not as sporadic outbreaks of formless anger and frustration but as a permanent and growing groundswell of demands for radical change. In such circumstances only drastic action domestically through the deployment of the coercive arm of government or the threat or reality of external attack is likely to be effective enough to preserve the current basic structures of society. The alternative is to recognize the dangers of going down that path and collectively engineer an alternative peaceful, far-reaching reform of current rules, institutions and practices. And *that* is a practical political project to which we return in the final chapter.

However, the decline in engagement with the electoral system is not simply a reaction to declining trust and the growth of 'a plague on both your houses' response. 'Disenfranchisement by stealth' has, as Stiglitz affirms, a long history in American politics. From the long shadow of Jim Crow to the saga of 'the hanging chads', arguments about who can and who cannot vote have influenced election outcomes. The rules around voter registration, even the time and location of voting has been manipulated to effectively stop some citizens from casting their ballot. Removing voting rights from felons is biased against groups that are most frequently convicted of serious crimes. As a result of both disaffection and disenfranchisement more than a quarter of Americans qualified to vote are not registered to do so. Of the remaining three-quarters, the proportion of eligible electors who do vote varies widely depending on the elective offices concerned, the issues of the day and the general climate of political trust and engagement.[7]

The other basic reason why people neither vote nor rebel concerns their lack of political power, or in other words, it stems from their effective *disempowerment*. We have already stressed this point in earlier chapters. The resources that dominant interests like corporations can bring to bear on policy makers and the interlocking nature of corporate and political elites effectively closes the political system to other interests and choices. However, as stressed in Chapter 8, it is the hidden or third dimension of power that ensures the effective disempowerment of the majority. 'There is another way for moneyed interests to get what they want out of government: convince the 99 per cent that they have shared interests. This strategy requires an impressive sleight of hand; [because] in many respects the interests of the 1 per cent and 99 per cent differ markedly' (ibid. p. 146). An effective strategy by moneyed interests to justify their overwhelming wealth and power is to frame their privileges in terms of fairness defined as 'desert'; they deserve the lion's share of the pie. This position, as we saw in Chapter 8, resonates sentiments of a conservative moral foundation. However, as inequality remorselessly increases it is an increasingly problematic – for elites – position to credibly maintain.

I noted in Chapter 10 Sen's arguments that the social choice approach could deliver coherent collective decisions if based on broadening the informational base on which interpersonal comparisons of well-being are based, by adopting a workable concept of 'partial comparability'. This, as he argues, is useful for avoiding some of the inconsistencies of formal voting systems, no small gain in representative democracies, while making room for the role of values in the formation of individual preferences. However, it is far from sufficient in saving such systems from unjust outcomes because the approach ignores the third dimension of power, namely the ability of dominant interests to manipulate individual preferences.

Stiglitz presents a range of useful social science research that documents how the sleight of hand is perpetrated. However, in keeping with his methodological individualist approach, he too tends to underestimate the culturally embedded and socially constructed nature of the manipulative processes at work. Stiglitz, like so many others, quotes from the final page of *The General Theory*, an ode to the efficacy of ideas in politics.[8] This position sits easily with Keynes's idealist ethics, imbibed at the feet of Cambridge ethicist, G.E. Moore, and his new liberalism.[9] Hence, Stiglitz's positive directions for policy reform, for example, in taxation and financial reform, imply a return to the neutral umpire view of the state. However, it is not enough to rationally outline the biased perceptions and beliefs at work and point to the logical solutions, assuming that a newly educated mass of voters will elect governments committed and able to carry out those reforms. It is necessary to de-rig the system first.

CONCLUSION

In one important sense, neoliberalism as a political project has been too successful. It has so changed the political economy of contemporary capitalism that the rocks have been exposed. The fiction of a trickle-down prosperity has run aground. The moral imperative of possessive individualism has outraged the deep moral convictions of people who know in their gut that this is not right. People are asking questions – classically ethical questions about *what is right*. In political terms, ethics thus assumes its twofold relevance: how do people's values affect their individual and collective behaviours; and how *should* they. The five Ds – disaffection, distrust, disgust, disempowerment and disengagement – now define the political landscape of contemporary democracies.

Conventional economic analysis offers little here. Real people are not representative agents. There are significant differences across and within societies concerning the specific content of their interests and values. These differences and their implications for policy are not captured by orthodox theory. The contributions of heterodox economists – useful as they are in decentering attention from the rational maximizing agent – still largely miss the point by abstracting away from the structural sources and collective processes of economic and political activity. The basic insights of classical economics – namely that the capitalist system is driven by the dynamic competitive pursuit of profit maximization under crisis-prone conditions and that the key unit of analysis is class not the individual – are missing.[10]

The rise of populist and nationalistic political sentiments in Western democracies is not the result of mistaken ideas and misled citizens. It arises from the deeply felt anger and fear of a growing majority of people who have lost trust in the people who govern them and the political and economic system that produces those leaders. The great tragedy of current developments is that in their confusion and anger, disaffected people in Western democracies people are turning to demagogic solutions, rather than focusing on rebuilding a strong political centre free of the neoliberal cant and policy prescriptions. I suggest that public policy driven by a determination to place the ethical imperative of identifying and reducing existing social injustices at the centre of political economic analysis, along with a realistic approach to mobilizing the resources and political support for doing so, can (and should) focus our attention. The final chapter makes some suggestions in that direction.

NOTES

1. The stress here is on the 'formal entitlement' to vote. In many cases, the effective power to vote was denied certain groups well into the century. For example, the Jim Crow regime that prevented black Americans from voting in some Southern states of the USA was in force into the 1960s and required federal government legislation and force to break.
2. See my comments on Mill in Chapter 4. Gray argues that Mill never managed to reconcile his universalistic and pluralistic conceptions of liberalism. 'In favouring liberal institutions as instruments of inquiry, Mill looked forward to a rational consensus on the best way for humans to live. In affirming that humans can live well in a variety of ways he was a proto-value-pluralist. Mill's project *On Liberty* founders between these two philosophies' (Gray, 2000, p. 30). Much the same claim could be made for Rawls's theory of justice.
3. Hobhouse's influential book, *Liberalism*, published in 1911 was an early precursor to 'social liberalism', sometimes referred to as 'the new liberalism'. H.G. Wells's lead character in his novel *The New Machiavelli* modelled a politician subscribing to this charter and Hobhouse's stress on government action to offset the structural inequalities embedded in capitalism influenced the policies of the Asquith and Lloyd George Liberal Party governments before and during World War I.
4. This is particularly the case in English-speaking democracies. Even when Labour parties were in government during part of this period – as in Australia, Canada and New Zealand – they held power on the basis of a commitment to the basic tenets of neoliberalism. In some European and Scandinavian countries, it is true, 'softer' variants of neoliberalism prevailed. In Germany, for example, a well-entrenched social market model has proved remarkably resistant to American-style policy models. However, in Germany's case it can be argued that the social market approach already imposes institutionalized features that effectively mirror the necessary elements of neoliberalism, especially with respect to the requirements of worker compliance and discipline. It is also the case that the strictures of the social market did not prevent complacent Germany politicians and the banks from playing a leading role in the global financial crisis.
5. The indirect system of electing an American President ensured, in these circumstances, Trump's victory in spite of the fact that Hillary Clinton received a clear majority of votes nationwide.
6. In fact, in April 2017, Prime Minister May did unexpectedly call an early general election. By now we know the result and some of the early consequences.
7. At the time of writing it appears that the 2016 US voter turnout was the lowest since 2004.
8. For those readers who have thus far managed to escape exposure, the famous statement is as follows: 'The ideas of economists and political philosophers, both when they are right and when they are wrong, are more powerful than is commonly understood. Indeed the world is ruled by little else. Practical men, who believe themselves to be quite exempt from any intellectual influence, are usually the slaves of some defunct economists' (Keynes, 1937/1973, p. 383).
9. For a discussion of Keynes's ethics, see Skidelsky (2009).
10. However, see Shaikh (2016) who offers an impressive analysis of what he calls 'real competition'; and 'turbulent regulation' in opposition to both orthodox and Keynesian macro-dynamics.

Epilogue

18. Recapturing the high ground

Leading active members of today's economics profession have joined together into a kind of politburo for correct economic thinking. As a general rule . . . this has placed them on the wrong side of every important policy issue, and not just recently but for decades (James Galbraith).

The tensions and contradictions within the capitalist political-economic configuration make for an ever-present possibility of structural breakdown and social crisis (Wolfgang Streeck).

In this final chapter I first pull the focus on the key conclusions and implications of the arguments presented throughout the book, concentrating on the dangerous trajectory on which we as a species are embarked. The book then ends with an attempt to answer the question – where to next for a progressive left?

REPRISE

Orthodox neoclassical economics as taught in the academy and practiced in the policy arena has developed in a self-perpetuating bubble that has entirely missed the most important real world developments in the global economy over the past three or four decades. By implicitly adopting a neutral umpire view of the capitalist state, based on an unsound bifurcation of the positive and normative dimensions of the discipline, economists have unwittingly helped usher in the neoliberal world order. In this order, the narrative of free markets has been a potent ideological cover for politically managed real markets that serve the interests and buttress the power of a dominant class of supermanagers and wealthy family networks. What we are witnessing in neoliberalism is a progressive decoupling of capitalism and democracy. This is an historic break in the life story of capitalism, which in the twentieth century found in modern representative democracy the ideal political vehicle for its maturation.

The models of orthodox economics reduce human agency to an idealized society of Robinson Crusoes, rational representative agents bumping into each other like random atoms, unaware of each other's shared humanity. By adopting an 'engineering' conception of economics, the role of values in conditioning human social behaviour and outcomes both intended and otherwise, is left out of the picture. I have argued that ethics matters at this ground floor level but also that ethical questions of what is the right thing to do and the right policy to implement should occupy practitioners and policy makers at a meta level. This represents *my* ethical perspective in a twofold sense. First, I argue for the necessity to ground economics policy in a coherent ethical tradition of which the three main ones are consequentialist, deontological and virtue based. Second, I opt for a version of the first tradition in the form of Sen's 'comprehensive consequentialist' approach to reducing wherever possible clear cases of social injustice by improving the capacities of structurally disadvantaged peoples to live lives that they value.

The key emphasis in the preceding sentence is 'where possible'. Capitalism in both its Western liberal democratic and Eastern authoritarian forms is an inherently unstable and unequal social order. Class inequalities are predicated upon and reinforce asymmetric power relations. What is possible in political economic terms will depend on the historically specific nature of the extant class structures and power realities. The neoliberal dynamic has left the world with an increasingly hardened pattern of economic and status inequality that has shrunk the space for progressive social democratic resistance – shrunk it but not, fortunately, to a singularity. The very fact of the multiple contradictions of neoliberalism as a form of economic oligarchy – in particular, its inability to limit the growth in inequality – offers scope for a progressive left response to emerge.

Societies like America can now much more easily be grasped as deeply class divided, represented by the large inequalities of income and wealth and by receding avenues for upward social mobility. America and many other advanced capitalist nations are like floating communities in the high tide era of the great ocean liners. A small dominant or ruling class occupies the upper decks and frequents the captain's dining room. A somewhat larger but still small upper middle class dwells on the deck below and dines with the ship's junior officers, occasionally catching a glimpse of what goes on above them. Moving down towards the bowels of the ship an increasingly anxious middle class occupy decks that seem less and less salubrious as the cruise continues. Below them an increasingly alarmed, diverse and fragmented lower middle class struggle to maintain their occupancy of decks prone to flooding. Even further down and equally fragmented an increasingly desperate working class scramble for whatever accommodation is left, dealing with chronic seasickness occasioned by life in a vessel tossed about in stormy seas. Last of all, a lumpen proletariat of the dispossessed, homeless and mentally ill is left out on the lowest, most exposed deck, clinging onto the rails until flung into the unforgiving waves.

The dominant class, as we have seen, comprise the 1 per cent. The upper middle class (this author included) cover roughly those who receive incomes in the 90–99th percentiles generated from careers in the middle ranks of the corporation, government service, academia and the professions. This class performs effectively in its auxiliary role to the dominant class, providing most of the intellectual muscle and virtually all of the ideological cover to ensure that the current class order prevails. Frank (2016) calls this manifestation of Plato's guardians the liberal class. Its members do very well in material terms but, according to Frank, are obsessed with relative status within rather than without the group. Universities and professions like medicine, law and architecture offer archetypal examples of rigid status orders. Increasingly the upper middle class is distancing itself further and further away from the rest of their fellow citizens, the bottom 90 per cent who live on the lower decks. However, they have become very active in democratic politics, especially in what had been the centre-left political parties. More than any other social grouping it is they who have connived in shifting these parties to the right, to the 'extreme centre', to a shared acceptance of the political programme of neoliberalism.

Thus, the emergence of 'the third way' in the British Labour Party and similar developments in other capitalist countries at the same time freed their leaders and supporters to focus on issues other than the reality of embedded and intensifying inequality stunting the life chances of the other 90 per cent. Identity politics – concerning issues of gay rights, ethnicity, gender and religion – assumed centre stage. These are all important society-wide matters that impact on the effective capacities of all people to live worthwhile and fulfilling lives; discrimination against these groups is real and devastating and therefore legitimate targets for progressive policies that identify and reduce existing injustices – but not to the exclusion of the task of confronting the class subjection of the bottom 90 per cent in which women, gay and other minorities are over-represented. However, the debates and policies generated all too often were conducted within and for the benefit of members of the upper middle class, who were easily rebranded the 'cultural elites' by conservative forces playing on the moral intuitions and material grievances of the bottom 90 per cent. By privileging identity over class the upper middle class has unintentionally diverted the righteous wrath of the majority onto itself and the political parties of the nominal left that its members control. It is impossible to even begin to get an understanding of Donald Trump's presidential victory without grasping this point.

To begin to fight back will be difficult because it will require those members of the comfortable upper middle who profess a commitment to reversing the trend to greater social and economic inequality to take front on the current socio-political order that provides for their many comforts. A well-meaning rhetoric of 'social inclusion' will simply not address the real, material exclusionary forces that make the lives of unemployed ex-factory workers, struggling farmers and small business people, slum dwelling minority members and single parent households a living hell. I am reminded of a sign that appeared on houses in the 1960s wherever freeways cut through poor districts of large cities – 'get me out of this hell'. Large numbers of people in today's capitalist central are demanding for someone, anyone, to do just that. Who can forget actor Peter Finch in the film *Network* (1976) advising television viewers to fling their windows open, put their heads out and yell, 'I'm mad as hell and I'm not going to take it anymore'? It is this socio-political reality that invites the demagogue in and places our democracies at peril.

PROSPECTS FOR A POLITICS OF RESISTANCE AND RENEWAL

In the wake of Brexit, Trump and the rise of right wing nationalism in France, Austria, Germany, the Netherlands and Belgium it has become popular to see a rising wave of populism as an inevitable, unstoppable social tsunami. This was certainly the view expressed by shocked elites in the immediate aftermath of the events of 2016. What is less appreciated is the real possibility that properly addressed, the political rage of the majority can result in a progressive resurgence of a successful moderate left programme – possible only if the extremes of political violence can be avoided and the nominally (historically) leftist major party in established democracies rediscovers its traditional role as governing for the 90 per cent. It is one of the great ironies of recent political history that it is the traditionally right of centre major party in both the USA and UK that claims to be the champion of the working class. For this strange state of affairs the leaders of the Democratic and Labour parties must accept major responsibility and now do something to end it.

Populism is a powerful force for stoking demagogic change but is an unstable basis for maintaining the oligarchic outcome, since the promises of the demagogue can never be adequately delivered. Abraham Lincoln's sage observation that politicians (in a democracy) can't fool all the people all the time inevitably comes home to roost. The unresolved rage of the dispossessed and disappointed will eventually turn on the political saviour who did not, after all, change their world for the better. Once that begins to be widely appreciated, the political momentum can swing behind alternatives designed to genuinely meet the needs and aspirations of the bottom

90 per cent – *because the reactionary forces have already raised the problems of increasing inequality and exclusion that they have demonstrably failed to resolve.*

The potential for a new progressive politics depends on two key conditions. First, the turn to demagoguery must not descend into violent suppression of popular resistance by either state organs or civil society groups that effectively suspend normal democratic institutions and processes. As Weber stressed: '(t)he decisive means for politics is violence' (Weber, 1919 [1970], p. 121). In America the political system and civil society is familiar with violent acts, mostly perpetrated by right wing individuals and militia. Externalizing violence through war with foreign enemies is also a likely and potent response by right wing leaders coming under popular pressures from voters. As long as the threat of foreign governments and migrants is kept white hot, the day of reckoning can be put off. Eventually, however, the failure to deliver on the real issues will only be resolved by either violence and repression, on the one hand or electoral defeat, on the other. The latter is not guaranteed and will eventuate only if the second condition is met, namely the creation of a coherent and practical progressive political programme of reform. What would that look like and how would it be delivered?

THE PROGRAMME

A successful programme of reform and renewal that would, for a time at least, reduce social injustices and ameliorate the socially destructive forces of contemporary capitalism, entails a number of components of which the most important are sketched below. The emphasis here is on both the temporary or time-conditioned nature of the outcomes and the stress on amelioration rather than resolution. As the second epigraph at the start of this chapter stresses, capitalism is at its core a dynamic, crisis prone social order. Nothing lasts forever; the price of justice is eternal vigilance. Moreover, the structural organizing principle of capitalism is contradiction in the form of class opposition. No politically imposed 'solution' in a capitalist democracy is immune to contradictory stresses and recurring class struggles. With that sober reflection in mind, the key steps are as follows:

1. *An ethical compass.* Any organized attempt to change the world for the better must have a clear conception of what a better world would look like if and when it arrives. I have argued in favour of establishing an ethic of responsibility that focuses on the actual consequences across

populations of government policies with respect to how they enhance or constrain the capacities of people to live well. Living well involves freedom from extreme want and the effective opportunity to choose valued life experiences in communal circumstances that reflect and support those opportunities. There is no sense in which the values and opportunities emerging will be identical or even similar across a capitalist society. To some extent there will always exist tensions and challenges over both embedded in class and identity location. Successful democracies deal with these stresses and recurrent crises better than other social orders (Runciman, 2013).

2. *A concerted political economic analysis.* Effective policy requires analysis of how capitalist societies in the current phase of globalization work. This is simple to say, of course, but devilishly difficult to do. A necessary first step is to unlearn most of what currently passes for economic analysis, and engage in a collective international intellectual effort to understand what is going on. Networks like the World Economics Association offer one such avenue. Central to analysis would be a focus on identifying how and where unjust outcomes are currently occurring. Where are there roadblocks preventing particular groups from realizing their capacities? What policies could reduce or avoid those roadblocks? What priorities should determine which roadblocks are attacked first?

   In order to follow this line of attack it is necessary to jettison the traditional metrics or indices of well-being – per capita GDP, official unemployment data, school retention rates, university graduate numbers and so on. By focusing directly on the policy areas themselves and analysing how current outcomes are progressing policy makers will get a clearer appreciation as to what is not working well. In the case of employment we need to know what jobs are being created, who is gaining access to them – and who is not – and what the conditions of remuneration, safety, health and security are. We also need to know what jobs are disappearing and likely to go in the near future so that policies of transition can be developed to avoid sudden spikes in worklessness. We need much better information on underemployment than is currently available, especially with respect to people with disabilities or particular constraints (for example, caring responsibilities) who are prevented from active participation. A series of policy-specific questions like this apply to the other key areas impacting on just outcomes, including health, education, transport and housing. Progress in these terms needs to be addressed on the basis of several basic foundations. A sensible economics must be ever aware of the ideological tools deployed to undercut its impact.

3. *The policy foundations*. In order to provide a framework to attack particular policy-dependent injustices it will be vital to achieve radical changes in the current distribution of income and wealth. Taking concrete steps to reverse the neoliberal lurch to inequality, rather than waiting for the contradictions of inequality to lead to crisis and collapse to do the work, will mean imposing substantial taxes on the wealth of individuals during life and after death and taxing super incomes at super rates, as once occurred in the twentieth century. This is baldly put because it cannot be avoided if substantial progress on reducing injustices is to be achieved. This conclusion will be wildly unwelcome by the 1 per cent and hardly welcome to the upper middle class elites. It will also place heavy demands on the political process (see comments further on). Radical tax reform in this direction is necessary to seriously address the particular policy fields noted earlier. But it also funds the companion foundation – an adequate guaranteed income ensuring that no one is prevented by lack of money alone from living well. Reich (2015) terms this policy 'the citizens' bequest', a universal entitlement given to young people when they reach adulthood, designed to fit them to fully participate in and contribute to society operating under the new rules and conditions of the capitalist economy. It will be obvious from earlier discussions that this is a necessary but far from sufficient condition and thus a foundation rather than completed dwelling. Furthermore, the stress is on 'adequacy' and security of the guarantee. The notion of a 'guarantee' means that the income flow is secure. The level of income will well exceed the current tendency to provide minimum support designed to keep the poorest in poverty or just above it. However, as long as capitalism powers the economy, the level of income guaranteed will hardly approach the charge of 'luxury'. Nor will redistribution approach absolute equality. The individual competitive struggle will inevitably favour people with specific talents and luck over others. All that can reasonably be sought by policy makers in the foreseeable future of capitalism as it exists is to confine the tendency to generate and reproduce greater injustices, while substantially increasing the capacities of citizens to participate in the new economy. What might happen if, at some future time, capitalism as we know it does self-destruct (as generations of both conservative and radical critics have predicted) or be destroyed by some external catastrophe, is beyond the scope of this book and this author. Over the longer term, the degree of redistribution required through the taxation system will decline as the *pre-distribution* of incomes becomes more equal – that is, as progressively more people acquire the skills and access the opportunities to use those skills.

There clearly will be transition problems in moving to a significantly more progressive taxation regime. The political backlash by the wealthy and powerful is to be expected. However, just as significantly, current tax arrangements and behaviour reflect a recent history of neoliberal values that encourage avoidance and evasion. This double defensive rampart must be assailed in order to achieve lasting and significant reform. If the battle over values can be won – that is, if an ethics of just outcomes prevails – paying taxes becomes a civic duty rather than an unfair burden. If most people believe that most people are paying their fair share of tax then most people will actually do so. The values-behaviour process becomes self-reinforcing and a political resource in overcoming the power of resistance by wealthy interests determined to avoid paying their share. To the familiar argument that redistribution kills incentive, innovation and growth, the answer must be – prove it! Such claims are currently advanced as self-evident truths based on the faulty economic models that have failed so completely to explain still less predict how real economies work. The ideological nature of these ritualistic claims is obvious but no less potent for that.

THE PROCESS

If one takes a comprehensive consequentialist approach to policy then one is committed to seriously addressing the process by which favoured policy outcomes are to be achieved. Many of the specific process issues have been discussed in the 'Implications' section of the chapters in Part III. However, two overarching directions need to be highlighted. *The first imperative* is to reconnect the self-conscious interests of the middle and working classes in order to develop political coalitions aimed at seizing and keeping control over democratic government. This will involve operating through the major social democratic political party and wresting control of the latter from elements of the comfortable liberal elites. This is necessary to reorient the policies of those parties away from the neoliberal agenda and an associated exclusive focus on identity politics. At the same time, attention must be devoted to continued oppositional political mobilization around localized issues on the ground, on matters that concern the lives of the majority in everyday life; examples are food prices, environmental degradation, police violence, deaths in custody, housing conditions, urban renewal, public transport, loss of agricultural lands, job losses and loss of local amenities like post offices and savings institutions. Channelling rage against the depredations of fraud and corruption in the dominant and political class through movements like Occupy can link disparate oppositional actions across society and across borders, thanks to modern media technologies.

Taking the case of America about to enter a Trump presidency, primary emphasis should be on jerking the Democratic Party sharply leftwards to focus on those issues that cost Hillary Clinton the 2016 election. The basis is there. Trump's victory was closer than immediately recognized. Trump held every state that Romney won in 2012. It was his narrow victories in the northern Midwest Rust Belt states that pushed him across the line. These are the states in which the main losers from economic restructuring live. These are the regions of anger and revenge containing the legions of the lost that the Democratic Party must win back. If Trump implements the key economic promises of his campaign – cutting taxes on the rich and raising tariffs on foreign goods – the failure of protectionist, tickle down policies will help the left cause. Alternatively, if Trump governs as normal, aping Calvin Coolidge's philosophy that 'the business of America is business', the same mass voter turn-off is inevitable – *if* the Democrats have developed a suitable alternative programme. The demographics continue to move in favour of the Democrats with the relative decline of the white population in the electorate. The task is to reposition in order to attract more of the growing Latino and other minority groups, while simultaneously winning back workers, farmers and small business operators. Thus, this programme has to concentrate on producing secure jobs with prospects for living lives that allow effective choices. Simply creating large numbers of insecure, part-time, low-wage jobs that force people to move in and out of employment and to hold more than one job will not do. This simply reproduces at an ever-expanding scale the current patterns of income and wealth polarization and status differentiation, fuelling the anger and despair effectively mined by Trump and his kind.

Alongside employment policies, progressive political forces must push for educational and infrastructure investments that fit the workforce for the new jobs that drive technologically advanced sectors of the economy in those industries where the secure and well-paid jobs are arising. However, members of the liberal elites engaged in education and the professions all too readily hijack such policies in order to advance their interests and status. The indicators of success here will relate to the numbers and types of jobs created and the degree of movement into them of unemployed and underemployed workers. It is likely that most investment will need to be focused at the preschool, elementary and technical sectors of training and on developing pathways for people moving though their careers.

A major reason for the increasing irrelevance of the Democratic Party in America has been the expulsion of organized labour from its base. This has in part followed from the decline of the trade unions in key sectors as the process of deindustrialization and deregulation has unwound in its strongholds. This has also happened in other advanced capitalist societies like Britain and Australia, but to nowhere near the same extent. Ways need to be found to increase the voice of organized labour within the Democratic Party in order to weaken the grip of the liberal elites of the upper middle class, at the same time that broader civil society movements are mobilized. The latter force is needed to exert the external pressure on those elite leaders to affect organizational and, hence, programme change. The unexpectedly strong appeal of Bernie Sanders during the 2016 presidential primaries points up the potential for broad mobilization in this direction.

This latter point underscores the importance of taking the struggle to the people and finding new ways of re-stoking the fires of countervailing power. Strengthening labour unions and organizations, encouraging localized opposition to developments that destroy or segregate communities and remove vital props to community life and questioning the taken-for-granted pronouncements of conservative leaders are necessary concomitants to the programme of retaking the party of the left. Reich (2015) proposes a number of ways in which countervailing power can be mobilized and directed towards these ends.

THE THREE FUTURES OF CAPITALISM

Humanity stands at a crossroads. As a species we face three possible futures. The first looks towards a renewed and reinvigorated social democracy enlivened by values that encourage behaviours marked by cooperation, sharing and greater equality of opportunity. Public policies would be consciously directed towards identifying and reducing the current indefensible scale of economic inequalities and social injustice. In this world, most of the dividends of the Enlightenment – freedom of expression and organization, political participation and equality before the law – would be preserved. The second future we face is the rise and consolidation of an authoritarian state capitalism, the outlines of which are today apparent in Russia, China and Singapore. In this society, the features of classical liberalism are foresworn in the name of security and social order. Existing hierarchies of privilege and power are frozen, leaving the vast majority of people – citizens in name only – to find their place in the rigid structures that prevail. The final future is a degenerate form of the second but with historic echoes of a tragic past – fascism. All three futures are closer than we think.

CONCLUDING THOUGHTS

Throughout this book I have argued in favour of developing a radical political economy that would explicitly embrace a conception of social justice in order to promote public policies for a social democratic future. Having lived my adult life through the neoliberal counter-revolution and witnessed the demise of the twentieth-century experiment in social democracy, I am in no doubt as to the immense difficulties in turning history around. As history teaches us, no ruling class willingly vacates the field. Today's dominant class and its guardians have a tenacious grip over economy and society, assisted by the current trajectories of technology and government. Prising loose their grip will be a mighty challenge. One useful asset in taking on the challenge will be to replace an increasingly inadequate economics discipline with a political economy built on a broad concept of ethically motivated subjects and politically conditioned outcomes. This approach will hardly recommend itself to those committed to a radical overthrow of capitalism or to an alternative society that has reversed the growth dynamic and abolished the use of money. They are entitled to pursue their path. I invite them to tell us how the transition will occur and what intellectual discipline and tools they would propose. In the interim, in the interests of the 90 per cent, I would humbly recommend the ideas and directions advanced in this book, as the need for change and reform is pressing.

References

Adelman, J. (2013) *Worldly Philosopher: The Odyssey of Albert O. Hirschman*, Cambridge, MA: Harvard University Press.

Akerlof, G., O. Blanchard, D. Romer and J. Stiglitz (2014) *What Have We Learned?: Macroeconomic Policy After the Crisis*, Cambridge, MA: The MIT Press.

Ali, T. (2015) *The Extreme Centre: A Warning*, London: Verso.

Amnesty International (2016) *Island of Despair*, https://www.amnesty.org/en/documents/asa12/4934/2016/en/ (accessed on 18 October 2016).

Arrow, K. (1951) *Social Choice and Individual Values*, New York: Wiley.

Arrow, K. (1963) 'Uncertainty and the welfare economics of medical care', *American Economic Review*, **53**: 941–73.

Arrow, K. (1969) 'The organization of economic activity: issues pertinent to the choice of market versus non-market allocation', in *The Analysis and Evaluation of Public Expenditure: The PPB System*, US Congress, Joint Economic Committee, Washington DC: GPO.

Arrow, K. (1971) 'Political and economic evaluation of social effects and externalities', in M. Intriligator (ed.) *Frontiers of Quantitative Economics*, Amsterdam: New Holland, pp. 1–30.

Arrow, K. (1972) 'Gifts and exchanges', *Philosophy and Public Affairs*, **14** (Summer): 343–62.

Arrow K. and G. Debreu (1954) 'Existence of an equilibrium for a competitive equilibrium', *Econometrica*, **22**: 265–90.

Arrow, K. and A. Fischer (1974) 'Environmental preservation, uncertainty and irreversibility', *Quarterly Journal of Economics*, **88** (2): 312–19.

Bachrach, P. and M. Baratz (1970) *Power and Poverty: Theory and Practice*, Oxford: Oxford University Press.

Barker, T. (2008) 'The economics of avoiding dangerous climate change: An editorial essay on the Stern review', *Climatic Change*, **89** (3–4): 173–94.

Barry, B. (1973) *The Liberal Theory of Justice: A Critical Examination of the Principal Doctrines in A Theory of Justice by John Rawls*, Oxford: Clarendon Press.

Barry, B. (1989) *Theories of Justice: A Treatise on Social Justice Volume I*, New York: Harvester-Wheatsheaf.

Barry, B. (2005) *Why Social Justice Matters*, Cambridge: Polity Press.
Becker, G. (1981) *A Treatise on the Family*, Cambridge, MA: Harvard University Press.
Beinhocker, E. (2006) *The Origin of Wealth: Evolution, Complexity and the Radical Remaking of Economics*, New York: Random House.
Bel, G. (2006) 'Retrospectives: The coining of "Privatization" and Germany's National Socialist Party', *Journal of Economic Perspectives*, **20** (3): 187–94.
Bentham, J. (1789 [1961]) *An Introduction to the Principles of Morals and Legislation*, New York: Doubleday & Co.
Bergson, A. (1938) 'A reformulation of certain aspects of welfare economics', *Quarterly Journal of Economics*, **52**: 310–24.
Berlin, I. (2000) *Three Critics of the Enlightenment: Vico, Hamann, Herder*, Princeton: Princeton University Press.
Berry, M. (1987) 'Inequality', in S. Encel and M. Berry (eds) *Readings in Australian Society*, Melbourne: Longman Cheshire.
Berry, M. (2013) *The Affluent Society Revisited*, Oxford: Oxford University Press.
Binmore, K. (1994) *Playing Fair: Game Theory and the Social Contract*, Cambridge, MA: MIT Press.
Birdsall, N. and J. Nellis (2006) *Winners and Losers: Assessing the Distributional Impact of Privatisation*, Washington, DC: Center for Global Development.
Black, D. (1948) 'On the rationale of group decision-making', *Journal of Political Economy*, **56**: 23–34.
Blaug, M. (1968) *Economic Theory in Retrospect*, second edition, Cambridge: Cambridge University Press.
Blaug, M. (1996) *Economic Theory in Retrospect*, fifth edition, Cambridge: Cambridge University Press.
Blinder, A. (2013) *After the Music Stopped: The Financial Crisis, the Response, and the Aftermath*, New York: Penguin Books.
Blocker, H. and E. Smith (eds) (1980) *John Rawls' Theory of Social Justice*, Athens, OH: Ohio University Press.
Blyth, M. (2013) *Austerity: The History of a Dangerous Idea*, New York: Oxford University Press.
Bowles, S. (2012) *The New Economics of Inequality and Redistribution*, Cambridge: Cambridge University Press.
Brandt, R. (1979) *A Theory of the Good and the Right*, Oxford: Clarendon Press.
Broome, J. (1989) 'Should social preferences be consistent?', *Economics and Philosophy*, **5**: 7–18.

Buchanan, A. (1988) *Ethics, Efficiency and the Market,* Tototowa, NJ: Rowman & Littlefield.
Buchanan, J. and R. Tollison (1984) *The Theory of Public Choice II*, Ann Arbor, MI: University of Michigan Press.
Campbell, H. and R. Brown (2003) *Benefit-Cost Analysis: Financial and Economic Appraisal Using Spreadsheets*, Cambridge: Cambridge University Press.
Carson, R. (1962) *Silent Spring*, Boston, MA: Houghton Mifflin.
Cartledge, P. (2016) *Democracy: A Life*, Oxford: Oxford University Press.
Cassidy, J. (2009) *How Markets Fail: The Logic of Economic Calamities*, London: Penguin Books.
Chipman, J. (nd) *Pareto: Manuel of Political Economy*, University of Minnesota, http://users.econ.umn.edu/~jchipman/DALLOZ5.pdf (accessed on 4 May 2016).
Cheung, S. (1969) 'Transaction costs, risk aversion, and the choice of contractual arrangements', *Journal of Law & Economics*, **12** (1): 23–42.
Clark, G. (2007) *A Farewell to Alms: A Brief History of the World*, Princeton, NJ: Princeton University Press.
Coase, R. (1960) 'The problem of social cost', *Journal of Law and Economics*, **3**: 1–30.
Cohen, M. (2016) *American Maelstrom: The 1968 Election and the Politics of Division*, Oxford: Oxford University Press.
Colander, D. (2007) 'Retrospectives: Edgeworth's Hedonimeter and the quest to measure utility', *Journal of Economic Perspectives*, **21** (2): 215–26.
Collier, P. (2007) *The Bottom Billion: Why the Poorest Countries are Failing and What Can Be Done About It*, Oxford: Oxford University Press.
Congleton, R. (2002) 'The median voter model' in C. Rowley (ed.) *The Encyclopedia of Public Choice*, AA Dordrecht, the Netherlands: Kluwer Academic Press.
Cooter, R. (1987) 'The Coase theorem' in J. Eatwell, M. Milgate and P. Newman (eds) *Allocation, Information and Markets*, Oxford: Oxford University Press.
Coyle, D. (2007) *The Soulful Science: What Economists Really Do and Why it Matters*, Princeton, NJ: Princeton University Press.
Crenson, M. (1971) *The Un-Politics of Air Pollution: A Study in Non Decisionmaking*, Baltimore, MD and London: The Johns Hopkins Press.
Daly, H. (ed.) (1973) *Toward a Steady-State Economy*, San Francisco, CA: W.H. Freeman.
Daly, H. and J. Cobb (1989) *For the Common Good*, Boston, MA: Beacon Press.
Diamond, P. and J. Hausman (1994) 'Contingent Valuation: Is some

number better than no number?', *Journal of Economic Perspectives*, **8** (4): 45–64.
Dorling, D. (2014) *Inequality and the 1%*, London: Verso.
Dorling, D. (2015) *Injustice: Why Social Inequality Still Persists*, Bristol: Polity Press.
Downs, A. (1957) *An Economic Theory of Democracy*, New York: Harper and Brothers.
Dutt, A. and C. Wilber (2013) *Economics and Ethics: An Introduction*, Basingstoke, Hampshire: Palgrave Macmillan.
Dworkin, R. (2011) *Justice for Hedgehogs*, Cambridge, MA: Harvard University Press.
Edgeworth, F. (1881 [1932]) *Mathematical Psychics*, London: London School of Economics Reprints.
Edwards, W. (1954) 'The theory of decision making', *Psychological Bulletin* **51** (4): 380–417.
Ehrlich, P. (1968) *The Population Bomb*, New York: Sierra Club & Ballantine Books.
Ehrlich, P. and A. Ehrlich (1991) *The Population Explosion*, New York: Tuchstone Books.
Etzioni, A. (1990) *The Moral Dimension: Toward a New Economics*, New York: The Free Press.
Euronews (2016) 'UN says one million migrants should reach Europe by 2016', http://www.euronews.com/2015/09/08/un-says-one-million-migrants-should-reach-europe-by-2016 (accessed on 17 October 2016).
Fehr, E. and S. Gächter (2000) 'Cooperation and punishment in public goods experiments', *American Economic Review*, **90** (4): 980–94.
Fehr, E. and S. Gächter (2002) 'Fairness in the labour market: A survey of experimental results', Working Paper No. 114, *Institute for Empirical Research in Economics, University of Zurich*, Switzerland.
Fehr, E. and K. Schmidt (2004) 'Fairness and incentives in a multi-task principal-agent model', *Scandinavian Journal of Economics*, **106** (3): 453–74.
Fleming, M. (1952) 'A cardinal concept of welfare', *Quarterly Journal of Economics*, **66**: 366–84.
Florio, M. (2004) *The Great Divestiture: Evaluating the Welfare Impact of the British Privatisations, 1979–1997*, Cambridge, MA: MIT Press.
Foley, D. (2006) *Adam's Fallacy: A Guide to Economic Theology*, Cambridge, MA: Harvard University Press.
Fournier, V. (2008) 'Escaping from the economy: politics of degrowth', *International Journal of Sociology and Social Policy*, **28** (11/12): 528–45.
Frank, T. (2016) *Listen Liberal: Or Whatever Happened to the Party of the People?*, New York: Metropolitan Books.
Frey, B. and F. Oberholzer-Gee (1997) 'The cost of priced incentives: an

empirical analysis of motivation crowding out', *American Economic Review*, **87** (4): 746–55.
Friedman, M. (1953) 'The methodology of positive economics', in M. Friedman (ed.) *Essays in Positive Economics*, Chicago, IL: University of Chicago Press.
Frontex (2015) *Detection of illegal border crossing statistics*, http://frontex.europa.eu/assets/Publications/Risk_Analysis/Annual_Risk_Analysis_2015.pdf (accessed on 17 October 2016).
Galbraith, J.K. (1958) *The Affluent Society*, Boston, MA: Houghton Mifflin.
Galbraith, J. (2009) *The Predator State: How Conservatives Abandoned the Free Market and Why Liberals Should Too*, New York: Simon & Schuster.
Galbraith, J. (2012) *Inequality and Instability: A Study of the World Economy Just Before the Great Crisis*, Oxford: Oxford University Press.
Galbraith, J. (2014a) *The End of Normal: The Great Crisis and the Future of Growth*, New York: Simon & Schuster.
Galbraith, J. (2014b) 'Unpacking the first fundamental law', *Real-world Economics Review*, **69** (7): 145–9.
Gaus, G. (2008) *On Philosophy, Politics and Economics*, Belmont, CA: Wadsworth Cengage Learning.
Gaus, G. (2013) *On Philosophy, Politics and Economics*, Belmont, CA: Wadsworth Cenage Learning.
Gauthier, D. (1986) *Morals By Agreement*, Oxford: Oxford University Press.
Georgescu-Roegen, N. (1971) *The Entropy Law and the Economic Process*, Cambridge, MA: Harvard University Press.
Gilens, M. (2012) *Affluence and Influence: Economic Inequality and Political Power in America*, Princeton, NJ: Princeton University Press.
Goldthorpe, J. (1963) *The Affluent Worker: Political Attitude and Behaviour*, Cambridge: Cambridge University Press.
Gould, S. (2002) *The Structure of Evolutionary Theory*, Cambridge, MA: Harvard University Press.
Gouldner, A. (1975a) 'The norm of reciprocity', in A. Gouldner (ed.) *For Sociology: Renewal and Critique in Sociology Today*, Harmondsworth: Penguin, pp. 226–59.
Gouldner, A. (1975b) 'Reciprocity and autonomy in functional theory', in A. Gouldner (ed.) *For Sociology: Renewal and Critique in Sociology Today*, Harmondsworth: Penguin, pp. 190–225.
Graaff, J. de V. (1957) *Theoretical Welfare Economics*, Cambridge: Cambridge University Press.
Gray, J. (1995) *Liberalism*, second edition, Minneapolis: Minnesota University Press.

Gray, J. (2000) *Two Faces of Liberalism*, London: Polity Press.

Greenwald, B. and J. Stiglitz (1986) 'Externalities in economies with imperfect information and incomplete markets', *Quarterly Journal of Economics*, **101**: 229–64.

Habermas, J. (1975) *Legitimation Crisis*, Boston, MA: Beacon Press.

Hacker, J. (2008) *The Great Risk Shift*, Oxford: Oxford University Press.

Hacker, J. and P. Pierson (2010) *Winner-Take-All-Politics: How Washington Made the Rich Richer and Turned its Back on the Middle Class*, New York: Simon & Schuster.

Hahnel, R. and K. Sheeran (2009) 'Misinterpreting the Coase theorem', *Journal of Economic Issues* **43** (1): 215–38.

Haidt, J. (2013) *The Righteous Mind: Why Good People are Divided by Politics and Religion*, London: Penguin Books.

Halpin, A. (2007) 'Disproving the Coase theorem?', *Economics and Philosophy*, **23** (3): 321–41.

Hare, R. (1981) *Moral Thinking*, Oxford: Clarendon Press.

Harsanyi, J. (1955) 'Cardinal welfare, individualistic ethics and interpersonal comparisons of utility', *Journal of Political Economy*, **63**: 309–21.

Hart, H. (1973) 'Rawls on liberty and its priority', *University of Chicago Law Review*, **40** (Spring): 551–5.

Hausman, D. and M. McPherson (1996) *Economic Analysis, Moral Philosophy and Public Policy*, Cambridge: Cambridge University Press.

Hausman, D. and M. McPherson (2006) *Economic Analysis, Moral Philosophy and Public Policy*, second edition, Cambridge: Cambridge University Press.

Hazlitt, W. (1825 [2004]) *The Spirit of the Age and My First Acquaintance with Poets*, reprinted in R. Woof (ed.) Grasmere: The Wordsworth Trust.

Henriques, D. (2011) *The Wizard of Lies: Bernie Madoff and the Death of Trust*, New York: Henry Holt & Co.

Hicks, J. (1939) 'The foundations of welfare economics', *The Economic Journal*, December, **49** (196): 696–712.

Hicks, J. (1946) *Value and Capital*, London: Clarendon.

Hirschman, A.O. (1977) *The Passions and the Interests: Political Arguments for Capitalism before Its Triumph*, Princeton, NJ: Princeton University Press.

Hirschman, A.O. (1984) 'Against parsimony: three easy ways of complicating some categories of economic discourse', *Bulletin of The American Academy of Arts and Sciences*, **37** (8): 11–28.

Hirschman, A.O. (2013) 'The changing tolerance for income inequality in the course of economic development', *The Essential Hirschman*, Princeton, NJ: Princeton University Press.

Honeywill, R. (2016) 'The man problem', *Ockham's Razor*, 5 June, Australian Broadcasting Corporation Radio National, Sydney.

Horowitz, I. (1967) *The Rise and Fall of Project Camelot: Studies in the Relationship Between Social Science and Practical Politics*, Cambridge, MA: MIT Press.

Hotelling, H. (1929) 'Stability in competition', *The Economic Journal*, **39**: 41–57.

International Monetary Fund (IMF) (2009) *Global Financial Stability Report*, Washington DC: International Monetary Fund, https://www.imf.org/External/Pubs/FT/GFSR/2009/01/pdf/text.pdf (accessed on 6 June 2016).

Jeffries, S. (2016) *Grand Hotel Abyss: The Lives of the Frankfurt School*, London: Verso.

Jones, O. (2011) *Chavs: The Demonization of the Working Class*, London: Verso.

Jones, O. (2014) *The Establishment: And How They Get Away With It*, London: Allen Lane.

Kahneman, D. and A. Tversky (2000) *Choices, Values and Frames*, Cambridge: Cambridge University Press.

Kaldor, N. (1939) 'Welfare propositions and interpersonal comparisons of utility', *The Economic Journal*, September, **49** (195): 549–52.

Kay, J. (2015) *Other People's Money: Masters of the Universe or Servants of the People?* London: Profile Books.

Keane, J. (2009) *The Life and Death of Democracy*, New York: W.W. Norton.

Keynes, J. (1923 [1971]) *A Tract On Monetary Reform, The Collected Writings of John Maynard Keynes, vol. IV*, London: The Macmillan Press.

Keynes, J.M. (1937 [1973]) *The General Theory and After, Part II Defence and Development, The Collected Writings of John Maynard Keynes, vol. XIV*, London: The Macmillan Press.

Krehbiel, K. (2004) 'Legislative organization', *The Journal of Economic Perspectives*, **18** (1): 113–28.

Krugman, P. (2008) *The Return of Depression Economics and the Crisis of 2008*, London: Penguin Books.

Kunkel, B. (2014) 'Paupers and richlings', *London Review of Books*, 3 July, **36** (13): 17–20.

Kuznets, S. (1955) 'Economic growth and income inequality', *American Economic Review*, **45** (1): 1–28.

Lanchester, J. (2010) *Whoops! Why Everyone Owes Everyone and No One Can Pay*, London: Allen Lane.

Lanchester, J. (2012) *Capital: A Novel*, New York: W.W. Norton & Co.

Quiggin, J. (2010) *Zombie Economics: How Dead Ideas Still Walk Amongst Us*, Princeton, NJ: Princeton University Press.

Rajan, R. (2010) *Fault Lines: How Hidden Fractures Still Threaten the World Economy*, Princeton, NJ and Oxford: Princeton University Press.

Rawls, J. (1971) *A Theory of Justice*, Oxford: Oxford University Press.

Rawls, J. (1993) *Political Liberalism*, New York: Columbia University Press.

Rawls, J. (1999) *The Law of Peoples*, Cambridge, MA: Harvard University Press.

Rawls, J. (2000) *Lectures on the History of Moral Philosophy*, Cambridge, MA: Harvard University Press.

Rawls, J. (2001) *Justice as Fairness: A Reappraisal*, Cambridge, MA: Harvard University Press.

Rawls, J. (2007) *Lectures on the History of Political Philosophy*, Cambridge, MA: Harvard University Press.

Reich, R. (2008) *Supercapitalism: The Transformation of Business, Democracy and Everyday Life*, New York: Alfred A. Knopf.

Reich, R. (2015) *Saving Capitalism: For the Many, Not the Few*, New York: Alfred A. Knopf.

Reinhart, C. and K. Rogoff (2009) *This Time is Different: Eight Centuries of Financial Folly*, Princeton, NJ and Oxford: Princeton University Press.

Reiss, J. (2013) *Philosophy of Economics: A Contemporary Introduction*, New York: Routledge.

Reiter, S. (1987) 'Efficient allocation', in J. Eatwell, M. Milgate and P. Newman (eds) *Allocation, Information and Markets*, Oxford: Oxford University Press.

Robbins, L. (1932) *An Essay on the Nature and Significance of Economic Science*, London: Macmillan & Co.

Romer, P. (1986) 'Increasing returns and long-run growth', *Journal of Political Economy*, **94** (5): 1002–37.

Rorty, R. (2005) 'Pragmatism', in E. Craig (ed.) *The Shorter Routledge Encyclopedia of Philosophy*, Oxford: Routledge.

Rothschild, E. (2002) *Economic Sentiments: Adam Smith, Condorcet and the Enlightenment*, Cambridge, MA: Harvard University Press.

Roubini, N. and S. Mihm (2011) *Crisis Economics: A Crash Course in the Future of Finance*, London: Penguin Books.

Runciman, D. (2013) *The Confidence Trap: A History of Democracy in Crisis from World War I to the Present*, Princeton, NJ: Princeton University Press.

Samuelson, P. (1947) *Foundations of Economic Analysis*, Cambridge, MA: Harvard University Press.

Sandel, M. (1982) *Liberalism and the Limits of Justice,* Cambridge: Cambridge University Press.

Sandel, M. (2009) *Justice: What's the Right Thing to Do?*, London: Penguin Books.

Sandel, M. (2013) *What Money Can't Buy: The Moral Limits of Markets*, New York: Farrar, Straus and Giroux.

Scanlon, T. (2003) 'The diversity of objections to equality', in T. Scanlon, *The Difficulty of Tolerance: Essays in Political Philosophy*, Cambridge: Cambridge University Press.

Schattschneider, E. (1960) *The Semi-Sovereign People: A Realist's View of Democracy in America*, New York: Holt, Rinehart and Winston.

Scheve, K. and D. Stasavage (2016) *Taxing the Rich: A History of Fiscal Fairness in the United States and Europe*, Princeton, NJ: Princeton University Press.

Schumacher, E.F. (1973) *Small is Beautiful: Economics as if People Matter*, London: Blond & Briggs.

Schumpeter, J. (1912 [1934]) *The Theory of Economic Development*, Cambridge, MA: Harvard University Press.

Schumpeter, J. (1943 [1987]) *Capitalism, Socialism and Democracy*, London: Unwin Paperbacks.

Scitovsky, T. (1941) 'A note on welfare propositions in economics', *Review of Economic Studies*, **9**: 77–88.

Sen, A. (1970a) *Collective Choice and Social Welfare*, San Francisco, CA: Holden-Day.

Sen, A. (1970b) 'The impossibility of a Paretian liberal', *Journal of Political Economy*, **78** (1): 152–7.

Sen, A. (1981) *Poverty and Famines: An Essay on Entitlement and Deprivation*, Oxford: Oxford University Press.

Sen, A. (1985) *Commodities and Capabilities*, Amsterdam: North-Holland.

Sen, A. (1987) *On Ethics and Economics*, Oxford: Blackwell.

Sen, A. (1992) *Inequality Reexamined*, Cambridge, MA: Harvard University Press.

Sen, A. (1998) 'The possibility of social choice', Nobel Prize lecture, Stockholm, December. http://www.nobelprize.org/nobel_prizes/economic-sciences/laureates/1998/sen-lecture.pdf (accessed on 3 September 2016).

Sen, A. (2009a) 'Introduction' to A. Smith, *The Theory of Moral Sentiments*, London: Penguin Books.

Sen, A. (2009b) *The Idea of Justice*, London: Allen Lane

Sen, A. (2012) 'Values and Justice', *Journal of Economic Methodology*, **19** (2): 101–108.

Sen, A. and B. Williams (eds) (1982) *Utilitarianism and Beyond*, Cambridge: Cambridge University Press.

Shaikh, A. (2016) *Capitalism: Competition, Conflict and Crises*, New York: Oxford University Press.
Shiller, R. (2008) *The Subprime Solution: How Today's Global Financial Crisis Happened and What to Do About It*, Princeton, NJ: Princeton University Press.
Shiller, R. (2013) *Finance and the Good Society*, Princeton, NJ: Princeton University Press.
Shweder, R., N. Much, M. Mahapatra and L. Park (1997) 'The "big three" of morality (autonomy, community and divinity) and the "big three" explanations of suffering', in A. Brandt and P. Rozin (eds) *Morality and Health*, New York: Routledge.
Singer, P. (2010) *The Life You Can Save: How to Do Your Part to End World Poverty*, New York: Random House.
Skidelsky, R. (2000) *John Maynard Keynes: Fighting for Britain, 1937–1946*, London: Macmillan Publishers.
Skidelsky, R. (2009) *Keynes: The Return of the Master*, London: Allen Lane.
Smart, J. and B. Williams (eds) (1973) *Utilitarianism: For and Against*, Cambridge: Cambridge University Press.
Smith, A. (1790 [2009]) *The Theory of Moral Sentiments*, New York: Penguin Books.
Standing, G. (2011) *The Precariat: A New Dangerous Class*, London: Bloomsbury.
Steil, B. (2013) *The Battle of Bretton Woods: John Maynard Keynes, Harry Dexter White and the Making of a New World Order*, Princeton, NJ: Princeton University Press.
Stern, N. (2006) *Stern Review on the Economics of Climate Change*, London: HM Treasury.
Stiglitz, J. (2001) 'Information and the change in the paradigm in economics', Nobel Prize lecture, December. http://www.nobelprize.org/nobel_prizes/economic-sciences/laureates/2001/stiglitz-lecture.pdf (accessed on 4 April 2016).
Stiglitz, J. (2010) *Freefall: America, Free Markets and the Shrinking of the World Economy*, New York: W.W. Norton & Co.
Stiglitz, J. (2012) *The Price of Inequality: How Today's Divided Society Changes the Future*, New York: W.W. Norton & Co.
Stiglitz, J. (2015) *The Great Divide: Unequal Societies and What We Can Do About Them*, New York: W.W. Norton & Co.
Stiglitz, J., A. Sen and J. Fitoussi (2010) *Mismeasuring Our Lives: Why GDP Doesn't Add Up*, New York: The Free Press.
Tawney, R. (1931) *Equality*, London: George Allen & Unwin.
Tett, G. (2009) *Fool's Gold: How Unconstrained Greed Corrupted a Dream,*

Shattered Global Markets and Unleashed a Catastrophe, London: Little, Brown.
Tett, G. (2015) *The Silo Effect: The Perils of Expertise and the Promise of Breaking Down Barriers*, New York: Simon & Schuster.
Varoufakis, Y. (2011) *The Global Minotaur: America, Europe and the Future of the Global Economy*, London: Zed Books.
Veblen, T. (1921) *The Engineers and the Price System*, New York: B.W. Huebsch.
Viner, J. (1948 [1973]) 'Bentham and J.S. Mill: the utilitarian background', in E. Phelps (ed.) *Economic Justice*, Harmondsworth: Penguin Books.
von Neumann, J. and O. Morgenstern (1944) *Theory of Games and Economic Behavior*, Princeton, NJ: Princeton University Press.
Walzer, M. (1983) *Spheres of Justice*, New York: Basic Books.
Weber, M. (1919 [1970]) 'Politics as a vocation', in H.H. Gerth and C. Wright Mills (eds) *From Max Weber: Essays in Sociology*, London: Routledge & Kegan Paul.
Wells, T. (2014) 'Recovering Adam Smith's ethical economics', *Real-World Economics Review*, 68, http://www.paecon.net/PAEReview/issue68/whole68.pdf (accessed on 11 November 2016).
Wight, J. (2015) *Ethics in Economics: An Introduction to Moral Frameworks*, Stanford, CA: Stanford University Press.
Wilkinson, R. and K. Pickett (2010) *The Spirit Level: Why Equality is Better for Everyone*, London: Penguin Books.
Winch, D. (1971) *Analytical Welfare Economics*, Harmondsworth: Penguin Books.
Wolf, M. (2014) *The Shifts and the Shocks: What We've Learned – and Have Still to Learn – from the Financial Crisis*, New York: Penguin Press.
Wolff, R. (1977) *Understanding Rawls: A Reconstruction and Critique of A Theory of Justice*, Princeton, NJ: Princeton University Press.
Wolff, R. and S. Resnick (2012) *Contending Economic Theories: Neoclassical, Keynesian and Marxian*, Cambridge, MA: MIT Press.
World Commission on Environment and Development (1987) *Our Common Future*, Oxford: Oxford University Press.

Index